Movie Comedians
of the 1950s

MOVIE COMEDIANS OF THE 1950s

Defining a New Era of Big Screen Comedy

Wes D. Gehring

McFarland & Company, Inc., Publishers
Jefferson, North Carolina

ALSO BY WES D. GEHRING AND FROM MCFARLAND: *Genre-Busting Dark Comedies of the 1970s: Twelve American Films* (2016); *Chaplin's War Trilogy: An Evolving Lens in Three Dark Comedies, 1918–1947* (2014); *Will Cuppy, American Satirist: A Biography* (2013); *Forties Film Funnymen: The Decade's Great Comedians at Work in the Shadow of War* (2010); *Film Clowns of the Depression: Twelve Defining Comic Performances* (2007); *Joe E. Brown: Film Comedian and Baseball Buffoon* (2006); *Mr. Deeds Goes to Yankee Stadium: Baseball Films in the Capra Tradition* (2004)

Frontispiece: *The Court Jester*'s Danny Kaye's constant attempts to remain upright, or face Mark Twain's 19th-century description of being an armor-bound turtle, "was like an ironclad coming into port." Kaye is flanked by his two *Jester* love interests, Angela Lansbury (left) and Glynis Johns.

LIBRARY OF CONGRESS CATALOGUING DATA ARE AVAILABLE

Names: Gehring, Wes D. author.
Title: Movie comedians of the 1950s : defining a new era of big screen comedy / Wes D. Gehring.
Description: Jefferson, N.C. : McFarland & Company, Inc., Publishers, 2016. | Includes bibliographical references and index. | Includes filmography.
Identifiers: LCCN 2016042282 | ISBN 9780786499960 (softcover : acid free paper) ∞
Subjects: LCSH: Comedy films—United States—History—20th century. | Motion picture actors and actresses—United States. | Comedians—United States.
Classification: LCC PN1995.9.C55 G4255 2016 | DDC 791.43/617—dc23
LC record available at https://lccn.loc.gov/2016042282

BRITISH LIBRARY CATALOGUING DATA ARE AVAILABLE

ISBN (print) 978-0-7864-9996-0
ISBN (ebook) 978-1-4766-2692-5

© 2016 Wes D. Gehring. All rights reserved

No part of this book may be reproduced or transmitted in any form or by any means, electronic or mechanical, including photocopying or recording, or by any information storage and retrieval system, without permission in writing from the publisher.

Front cover image of Bob Hope breaking up Bing Crosby on the set of *Road to Bali*, 1952 (Paramount Pictures)

Printed in the United States of America

*McFarland & Company, Inc., Publishers
Box 611, Jefferson, North Carolina 28640
www.mcfarlandpub.com*

For all my mentors through the years—
starting with my parents

Table of Contents

Preface and Acknowledgments   1
Prologue, with Notes on Abbott & Costello   3

1. Judy Holliday: *Born Yesterday* (December 27, 1950)   7
2. Martin & Lewis: *Sailor Beware* (February 1, 1952)   21
3. Bob Hope: *Son of Paleface* (October 2, 1952)   35
4. Charlie Chaplin: *Limelight* (October 25, 1952)   48
5. Red Skelton: *The Clown* (January 29, 1953)   61
6. Hope & Crosby: *Road to Bali* (January 30, 1953)   72
7. Tom Ewell/Marilyn Monroe: *The Seven Year Itch* (June 4, 1955)   84
8. Jack Lemmon: *Mister Roberts* (July 15, 1955)   96
9. Martin & Lewis: *Artists and Models* (December 22, 1955)   107
10. Danny Kaye: *The Court Jester* (February 2, 1956)   123
11. Tony Randall: *Will Success Spoil Rock Hunter?* (September 12, 1957)   136
12. Lemmon & Curtis/Monroe/Joe E. Brown: *Some Like It Hot* (March 30, 1959)   149

Epilogue: The Question of Quality 1950s Film Clowns   170
Filmography   181
Chapter Notes   183
Bibliography   193
Index   199

Preface and Acknowledgments

> We should all thank God for TV.... We [filmmakers] have always been the lowest of the low but now they have invented something which we can look down on [TV].—Billy Wilder[1]
>
> Eisenhower assured us that Russia wouldn't attack ... so I don't think the Army has any-thing to worry about because I don't believe McCarthy even has the H-bomb.—Bob Hope[2]

To paraphrase a 1950s Hollywood crack, "I had more help on this project than a Hollywood starlet with a stuck zipper." Ironically, my needs were minuscule compared to the era's McCarthy-induced blacklisting and the pioneering TV competition which damaged and/or ended the careers of so many American filmmakers in this most collaborative of art forms.

Regardless, even without having to fight such battles, the completion of this book merits many "thank yous." Naturally, acknowledgments invariably produce the fear that someone has been missed. Consequently, if omissions have occurred, let me offer my profound apologies at the onset of this process. I must begin with my department chairman, Tim Pollard. He has provided the most generous support for the text, and several other book projects. Moreover, he is also responsible for creating a winningly congenial working environment for both writing and teaching. Without such a setting, to paraphrase a Dean Martin lyric, "I'd be a walking case of the blues."

As always, Janet Warrner has provided important editorial assistance, while Kris Scott was responsible for the computer preparation of the work. Plus, Chris Flook was invariably available to assist in questions involving the reproduction of stills. Along related lines Indiana University Art Museum's Associate Registrar Heather A. Hales facilitated permission from the gallery to reproduce its Marsden Hartley 1941 painting *Three Friends* (1941, see Chapter 10).

Two Ball State emeritus professors, film scholars Conrad Lane and David L. Smith, provided invaluable discussions about the project, as did the former BSU endowed chair and award-winning filmmaker Robert Mugge. And BSU's interlibrary loan staff was invaluable in tracking down my every request: Kerri McClellan, Lisa Johnson, Elaine Nelson,

Karin Kwiatkowski, and Jodi Sanders. Moreover, given this was the final installment of a film clown trilogy (1930–1960), following *Film Clowns of the Depression: Twelve Defining Comic Performances* (2007) and *Forties Film Funnymen: The Decade's Great Comedians at Work in the Shadow of War* (2010), several major libraries contributed to this study: New York City's main public library at Fifth Avenue and 42nd Street (guarded by its monumental marble lions, "Patience" and "Fortitude"); the New York Public Library for the Performing Arts at Lincoln Center; the Cinema Arts Library at the University of Southern California in Los Angeles; and the Margaret Herrick Library, Academy of Motion Picture Arts and Sciences, Beverly Hills, California.[3]

Naturally, none of this would be possible without the love, support, and patience of my family and friends. With such nurturing parents, an encouraging muse (Cassie), film-loving daughters (Sarah and Emily), and a growing brood of little movie fans (Michael, Emmett, Kadri, Lily and Ruby), much can be accomplished, *and rediscovered*. For example, at two years of age a fully engaged grandson (Michael) sat on my lap and watched all of Chaplin's *The Circus* (1928), bringing back my earliest joys at first encountering the Tramp. I was reminded of the brilliant use of children at the *Peter Pan* premiere in *Finding Neverland* (2004)—joyfully rekindling dormant memories from long ago.

Prologue, with Notes on Abbott & Costello

> To paraphrase poet/critic Katy Lederer, "[Sometimes a clown can be] so spiritually off-balance that he had no other choice but to extend his lyric syntax like a rope to an eternity to which he tried— sometimes comically and other times tragically—to cross."[1]

This book completes my trilogy of personality comedian decade books, following *Film Clowns of the Depression: Twelve Defining Comic Performances* (McFarland, 2007) and *Forties Film Funnymen: The Decade's Great Comedians at Work in the Shadow of War* (McFarland, 2010).[2] For me, these books represent revisiting a pre-analytical film comedy period rooted in my older baby boomer youth. It was a time when pioneering TV was largely populated with Hollywood's castoffs of the 1930s and '40s, as the large screen battled the upstart small one. Television then was rather like *Turner Classic Movies* with commercials. Thanks to a comedy-loving father, I was privy to the *gold standard*—"late night" feature film comedies. These viewings and Saturday afternoon TV matinees exposed me to everyone from the Marx Brothers and W. C. Fields to Mae West and Hope & Crosby's *Road* pictures. Plus, before and after school children's programming was largely filled with 1930s short subjects of the Little Rascals, Laurel & Hardy, the Three Stooges, and many others. There were also brief surreal live TV performances that were sometimes as absurd as the then contemporary-inspired sketches of Ernie Kovacs' (1919–1962) "The Nairobi Trio," a robotic ape band performing in trench coats, gloves, and Chaplinesque bowler hats. The routine was topped off by the drummer hitting the distracted conductor's head with a drumstick.

Well, this group had nothing on Adolph Proper (1886–1950), whose act was continued until 1970 by Sammy Levine. Called "The Banana Man," the popular Proper appeared in at least one short film subject, *Seeing Red* (1934), and Levine later frequently turned up on the early morning children's TV program *Captain Kangaroo* (1955–1992). Producing odd sounds while laughing bizarrely, Levine's shtick also involved playing fake musical instruments and simulating their sounds, while producing huge amounts of fruit from his dark trench coat pockets. This often included up to 300 bananas. Bit by bit this pocketed produce department was placed in a small, wheeled boxcar-shaped container from which Banana

Man would periodically lift another box and attach it to the first one. Eventually he would have three or four miniature banana wagons, and while never stopping that crazed laughter, he would slowly exit the stage with what had turned into a train. This was how my pre-kindergarten day often started. As dark comedy humorist Jim Knipfel observed, with only partial tongue-in-cheek intent, of a similar odd old act on TV, "Wasn't this condoning, even encouraging, schizophrenia as a viable lifestyle option?"[3]

The moral of the story, besides possibly explaining the 1970s' increased acceptance of psychiatry, is that for many baby boomers comedy felt like three decades of funny all accordioned together. Though I referenced these books as a trilogy, the texts examine one continuous line of laughter. So while the millennial generation (born between the early 1980s and 2000) have a history of comedy at their fingertips, boomers experienced something similar, but with little control other than an arbitrary TV dial, and a liberal dad.

Going hand in hand with 1950s baby boomer exposure to old film comedy rebroadcast on TV was the *Colgate Comedy Hour* (1950–1955), and rotating hosts which often included Martin & Lewis, Abbott & Costello, and other contemporary film comedians. While the former team is well represented in this text, the latter duo is not included. Had this been a book focused on early television comedy, Abbott & Costello would have made the grade. However, while their early 1950s film work was popular for a time, its quality had greatly deteriorated. And this comes from a fan, who devoted a chapter to the team's *Buck Privates* (1941) in the aforementioned text on 1940s film comedians.

Abbott & Costello were essentially inspired vaudevillians who were sandwiched into pictures two ways. The first half of the 1940s gerrymandered their often brilliant routines, such as the immortal "Who's on First" bit (see their *Naughty Nineties*, 1945) around personality comedy's invariably loose storyline. Secondly, in the latter half of the 1940s, and into the early 1950s, the duo were comically subjected to encounters with a myriad of movie monsters. Conveniently, their home studio (Universal) controlled the rights to the majority of filmdom's scary creatures. What resulted were some engaging 1940s pictures, especially the quintessential *Abbott and Costello Meet Frankenstein* (1948, with Lon Chaney, Jr., and Bella Lagosi), and to a lesser extent, *Abbott and Costello Meet the Killer Boris Karloff* (1949, with their titled co-star Karloff).

Between the novelty of the team in horror film parodies and co-starring actors associated with the genre, the pictures initially worked. Unfortunately, Universal ran the formula into the ground, cut production values, and essentially stopped casting the name actors synonymous with terror. The best of the 1950s ongoing series was *Abbott and Costello Meet the Invisible Me* (1951), which made an early proposal for this text. However, in a final pre-screening of all selections, the picture just did not measure up. Maybe, if Universal had polished both the material and the budget, such as luring *the* early sound film "invisible man" (Claude Rains, see James Whale's classic *The Invisible Man*, 1933, Rains' movie debut), the picture would have made the cut.

If I needed an Abbott & Costello defense, I would cite Andy Borowitz's book *The 50 Funniest American Writers: An Anthology of Humor from Mark Twain to the Onion* (2014).[4] It is a solid addition to humor scholarship despite, from my vantage point, the surprising exclusion of Robert Benchley and Kurt Vonnegut. Choices. Someone's favorite is inevitably left out. Consequently, if a reader has been offended by an omission, please accept a moment of sincere author contriteness. I am only placing words in a row on paper better to explain possible perspectives on a subject which has obsessed me since I first saw an image of Charlie Chaplin's Tramp so many years ago.

Regardless, as one would assume, there are basic parallels between this text and its two predecessors. Most obviously, 12 pivotal personality comedian films have again been selected from a focus decade. Plus, since few clowns are capable of performing the cinema hat trick of writing, directing, and performing, unique writer/directors again surface to help mold performers and/or performances. In this study, two such auteurs make an exceptional impact on several of the featured films. The most significant is Frank Tashlin. First, he had a direct involvement in three of the highlighted features: *Son of Paleface* (1952), *Artists and Models* (1953), and *Will Success Spoil Rock Hunter?* (1957). Second, Tashlin's satirical cartoon-oriented ambience, especially given his number one protégé, Jerry Lewis, had a major influence on the very nature of 1950s screen personality comedy.

The second extraordinary auteur of the decade in this area is Billy Wilder. His influence was less than Tashlin's only because personality comedy was not his only genre focus. In contrast, between the mid–1940s and the early 1960s, Tashlin worked with (sometimes without screen credit) an array of comedians who included the Marx Brothers, Bob Hope, Red Skelton, Martin & Lewis, Jerry Lewis, and Danny Kaye. However, when Wilder did key on personality comedy, as in this text's *The Seven Year Itch* (1955) and *Some Like It Hot* (1959), he was capable of work which far transcended a single decade. He was also able, through incredible patience, to draw two performances out of Marilyn Monroe which elevated her above the era's unfortunate phrase of "dumb blonde." (A further goal of this text has been a three-part breakdown of that phrase and how it did *not* apply to Monroe and Judy Holliday, while Tashlin cruelly but comically used it on Jayne Mansfield.)

While all decades represent transitions, this final text in my personality comedian trilogy represents two distinctive breaks with what came before. First, the 1950s was the decade when essentially all major film clowns had neither a set comic garb, nor make-up, be it Chaplin's Tramp costume, or Groucho Marx's greasepaint mustache and equally accented black elevator eyebrows. Moreover, the film clowns did not limit themselves to comic parts, but also "essayed" serious roles—best exemplified in this volume by Jack Lemmon's long and varied career. Competition from television necessitated and/or demanded the change. Because suddenly yesteryear's costumed comics were there for free on television. Moreover, the garb of small screen clowns was not to be topped, whether it was primetime's Red Skelton and his menagerie of characters, such as Freddie the Freeloader and Clem Kadiddlehopper, or children's programs like Pinky Lee and his "uniform" of a loud plaid suit and baggy checkered pants and a goofy undersized hat (a precursor to Pee-Wee Herman). Moreover, there was a sheer war for viewers going on between TV and the movies. For example, when Charlie Chaplin was asked his opinion of the new medium at the time of *Limelight* (1952, see Chapter 4) he observed:

> I hate it. I will not permit it in my house. The idea of actors letting themselves be shown on that lousy, stinking little screen!… [It] should be done away with. It is ruining the country.[5]

Second, McCarthyism put a certain satirical clamp on comedy which was unknown to the 1930s and 1940s. Only the proliferation of the new TV culture provided a safety valve of sorts for the satirically inclined—especially Tashlin. Either way, McCarthyism and TV almost created a metaphorical comedy dam on cinema personality comedy, be it blacklisting, or a talent drain to the small screen, or simply a shake-up of screen comedy in general. Did this result in a certain dumbing down of large screen clowns? The text examines the question and invites the reader to make the final decision.

Of course, at the time, this young comedy sponge was too busy laughing to be aware of such decidedly serious subjects. And while film might have been fighting TV it was a portal to the past for baby boomers. Yet, as I ponder this trilogy trail I have been revisiting for several years now, I am taken with an "opinion piece" in today's *New York Times* (March 20, 2016). "Penned" by the gifted writer Katie Roiphe, the essay is titled "Dying, with Nothing to Say." She elegantly bemoans the fact that few people are blessed with the chance for meaningful last words. Or, if so gifted, can one illuminate a lifetime in the briefest of moments?

I cannot fault her essay and its moving conclusion: "It may be the last chance for the dying person to clarify, but clarity doesn't necessarily come. In this way, death is a lot like life."[6] Yet, I believe one can metaphorically reframe the phrase "last words" to a more comforting suggestion—the expression might better be defined by how one lives each day. My professorial philosophy is taken from Robert Frost's adage "I am not a teacher; I am an awakener." The key element of that axiom suggests you become what you do each day. Legendary coach John Wooden was fond of quoting, in part, his father's suggestion "to make each day a masterpiece." Consequently, an individual continually lives one's "last words." Thus, in part, this trilogy journey into my past is an attempt at the last words of a passionate laughter-filled youth fueled by a comedy-mentoring father. Indeed, while he is still alive at 88, his "last words" for me, if he leaves first, will be a montage of laughter moments, be it the anti-establishment Marx Brothers, or Laurel & Hardy as defined by Laurel, "two minds without a single thought."

∼

However, anyone thinking my personal pinballing into the past is simply a memory lane trip would be mistaken. As art historian Holland Cotter has observed, history is a grand sorting machine, loading on events … dividing time into nameable, datable piles…[7] This is merely a modest sorting, and hopefully binding, of a past from my ground level view. Thus, the trilogy has been most directed at re-navigating a pivotal portion of my youth, something critic Geoffrey H. Hartman would call the "wild surmise," and which I am now cerebrally better equipped to understand.[8] Hopefully, as someone who has attempted a lifetime of wordsmithing, I will now also be better able to articulate this early me, from so long ago. That is, to paraphrase Kurt Vonnegut, "writing allows patient people to edit themselves into something like intelligence."[9] We shall see.

1

Judy Holliday
Born Yesterday (December 27, 1950)

> *Born Yesterday* might easily be called *Pygmalion Goes to Washington.*—Film scholar Maria DiBattista[1]

As Maria DiBattistia's alternate title suggests, Judy Holliday's (1922–1965) *Born Yesterday* character, Billie Dawn, is in makeover mode inside Frank Capra–land, à la *Mr. Smith Goes to Washington* (1939). As with most personality comedians, their persona have a fault line to another comedy genre.[2] For example, throughout Bob Hope's film career he had a propensity for parody, especially of Westerns (see Chapter 4's *Son of Paleface*, 1952).[3] Holliday's clown is best linked to Capraesque feel-good populism, a patriotic world of unlimited possibilities.[4] However, the title *Born Yesterday* also implies Holliday's Dawn arrival in the capital as a poster child for the unschooled. Indeed, her hair color invites the further denigrating phrase "dumb blonde." Period *New York Times* critic Lewis Nichols fleshed it out further: "No thought ever could have passed through her mind."[5]

Though personality comedy is the only humor genre in which character trumps the importance of the narrative, a thumbnail sketch of *Born Yesterday* provides the basic perimeters of Holliday's transformation. Fittingly, her character name, "Dawn," hints at a pocket definition of populism's most central theme—second chances. She is the mistress of crude, gangsterish, junkyard millionaire Harry Brock (Broderick Crawford), who has come to the capital to further expand his domain. Given that Brock has in his pocket a congressman, with another appropriate name, Norval Hedges (Larry Oliver), and enough money to control additional D.C. powerbrokers, Brock wants to *buy* increased power.

Though Crawford's vulgar street-wise wannabe mogul is no study in refinement, he is advised that his equally crude chorus girl companion (Dawn) could be a detriment to his wheeling and dealing in D.C.'s surface culture. Thus, when leftist *New Republic* reporter Paul Verrall (William Holden) comes calling for presumably a negative story, he instead finds himself drummed into being Dawn's babysitter/tutor, as Crawford's character does his illegal thing. However, just as *Mr. Smith*'s Jean Arthur, a political aide to a crooked senator, finds herself assigned a similar task to Jimmy Stewart's overly naïve junior senator, only to fall in love with him, a comparable fate awaits Holden's reporter. And in both cases, love and patriotism prevail. But *Born Yesterday*'s is more driven by Holliday's personality comedy makeover.

With this framework in place, it is time to hone in on Holliday's persona, a character she perfected by first playing Dawn on Broadway for over three years (1946–1949). Yet, calling her a "dumb blonde" is an unfortunate description. For example, even a critic during her original stage run observed:

> In one line, she managed to forge the image of an intellectually vacuous young woman with a peasant shrewdness and a hard honesty: "Do me a favor, will ya, Harry [her junkyard king], drop dead."[6]

And two decades after the play's adaptation, English theatre critic and playwright Kenneth Tynan wrote in *The New Yorker*:

> Like most of the funniest performers in the world, she has an attitude in her films of alert skepticism. There is something fishy about the planet, she implies. She is ready to be grateful for its smallest mercies and she is infinitely educable to our ways but we may all, she hints, be nuts.[7]

Yet, Holliday's voice and physical appearance keep bringing her back to the land of dumb blondes. For example, her speech fluctuates between gravel and Fanny Brice's Baby Snooks character. Coupled to that is a "Face right out of Renoir ... [and a] body from Rubens."[8] What was this girl to do? Though Holliday won an Oscar for bringing Dawn to

William Holden (center) as tutor/advocate for Judy Holliday against bully Broderick Crawford in *Born Yesterday*.

the cinema in only her second high profile picture appearance, she soon grew tired of the dumb blonde persona, "I started off as a moron ... worked my way up to imbecile ... and have carved my current niche as a noble nitwit."[9] She showed entertaining signs of working toward a more intelligent screen personality in her last film—*The Bells Are Ringing* (1960, for which she had also won a 1956 Tony). But with a short filmography and an ongoing battle with breast cancer (dying at 42), one can only speculate on what might have been.

Ironically, another 1950s dumb blonde, Marilyn Monroe (see Chapters 7 and 12), wanted to break out of that image, too. Paradoxically, she also showed evidence of doing just that in her last film, *The Misfits* (1961, just a year after Holliday's *Bells*). Sadly, Monroe also died early (a 36-year-old victim of suicide, 1962), before a *what if* could be played out. Yet, the personae of both actresses had many differences. Indeed, Holliday's pioneering biographer, Will Holtzman, observed:

> Both women had come to the public's attention for playing what were essentially, for want of a better term, dumb blondes. Judy's characters were more under-educated diamonds in the rough, whereas Marilyn's were overheated baby dolls. Marilyn bore a certain similarity to her roles, but Judy could not have been less like hers.[10]

The only qualifier to this comparison is Holliday's inherent populist nature, which she invariably showcased in both her personal and professional lives. Otherwise, Holtzman's comparison is dead-on.

Speaking further to this juxtapositioning, naturally both women were brighter than their performing alter egos—partly an outgrowth of a particularly chauvinistic era. That is, in the post-war 1950s the men were back from the service and not to be intellectually threatened, despite women having carried on nicely in the job market. Moreover, Holliday's IQ was 172—borderline genius. Consequently, as her previously quoted comments suggest, being tied to such an image must have been exceptionally difficult.

Additionally, another key difference existed between Holliday and Monroe. Though their screen alter egos were childlike, Holliday was more the tough kid, like the early 1930s roles of another blonde icon, Jean Harlow, especially from *Dinner at Eight* (1993). In this film, a mindless Harlow is also tied to a crookedly brutish nouveau-riche businessman (Wallace Beery). Indeed, Holliday's *Born Yesterday* dressing down of Crawford is patterned upon a similar *Dinner* berating of Beery by Harlow's dumb blonde—because, in directing both movies, George Cukor saw the parallels and borrowed from himself.[11] In contrast, Monroe's waif is devoid of Holliday's moxie, and exuded a little girl lost aura, complicated by an urchin trapped in a sultry body. This is further accented by their voices—Monroe's is all breathless innocence; Holliday's pipes might peel paint off the wall.

One could better explain the differences between the Holliday and Monroe personas in a clinical manner. Humor conduct is equated with an awareness of a character's needs and/or values. Abraham Maslow's *Motivation and Personality* (1954) hierarchy of needs remains *the* standard:

1. The need for *basic life*—food and shelter.
2. The need for a *safe and secure environment*.
3. The need to *belong and to be loved*.
4. The need for *esteem*, where status, responsibility, and recognition are important.
5. The need for *self-actualization*, for personal growth and fulfillment.[12]

If one then compares these actresses in their greatest roles, Holliday's *Yesterday* and Monroe's *Some Like It Hot* (see Chapter 12), these differences are strikingly apparent.

In *Yesterday*, both Harry and Dawn are comic primitives, with Holliday's character even affectionately coining a description of him which is equally applicable to her: "He's always lived at the top of his lungs." Harry is rough with her, but he also confesses his love on two occasions. They both ascended from the gutter and share an appetite for sex and gin rummy. Plus, for seven years all her expensive needs have been met. In Dawn's own way, it is a tit for tat world. For example, after Harry has observed, "she's a little on the stupid side," and hired Holden's reporter as a tutoring distraction, Dawn propositions Paul: "It's only fair, we'll educate each other." Earlier in their discussion she demonstrates having passed Maslow's first three stages—basic needs, security, and belonging to someone:

> DAWN: I'm stupid and I like it.
> PAUL: You do?
> DAWN: Sure. I'm happy. I get everything I want, two mink coats, everything. If there's something I want I ask…. As long as I know how to get what I want, that's all I want to know.

Paul will only get through to Dawn when Maslow's final categories are introduced—respect and personal growth. (As noted above it is another case of "the seven year itch.")

In contrast, Sugar (Monroe's singer) in *Hot* struggles even with Maslow's opening points. First, since she drinks and only has a mediocre voice, she battles for the basic needs of food and shelter. Second, this situation naturally dovetails into a lack of safety and security. Third, Sugar has a weakness for tenor saxophone players who only take advantage of her. Thus, she neither belongs nor is loved. She is a cover girl for the total dependency of a child.

Regardless, the foundation for Holliday playing a cinematic Dawn is anchored to the film *Adam's Rib* (1949) and ironically relates to her dumb blonde scenario. Columbia Pictures had purchased the rights to *Yesterday* for a then astronomical $1 million, despite the paradox that author Garson Kanin had based the tale's vulgar junkyard tycoon, *Harry* Brock, on the studio's production chief *Harry* Cohn. To Cohn's credit, he was unphased by this Hollywood in-joke. But he was bothered about who to cast as the lead, since Holliday essentially had no movie resume. Consequently, he was set to use Columbia's reigning leading lady, Rita Hayworth. Yet, Hayworth's sexy bright persona was no Dawn. And it became a moot point when she defected from the screen to marry Pakistan Prince Aly Khan. Cohn was less than pleased, and even following Holliday's casting (after many others were screen tested), Cohn demonstrated why he had been the model for the crude junkyard king when he observed, "If only that cunt Hayworth hadn't married that Moslem playboy."[13]

Katharine Hepburn kept a home in New York and had become a big fan of Holliday's Broadway Dawn. The legendary actress also knew that *Adam's Rib* was a great script, arguably the best of the nine teamings she had with her then secret off-screen partner, Spencer Tracy. What is more, she was aware of a small but vital part yet to be cast in the film. With some building up, it might be the perfect part to convince Cohn to cast Holliday. Tracy, Kanin, and the picture's director, George Cukor, all fell in line—it was hard to deny Hepburn on a mission. Accordingly, in her memoir she wrote, "Garson and I went East to … get Judy to play a tiny part in our movie … [with] a great scene."[14] And Cukor later confessed the lengths to which Hepburn went to make this happen:

> She's [Hepburn] the one who took me to see her [Holliday] in the play of *Born Yesterday* on Broadway. Judy didn't think she had a chance to do the movie. She kept saying that Harry Cohn wouldn't give her a crack at it.... But Kate was very generous with [building up Holliday's role at the expense of her own part]. It was a very touching friend-ship ... [Hepburn] appreciates people with talent. She always got very excited about it.[15]

Adam's Rib involves husband and wife lawyers (Tracy and Hepburn) who find themselves on opposing sides in a domestic shooting case. Holliday's dumb blonde (with "peasant shrewdness") suspects her screen husband Tom Ewell (see Chapter 7) is having an affair and follows him to his mistress' (Jean Hagen) apartment. Breaking in on them she produces a gun and proceeds to shoot with averted eyes in the general direction of the lovers. Though Ewell's character is slightly wounded, what should be an open and shut case for Tracy is turned into a feminist referendum by Hepburn, the activist attorney. Naturally, Holliday's character is found not guilty. But Hepburn's plan for getting Holliday her *Yesterday* part hinges on the scene when the two actresses first appear together on screen.

Tracy's definitive biographer, James Curtis, best describes this all important sequence, bolstered by an added quote from Ewell:

> When it came time for Holliday's big scene, Amanda's [Hepburn] jailhouse interview of the would-be murderous [Holliday], Hepburn asked that Cukor set up [the camera] so that it showcased Judy ... [with Hepburn] in profile, framing the left edge of the shot. Eve March ... [Hepburn's screen secretary was] to the right, though the whole thing played in one continuous five-minute take. "She [Hepburn] was wonderful with Judy Holliday," said Tom Ewell. "She worked like a dog to throw the emphasis on her with extra lines and close-ups. No other star ever did that."[16]

Hepburn even had blurbs planted in the trade papers that Holliday was stealing the picture from the stars. As an addendum to Hepburn's generosity and eye for talent, especially to better sell Holliday, Ewell later shared, "Hepburn called me personally in New York and said, 'Look, if you do this film, I'll do anything I can to be your press agent.'"[17] Hepburn was right in her assessment of Ewell as a foil for Holliday. He brings a comic anti-hero element to an inherently unsympathetic part. Regardless, even the already supportive Cukor was bowled over by the uneducated ethic New Yorker housewife performance Holliday created: "I'll never forget that extraordinary scene she [Holliday] did in *Adam's Rib*, in the woman's prison, with Hepburn."[18]

Of course, Cukor was pivotal, too, by maintaining that continuous five-minute take, with only a few brief cut-aways added later. And Holliday delivered, with a natural ease, growing sympathy for her viewers. Though the Broadway star was initially nervous during early takes, Hepburn helped her use the emotion (a natural response to a jailhouse interview), and this showstopper was all the better for it. Moreover, anticipating Holden's *Yesterday* part, Hepburn was able to guide Holliday's Dawn to the respect and personal growth of Maslow's earlier chart. Indeed, it transitioned into a defense, since Hepburn used it as an explanation for the shooting—Dawn was merely protecting Marlow's first three fundamental needs—home, security, and being needed by someone. Holliday's performance received a Golden Globe nomination for Best Supporting Actress. And more importantly, Hepburn's plan (which also involved making sure nothing was lost in the editing room) was the catalyst for Holliday's movie casting as Dawn.

The *Adam's Rib* prologue to Holliday and *Yesterday* has been belabored for several often ironic reasons. First, it simply represents a fascinating backstory to one of the most memorable performances in Broadway history gerrymandering its way to Hollywood à la the passion and sacrifice of Hepburn. Second and paradoxically, it highlights a dumb blonde persona (however progressive compared to Monroe) appearing in a *groundbreaking feminist film*. Third, considering this self-contradiction, the accomplishment was shepherded through by Hepburn, arguably Hollywood's greatest period feminist.

Fourth, there is a sardonically mocking perspective to the fact that while *Yesterday* was written in the mid–1940s, it was a cinematic harbinger of feminism's 1950s backsliding, compared to an assertive 1940s capstone film like *Adam's Rib*. With exceptions, such as Hepburn, the era was more repressive to women (especially smart women) than just a few years before. Men felt threatened by just how well women had performed in the previous decade's war-related job market. As Mary Keefe, the model for Norman Rockwell's iconic 1943 *Saturday Evening Post* cover "Rosie the Riveter," later observed, "[Rockwell] was trying to get people to realize that all women could help out [substantially] with the war effort when the men were away."[19] Indeed, arguably the most famous line from 1950s television was Ralph Kramden's (Jackie Gleason) signature argument-related hand clenched threat to his stay-at-home wife Alice, (Audrey Meadows), "Boom zoom to the moon, Alice," in the ironically titled television program *The Honeymooners*.

Fifth, there is almost a peculiarity to the fact that Holliday's soon-to-be Oscar-lauded Dawn (upsetting Bette Davis' assertive and favored *All About Eve* character) was presented to the public only in a slightly altered *Adam's Rib*'s form. Nevertheless, while Hepburn (who enjoyed being on the set even if she was not in the sequence) helped coach Holliday, it was, of course, only natural that the younger actress would bring elements of Dawn to her *Adam's Rib* part. Still, there was no denying that Holliday delivered in that single long take, spilling out her character's frustrating life in a poignantly comic *and* pathetic monologue. One is reminded of a conversation from the neglected *Nurse Betty* (2000), when a blonde (Renée Zellweger) not unlike Holliday's character is described as not so much "wanting a better life" but just "wanting a life."

Nonetheless, maybe Hepburn's greatest assist at this point was simply helping Holliday calm down during early interview takes. Though in yet another paradox, as previously noted, some of actress Holliday's initial anxiety was employed in the lengthy sequence, given the normal/realistic apprehensiveness of a jail setting. In any event, the elements that came together in this highlighted Holliday interview were so effective one could almost put a period between each word for its naturalness. Indeed, in feminist fairness, one might argue a minority report for Holliday, even when compared to steamroller Hepburn. For example, pioneering women film historian and critic Molly Haskell manages to put an empowering perspective on Holliday:

> As Hepburn was smart, Judy Holliday was "dumb" … yet the suffusing glow and impact of her [Holliday's] personality belie her dumbness…. In *Adam's Rib*, *Born Yesterday* … [and other pictures], she comes on slowly, with her beady eyes and poker face [for protection], and builds gradually into something that lights up the screen. Staunch and fluffy as a muffin, pigheaded, suspicious, with an oh-ho-you're-not-going-to-fool-me laugh, she listens intently and then comes out with a remark from left field that is sublimely logical to her. She is moony and mulish…. [Yet] in her militantly sheeplike way, was as much and as invincibly her own person as any crusading feminist.[20]

Haskell likening her to being "doughy" yet having an intense protectiveness captures an *every woman* scenario, consistent with her populist connection. There was no confusing her with a vacuous sexy glamour girl. She was not, however, "that fat Jewish broad"

Cohn referred to behind her back.[21] Still, comedians are generally best served by not being conventionally attractive. Plus, the standard first rule of personality comedians is to look and/or sound funny. Holliday, already had a cartoon Bronx voice whose volume and mangled syntax could shatter glass, yet still managed to hold its own in a period when *loud* passed for the norm, from Lou Costello's "HEY ABBOTT!" to Jerry Lewis' "HEY LADY!" (see Chapters 2 and 9). Indeed, with Holliday's "moony" face, frizzed platinum hair, and high pitched horn of a voice, she was not unlike the wise fool Harpo, who was the sound effects "silent" Marx Brother. In truth, to paraphrase some people on the Columbia lot, she resembled "Harpo meets Harlow." On the flip side, à la miming Harpo, a signature *Born Yesterday* scene is Dawn's largely silent gin game. In any event, Haskell could have been describing Harpo when she wrote of Holliday that there are long periods when "she listens intently and then [responds with an action] from left field that is only sublimely logical to her." And though Holliday was performing in a transitional period when comedians no longer wore a set humorous "uniform" from picture to picture, like Harpo's trench coat, Dawn's initial nouveau rich *Born Yesterday* wardrobe was as comically garish as any clown's attire.

Additionally, Dawn's other basic *Born Yesterday* traits are textbook characteristics of the personality comedian.[22] She is an *underdog* based upon being an illiterate former chorus girl whose mistress situation is fast approaching an expiration date. Naturally, this is often coupled with being an *outsider*, which makes her predisposed to a nomadic existence. That is, a picaresque life simply means one either does not fit in anywhere and/or is teamed with an equally nonmember of normal society. Indeed, a final personality comedian trait is just that—morphing into a temporary *team-like* scenario, instead of the old school permanent coupling of a Laurel and Hardy. For example, Dawn begins *Born Yesterday* with Crawford's loudmouthed Harry as a comedy partner, though her verbal blasts were more ingratiatingly appealing. Still, their team shtick could vary from ear-piercing shrieks out the hotel windows (across a courtyard) of the adjoining wings of their luxurious suite, to their comic, nearly silent gin game, which she always wins. In addition, their basic humor premise paralleled that of Laurel and Hardy. Like Harry, Oliver ruled it over Stanley by his alleged superior intelligence (despite writer Laurel correctly defining their relationship as "two minds without a single thoughtht"[23]). But Harry simply shouted louder; he was not really more intelligent. Dawn had just never applied herself. And as was frequently the outcome in a Laurel and Hardy film, Dawn (like Stanley) came out ahead.

In time *Born Yesterday* gravitates toward a second temporary team—Dawn and Paul, William Holden's intellectual reporter. He will mentor her towards recognizing and beginning to achieve Maslow's "need for esteem" and "self-actualization." But before transitioning to Paul's guiding influence on Dawn's metamorphosis, with its sizable populism component, one needs to briefly scrutinize the team's dynamics. Harry and Dawn, like so many comedy collaborations, is anchored in one of various bully scenarios. There is Hardy's mild browbeating of Laurel, Abbott's more intimating behavior towards Costello, and Moe's oppressing of the other Stooges. In contrast, Dawn and Paul follow the standard Martin and Lewis team formula—copycat admiration. For Lewis, this essentially meant comically attempting to emulate a cool older "brother." Martin is more model than teacher, though he sometimes doubles as a tutor, too, such as trying to teach Lewis to box in *Sailor Beware* (1952, see Chapter 2). While Martin could also be mean to Lewis, too, as in *The Stooge* (1953), this was atypical of the team's relationship. Indeed, their studio (Paramount) was so concerned about how unrepresentative it was of the duo that the picture was shelved for two years! Moreover, Lewis' greatest film, after his 1956 break with Martin, was *The Nutty Professor* (1963), in which he narcissistically plays both a nerdy academic and a sensual playboy obviously patterned on Martin. (Fittingly, Holliday's best film after *Born Yesterday*, *Bells Are Ringing*, had Martin for a co-star.)

Consequently, *Born Yesterday*'s narrative braiding of a second comic team dynamic is ultimately understated. However, it begins broadly by borrowing from an early 20th century vaudeville routine commonly referred to as a "Dumb Dora" sketch, in which a straight man is constantly befuddled by a daffy woman companion. For example:

> LOUISE: The doctor said I'd have to go to the mountain for my kidneys.
> BOB: That's too bad.
> LOUISE: Yes, I didn't even know they were up there.[24]

It is now most associated with the comedy team of George Burns (1896–1996) and Gracie Allen (1895–1964), who successfully transferred it to radio (1933–1950) and then television (1950–1958). But cartoonist Chic Young of later *Blondie* comic strip fame had created a *Dumb Dora* strip in the 1920s, and the concept has never really gone away, be it screwball comedy heroine Carole Lombard in *My Man Godfrey* (1936), or loopy Goldie Hawn on *Rowan & Martin*'s *Laugh-In* (1968–1970). So how does this relate to *Born Yesterday*'s second comedy duo—Holliday and Holden? What follows is one of their early exchanges:

> PAUL: Nobody's *born* smart, Dawn. You know what the stupidest thing on earth is? An infant.
> DAWN: What've you got against babies all of a sudden?
> PAUL: Nothing, I've got nothing against a brain that's three weeks old and empty. But after it hangs around for thirty years and hasn't absorbed anything, I begin to wonder about it.
> DAWN: What makes you think I'm thirty?

Now, while this passes for a "Dumb Dora" bit, Paul neither milks the laugh by a true straight man's comic bewilderment and/or a rolling of the eyes, nor does he barrel ahead with more setups for other vapid responses. Just a few of these exchanges, or Dawn simply stating, "I'll think it over but I can tell ya now, the answer's no," quickly establishes that Paul has his work cut out for him. And just like the aforementioned blank slate of a baby, if Paul is to use education to jump-start Dawn's ability to think, he can neither laugh nor be condescending towards his non-traditional student. Moreover, even at the beginning of this college of one, Dawn suggests hope by having one immediate educational goal in mind, despite her crude utterance: "I want to talk good."

Despite occasional gray matter impairments, such as Dawn not having a clue about the existence of the Supreme Court, Holden's Paul provides a quick civics lesson in American democracy as he doubles as a D.C. tour guide. Their itinerary includes viewing and reading the Gettysburg Address, the Constitution, and the Declaration of Independence, and stops at the National Art Gallery, plus the Lincoln and Jefferson memorials. This sometimes montage look at these bulwarks of democracy are reminiscent of title character Jimmy Stewart's quick outings to many of the same sites in *Mr. Smith Goes to Washington*. Of course, Smith already knew their significance but his enthusiasm at his initial viewing anticipates Dawn's double-whammy fervor at first seeing them while having a simultaneous epiphany over their importance. Consequently, the Dawn and Paul duo quickly moves from the toned-down "Dumb Dora" laughter scenario to populism's feel good approach ... yet still driven by the sheer comic personality of Holliday.

Her Dawn is a quick study, a point underlined by Hollywood's propensity to slap glasses on someone suddenly absorbing information. With Holden already wearing them, no doubt making him a regular professor in la la land symbolism, Dawn is soon sporting spectacles, too. Regardless, Paul's prize pupil soon recognizes that all men being created equal also negates any right to be a bully, like Crawford's Harry. Coupled with that, Dawn is now cognizant that Harry is never really happy—all he wants is money. With that awareness, one could say Dawn is embracing a tongue-in-cheek axiom by leftist author/critic Clive James which could double as a playful clarification of the genre (populism) forever lurking in this clown film:

> Common sense and a sense of humor are the same thing, moving at different speeds. A sense of humor is just common sense, dancing. Those who lack humor are without judgment and should be trusted with nothing.[25]

At this point the film gets a little diabetically democratic à la *Mr. Smith* being defined as "Capra-corn." But the flag waving is minimal, never becoming, to borrow a recent line from a Robert Downey character, "Eugene O'Neill long." (Reining in Capra would have been a challenge for Kanin, who was fond of saying, "I'd rather be Capra than God, if there is a Capra.")

Absorbingly, just as Stewart's Mr. Smith drew his greatest strength from his religious-like visits to the Lincoln Memorial, Dawn's go-to patriot place is the Jefferson Memorial and its stipulation for equality. She now hates what Harry stands for and receives her emancipation when she can tell him to "drop dead!" Of equal importance is her recognition that education is the nucleus of freedom: "A world full of ignorant people is too dangerous to live in."

Returning to the close of Clive James' simplistic euphemism for populism, "Those who lack humor are without judgment and should be trusted with nothing," Dawn is able to topple Harry's junkyard kingdom. When Dawn was in her metaphorical Pinocchio period, she was not only a puppet to Harry's puppeteer, he had incautiously placed the "strings" to his empire in her name for protection. If his latest criminal deals were exposed, what the still-learning Dawn described as "the biggest swindle since the 'Tea Pot [Dome] something [Scandal,' when President Harding's administration was connected to oil company bribery, 1922–1923]," Dawn, not Harry, would go to jail. But now the liberated former chorus girl owned everything, and Crawford's character was finished.

Consequently, as a clown comedy frequently colored by populism, both genres triumphed—the common individual/personality comedian had defeated an evil minority (Harry and his "yes" men). Of course, *Born Yesterday* always managed to emphasize Dawn's wacky romance more than the populist *Mr. Smith* or even Capra's *Mr. Deeds Goes to Town* (1936), in which one more reporter plays advocate for a disadvantaged individual. Thus, *Born Yesterday*'s primary genre, whether talking *Pygmalion* or populism, is clown comedy, in Holliday style. As *Variety*'s review stated:

> Almost alone, she makes "Born Yesterday" a smart ticket buy for filmgoers, and the dumb, sexy character she portrays is one the public will take to its heart.[26]

And she takes the team premise for Martin & Lewis an extra step, what begins with Holliday's copycat admiration/emulation (from glasses to old glory) of Holden's character turns to love.

"Student" Judy Holliday falling for "teacher" William Holden in *Born Yesterday*.

Fortunately, the personality comedian emphasis of *Born Yesterday* was a plus, since populism was losing favor by the 1950s. That was the decade when the apparent hyperbolic Lincoln quote, "You can fool all the people some of the time, and some of the people all the time, but you cannot fool all the people all the time," had become questionable, though that had certainly not been the case with Dawn.[27] Still, World War II had shown that multitudes around the globe were hypnotized by the likes of mass murderers like Hitler and Mussolini. Furthermore, after the conflict, a cold war with the Soviet Union had descended on the world, and organizations like the House Un-American Activities Committee (HUAC) and the Catholic Legion of Decency began fanning communism fears among the populous. Sadly, many individuals were fooled. Ultimately, Hollywood itself would be stained by a 1950s Blacklist, banishing seemingly everyone with the previous leftist leaning from employment. The HUAC lunacy, soon to be dubbed McCarthyism (after junior Senator Joseph McCarthy), would eventually demand witnesses to name names of other possible liberals. Incredibly, this craziness would even impact Holliday and *Born Yesterday*, which will be addressed shortly.

Related to this harassment, one must first diagram populism's cyclical decline at this time. Even Capra, the patron saint of a genre which could double as America's ethos, had already revealed populism's Achilles' heel in *Meet John Doe* (1941). Archetypal American actor Gary Cooper plays a trustingly naïve character, who, for a time, innocently becomes a front for a fascist organization bent on controlling America. Surprisingly, even *It's a Wonderful Life* (1947) would have some revisionists question its meaning. For example, author/critic David Thomson writes:

> The American dream ... [in *Life*] was so close to ... [a] nightmare. The film that failed in 1947 had become a token of uplifting fellowship, yet it was a film noir full of regret, self-pity, and the temptation of suicide. How could so many people convince themselves that it was cheery?[28]

The evil institutionalism of Mr. Potter wins, and similarly goes unpunished, though the people eventually come together. Regardless, Capra, as in *Deeds*, had suggested ever greater populist diligence in his 1948 adaptation of Howard Lindsay and Russell Crouse's Pulitzer Prize–winning play *State of the Union* (1945–1947). The screen version features many traditional Capra components, from starring arguably America's most iconic leading man (Spencer Tracy), to including sequences of D.C.–based idealism—especially the scene in which Tracy eloquently describes what the White House symbolizes to both the country and the world in general.

However, *Union* also shows various corrupt political machines and the proverbial smoke-filled rooms which attempt to mislead the public. Moreover, even Tracy's character, the ironically named Grant Matthews (Ulysses S. Grant was a mediocre president), is flawed—unfaithful for a time to both his wife and his democratic values. (*Mr. Smith*'s first name is *Jefferson*.) Tracy's Grant had been briefly tempted to become president *whatever* the cost. Of course, when Grant comes to his personal and professional senses, he drops out of the race and gives a Capraesque populist speech broadcast nationwide by a then groundbreaking use of television. But the spirit of *Mr. Smith* would have then had Grant's character taking on the corrupt kingmakers while becoming chief executive. However, here he places the democratic onus on the electorate. And while he has inspiringly warned the people, via his televised American pep rally talk, the fraudulent institutions will still strive to mold public policy. Given that a popular period axiom for the conclusion of science fiction films was "Watch the Skies! [For Danger]," a populist counterpoint warning might have been the title "Messiah or Dictator," from the screen adaptation of *All the King's Men* (1949, to be addressed shortly).

Nevertheless, one must first scrutinize the immense critical and commercial success of Holliday's Oscar-winning performance in *Born Yesterday*. The reviewers essentially said *she was the film*. Indeed, the *Variety* critique which noted, in part, "Almost alone, she makes 'Born Yesterday' a smart ticket," sounds almost modest compared to so many other reviews.[29] For example, the *New York Herald Tribune* declared:

> To say that Judy Holliday repeats her stage success in the role of Billie Dawn in the movie version of ... "Born Yesterday" would be to understate the case. In this outing ... the comedy about the intellectual birth of a millionaire's moll is the next thing to a Holliday monologue.[30]

The *Hollywood Reporter* critic was more blunt: "Without her triumphant performance of Billie Dawn, the honey-haired chorus girl who topples the power of a money-mad tycoon, 'Born Yesterday' would be dead tomorrow."[31] The *New York Daily News*' veteran screen critic, Kate Cameron, politely shortened the same sentiment in her late December (1950) critique: "Judy is the main show and her performance is one of the funniest I've seen on the screen this year."[32] And the *Christian Science Monitor*, entitling their review, "Judy with a Punch," went so far as to put her watershed performance into an historical perspective:

> [*Born Yesterday* brings to the screen] the most raucous and most hair-raising talent for low comedy since [Oscar-winning] Marie Dressler [1868–1934], Sophie Tucker [1887–1966], Mae West [1893–1980], Martha Raye [1916–1994], or (for that matter), W. C. Fields [1880–1946].[33]

The *Saturday Review* underlined Holliday's seemingly instant historical eminence as reviewer Hollis Alpert said, "Billie Dawn is [now] seen as an 'American institution.'"[34] *New Yorker* critic Kenneth Tynan was even more specific than "low comedy" when he described a key character of Holliday's humor as paralleling that of another legendary performer:

> Apart from Beatrice Lillie [1894–1989], no one can ever have expected a more ungodly disbelief in fashion. Judy Holliday is perfectly polite to her clothes but they seem visited on her, like mannered guests whom she can't wait to be rid of.[35]

And nowhere was this more true than in *Born Yesterday*.

Additionally, Holliday's celebrity grew further when the backstory resurfaced of how she came to be cast in the original Broadway production of *Born Yesterday*. It was life imitating hoary art as minor player Holliday replaces the lead, learns the part in no time, and is a major star overnight. Hackneyed but true. Garson Kanin had written the play specifically for frequent Capra screen heroine Jean Arthur. But she dropped out while the play was being fine-tuned on the road before a much anticipated opening on the "Great White Way." The official explanation was ill health, but her definitive biographer, John Offer, more honestly confessed, "The real reasons for Arthur leaving *Born Yesterday* remain obsure."[36] The actual truth was that a disinterested diva used some questionable physical issues to drop out.

Arthur's mistake was Holliday's break. And the *New York Herald Tribune* reminded the public of that fact after the exceptional opening of the film adaptation five years later:

> [Producer Max] Gordan and Kanin frantically mulled over a list of possible actresses [and] recalled a girl named Judy Holliday. [Though hardly well known] Miss Holliday was interviewed and signed for the part, and went into grueling and virtually continuous rehearsals for the next seventy-two hours. She was an instantaneous hit when the show opened in Philadelphia, and her triumph was repeated in New York.[37]

Fittingly, though the popular film adaptation was previewed on the West Coast in November 1950, it still managed to be the sixth top grossing film of 1951, nearly equaling a close box office spread of all the films above it except number one *David and Bathsheba*, followed by *Show Boat* (both 1951).[38]

Despite this megahit, which most critics largely credited to Holliday, her stardom was suddenly threatened just as it was getting started. Almost immediately the movie was attacked on both coasts for political reasons. In the West, *Born Yesterday* was condemned in *The Tidings*, a Los Angeles Catholic diocese newspaper reprinted in 22 church-related publications. *Tidings* editor and critic Thomas H. Mooring wrote a critique entitled, "Clever Film Satire Strictly from [Karl] Marx," stating:

> "Born Yesterday" [is] the most diabolically clever political satire I have encountered in almost thirty years of steady film reviewing. Never have human symbols been more subtly molded to carry destructive comment through disarming comedy.[39]

While Moorings' claims appeared in late 1950, in early 1951 the film was picketed at some New York theatres by two Catholic veteran groups sponsored by the church's Anti-Communist Committee. The organization asked the public

> to boycott ... [each theatre] house because, it was stated, both Miss Holliday and Garson Kanin, author of the play upon which the pic[ture] was based, were linked with organizations listed as subversive by the Attorney General's office.[40]

Given the Capraeque nature of *Born Yesterday*, including its *Mr. Smith*–like visits to so many of America's D.C. shrines, how could such a claim be made? One might even recycle a popular period catchphrase, "That's the $64 question," inspired by a well-liked 1950s NBC radio program, *The $64 Question* (later to become the *$64,000 Question* on CBS television). The answer is threefold. First, Kanin and Holliday had supported liberal causes which also included members of a still legal communist party, from championing the "Hollywood Ten" (writers and directors cited for Contempt of Congress for refusing to testify to HUAC, 1947), to campaigning for Henry Wallace's 1948 Progressive Party presidential run. (He had previously been a former vice-president under Franklin Delano Roosevelt, as well as having served in the cabinets of Roosevelt and President Harry S Truman.) And world events in 1949–1950 further fueled right-wing paranoia about communism in America, from China's decades-long civil war ending with a communist victory in 1949, to the beginning of the Korean War in 1950.

Second, Holliday and Kanin were made more vulnerable by democratic events which occurred the same year *Born Yesterday* appeared. In 1950, the Hollywood Ten began serving one-year prison terms for contempt of Congress. Also, a pamphlet-style booklet called *Red Channels: The Report of Communist Influence in Radio and Television* appeared. It was published by the anti-communist journal *Counterattack* in June of that year and listed 151 entertainment-related people alleged to be either communists or communist sympathizers. Holliday and Kanin were both included. They were among good company, including Charlie Chaplin, Orson Welles, Leonard Bernstein, Arthur Miller, Dorothy Parker, Peabody Award–winning CBS journalist William Shirer, Edward G. Robinson, Dashiell Hammett, Lillian Hellman, Ruth Gordon (Kanin's actor/writer wife), Zero Mostel, and Pete Seeger.

Most of these alleged "pinko" ties went back to a time when responsible people were fighting fascism around the globe, especially starting with the Spanish Civil War (1936–1939), the prelude to World War II. The anti-fascist coalitions of the 1930s and 1940s were usually a motley collection of progressives, socialists, communists, and other liberal groups. Indeed, thousands of Americans joined the Abraham Lincoln Brigade in order to journey to Spain and help the International Brigade fighting the fascist coup of General Francisco Franco. He had overthrown an elected leftist Popular Front government, with substantial support from Nazi Germany and fascist Italy; the Soviet Union was the only major country aiding the Popular Front.

Not surprisingly, many progressive Americans did everything they could for this cause, and/or later advocating a second front during World War II to aid the Soviets when invaded by Nazi Germany. (Military and civilian casualties for Russia eventually numbered over 20,000,000—the most of any country involved in the war.) Even tangential involvement in these or similar liberal activities, such as signing a petition, writing a letter, attending a rally, donating money and so on, could and did land one's name in *Red Channels*, or as it was satirically nicknamed, "the red hunter's *Reader's Digest*." Though not a communist, Holliday came from a socialist family and had supported many of these suddenly toxic causes. The looney injustice of all this is best summarized by an excerpt from a Lillian Hellman letter to HUAC: "I cannot and will not cut my conscience to fit this year's fashions."

Third, *Born Yesterday* included Dawn digs at fascism, especially against Harry's corrupt junkyard mogul. Well, in those exceedingly conservative times, any depiction of a dishonest businessman could be decoded as a communist attack on capitalism. Plus, the actor playing this so-called fascist character, Broderick Crawford, had won a Best Actor Oscar the previous year for portraying a homegrown fascist in the Academy Award–winning Best Picture *All the King's Men* (1949). It was based upon Robert Penn Warren's Pulitzer Prize–winning "novel," and was really a veiled biography of Louisiana's demigod Senator Huey Long. Ultimately, maybe if *Born Yesterday* had not been such a hit, there would have been less red-baiting of Holliday, since HUAC-orientated organizations liked nothing better than to ruin and/or humiliate stars by later also pressuring them to name names of other alleged fellow travelers.

Not surprisingly, Holliday was called before HUAC in early 1952. Cohen, for all his coarseness, was one of the only Hollywood bigwigs to fight for his performers, and Holliday was well-tutored on how to get through her HUAC grilling. Paradoxically, however, her greatest asset was playing the dumb blonde she so despised, or as biographer Gary Carey described it, "she would give her final and maybe her best performance as Billie Dawn in a Washington, D.C., courtroom."[41] For example, when asked if she knew Albert Einstein had a communist-front record, Holliday responded with perfect Dawn illogic:

> Then I'm sure ... Einstein [and others] got into it the way I did, because I am sure none of them are communists. I mean if you are communist, why go to a communist front? Whatever you are, be it![42]

Thankfully, the communist attacks on Holliday and *Born Yesterday* were seen as pure lunacy by most viewers, or as the Motion Picture Association of America (MPAA) said, in part, in a telegram to all Catholic publications which ran Mooring's damning review, "[The film] gives warmth and positive support to the democratic ideals, principals and institutions of America."[43] Film historian Mark Merbaum would later write, "The serious moral of *Born Yesterday* is not slighted but it was the humorous aspects of the film that made it the triumph it was ... [especially] the performance of Judy Holliday."[44] Nevertheless, the belaboring of how her personality comedy succeeded in an often populist framework was done for two reasons. First, while the latter genre was about to go dormant for much of the decade, how ironic that a quasi-populist picture like *Born Yesterday* should be criticized by some for simply doing what populism is all about—warning people against institutionalized corruption and the attempted manipulation of the people. Traits visible in the film. This makes *Born Yesterday* even more timely today, and does not bode well for the rest of the 1950s. Second, the fact that even such an All-American picture could meet with such criticism at the beginning of the decade suggests why the 1950s has such a dumbing down reputation—the conservative political establishment was humor-deprived and threatened.

Nevertheless, *Born Yesterday*'s success along personality comedy lines launched an outstanding new talent. And even though it was the rigid 1950s, character-driven comedy at its best, as in Holliday's performance, is when a figure like Dawn can find and encourage a capacity for change ... even in the narrow confines of her era.

2

Martin & Lewis
Sailor Beware (February 1, 1952)

> Dean's [talent] was making the audience his friend—*especially* compared to how they felt watching [fellow Rat Packer] Frank [Sinatra] or Jerry [Lewis]. Dean took the edges off of Jerry's hysteria and Frank's egoism. He made each one go down easier. Standing beside each of them with a look of bemusement and mild shock, he was *us*—but cool and breezy and quick-witted and easy on the eyes: entertaining even on his own.—Critic Shawn Levy[1]

The above quote is important to keep in mind, because during the years in which the duo were teamed (1946–1956), Jerry Lewis was given the most critical attention *and* credit for their achievements. And the team had a mega rock star-like success during their decade together. Indeed, from 1951 to 1954 Martin & Lewis were either number one or two at America's box office turnstyles.[2] Even their acrimonious final two years together, when they spoke only when performing, still found their movies solidly lodged in Hollywood's top 10 box office listings—seventh in 1955, and sixth in 1956.[3] Plus, their contractual club dates and television appearances remained SRO (standing room only) until their last professional obligations were fulfilled. Even then fellow performers begged them not to quit, with Abbot & Costello putting that request in a published plea in a trade paper.

Ironically, Martin & Lewis' popularity still rivaled the first time they played Broadway's Paramount Theatre (July 1951). Pandemonium ruled. Fans, many of whom had camped out for tickets, filled Times Square and stopped traffic. Plus, the team's films were periodically re-issued to theatres during my teen years in the 1960s and early 1970s. My biggest surprise related to their long shelf life was watching a dubbed German version of *Sailor Beware* in a 1970 Frankfurt (Germany) theatre during a European backpacking trip. Astonishment quickly returned when I discovered that while all dialogue was in German, the film's songs remained in English. *Sailor Beware* was a trailblazer in their work being dubbed into other languages. For example, the picture was the first adapted into French. Thus, one might argue that France's famous obsession with Lewis began with this movie.

So why all this backstory before directly addressing *Sailor Beware*? After all, unlike the neglected Judy Holliday (1921–1965), Dean Martin (1917–1995) and Jerry Lewis (1926) still command high profile status, especially given their subsequent long solo careers. The answer is provocatively multi-faceted. First, as the opening quote should have made clear, despite the multiple talents of Lewis, this chapter is, in part, a revisionist examination of Martin during their team years. Second, and directly related to this point, the Martin & Lewis collaboration is best divided into two parts—the "team" period, and the Lewis dominated years. Lewis himself acknowledged the timing of the rupture in his incongruously titled self-serving book, *Dean & Me (A Love Story)*: "We didn't disagree about much for the first half of our decade together."[4] *Sailor Beware* was the fifth of their 16 movie collaborations. It is the duo's best *team* film, and arguably their premier picture.

Second, Lewis initially remained a major independent presence after their breakup. Yet, paradoxically, his best 1950s "solo" outing occurred in *Artists and Models* (1955, see Chapter 9), when he was technically still part of Martin & Lewis. (Antithetically, even here, Lewis is best when temporarily teamed with Shirley MacLaine—more proof of the need to take "the edge off of Jerry's hysteria.") Third, *Sailor Beware* is more in the old school vaudeville tradition of a Bob Hope & Bing Crosby *Road* picture. Indeed, Martin & Lewis even have a showstopper theatre-based comic song and dance duet (to be addressed shortly), which is a staple of the *Road* series. Appropriately, *Sailor Beware*'s director, Hal Walker, performed the same task on the best of the Hope-Crosby teamings—1946's the *Road to Utopia*. Moreover, he again turned up as the director of the *Road to Bali* (1953, see Chapter 6). And shortly after *Sailor Beware*'s release, Hope & Crosby make a cameo in Martin & Lewis' *Scared Stiff* (1952), with the younger duo returning the favor in the *Road to Bali*.

Fourth, as noted in the Prologue and expanded upon in later chapters (3, 9, and 11), when Martin & Lewis scripts tend to overly favor the latter half of the partnership, the transition is greatly assisted by the cartoon orientated director Frank Tashlin (1913–1972). He megaphoned the team in two of their final films, *Artists and Models* and the sardonically titled last picture—1956's *Hollywood or Bust*. (As demonstrated in other decade structured studies of seemingly fully formed comedians, one or two special directors can still provide a notable impact.[5])

Dean Martin (top) and Jerry Lewis in the happy early years (circa 1950).

With these parameter points

in place, it is now appropriate to provide a *Sailor Beware* sketch of the paper thin plot which best serves the character-driven personality comedy genre.[6] Al Crowthers (Martin) and Melvin Jones (Lewis) are two strangers who meet at a San Diego Navy recruiting station. Neither plans to be accepted on medical grounds. Melvin's "uvula becomes edematous" (swells up) when he gets too close to women's cosmetics and the boy/man cannot breathe. As Lewis' character deadpans, "that could be fatal." (Repetitions of his uvula/edematous condition are a standing joke in the movie.) In Al's case, his "trick knee" has resulted in multiple flunked physicals—which allows him to have long, drawn out, passionate goodbyes with a bevy of beauties. (Indeed, the first time Martin meets Al, Dean's character is in an amorous embrace with an unbilled cameo by movie star Betty Hutton, the lead of such classics as Preston Sturges' 1944 *Miracle of Morgan's Creek*, and George Sidney's *Annie Get Your Gun*, 1950). Even moronic Melvin (Lewis later referred to his persona as "the idiot"), stutters, "wasn't that...," setting-up Al's comic malapropism finish to the question, "Hetty Button."

Naturally, however, both Martin & Lewis pass their physicals, with the standard service comedy pranks, from the childish Melvin being embarrassed to disrobe in public, to being subjected to an amusingly long needle. More importantly, an ongoing source of comedy is provided by establishing a mean commander, Robert Strauss' CPO (chief petty officer) Lardoski, another given in military clown comedies. A personality comedy genre basic is also evoked by being nomadic. That is, after squeezing all the comedy from the San Diego setting (including basic training and going on leave), the Martin & Lewis company is shipped to Honolulu to exhaust the humor possibilities in Hawaii. As an addendum to the travel motif, frequently the mode of transportation comes into comic play, too, from the Marx Brothers' misuse of an ocean liner in *Monkey Business* (1931), to Steve Martin and John Candy's misadventures with many means of transportation in *Planes, Trains & Automobiles* (1987).

In *Sailor Beware* Martin & Lewis' company is transferred to Honolulu via submarine, which also provides several personality comedy situations for comic sequences. The most entertaining scene involves Melvin being left alone on deck as the ship submerges. Recycling an inventive sequence from Sydney Chaplin's (Charlie's brother) *Submarine Pirate* (1915), Jerry's anti-hero eventually seeks safety atop all that remains above sea level—the periscope. The sequence is milked further by having Melvin squish his face against the glass of the periscope's upper prism viewer. Seen from below by the captain, his officers, and the theatre audience, Melvin's mashed sucker-like lips and face make for an ongoing sight gag. In fact, the best below surface guess is, "[It] looks like a sea monster to me, Captain."

Once in Honolulu, the plot keys upon a bet made before the company left San Diego. Strauss' CPO bully, comically thinking Melvin was a lady's man, had gambled with Al, and most of his fellow sailors, that Jerry's dopey sailor would *not* be able to kiss the Hawaiian-based sexy French nightclub singer Corinne Calvert (an actress playing herself, 1925–2001). Coupled to this simple plot is an unlikely boxing match victory by wimpy Melvin, and some songs by Al, since his civilian job had conveniently been a nightclub singer, too. And as in the vast majority of clown comedies, everything works out in the end.

As the *Brooklyn Eagle* noted of this framework, "There's no getting away from it [everyone else in the movie is a 'stooge'], these boys [Martin & Lewis] take over a screen, and Lewis takes more of it than Martin."[7] Yet, in this still fairly balanced *team* comedy, too many of the reviews take *Variety*'s perspective, "with such a vital comic as Jerry Lewis, it is difficult to plot a substantial story to sustain interest in between his funnily [strange] frenetic routines."[8] The *New York Journal American*'s critique openingly states, "If you thought Jerry Lewis was funny in the previous Dean Martin–Jerry Lewis films, wait until you see him in *Sailor Beware*."[9] There is a consistent "Lewis, Lewis, Lewis" to these reviews. Nevertheless, there were a few critics who saw the full package, such as the *New York Daily News*' Kate Cameron:

> The more you see of the average comic on screen, the unfunnier he becomes. But with Dean Martin and Jerry Lewis, the reverse is true. These two zany comics grow more amusing with each picture…. A [Lewis] fight sequence and a scene in which Martin tries to teach Lewis how to enunciate properly are the funniest in the picture.[10]

Lewis' fight sequence is brilliant, as he, in part, amusingly backpedals like Muhammad Ali on steroids, or gets on his knees and punches his opponent's feet. Even Bosley Crowthers' rare *New York Times* pan of the picture praises the scene, though he qualifies full credit to Lewis by indirectly reminding readers of Charlie Chaplin's tour de force boxing scene in *City Lights* (1931):

> His [Lewis] fast and elaborate footwork to stay away from his baffled foe, while he shadowboxes like sixty [very fast and often tripping himself], is graphic and genuine fun. But then, of course, he did have the fair example of Charlie to study for this routine. [The aforementioned *City Lights* scene still sets the comic bar for all boxing sequences.][11]

That being said, critic Cameron's other highlighted *Sailor Beware* routine, about Dean teaching Jerry to box is part of a lengthy locker room rubdown routine which, in its entirety, is the picture's quintessential comedy sketch. This status comes from being the picture's funniest and most sustained reign of laughter. In fact, it is so lengthy that the sequence is best showcased in pivotal excerpted points. Moreover, the following abbreviated bits demonstrate Dean's multiple talents, starting with his being much more than a straight man—Lewis' later limited take on Martin[12]:

> DEAN: Put on the [boxing] act right now [in order to scare Melvin's near by opponent]. Go ahead. Listen, Melvin, how long you been fighting?
> JERRY: Ah, ah, ah, ah, ah, ah [Dean slaps the back of Melvin's head to get this supposedly veteran punch-drunk fighter back on track]. I been fighting now for about sisteen [sic] years.
> DEAN: Sisteen [sic]?
> JERRY: Yeah. Oh, it's about sisteen [sic] years.
> DEAN: Sisteen [sic]. What do you mean?
> JERRY: Sisteen. Fourteen, fifteen, sisteen, sisteen [sic].
> DEAN: Oh, sure. How many fights have you had altogether?
> JERRY: Ah, ah, ah, ah, ah, ah [Dean again slaps the back of Melvin's head to get this human broken record back on track]. Altogether now, when you add them up, I had 101 fights. 101….
> [The routine continues along these lines and then their comic interaction reverses.]
> DEAN: Well, who was your toughest fight?
> JERRY: The toughest fight I had was with Gene Tierney [a sexy period actress].
> DEAN: [Now, a surprised Dean stutters] Ah, ah [and Jerry slaps the back of his head]. That was the toughest fight?
> JERRY: Gene Tierney.
> MARTIN: You mean [former heavy weight boxing champion] Gene Tunney.
> JERRY: You fight who you want, I fight who I want….

Later in this inspired routine Dean adds some soft bodily comic action with the dialogue, after Lewis' Melvin confesses he was once offered money to throw a fight:

> JERRY: He says to me, "Kid, I'll give you a tousand [sic] dollars if you—
> MARTIN: No, he said he'd give you a thousand dollars.
> JERRY: He said he'd give me a tousand [sic] dollars.

This ongoing back and forth of Dean repeating "thousand dollars" to Jerry's "tousand dollars" culminates with an Oliver Hardy-like patient exasperation by Dean at Jerry's variation on Stan Laurel's pea-brain nature. Dean's Al eventually results to a "T-H-O-U-S-A-N-D" spelling lesson and an amusing attempt with his hand to assist Melvin's wayward jaw and tongue to enunciate properly. Finally, a compromise is reached with Jerry's character understandably saying "ten hundred dollars." As the drawn-out routine continues, Dean is even more the comedy catalyst. Precipitated by Jerry's rival and handlers (one of whom is an unbilled and yet to be iconic James Dean) leaving the locker room, Dean governs the *team* comedy with Jerry. What follows is yet another excerpt from the sketch, when the locker room rubdown ruse (scaring the adversary) is complete and Dean gives Jerry some boxing tips:

> DEAN: Put up your guard.
> JERRY: Yeah [he raises his gloved hands and Dean lightly hits him in the stomach].
> DEAN: Right, put this up [the gloved hands]. Now I hit you in the stomach. Why? Why?
> JERRY: Well, you hit me. [Jerry lowers his guard and Dean lightly hits his head.]
> DEAN: Why? 'Cause it wasn't protected. Always protect your stomach.... [This soon proceeds into] Up, down, up, down. Protect. [And Dean comically peppers Jerry with soft blows to the head and tummy quicker than Jerry can raise and lower his gloved hands.]

This continues to be a laugh-producing Dean sequence as he teaches Lewis another boxing lesson—grabbing Jerry in a clutch and demonstrating how an opponent can easily free an arm and glove and pepper the back of one's head with "rabbit punch" after "rabbit punch," which Dean comically proceeds to demonstrate on Jerry with cartoon-like speed.

Fittingly, this lengthy comic prologue, which is a testament to how *both* Martin and Lewis could play the focus comedian in such an ambitious sketch, leads into Melvin's aforementioned bout. Surprisingly, if these are the film's two signature sequences, a close third is also a Dean highlighted routine for the duo. The mainspring for this musical sequence is a missing act at a Honolulu nightclub where the two are on leave. Given Al's civilian entertainer background, Martin's character is pressed into duty, with Melvin tagging along. It begins with an amusing failure when the team attempts to sing a two-part harmony of "The Sailor's Polka," a number Dean performed on the submarine trip to Hawaii. But despite Melvin's off-pitch screeching, he whines that Al has the easier part. Yet, when they switch, there is still the same comic musical misfire.

The situation anticipates a future real Rat Pack Las Vegas nightclub closing, with just Martin and Sinatra on stage casually winding down their act with joking general patter. However, Martin always gets the bigger laughs, which mystifies Sinatra. Thus, one night he asks Dean if they can switch lines. His accommodating friend does so, which at one point actually reduces Martin to being a straight man. Yet, Sinatra still does *not* crack up the audience, while Martin's minimal expressions get the guffaws. Later, a puzzled Sinatra asks Dean, "How come you always get the laughs and I don't [even when you are setting up the joke]?" Martin's simple response, "You're not funny."[13] Returning to Jerry's aforementioned request to switch parts in the "The Sailor's Polka," if Melvin had asked Sinatra's question but substituted "songs" for laughs, Martin could have provided a similar answer, "You can't sing." *And yes*, I know in this case Lewis is deliberately chirping like a boy/man because Melvin is suffering from history's worst case of a changing adolescent voice.

So what is the point? When Lewis the performer eventually thinks his range is beyond being a shower singer, it weakens the late Martin & Lewis pictures (the squeak/smooth contrast is part of their comedy), as well as hurting Lewis' solo career. Yes, he had a modest 1958 hit recording of the Al Jolson song, "Rock-a-Bye Your Baby with a Dixie Melody," but it was a fluke novelty number tie-in with his movie *Rock-A-Bye Baby* (1958). Indeed, when that film is screened today, the Chaplin wannabe Lewis' number turns the plot into bathos. Ironically, the filmmaker seems to underscore these singing limitations in his best solo outing, *The Nutty Professor* (1963) ... as well as his need for Martin. The film is a contemporary parody of Robert Lewis Stevenson's *Dr. Jekyll and Mr. Hyde*. Lewis' buck-toothed nerdy professor Julius Kelp invents a serum which transforms him into the cool handsome singer Buddy Love, à la Dean Martin. As the confident Buddy he pursues a pretty student (Stella Stevens) and musically mesmerizes her and the student body. But once the formula wears off, invariably when he is singing, his squeaky pipes would not be out of place in Melvin's attempts at "The Sailor's Polka." Regardless, Lewis' delusions about his singing abilities can best be lumped into the growing ego which caused the split with Martin. For example, comedy historian Ronald L. Smith quotes the comedian's later description of the "large number [of people] who simply can't stand his ... [solo work], 'People hate me because I am a multifaceted, talented, wealthy, internationally famous genius.'"[14] By this time the overlap in the original Martin & Lewis fan base would probably fit in a phone booth.

Nevertheless, with "The Sailor's Polka" being a bust within the movie story, Dean's Al decides the duo should perform the smile-producing "Old Calliope Song," once heralded to entertainment starved small town America that the circus and/or the minstrel show had arrived. Except this time the singing is largely left to Dean, while Jerry adds the sound effects—his outlandish takes on various musical instruments. Again, one has an amusingly protracted sequence which eventually segues into a charming Martin & Lewis soft-shoe number. This is traditional *team* comedy at its best. And keep in mind, with or without Lewis, Martin's movie numbers were frequently laced with comedy, anticipating his later hit TV program, *The Dean Martin Show* (1965–1974).

While *Sailor Beware*'s best sequence was Lewis' impressive boxing routine, the lengthy build up to the fight which displayed the duo's multifaceted *team* talents, and the charmingly extended "Calliope" routine, the film featured an assortment of additional comedy pluses. For example, Lewis took the satirization of the strong American male, patented so effectively by Eddie Bracken in Preston Sturges' *The Miracle of Morgan's Creek* and *Hail the Conquering Hero* (both 1944), to new heights. Plus, Lewis added the natural plasticity of his face and body to Bracken's ultimate anti-hero. Nonetheless, here is how Sturges' Bracken is a

> precursor of the Jerry Lewis characterizations of the '50s and '60s. He is a complete failure—physically handicapped ... [with health issues], rather confused mentally, and cursed with a pusillanimous [fearful] character.... He represents to us the weakest and, therefore, most disturbing side of our personality.... (This ... may explain why many reject characters like the ones played by Bracken and Lewis so violently. He is a side of us we do not readily like to admit to.)[15]

This scenario suggests Martin's presence in the team benefitted Lewis *beyond* helping take "the edges off Jerry's hysteria." That is, Dean's all-male unflappableness also provided yet another kind of balance to Jerry's problem child persona. Indeed, during the production of *Sailor Beware*, an article written for the pocket-sized magazine *Quick* even described Martin's singing style as "muscular sexiness."[16] Both perspectives would fit Lewis' early harsher description of the duo, "for the first time here we have a [team composed of] a handsome man and a monkey," with occasional elevated descriptions of his character as an idiot.[17]

In fact, their early equal partner dynamics as a duo were unique. Most previous teams had a player at negative odds with other character(s). In the silent era, America's first internationally known comedian, the rotund John Bunny (1863–1915)—fat, funny, and forgotten—was often paired with a hen-pecking wife played by the Olive Oyl thin Flora Finch (1867–1940). Their short subjects, sometimes nicknamed "Bunnyfinches," represented the first comedy team, and cinematically started the comic contrast of fat and thin.

A thumbnail sketch of other more familiar teams would naturally include Laurel & Hardy. And while Stan Laurel (1890–1965) was fond of calling them "two brains without a single thought," Oliver Hardy (1892–1957) definitely lorded it over Stan.[18] Again, one has the size contrasts. Abbott & Costello continued the fat-thin visual gag on a more aggressive level, with Bud Abbott (1895–1974), the consummate straight man, often bullying Lou

Dean Martin (left) and Jerry Lewis as a *team* entertainingly playing the "Old Calliope Song" in *Sailor Beware*.

Costello (1906–1959). While previous examples showcased two comics, Lou was the laugh beneficiary of their duo.[19]

The same dominating tendency occurred with the multiple Marx Brothers. Groucho (1890–1977) belittled brothers are best seen as teams within teams. For example, Chico (1886–1961) often works together with Harpo (1888–1964) against Groucho, or simply had mastery over the latter Marx when they were paired. Moreover, when brother Zeppo (1901–1979) appeared in their Paramount pictures (1929–1933), he was subserviently coupled with Groucho. In addition, when Margaret Dumont (circa 1889–1965)—who co-starred in so many of the team's movies she was nicknamed the "fifth Marx Brother"—was on the screen, she was paired with an insulting Groucho.[20]

In the Three Stooges, Moe Howard (1897–1975) ratcheted up the mean level over partners Larry Fine (1911–1974) and brother Curly Howard (1906–1952). After Curly's 1946 stroke, he was replaced by yet another brother, Shemp Howard (1900–1955). With Shemp's 1955 death, the trio lineup would continue with a series of Curly/Shemp replacements. The act essentially ended with Larry's 1970 stroke. Yet, whatever the configuration, Moe continued to be the catalyst for an almost brutally surreal/cartoon-like physical slapstick against his comedy partners.

Even the sometime *Road* series team of Bob Hope (1903–2003) and Bing Crosby (1904–1977) had the latter figure constantly doing awful things to his ski-nose "buddy," from selling Bob to a slave-trader during the *Road to Morocco* (1942), to constantly putting him at circus performing risks in their *Road to Zanzibar* (1941). Moreover, the only time Hope ever got the girl (*Road* leading lady Dorothy Lamour), the surprise ending of the *Road to Utopia* (1946) reveals that he has been cuckolded by Bing. That is, the picture is shown with the framing device of Hope and Lamour as an elderly married couple ... closing with the viewer's first sight of their grown son—played by Crosby.

In contrast, Martin & Lewis' formula keys upon a sickly childlike nerd attempting to be like his cool older brother, with the Martin figure only too happy to serve as a model and/or protector for the "kid." Interestingly, Lewis actually felt like that after first meeting Martin, even *before* their teaming, "I'm thinking he's going to be someone special: the big brother I never had."[21] Much later, Lewis credited this sibling scenario with how they became a team:

> I was thrilled to be on the same show [nightclub bill], at last, with my fantasy big brother. But it wasn't enough for me to just be in the same place with him at the same time. Like all little brothers, I craved attention. And one night during the third show, as Dean stood on the ... stage entrancing the audience (but especially the ladies) with his honeyed version of "Where or When," I figured out how to get it ... [I upstaged his number as a crazy waiter.] I had made a calculation about Dean.... I figured him for a guy who didn't take himself too seriously, who saw all of life as one big crazy joke ... [Dean went along] ... slowly, milking it for all it was worth—[he] turned to face the monkey who had ruined his song. Our eyes met ... [and] I saw the indulgent smile of the older brother I had always longed for.[22]

And thus a spontaneously chaotic act was born. Ironically, Jerry's comment about Dean being a figure "who didn't take himself too seriously" would later be the genesis of how Martin eventually blew by Lewis in the entertainment world.

Nonetheless, the guardian older brother scenario is a given in the Martin & Lewis team, especially in the early years. For example, late in *Sailor Beware*, the constantly troublesome Melvin has Al going to great lengths to keep an eye on the dopey fellow he has looked out for since film frame one. Thus, even as Martin is about to go on stage, he tells

Melvin, "You're staying with me if you have to stand next to me while I sing." Though this is a unique relationship in comedy team history, there is a certain behind-the-scenes parallel with Laurel & Hardy. In both cases, the dominant individual on the screen (Hardy and Martin) had little interest in the work behind the scene. Each was seemingly most interested in getting to the nearest golf course. In contrast, Laurel and Lewis were obsessed with the filmmaking process, especially the story's tone. In fact, Lewis would later even write a book entitled *The Total Film-Maker* (1971).[23]

This arrangement has potential red flags. The behind-the-scene partner could destroy the team's balance by tipping the scales in his favor. Happily, this was *not* the case with Laurel & Hardy. After being teamed and molded by writer/director Leo McCarey, Laurel was brilliant at both keeping their sketch material funny and maintaining the team's equilibrium.[24] Sadly, this was not the case with Lewis. He came down with what film historians have called the "Charlie Chaplin Disease."[25] Chaplin not only starred in his pictures, he wrote, directed, and composed the music for them. Since then, only Woody Allen has approached Chaplin's level of sustained comic genius, sans the musical compositions. But the history of film comedy is full of those who have failed trying, from silent star Harry Langdon, to Eddie Murphy's *Harlem Nights* (1989). It is just too many hats to wear. A solo Lewis would briefly come close with *The Bellboy* (1960). But he would quickly crash and burn both artistically and commercially.

Lewis' opening of this comic Pandora's Box escalates in the years after *Sailor Beware*. And they are, as suggested earlier, further innocently inflated by his work with Frank Tashlin, whose cartoon style was more geared to Lewis' persona. Yet, Lewis' obsession with Chaplin would also encourage him to attempt to enter the ephemeral world of Charlie pathos, such as the close of *City Lights* (1931).[26] That is, the Tramp's idealized and once blind child/woman has been enabled to see Charlie. Yet when she first beholds her bedraggled benefactor, her response is poetically described by pioneering critic James Agee:

> [Chaplin's Tramp] recognizes himself, for the first time, through the terrible changes [disappointment] in her face. The camera just exchanges a few close-ups of the emotions which shift and intensify in each face. It is enough to shrivel the heart to see, and it is the greatest piece of acting and the highest moment in movies.[27]

Lewis never remotely got close to this poignancy, though no other comedian has either. But one can see Lewis already reaching for this comic talisman as early as his first solo picture, *The Delicate Delinquent* (1957). Here, as elsewhere, Lewis' ongoing attempts at pathos invariably turn to bathos. And over time, his Martin & Lewis period essentially had him and his sycophants turning Martin into a supporting player—only able to look in on the comedy. The *Delinquent* script finally caused Martin to pull the plug on this once *unique team dynamic* ... which had not been right for some time.

This telescoping into the future is not what makes a *Sailor Beware* screening bittersweet. All the nuances of an exceptionally funny *friendly* sibling duo are there. Lewis' later left-handed praise of Martin as a gifted straight man was merely more comic condescension towards his *big brother*. Martin was never merely a straight man—bemused expressions saw to that. Moreover, *Sailor Beware* had Jerry playing straight man, too. For instance, after the aborted "Sailor's Polka" number, and Dean's Al suggested they move on to "The Old Calliope" standard, Melvin plays setup for Al: "Oh, we're gonna do another one together both?" Dean, the grammatically correcting older "brother" observes with comic affection,

"'Together both?' That's as bad as, 'Up the street, the soldiers, they're marching down.' Now come on, let's sing the song." This is *team* comedy.

Sadly, the majority of Martin & Lewis texts suggest their best team comedy is forever lost in their nightclub performances, or just horsing around on a movie set. For example, James Dean later told his then girlfriend, Liz Sheridan (Jerry Seinfeld's future TV mother):

> I did a tiny part in a Dean Martin–Jerry Lewis movie. Those two guys are really crazy—at breakfast on the set one morning, they ran around pouring pancake syrup on everyone's head, cast and crew and everyone. It held up production for hours. I thought it was hilarious. The director [Hal Walker] was mad as hell but they didn't seem to care. Someone told me that they're always doing stuff like that.[28]

Of course, Martin & Lewis did not have a complete corner on *Sailor Beware* set antics. Another came from a most unusual source, the picture's exotic Corinne Calvet, the number one pinup girl in postwar France, and Martin's love interest, once the film reached Hawaii. She had also co-starred in the team's first picture, *My Friend Irma Goes West* (1950). Calvet had "found Dean friendly, a man of the world, self-assured and quiet"—just the opposite of her impression of Lewis.[29] Appropriately, Martin had also played "big brother" to her rescue on that set when Lewis was harassing her as a human monkey. Flash forward to *Sailor Beware* and while talking to Dean she was again harassed—this time by the picture's lecherous producer, Hal Wallis. He accused the shapely Calvet, whom he had previously attempted to seduce, of wearing falsies and repeatedly demanded she take them out:

> CALVET: "Mr Wallis, are you calling me a liar?" I spoke in a menacing tone as I approached him. I grabbed his hand, and in front of everyone, put it inside my dress and made sure he felt that I had nothing there but my own breast. "Are you finding anything there but my flesh? No? Then thank you." Dropping his hand, I returned to stand next to Dean Martin, who looked extremely amused.
> MARTIN: "Bravo," he said softly. "That was magnificent."[30]

Sadly, like Martin & Lewis' best moments, this sweet revenge by Calvet was not caught on film. Regardless, maybe the best recorded examples of the team occur on NBC television's *Colgate Comedy Hour* (1950–1955), a live variety show frequently hosted by the duo. For instance, in a 1955 episode promoting their latest movie, *You're Never Too Young* (1955), one of their sketches segues into a song and dance number which would not be out of place in *Sailor Beware*.[31] Moreover, Dean steals the most inventive routine, a parody of CBS' *Person to Person* program (1953–1961), in which renowned newsman Edward R. Murrow would do live interviews with celebrities from all walks of life. However, the entertainment hook for these "visits" was that Murrow would be in a large comfortable chair in the studio, while his guests were at their homes.

The Martin & Lewis spoof is entitled *Person to People*, with Dean playing Tedward R. Burrow, and Jerry appearing as a Hollywood comedian acting like Jerry's self-described "idiot" persona. An important addendum to the parody is that Murrow was a *heavy smoker* and he conducted the sessions in what seemed like a cigarette haze. Thus, the segment opens in a total tobacco fog, with a cigarette puffing Dean finally emerging from the smog. And while Jerry is funny, he is basically just doing a variation of his movie alter ego. Nevertheless, it is Dean who is executing the real spoofing performance, such as amusingly stumbling over his own questions, something the ever so articulate Murrow would never do. Along the same lines, each time the camera returns to Burrow/Dean for a new question, he is in a different comically cozy smoke-filled position, from dangling a leg over his sizable chair arm, to assuming a horizontal hammock-like pose—things anathema to the distinguished Murrow. (He much preferred hard news, and only hosted the program so CBS would allow him more autonomy.) The inspired sketch even ended with a comic nod to Dean. *Person to Person* usually involved meeting other members of the focus individual's family. This bit concluded with a peek at Burrow's family, in which six heavy smokers suddenly appear.

Fittingly, given Dean's spot-on parody of Murrow, Martin & Lewis had appeared on the program the previous year to plug another of their films, *Living It Up* (1954).[32] While the duo seems chummy in Lewis' den and adjoining "playhouse" (which included their awards and his personal film equipment), the cracks are apparent in this now veneered "friendship." Murrow even brings up the feud about which the public had been hearing. (This was also the year that *Look* magazine gave the team a cover photo ... only to crop Martin out of the shot.) Lewis quickly glossed over the feud scenario, saying it was not unusual for people to have disagreements.

Yet, when Martin & Lewis move the interview to the "playhouse," it comes out that they had just been shooting one of Jerry's amateur weekend movies, and Dean had ducked out to play golf. And suddenly the normally animated Lewis says, without an ounce of comedy before or after the comment, "We had to kill him. We had to kill him." There is an awkward pause, which a punningly appropriate show business phrase would call "dead air time," before Dean jovially confesses to going AWOL to golf, after which he seems to have the need to explain Jerry killed the gangster he was playing.

Murrow eventually asks what is behind their work. Dean deadpans, "The money," before seguing into a pat answer about entertaining people. Yet, the remark anticipates the much reported 1956 comment Dean made to Lewis at the time of their split. After somehow engagingly honoring his contractual obligation, the strain and hurt Dean felt the last few years produced the utterance, "[You're] nothing to me but a fucking dollar sign." Later a calmer Martin blamed the key to their split upon the aforementioned "Chaplin Disease":

> He read a book about Chaplin. At some point, he said to himself, "I'm exactly like Chaplin," and from then on no one could tell him anything. He knew it all. Before that, if we made up a sketch or a joke, he asked me if I thought it was funny because he knew I wouldn't con him. I had never broken up deliberately.... When he didn't get the kind of laughs from me that a second Chaplin should have had, he began to try his stuff out on six guys we had around us as court followers. You might call them professional idiots. I could say, "My father's got pneumonia," and they'd guffaw. So Jerry didn't come to me any more for my opinion. He tried out his stuff on our idiot clique.[33]

This more measured telling of Lewis' team derailment dovetails back into a final insight from the Murrow interview. That is, when Lewis is asked what was behind their work, a brief paraphrasing of his observations has already essentially cut Martin out. "Dean is more the authoritarian figure in our movies and I'm the underdog—a situation in which most people in an audience could relate." So much for all that *brotherly* talk.

Despite the team's personal travail, their frequent early 1950s TV appearances, from hosting the *Colgate Comedy Hour*, to the Murrow interview in order to promote their latest film, make for an ironic comparison with Judy Holliday's career at this time. She was essentially blacklisted from the small screen during this portion of a bipolar decade, given her liberal 1940s politics (see Chapter 1). Through no fault of Martin & Lewis, the paradox continues when one quantifies how the government's HUAC (House Un-American Activities Committee) did damage to her employment, while this same government was a boon to the making of *Sailor Beware*. That is, the film's home company (Paramount) had the complete cooperation of the United States Navy, including all-important access to a real submarine. Given the recent conclusion to the unpopular Korean War (1950–1953), Martin & Lewis' film was also unofficially helping out Navy recruitment. For example, beyond *Sailor Beware* itself, PR material for the picture included a picture of Dean and Jerry standing on either side of a poster which said, "The NAVY Needs MEN."[34]

Plus, while some conservative groups incredibly managed to find communist elements in Holliday's *Born Yesterday* (1950), implying she was either dangerously red or suspiciously pink, *Sailor Beware* had Martin & Lewis in an all–American service comedy. Moreover, the team was also receiving additional kudos for their charity work, what eventually turned into Lewis' annual muscular dystrophy MS telethon. Throw in Martin's budding recording career, with major hits like "That's Amore," and it seemed the duo could do no wrong. The year prior to *Sailor Beware*, their combined earnings were over $1 million, which would be the equivalent of nearly $9 million today.[35] And even if this phenomenal figure made someone a jealously curmudgeon for what my grandfather used to describe as "a life lived up to the nostrils," Lewis responded with a patriotic answer. After acknowledging that even though American taxes took a hefty 90 percent of that amount, he said, "It's all right. The government needs tanks."[36]

Given this multi-faceted popularity base and the *team* comedy still at work in *Sailor Beware*, the film was another critical and commercial hit. As chronicled early in the chapter, despite reviewers generally focusing their praise on Lewis, sometimes it was qualified, such as *New York World-Telegram and Sun* critic Alton Cook observing:

> But there is no point in discussing the minute details of the picture. Its appeal depends entirely on how much and how long you relish the antics of Jerry Lewis.[37]

Also, even when a critic is both a Martin & Lewis fan and actually attempts to balance their contributions to *Sailor Beware*, as is the case with the *New York Herald Tribune*'s Otis L. Guernsey, Jr., there is a need to document the team's exceptional appeal. What follows is his review opening:

> The comedy team of Dean Martin and Jerry Lewis is one of the extra-ordinary show-business phenomena of the day, and it has been pretty well established that it doesn't matter much what they do so long as they do it in their popular and raucous style.[38]

Near the close of Guernsey's critique, he essentially reiterates this view with some abbreviated comedy of his own: "[Their drawing power] packs audiences in as though they hadn't heard a good joke in years."[39] More amusing yet was the *New York Times*' Bosley Crowther being duty bound to report the "phenomenon," yet honest enough to admit, "Frankly, we do not get it."[40] Yet, chronicle he must:

> Whatever it is Dean Martin and Jerry Lewis have got that makes people howl with laughter and toss with rocking frenzy in their chairs, there must be plenty of it in ... "Sailor Beware." For this coolly objective reviewer is duty bound to report that people were doing plenty of both things at the Mayfair Theatre yesterday.[41]

Paramount further fed the public's obsession with the team and *Sailor Beware* by sending them on a series of theatre appearances around the country coinciding with the movie's opening. The *Hollywood Reporter* noted their ambitious itinerary:

> They open today [Tuesday, February 12, 1952] at the Fox [Theatre], San Francisco, for a week, and while there will tape two of their NBC radio shows. [*Sailor Beware* co-star] Corinne Calvet will join them

Dean Martin (top) and Jerry Lewis promoting the United States Navy (1952).

for a taping on Friday and [film noir star] Lizabeth Scott on Sunday.... The comics will appear in Minneapolis for a week at the Radio City Theatre, opening Feb. 22.[42]

Other stops included Cincinnati and Boston. Not surprisingly, the movie was an enormous commercial smash, one of the top five box office hits of 1952.[43] More people saw *Sailor Beware* that year than such now-renowned 1952 productions as *The African Queen*, *High*

Noon, and *Singin' in the Rain*. Conceivably Martin & Lewis' best film, it was the most profitable of all their pictures.[44]

This neglected gem is later compared to Martin & Lewis' *Artists and Models* (1955, see Chapter 9), and what could be called the "Frank Tashlin and Solo Jerry Lewis Period." But for now it is enough to say that *Sailor Beware* represents a great example of the duo as a true *team*, whether fully recognized or not.

3

Bob Hope
Son of Paleface (October 2, 1952)

> *Brooklyn Eagle* critic Jane Corby found the movie's most inspired scene was when two desert buzzards were hitchhiking on the back of Hope's vintage car, with one already having a napkin around his neck. Greenhorn Hope complains, "You'll make the whole thing [film] unbelievable." But of equal fun and foreshadowing is that earlier he had referred to the buzzards as "Martin & Lewis."[1]

As noted earlier in the text, most personality comedians, like Hope, combine their clown personae with another comic approach. Hope's go-to other genre was most often parody. And since his prime film years almost exactly parallel the golden age of sound Westerns (roughly 1939 to the late 1960s), some of Hope's best work parodied this genre. *Son of Paleface* is a sequel to the comedian's first sagebrush spoof, *The Paleface* (1948), and fittingly, these were his two all-time top grossing films, as well as two of the most profitable pictures of 1948 and 1952.[2]

And while the text documents how the massive popularity of 1950 TV eventually forever changed the American film industry, Hope managed to use the small screen as a boost to *Son of Paleface*. That is, one of his co-stars was Roy Rogers, the most popular television cowboy (with Hopalong Cassidy and the Lone Ranger) of the early and mid–1950s.[3] This was no small accomplishment, given that Westerns were as popular on TV as they were in the movies, with an amazing 20-plus horse operas in prime time during much of the 1950s and 1960s. To paraphrase a popular Hope joke during the period, "There are so many Westerns on TV, I have to brush the hay off it before I can turn on my set." Moreover, as the *Hollywood Reporter*'s review stated:

> Casting Roy Rogers was a stroke of genius on [producer Robert L.] Welch's part; the cowboy star's [Rogers'] straight-faced earnestness served as a wonderful contrast to Hope's antics.[4]

Rogers' straitlaced persona, preferring his horse to sexy co-star Jane Russell, also added a satirical barb at movies' more adult fare over period television.

Indeed, *Son of Paleface* went all out to comically wage war on its new rival (TV). For example, the picture includes a gag, to be addressed shortly, in which Hope's character sneers,

"Let's see television top this!" Moreover, the film came at you in brilliant Technicolor. In contrast, there were only a handful of color TV sets in 1950s America, and none had the lustrous gloss of Technicolor. Be that as it may, Roy "King of the Cowboys" Rogers, talented horse Trigger, and cowgirl wife Dale Evans (who had also penned their TV show's popular theme song "Happy Trails to You") were also a very popular live touring ensemble. In fact, the day (October 1, 1952) the film opened at New York's Paramount Theatre, with Hope in appearance one day only, Rogers and company were in the midst of a very popular engagement at New York's Madison Square Garden.[5]

Son of Paleface's plot, as with all character-driven personality comedies, is not that important. As the *New York Times*' critique observed:

> As was always the case with those [Hope and Bing Crosby] "Road" shows, the important thing here is not the yarn but the farcical inspirations that pop up as it goes along. And these arrive in abundance.[6]

Still a cinematic hall tree of a story outline helps put the picture in perspective. Hope had starred as pioneer dentist Painless Potter in the original *Paleface*, which had also co-starred Russell. And just as Rogers had assisted the box office of the sequel, Russell, had done the same, too — but for entirely different reasons. At the time of *Paleface* she was only known as the voluptuous star of Howard Hughes' controversially sexual Western, *The Outlaw* (1943, released more broadly in 1950). The picture's famous censorship battles were largely a product of Russell's 38-inch bust line, and how Hughes had both discovered her (in a nationwide chest hunt), and the way in which he showcased her. Though the film is tame by today's standards, it was purposely provocative at the time because Hughes enjoyed pushing censorship issues, as he had done with the topics of violence and incest in *Scarface* (1932). Indeed, Russell was so well-endowed that the multi-talented and publicity savvy Hughes had even designed a special bra for his 20-year-old protégé when the film was briefly shown in 1941. Hope once famously introduced her as "the two and only Miss Russell."

Hope had, however, given Russell her chance at mainstream movie success by casting her in *Paleface*. (*The Outlaw*'s original director was the great Howard Hawks, though Hughes ultimately received solo screen credit, and the picture is not without some redeeming qualities.) Regardless, given that *The Outlaw* was a famous and/or infamous Western, it also enhanced the sagebrush parody aspirations of *Paleface* and its sequel. Thus, Hope's picture had maintained a basic parody component by casting performers (Rogers and Russell) associated with the genre under affectionate attack.[7]

In *Paleface*, Hope had also introduced that year's Oscar-winning Best Song, "Buttons and Bows." In the sequel Rogers and Russell perform a more parody-oriented version of the song via anti-hero Hope's periodic singing interruptions, such as "I'm so hated I hate myself." Nonetheless, this time the film opens with Hope playing Potter *Junior*, a pretentious Harvard student attempting to kiss beautiful gold digging Penelope (an unbilled Jean Willes) just after graduation. Like Buster Keaton's coldly calculating *Cops* (1922) sweetheart, who will have nothing to do with him until he makes good, Hope's tease is the same.

Penelope sends him West to claim the inheritance allegedly left by his late father in the Dakota town of Sawbuck Pass. He arrives in a struggling 1890s primitive auto, as a foreign to the West as the driving slicker and goggles attired Junior. Moreover, his "Out of the way, I'm a Harvard man" attitude is of hopeless significance in Sawbuck Pass. Indeed, its pointlessness becomes an ongoing gag throughout the film, because a monogramed "H"

Bob Hope (right) in his comic ego mode, with the sexy Jane Russell and squeaky clean Roy Rogers in *Son of Paleface*.

appears on all of his clothing, from sweaters and slickers, to jammies and underwear, not to mention Harvard pennants frequently turning up ... even among the Indians.

Sexy Amazon-sized Russell, nicknamed Mike, leads a gang behind a series of gold robberies. Federal agents Roy Barton (Rogers) and Doc Lovejoy (Lloyd Corrigan), masquerading as medicine men, are out to capture the culprits. At this point, all they know is that the crooks are led by a mysterious bandit known as the Torch (Russell), which is how the gang signal their night raids. Mike's cover is as a singer at a Sawbuck Pass saloon named the Dirty Shame. Given that Hope's seemingly soon-to-be-rich Junior immediately falls for gold thief Mike, and agent Rogers has a hunch she is the Torch, this singing cowboy (with a rifle hidden in his guitar) is only too happy to use Junior as bait to capture her.

Of course, beyond comically tweaking everything associated with a given genre for maximum spoofing effect a good parody usually also assumes a scattergun effect—kidding *everything* remotely related to the movies. For example, in Mel Brooks' burlesque Western *Blazing Saddles* (1974), the picture's conclusion manages to break into a nearby musical comedy set, and eventually reveals the whole Warner Bros. lot. A classic *Son of Paleface* example would include Hope's solo film tendency to spoof his "Road" picture partner (Bing Crosby) with a comic cameo. Consequently, before the picture is hardly underway, the film cuts to an unflattering shot of a cross-looking Crosby presumably driving home from the studio. In voiceover Hope observes:

> Uhr, oh, what's this?... [It] is an old character actor on the Paramount lot whom we try to keep working. He's supporting a large family but I guarantee this fellow won't be in the picture tonight.

What is comically funny and promising about this random picture parody dig is that it occurs so early in *Son of Paleface*. Normally, Hope's shish-kebabbing of Crosby surfaces well into the movie as a comic surprise. For instance, Crosby is an upset prison executioner at the close of the film noir parody *My Favorite Brunette* (1947) when he discovers Hope is going free. Consequently, since the *Son of Paleface* dig at Crosby is both so quick and clever, one expects a cameo topper further into the picture. Fittingly, that proves to be the case. When Junior finally has his heavenly hotel bath, and is still in his swimsuit (with the letter "H"), he spots an old-fashioned photographer in the outer room, with his head under the camera cloth:

> JUNIOR: [In a perturbed voice] "Who do you think you are, Cecil B. DeMille?"
> PHOTOGRAPHER: "Somebody call me?" [DeMille emerges from under the cloth. His film that year, 1952, *The Greatest Show on Earth*, would win the Best Picture Oscar.]

For Hollywood insiders, DeMille's photography assistant in the scene added even more fun, since he was played by *Son of Paleface* producer and co-writer Robert L. Welch. (Hope makes a cameo in DeMille's picture, too.)

Nevertheless, Junior's first visit to the Dirty Shame Saloon is parody pivotal for several reasons beyond the "Buttons and Bows" number. First, parody is most fundamentally funny because its central character falls so short of the standard genre hero. Hope could not be further from the manly cowboy icon and worn leather garb of Randolph Scott, a Western figure Mel Brooks elevates to such God-like status in *Blazing Saddles* that merely mentioning him produces a hallelujah chorus echo of his name. Hope's Western outfit is what any "Junior" cowboy might wear to a Halloween party. He has a 20-gallon hat minimum, wool chaps in which the sheep might still be lurking, spurs so big and sharp he walks to the saloon like a girl in her first pair of high heels, and a six-gun so small he cannot remotely spin it on one of his fingers. Parody should be funny without being an expert on the genre, and Hope's cowboy costume at the Dirty Shame Saloon is hysterical, even if Westerns are not your thing.

Second, despite Hope's self-deprecating kiddie cowboy saloon attire and matching cowardly tendencies, his persona could easily pivot to briefly being a cool, egotistical, womanizing wise guy. Thus, after randomly fingering the string of Rogers' guitar, he is equally capable of reducing the movie's designated swashbuckling male to child cowboy status by telling him, "Aren't you glad you wrote that letter to Santa?" (The line is also reminiscent of a Groucho crack from 1931's *Animal Crackers*. When a gangster shows the mustached one his gun, the comedian says, "Cute. [Did] Santa bring it for Christmas? I got a fire engine.")

Third, Hope's Junior gets a further satirical dig in at Rogers and cowboy stereotypes in general when he follows his Santa quip with a reference to Jane Russell's sultry saloon girl. That is, after Rogers seems impervious to beddable Russell, Hope's Junior asks him, "Don't you like girls?" A stone-faced Rogers responds, "I'll stick to horses." This response produces arguably movie Hope's most comic incredulous expression. Moreover, it ever so briefly pushes Rogers' character past asexual childhood into stereotypical cowboy perversity. Regardless, director and co-writer Frank Tashlin confessed a more commercial reason for keeping Rogers away from cinema romance:

> The script called for Miss Russell to fall in love with Mr. Rogers. A serenade below her balcony was to culminate in an embrace. But at the last moment this was *eliminated* from the script ... by breakfast-food lobbyists [Rogers' TV show was sponsored by Post Cereals] who claimed Young America might change their eating habits if ever their hero was seen caressing anything but his horse's furry nozzle.[8]

Third, the silliness of Hope's cowboy costume is only matched by a beer mug the size of a horse's leg he receives at the Dirty Shame Saloon. After somehow downing the beer, the following cartoon-like things occur to this "Junior": one of his Harvard monograms begins to peel off, his pipe uncoils, a firecracker effect occurs at the end of the now straight pipe, steam comes out Hope's ears, his body begins to spin like a top, then just his torso whirls while his head remains stationary. This is followed by Hope's noodle rapidly revolving while his body remains immobile, his head next disappears into his torso (with his giant cowboy hat resting on this kiddie cowboy's shoulders), and the craziness concludes with a funny noise as his head pops up.

As addressed in the Prologue and the previous chapter (as well as further embellishments in Chapter 9), such cartoon-like antics are Tashlin flourishes, borrowed from his comic strip and animation background. For Hope's definitive biographer, Richard Zoglin, fooleries like this, or Junior anticipating Mary Poppins by flying his horseless carriage across a broad abyss with an umbrella assist "demeans" the comedian—"Never before has he seemed so incidental to his gags."[9] I would agree that such material represents a dumbing down of the comic. For instance, Hope's hysterical *Brunette* response to a strong drink, sans special effects (especially when contrasted with noir idol Alan Ladd handling the same drink in a cameo), is funnier than Junior's manufactured meltdown.

However, with that being said, there is enough of Hope's normal smart aleck persona to maintain an entertaining balance. Moreover, Tashlin's bits are funny, but for everyone showcased, there are two or three typical Hope witticisms. These include such aforementioned jests as the Martin & Lewis buzzard reference and reducing Rogers' guitar to a present from Santa, to countless unmentioned wisecracks, including his response to just how cowardly he was: "Well, I was captain of the Olympic team," to his dream of a honeymoon with Jane Russell:

> Say, it's gonna be real fun honeymooning in Niagara Falls. My daddy spent a whole week there on his honeymoon, laughing, loving, drinking champagne. He had so much fun, he kinda wished Mother had been with him.

TV sponsors required Bob Hope to be Jane Russell's *Son of Paleface* lover.

Further, it was not as if a kiddie cartoon world had never before visited a Hope film. For instance, his teaming with Bing Crosby on the *Road to Utopia* featured a talking fish, a verbally complaining bear, and an actual visit from Santa Claus (Ferdinand Munier) and his reindeer-driven sleigh. (Of course, Hope and Crosby's presents were to have been two slinky, sensual girls.) Besides, between Hope being a long-established comedian with an excellent handle on the parameters of his persona, as well as the one calling the shots on *Son of Paleface*, the term "demeans" the comedian is an overstatement. Tashlin said after getting his first directing credit on the film:

> Putting Mr. Hope through his paces has difficulties for the director. His thirty-picture memory draws a bead on the particular joke you are trying to sell him. He remembers a similar routine in "Road to Singapore" [1940]. A fast rewrite is called for and the material is given what you hope is a new twist. No, Mr. Hope recalls that he did that twist in "Sorrowful Jones" [1949]. His narrowed eyes, squinting at you down that much maligned nose, is a withering experience. Your puttees [leather leggings for directors] curl and your megaphone sags. Lunchtime is spent in digging for a new piece of business and Mr. Hope's approbation [approval].[10]

Tashlin and any dumbing down factor become more of a potential problem with his Jerry Lewis collaboration (see Chapter 9). Interestingly, however, *Son of Paleface* has a priceless gag which is dependent on both a Hope wisecrack *and* some Tashlin special effects. Late in the movie Junior's horseless carriage loses a wheel during a chase and Roger rides to the rescue by lassoing the axle and pulling it up to keep the speeding vehicle from crashing. But then he hands the rope to designated driver Hope to somehow hold it up and now maintains the miracle while Roger goes after the wayward wheel. Junior subsequently tops this comic sight gag by plaintively yelling after Rogers, "Hurry up; this is impossible." Of course, one could also give the gag a possible assist from Buster Keaton, too. In the silent comedian's surrealistic short subject, *The Blacksmith* (1920), Buster manages to keep up another vintage car's wheel-less axle by attaching a child's balloon.

Also, keep in mind that *Son of Paleface* had another classic children's component, à la cartoons, which had nothing to do with special effects—Roy Rogers' horse Trigger. In ads for the picture, Trigger's billing frequently matched the size of Hope's co-stars.[11] Moreover, the horse's press sometimes rivaled the film's star. The *New Daily News*' review was entitled, "Bob Hope & Trigger Paramount Co-stars," while the *Brooklyn Eagle*'s critique was labeled "Bob Hope Aided by Trigger In a Western-Style Comedy."[12] However, Trigger's pièce de resistance occurs when the comedian and the horse must sleep together and fight over the covers. *Eagle* critic Jane Corby observed:

> Trigger shows himself a talented equine comedian. He steals the show from Hope in one scene, where [sic] they share the same bed, with Trigger proving adept at blanket-snatching.[13]

The scene tops Harpo Marx's surprise *Duck Soup* bedding down with a horse in three ways. First, in contrast to the earlier simple but brilliant sight gag, Hope and Trigger's sequence mixes the same surprise with a funny drawn out blanket back and forth fight. Second, while there is no context for a winner-loser scenario involving Harpo and company, Trigger looks to be *Son of Paleface* blanket champion, because he refuses to quit. Indeed, his method of pilfering the covers by using his teeth proves so effective that eventually Junior shifts to this teeth technique, too. Third, even though Hope's battle of the blankets occurred 20 years after the always provocation Marx Brothers' movie, because of Trigger's association with Rogers, whose "films have been as clean as Eisenhower's hound's tooth," the *Son of Paleface* sequence managed to be more suggestive to some period critics.[14] Indeed, it might even be part of the unspecified "blue notes" (indelicate) situations, which one critic described as having "crept" into the film, versus Rogers' normally lily-white Westerns."[15]

Ironically, while Tashlin's cartoon comic talents have been mildly criticized here as arguably dumbing down the humor, the use of Trigger also speaks to the writer/director's

Trigger gets special treatment on the *Son of Paleface* lot, with Jayne Russell, Bob Hope (center) and Roy Rogers.

earlier sensitive-to-animals sardonic children's books. For example, Tashlin fables always involve put-upon wildlife and conformity, like *The Bear That Wasn't* being forced to think he is human.[16] Thus, having Rogers and Trigger was a subliminal bonus for Tashlin. That is, he could play at being a fifth columnist satirist, too. Most period critics praised the human-like comic tricks of the "beautiful, intelligent and comic Trigger."[17] Yet, Tashlin could also double down the derision by suggesting Rogers' stallion, like *The Bear That Wasn't*, is being forced to conform to a human mindset. The *New York Herald Tribune* reviewer suggests as much:

> Roy Rogers, playing a Federal agent, stands as stiff as a [parody] target and lets himself be riddled with jokes about a typical Western idol. [And] poor Trigger ... does his stunts so well that he brings himself into the [ongoing spoofing] joke.[18]

Yet, this anthropomorphic use/misuse of Trigger need not convince one that the horse won and/or was even smarter. With one's tongue firmly in cheek, and a minor tweak, the closing line of *The Bear That Wasn't* also applies to Trigger: "No, indeed, he knew he wasn't a silly man, and he wasn't a silly man, and he wasn't a silly ... [horse] either."[19] Yes, in the world of anthropomorphic satire, man invariably places second. This is impeccably captured in a book title by a master of this variety of mockery—Will Cuppy's *How to Tell Your Friends from the Apes*.[20]

Nevertheless, whatever Junior's thoughts about Trigger, the pivotal character for Hope's parody cowboy is Sawbuck Pass' grizzled old-timer Ebenezer Hawkins (Paul E. Burn). He both saves Junior from an army of angry citizens to whom Junior's father owed money, and helps Hope find his shifty father's hidden gold. The spirit of Potter Sr., as played by Hope, also appears in a cameo, in order to briefly give his anti-heroic son a pinch of bravery. Ironically, the "H" on his clothing does *not* stand for Harvard ... but rather hell. Yet when it becomes clear the other place is full of sexy women, Junior loses his fear of dying just in time to outrun a tribe of Indians. After all, if one is pulling out every Western parody stop, this is as necessary as sagebrush. The *New York Journal American* credited it with being the logical (almost) conclusion to a funny fast forward film:

> [It] never once lets down, from its comic opening titles to its wild and woolly finish when Hope stops pursuing Indians by tossing [Tashlin inspired] banana peels in their horses' paths.[21]

Yet, that is not quite all. Undoubtedly, one of those aforementioned "blue notes" occurs at the very close with Hope's last line. This backside of the story is predicated by Jane Russell's character being a gold thief for much of the picture. Thus, while Junior wins her hand and Rogers rides off into the sunset like all good Western stars, Hope's novice cowboy still must wait several years until Russell gets out of prison. (Hollywood's censorship code was weakening, but criminal activity still necessitated some sort of punishment.) Luckily for Junior, however, he was still allowed conjugal visits. Consequently, the film's real close occurs when Russell is released ... preceded by a whole parcel of little Potters. Fittingly, for an industry still largely at war with television, Hope turns to the camera and says, "Let's see 'em beat *this* on television!"

Though Hope's tagline might seem tame today, keep in mind that during this same year (1952) CBS television was having conniptions over how to handle the real-life pregnancy of Lucille Ball, star of their smash hit *I Love Lucy*. In a medium in which one could not even say the word "pregnant," cigarette sponsor Philip Morris insisted her condition go unacknowledged, with the actress hiding her pregnancy behind the furniture. Only through the Bob Hope–like tenacity of Lucy's husband and co-star, Desi Arnaz, was the situation finally written into the script. He had bypassed the American Philip Morris executives and gone directly to the company's British chairman of the board, Alfred Lyons. Agreeing with Arnaz, Lyons sent the following memo to key company administrators: "To whom it may concern: Don't fuck around with the Cuban [Arnaz]!"[22] The subject is belabored here, because as this text continues to document, 1950s television was constantly intertwined with American movies. Examples include blacklisting Judy Holliday (see Chapter 1); television pressure reconfiguring the *Son of Paleface* script to make sure Rogers, to paraphrase Mae West, "continue to be as pure as the driven snow, lest he drift," and Hollywood powerbrokers concerned about their film stars being overexposed on the small screen (to be addressed shortly). Regardless, Junior's concluding television crack was so popular with critics that many could not resist citing it, with the *New York Times* adding further admiration: "[The] Best gag is the climatic snapper."[23]

Consisted with this lack of a spoiler alert, *Son of Paleface* was a monster critical and commercial success. And the often hard to please *New York Times* actually shouted the loudest. Calling it better than the original—high praise for any sequel—critic Bosley Crowther credited it with being

> much more adroitly [done] and with humor that is a broad as it is long, so that what is delivered in this colored package is a wild farce that comes so close to the style of those old "Road to—" pictures of Mr. Hope, Bing Crosby and Dorothy Lamour that you might almost shut your eyes (if you can manage) and think you are enjoying one of the same.[24]

If the *New York Times*' critique wins the checkered flag for the most pre-eminent *Son of Paleface* praise, the *Hollywood Reporter*'s review was a close second. Indeed, the anonymous critic writes with such unfettered joy, his assessment is reminiscent of an energy level description of a young Robin Williams—"like an untied balloon that had been inflated and immediately released."[25] Appropriately, the critique even begins in a matter which might describe the organized chaos of a Williams stand-up act:

> There is absolutely no sense to *Son of Paleface*, but there is an amazing amount of fun. It isn't often that the laughs start even before the credits come on, but with Bob Hope anything can happen and in this zany film it does.... Hope is at his very best in this madcap farce which, stated simply, means he's one of the funniest men alive.[26]

Simply put, *Son of Paleface* kudos were the 1952 norm in publication after publication, such as the *New York Herald Tribune*'s almost poetic overview, "[It] is as joyfully unpredictable as a stroll through an amusement park fun house."[27] Hollywood's trade bible, *Variety*, added:

> [It is a] hilarious, rambunctious follow-up to "The Paleface" ... [This sequel] is the broadest kind of slapstick, drawing advantageously on the silent-day masters of the pratfall [by way of Tashlin] for 95 minutes of uninhibited mirth that certainly should hit a nifty boxoffice pace all along the line.[28]

The *New York World-Telegram and Sun* opened by giving special credit to the film's producer and co-screenwriter:

> Paramount's two big Bobs, Hope and [Robert L.] Welch, have another hilarious hit in "Son of Paleface," the new picture at the Paramount Theatre. Since this star-producer team joined forces for "The Paleface" four years ago, they have had an unbroken run of profitable laughter.[29]

Look magazine's ad man's dream of a photo spread was titled "Bob Hope *and Friends*."[30] And the opening to Rose Pelswick's *New York Journal American* review could be credited with being the typical cookie-cutter genesis to how so many critiques began, with the optimum word "hilarious" being tucked in somewhere:

> If you howled at the Bob Hope comedy hit, "The Paleface," wait till you see its Technicolored follow-up, "Son of Paleface," which came yesterday to the Paramount. Hope is tops, and the piece fashioned around him is nothing short of hilarious.[31]

3. Bob Hope

Bob Hope was the number one reason for laughter in *Son of Paleface*.

All movies are a quasi-documentary of the period in which they were made, a time capsule of sorts. And naturally, that is the case with *Son of Paleface*. Indeed, my two favorite lines from the movie address two basic fears and/or worries for Hope. His reference to the hungry buzzards hitching a ride on the back of his horseless carriage as "Martin & Lewis" is funny yet poignantly telling at the same time. Though the *Hollywood Reporter* had just called Hope "one of the funniest men alive," Martin & Lewis had already passed him on Hollywood's top ten box office list. While Hope logged in at an impressive number five the year *Son of Paleface* was released (1952), Martin & Lewis held down the vaulted number one spot.[32]

My second *Son of Paleface* favored line is Hope's closing taunt of TV. By this time the comedian's position on the medium was a work in progress. Paramount, like all Hollywood studios, wanted its stars to stay clear of the small screen—"vaudeville in a box," as it was often called. Hollywood's powers that be neither wanted to contribute to the growing success of this new competitor, nor risk losing the movie magic of its reigning stars by over exposure. Yet, Hope felt he could handle the risk; the year (1950) the comedian took a small plunge into television, he was second only to John Wayne at America's turnstile's, with nary a Martin & Lewis in sight.[33] He had been Martin & Lewis' special guest the previous year when the duo essentially moved their radio show to television. Moreover, maybe Hope just wanted to stay current with a few small screen appearances. Still, there was a perceived movie risk. In 1949 he had also appeared on television's *Toast of the Town* (soon to be retitled the *Ed Sullivan Show*). The result, according to one of Hope's many books, *Don't Shout, It's Only Me* (1970, with Melville Shavelson), was film business ugly:

> I got poison pen letters from movie exhibitors. They feared and hated television and said it was ruining their business. They threatened to stop booking my pictures and end my career, because people were staying home to watch Ed Sullivan.[34]

Still, in 1950 Hope choose to do a series of television specials for NBC. He later admitted to being very "nervous" about "the frightening new medium of television" as he began to do his first monologue:

> How do you do, ladies and gentleman. What a fine-looking audience. (*Looks audience over and counts with his fingers.*) Oh, I thought I was still at the Paramount Theatre, working on percentages [parts of his nerves were feeling he had to be overly visual].... I decided I'd better get into television before Milton Berle used up my material. [Berle was then so popular on the small screen he was called "Mr. TV" and "Uncle Miltie." He was also famous for stealing material.][35]

As demonstrated by *Son of Paleface*'s colossal hit status, and Hope's continued top 10 box office standings, the comedian weathered most movie fallout about his early involvement in television. Yet, Hope biographer Raymond Strait revealed it was not a totally flack-free situation:

> After an absence of several years, Bob Hope returned to [host] the Academy Awards ... on March 19, 1953. [He emceed the ceremony a record 19 times throughout his career, over three times more than anyone else.] Hope had been snubbed [for several years] by the Academy Committee because he had signed up with NBC [1950] to do television shows.[36]

Two ironies graced the situation. One, it was the first time the ceremonies were televised, and Hope could hardly let that pass:

> Good evening, ladies and gentlemen ... I'm very glad to be here at the wedding of television and motion pictures.... And just like many other weddings ... it's comforting to know that Las Vegas is so handy. [At this time, it was a city in which divorces were easy to get.][37]

Second, Hope had decided by then that he would forever limit his small screen appearance to only periodic specials. And the aforementioned Berle might have been an indirect factor. According to actress and one-time Hope companion Marilyn Maxwell:

> He thought Milton Berle was a prostitute to television [working too much for too little.] I don't think I ever heard him say a nice word about Miltie throughout the years I've known him [Hope].[38]

Plus, by the time Hope hosted the 1953 Oscars, "Mr. TV," that federal bank of narcissism, no longer merited such a title. He was just another comedian in what was becoming television's golden age of funny people.

Before moving on to Chaplin and Chapter 4, there is one final elephant in the room that has graced—or is that disgraced—what has come before: McCarthy Age blacklisting. Movie novice Judy Holliday's early television opportunities were cut off by this blight. Martin & Lewis were young, trendy, and apolitical, with *Sailor Beware* being mutually helpful to both the team and the government. But Hope was a veteran star still at the height of his game. What was his response? For baby boomers on the fence about Hope—fans of his inspired early film work and put off by his later hawkish position on Vietnam—the answer is a positive tie-breaker.

Son of Paleface's 1952 release date was in a presidential election year, and neither filmmakers nor fans in general were anxious to be labeled "leftist." For four years professional harm, as in loss of one's career, could come to anyone "who might ever have spoken to someone who knew someone who once stumbled into a communist meeting."[39] But by 1952 Hope had had enough of demagogue McCarthy and began targeting him. Even some nasty letters did not deter him from pricking this homegrown fascist. For example, "Senator McCarthy is going to disclose the names of two million communists. He just got his hand on a Moscow telephone book."[40] Other cracks ranged from "Congress is appropriating money for Red Skelton to dye his hair black," to describing the Army-McCarthy hearings as "a new kind of television show. It's sort of a soap opera where everyone comes out tattletale gray."[41] But maybe Hope's best McCarthy summary joke was later selected by the comedian's daughter for inclusion in the collection, *Bob Hope: My Life in Jokes* (2003):

> No wonder there's so much confusion in Washington.... Everybody back there spends all their time under their desks.... If they're not practicing for an H-bomb attack they're hiding from McCarthy.[42]

Sadly, as the next chapter chronicles, the McCarthyism of 1952 was hardly done waging havoc on Hollywood, including the creator of its greatest icon—Tramp originator Charlie Chaplin.

4

Charlie Chaplin
Limelight (October 24, 1952)

> Neither comedy nor tragedy all together, it is a brilliant weaving
> of comic and tragic strands, eloquent, tearful and beguiling
> with supreme virtuosity.—*New York Times* critic Bosley Crowther[1]

Charlie Chaplin remains the greatest auteur, comic or otherwise, in the history of cinema. As *Variety* comically noted at the time of its strongly positive review of this 1952 film, "Production-wise, 'Limelight' is a one-man show since Chaplin does almost everything but grow his own rawstock."[2] That is, Chaplin wrote, directed, produced, scored, and starred in his films. For *Limelight*, he also composed a ballet and anchored the story in a then unpublished novella started in 1948, *Footlights*. Chaplin biographer David Robinson and other scholars have since reconstructed the work from multiple Chaplin drafts and published a 2015 edition which closely explores the novella and the film.

With such hosannas a younger reader might expect a direct cut to the last of Chaplin's truly substantial movies, *Limelight*. Yet, the House Un-American Activities Committee (HUAC) and the ugly rise of 1950s McCarthyism derails such a simple path. Chaplin's controversial personal and public life during the 1940s had placed the artist in the most paradoxical of situations. On the eve of his Hitler black comedy, *The Great Dictator* (1940, in which he played both the tyrant Hynkel "the Phooey," à la The Fuhrer, and the Jewish German Tramp–like barber), he was arguably the most famous and popular entertainer in the world.

Slightly over a decade later, he was then the most polarizing performer in the United States. What happened? *Dictator*, the groundbreaking dark comedy, had become his greatest commercial hit, but many critics did not fully understand and/or appreciate mixing horror with humor. Thus, while some totally applauded the picture, many reviewers, like the *Los Angeles Times*' Edwin Schallert, were puzzled by black humor's rapid jumps from shock to slapstick and mime. And out of confusion, or fear that Chaplin had gone too far, such reviewers played it safe and reverted to praise for the traditional bits and pieces:

> [T]he best moments ... stem from roots ... imbedded in the soil of the silent picture. He proves this spectacularly in a remarkable [ballet-like Hynkel] scene performed with a globe.... It might be called a kind of bubble dance [about his wish to control the world].[3]

Another reason for iffy American acceptance of *Dictator* as a whole (versus the normal alleluias without question for the latest Chapin release) was that the comedian was not just rocking the comedy boat about a belligerent dictator (*Time* magazine's 1938 Man of the Year); the filmmaker was also subtextually attacking more broadly controversial subjects, such as the major anti–Semites who existed in the United States.[4]

Chaplin's popularity stock was also damaged in the 1940s by way of a messy sexual scandal with an actress named Joan Barry. During a brief affair, Chaplin became convinced she would be a perfect lead for a film adaptation of *Shadow and Substance*—Paul Vincent Carroll's 1937 play about an Irish girl who sees visions of saints and ultimately brings more sophisticated church members back to a basic faith. Winner of the New York Drama Critics' award for Best Foreign Play in 1938, Chaplin invested a great deal of time (adaptation work) and money, from optioning the rights, to acting classes for his protégé. But after a myriad of problems with her, from missing classes and rehearsals to a hitherto unknown drinking problem, Chaplin dismissed Barry. She then began to harass him, doing everything from shattering windows in his home, to actually breaking in and holding him at gunpoint ... until he could calm her down.

Yet, Barry's coup de grace was getting Chaplin named in a paternity suit. Now, sexual scandals were nothing new to Chaplin. But in the past, between the Tramp's salad days, when his popularity seemed to be a balm for every transgression, and the fact that the comedian tended to marry his pregnant lovers, his career was like Teflon. Nonetheless, between essentially abandoning his Charlie persona sanctuary, and being certain he could not be the father of Barry's child—Chaplin decided to fight the charge in court. The resulting trial—which Chaplin lost—was a sham, because blood tests proved conclusively that he could not have been the father. (Blood tests were not then accepted as positive proof in California court cases ... but this specific injustice would eventually be instrumental in helping change the law.)

Yet, given his fondness for young women, the 54-year-old Chaplin did himself no favors by marrying 18-year-old Oona O'Neill, daughter of playwright Eugene O'Neill, a few months after Barry filed her late 1942 paternity suit. At the time, who could predict that Oona would be the love of the comedian's life until his 1977 death? Consequently, the press pounced. Chaplin would later confess, "I would sink into a deep depression, feeling that I had the acrimony and the hate of a whole nation upon me and that my film career was lost."[5] At the time, therefore, it seemed as if Chaplin almost had a penchant for being a most willing deer in the headlights. His proclivity for romance/sex could be likened to him actually wanting what the French call "a little death," an idiom for an orgasm.

Additional 1940s chipping away of his popularity was his unwavering Second Front support for our World War II ally the Soviet Union (1942–1945), following Nazi Germany's 1941 invasion of Russia. He felt they were bearing an unfair burden of the war, which later facts proved. (The Soviet Union suffered more than 20,000,000 military and civilian causalities during the conflict, far more than any other country.) Yet, at the time, ally or not, most Americans and Brits, including Prime Minister Winston Churchill, were only too happy to see Nazis and communists killing each other off. A Second Front "had" to wait until mid–1944.

Further popularity paring away in 1940s, beyond the pinko slurs and morality attacks, involved the reactionary right also pummeling Chaplin for never having become a United

States citizen, despite living here for 30-plus years. Yet, there was nothing unusual about this in the international artistic community. For example, Stan Laurel of Laurel & Hardy fame proudly retained his British passport from his arrival in California in 1910 to his death there in 1965, was never accused of 'failure' to become a United States citizen, and it irked him considerably to read the press attack Chaplin in this respect.[6]

In 1947 Chaplin further redefined dark comedy with *Monsieur Verdoux* by changing teams—*Dictator* used the genre in an attempt to stop the killing, while *Verdoux* applied the murderous practices of big government to a small "entrepreneur." There are no bells and whistles; Chaplin is blunt. If the individual is no longer safe, he must do what he must. Verdoux, based upon a real character, marries and murders widows for their money. The subject matter, and the picture's lack of the Tramp—what Chaplin called his "talisman," though it is unlikely even "Charlie" would have put across *Verdoux* at the time—were hardly a hit in America.[7] Still, Chaplin had never known an American critical and commercial failure of any picture in which he had starred ... quite the record for an always provocative personality whose career began in 1914. (However, the film was both popular and influential in Europe, attaining classic status long before it did in the United States.)

Chaplin's provocative private life continued during the decade, such as joining Judy Holliday and Garson Kanin in supporting 1948 Democratic splinter party candidate Henry A. Wallace for president. This far left, liberal innocent and former vice-president under Franklin Delano Roosevelt, ran a campaign hurt by its open support from the American Communist Party. Yet, the 1950s opened promisingly. It was as if Chaplin was responding to *Christian Science Monitor* critic John Beaufort's close to a negative review of *Verdoux*:

> One can perhaps be forgiven for hoping that Mr. Chaplin will revive the baggy pants, the bowler, the cane, and will give us more of the old, wise and wonderful foolishness [of Charlie].[8]

That is, Chaplin revived his "talisman," à la *City Lights* on Broadway in April 1950, and while he feared demonstrations and picket lines (often the fate of *Verdoux*), the film wiped away "any possible bad taste by *Verdoux*, confounded the Chaplin detractors, [and] *Life* magazine proclaimed the twenty-year-old film 'the best picture of the year.'"[9] Moreover, in 1951 Theodore Huff published his celebratory opus of a Chaplin biography.[10] In 1952 *Life* further encouraged the comedian's resurgence in a feature pictorial article just prior to the completion of *Limelight*, "Chaplin at Work: He Reveals His Movie-Making Secrets":

> Today, at 63, Chaplin is a small, graceful, white-haired man who still walks with the mincing gait of the universal tramp, still uses the familiar gestures of the early pantomime. His work schedule, his stubborn, tempestuous and infinitely exacting methods wear out men far younger than he.[11]

Was there a Chaplin phoenix in the making?

After all, in the four previous decades one could arguably credit Chaplin with creating the most significant comedy of each period. The 1910s gave viewers another groundbreaking type of dark comedy—one which they could embrace—*Shoulder Arms* (1918, using the genre to win a war[12]). During the "Roaring Twenties," one might argue between *The Kid* (1921) and *The Gold Rush* (1925), though he also produced his all-time funniest film, *The Circus* (1928, which won a special Academy Award for "versatility and genius in writing, acting, directing and producing"[13]). The Depression 1930s belong to *City Lights* (1931), despite *Modern Times* (1936) being his most cannibalized film by other comedians.[14] And though controversial at the time, the 1940s nod would most likely go to *The Great Dictator*.

Who is to say, had not negative fact checkers par excellence, at HUAC and in the United States government in general, resisted acting in such unwarrantedly damnable manner (to be addressed shortly), *Limelight* might have been given the 1950s exposure to qualify as the best American comedy for a fifth consecutive decade. What is now often forgotten is that the original early reviews of *Limelight* were generally superlative. Largely limited to a relatively brief New York run, once Chaplin's re-entry visa was revoked after leaving the country for the picture's London premiere, his notices were strictly scrapbook quality. Besides those which open the chapter, Alton Cook's *New York World Telegram* critique said it all in the title, "Chaplin's *Limelight* a film Masterpiece."[15] Archer Winsten's *New York Post* review called *Limelight* "the fitfully glowing twilight of a true motion picture genius [and] the power is still there."[16] Plus, Otis L. Guernsey, Jr.'s *New York Herald Tribune* critique stated:

> [T]he sense of longing that [Chaplin] has established throughout *Limelight* hangs over [any] flaws like a luminous cloud of sympathetic genius, in a haunting movie experience…. [I]ts camera work is often imaginative and its music [which later won a delayed Oscar for Best Original Score, co-written by Chaplin] seems to ache right along with the sensibilities of the characters. In it Chaplin's brilliance is visibly and palpably at work.[17]

Ludicrously, two days after Chaplin and his family (Oona and a growing number of children) left for England, United States Attorney General James P. McGranery ordered Immigration authorities "to determine whether the famous comedian should be readmitted."[18] The métier of absurdity on why this action being taken involved Section 137 of the United States Aliens and Citizenship Code: "'This paragraph is aimed at persons who advocate the overthrow of the Government,' with a Justice Department spokesman adding, 'I would say that we have a pretty good case.'"[19]

Chaplin was about to overthrow the government? That was pure insanity squared, well beyond even the charted blackness of his dark comedies. Chaplin might have had the swagger of an independent artist, but he was no political rebel. Besides, as novelist/critic Cristine Nehring reminds us, even true revolutionary zeal necessitates holding "ourselves to a kinder, gentler, higher standard."[20] Regardless, the idiocy of the accusation was essentially how the *New York Times* covered the situation—beyond Chaplin backing any pinkishly liberal causes, McGranery was really still "incensed at Mr. Chaplin over the latter's [1942] involvement in a paternity case Joan Barry brought … against him."[21] *But*, as previously noted, blood tests proved Chaplin could *not* have been the father. He would easily have won a reentry appeal. Yet, Chaplin was now tired of a decade of arch conservatives casting him as the patron saint of America's ethical and political pariahs. Thus, following a Verdoux-worthy delaying game of cat and mouse with the press about "his plans to return … [to America]," in order to buy time to get his assets out of the United States, he cut ties with the country for good.[22] Then, after being feted throughout Europe for both *Limelight* and being a victim of American injustice, he eventually would set up permanent residence in a Swiss chateau, just outside the village of Vevey, in January 1953.

So what was the story of *Limelight*, which was caught in the middle of "The Little Tramp" becoming "The Little Red"? The visceral American rejection Chaplin had suffered from *Verdoux* brings to mind a short defense mechanism penned by Elie Wiesel in his book *Open Heart* (2011): "To chase [away] this onset of anxiety, I let my thoughts take me back to a distant past [of my childhood]."[23] It turns out that this alleged radical, who had formerly seemed indifferent to destroying one's sympathy for him, had written a valentine to his past, somewhat filtered through his own recent travail.

Limelight goes back in time to the London of his youth, 1914, also the year his Tramp first appeared on the screen. Chaplin plays Calvero, a stage clown who has lost his audience, not unlike the comedian's position with the '50s American public. The film opens with Calvero coming home to his flat (in the Kennington slums of Chaplin's youth) pleasantly plastered. Noting an odd odor in the hall, he smells his cigar, and checks his shoes, à la a crude Keystone dog-dropping bit he might have done during his cinema beginnings. Suddenly the washed-up entertainer realizes he smells gas. He breaks through the door of a boarding house neighbor and saves from suicide a young ballerina (Claire Bloom), who through an illness has succumbed to a psychological "transferal disorder," making her believe her legs are paralyzed.

Calvero turns his modest quarters into a chaste nursing arrangement with Bloom's character Terry, despite a snooping landlady (Marjorie Bennett). Within the movie, the aging clown winningly describes the lack of any sexual subtext with the aphorism, "When you reach my age, a platonic friendship can be maintained on the highest platonic level." The situation also works as an understated in-joke, given Chaplin's Lothario-like reputation with young girls, especially with his leading lady (Bloom) bearing such a striking resemblance to his fourth wife Oona O'Neill—only five years older than Bloom and already the mother of four Chaplin children. (Three of them, Geraldine, Michael, and Josephine, appear in brief cameos at the beginning of *Limelight*.) The lookalike effect of Bloom and O'Neill is actually acknowledged in the film by Mrs. Chaplin (also a former ballerina) doubling for Bloom in a scene.

The casting of Bloom as Terry, as well as the nuances of the past, reflected the beauty and haunting vulnerability of both Chaplin's mother and the comedian's first love, Hetty Kelly. The young British comic fell hard for a fellow teenager, but his first trip to America (1910) for a Karno stage troupe separated a budding romance just as a relationship was blooming. Then his American popularity, first in their version of the music hall tradition (vaudeville) and later in early silent movies, doomed *the* love which was not to be. A second chance friendship was denied when Kelly then died young during the Spanish influenza epidemic, which engulfed the globe following World War I. Until Chaplin's marriage to Oona in 1942, many aficionados of the comedian felt the iconic star's loss of Kelly drove his obsession, on-screen and off, to find the perfect young heroine.

When Richard Attenborough did his biography film *Chaplin* (1992, with Robert Downey, Jr., in the title role), he suggested the comedian's search for a Hetty Kelly–like companion finally ended with his marriage to fourth wife O'Neill. To emphasize Chaplin's eventual success in solving what American narrative art calls "the beloved dead girl pattern," Attenborough cast the same actress (ironically

The once famous clown Calvero (Charlie Chaplin) comes home plastered in *Limelight*.

named Moira *Kelly*) as both Hetty Kelly and Oona O'Neill. Not surprisingly, in Bloom's 1982 memoir *Limelight and After*, the very title of which both denotes the importance of Chaplin's film to his public and to her career, she delicately describes the complexity of the part she was asked to play:

> [Chaplin and I] went to a theatrical costumer to outfit me for the *Limelight* screen test. Chaplin had already decided upon every last detail of every garment I was to wear. He remembered the way his mother had worn such a dress, and the way his first girlfriend [Kelly] had worn such a shawl, and I completely realized, then, that some composite young women, lost to him in the past, was what he wanted to bring to life.[24]

Given that Chaplin's style since the early silents was to act out each role for every performer (no matter how small the part), and for them to follow his directions *exactly*, one would assume Bloom's "composite" Terry greatly reflected every important shading of the real women who occupied this densely populated character. Yet, since cinema was at that time very much into Method acting, such as Marlon Brando seemingly becoming the animalistic Stanley Kowalski in *A Streetcar Named Desire* (1951), one might also assume an instant conflict between Chaplin and the young Bloom, just as the comedian as director clashed with Brando during the making of *A Countess from Hong Kong* (1967). But the junior Bloom was both relieved and charmed, as her memoir title suggests:

> I was close to a panic [about the screen test] until I saw that Chaplin intended to give me every inflection and every gesture exactly as he had during rehearsal. This didn't accord with my highly creative [budding Method aspirations] but in the circumstances [young, anxious to embrace the break of a lifetime, and in awe of this legend] it was just fine. I couldn't have been happier—nor did I have any choice. Gradually, imitating Chaplin, I gained my confidence, and by the time we came to the actual filming I was enjoying myself rather like some little monkey in the zoo being put through the paces by a clever, playful drillmaster.[25]

Without belaboring autobiographical links to the comedian's youth, several more ties merit noting. For instance, a pared-down *Footlights* provides some important Calvero details absent from the movie. For example, one "reading" of Calvero's alcoholic decline as a performer can be tied to the infidelity of an earlier, never seen wife. Originally, a young Chaplin had resented being largely abandoned by his hard-drinking, popular, stage entertainer father, *but* through the years his view of Chaplin, Sr., had softened, given that a contributing fact to his father drinking himself to death before the age of 40 was probably due to the promiscuity of his wife—Chaplin's beloved mother. A first-page description of *Footlights*' Calvero was equally true of Chaplin: "Calvero was not gregarious. He was shy and reserved and difficult to know. At times [he was] melancholy and austere."[26]

Calvero was essentially about a clown's fall from grace. Though set in Chaplin's youth, one cannot get around it being a subtextual tale of the 1952 comedian, even before the whole re-entry visa folly. That being said, however, there are numerous other partial influences from which to draw. For instance, during Chaplin's first Karno trip to America, he was mesmerized by the Broadway and vaudeville headliner Frank Tinney (1878–1940). Tinney's masterful timing and delivery squeezed big laughs out of old material, such as the following question and response: "'How about lending me a dollar for a week, old man?'" Pause. "'Who's the weak old man you want it for?'"[27]

Along similar lines, one cannot help but see similar bonds between Calvero's confident poise in successfully presenting his sentimental but winning flea act in *Limelight*. Though prominently featured in *Footlights*, the flea sketch was originally written during Tinney's

The Calvero (Charlie Chaplin) routine which includes the flea sketch in *Limelight*.

heyday. While Chaplin had filmed a portion of it during the silent era, the routine had never seen the *public* light of day until the artful grab bag that was *Limelight*. Much later Chaplin was shocked by a Tinney performance without his earlier comedy flair. Years later Chaplin said this had been a factor in making his film. Of course, who is to say that a then elderly Chaplin was rewriting his own life—not wanting to confess just how close he had felt to the now forgotten Calvero.

Nevertheless, *Limelight*'s faded star has additional potential roots. Barry Anthony's *Chaplin's Music Hall: The Chaplins and Their Circle in Limelight* (2012) makes a case for Calvero being drawn, at least in part, from the once popular British stage performer Lee Dryden (1863–1939), the father of Chaplin's half-brother Wheeler Dryden (1892–1957).[28] Like Calvero, Dryden had once been a 19th century stage star, only later to find his fame so faded he was reduced to work as a street musician; this also occurs to Calvero. Also like Chaplin's *Limelight* alter ego, the senior Dryden enjoyed a late-in-life final triumph at a benefit in his honor. And if truth be told, Chaplin, like *any* young trouper, would have vivid early memories of failure from which to draw. That is, any sense of a Cold War loss of his public

> must have revived his nightmare memory of 23 December 1907 when, as an 18-year-old hopeful, he had tried out an act as "Sam Cohen—The Jewish Comedian" in front of the predominantly Jewish audience at the Foresters' Music Hall [London].... After the first couple of jokes the audience started throwing coins and orange peels, and stamping and booing.... The horror of it filtered into my mind.... [Once mercifully done I] left the theatre and never returned.[29]

Obviously, Chaplin would have been mindful of all these things and a myriad of others. This was especially true with regard to Dryden, since his childhood métier paralleled a portion of the older entertainer's career. Plus, Chaplin had reconnected with the younger Wheeler when they were adults. (Wheeler was even eventually employed by the Chaplin studio; his tasks included working as an assistant director on *Dictator* and as a producer on *Limelight*.) Of course, one could argue that any of these tales are also smoke screens to soften Chaplin's unjustified decline in popularity by 1952—which is at the heart of his parallel with the much diminished fame of Calvero. Still, even by the 1930s Chaplin's gestation period for a picture measured in years, and all these aforementioned factors could be said to have represented an amalgamation of Calvero's "family" roots.

Speaking of family, besides the aforementioned young Geraldine, Michael, and Josephine briefly seen at the film's beginning, Chaplin's second son by second wife Lita Grey, Sydney (1926–2009, named for his half-uncle), played a major supporting role as Bloom's eventual lover. Chaplin's oldest son by Grey, Charlie Jr. (1925–1968), had a small role as a comic policeman in a *Limelight* ballet sequence, and Oona had the briefest of cameos. If not for the ultimate McCarthy mess, the film had the capstone feel of a touching, almost Chaplin home movie close to a career. However, beyond *Limelight*'s *Footlight* foundation, the aforementioned notation of infidelity plays a larger part in the novella. In the film, Terry's paralysis is vaguely blamed upon a psychological condition now known as transferal disorder. Yet, in the text there is a series of reoccurring paralysis episodes starting before Calvero appears, related to Terry's guilt over a privileged life (the opportunity to study ballot) at the sacrifice of a sister turning to prostitution.[30]

Subtextually, one could say prostitution dovetails into venereal disease in this autobiographical story. The day following the suicide rescue of Terry by Calvero, she attempts to vaguely explain things to him by saying she has been ill. He immediately assumes, in the most delicate manner, that a sexually transmitted disease (STD) is the problem:

> You should [just] do something about it. If it's a blood disease, there's a cure for it—a new drug—performing miracles! Curing thousands.... But if it's anything of that nature, you can be helped ... [she assures him that is not the case; to which he replies:] I'm on old sinner. Nothing shocks me.[31]

Keep in mind that in the story's recent Victorian past, an estimated one in four London women were involved in periodic prostitution. Plus, according to Chaplin scholar and doctor

Stephen Weissman's study, *Chaplin: A Life* (with an "Introduction" by Geraldine Chaplin), there is little doubt that Chaplin's mother's eventual fatal dementia was caused by venereal disease.[32] Undisputedly, Chaplin's views on such subjects would have undergone great change since his youth. Indeed, Chaplin's casual *Limelight* connection has come full circle by the picture's close. On the night of Calvero's comeback theatrical conclusion to the story, the filmmaker takes the time to show how very attractive A-level hookers pick up "johns" at major social events. They merely position themselves close to a rich older mark in the theatre, and with the most inviting of innuendo glances the prey is quickly reeled in.

The story is really a dual focus narrative. First Calvero inspires Terry back to the theatre and dance, and then his aging clown briefly loses his spark before she helps orchestrate one last hurrah as the great comedian Calvero, before dying in the wings. Paradoxically and poignantly, however, the movie's greatest scene is the duet between Chaplin's Calvero and another then-neglected real life clown, Buster Keaton. Buster had been one of the pantheon comedians of the silent era—Chaplin's only serious artistic rival, though that had gone unappreciated at the time. Not as commercially successful as silent clown rivals Chaplin and Harold Lloyd, Keaton's signature "Great Stone Face" minimalism in a chaotic world now makes his persona more existentially relevant with each passing year.

Sadly, Keaton's long neglect had been due to a number of factors—the coming of sound, control issues with MGM, an ugly divorce, and alcoholism. Yet, by the late 1940s, thanks in part to a seminal cinema essay also by one of Chaplin's greatest champions, James Agee's "Comedy's Greatest Era" (1949), Keaton's fortunes were beginning to improve.[33] Teaming with Chaplin in *Limelight*'s funniest sketch—a zany duet with Calvero on the violin and his nearsighted partner (Keaton) struggling to play the piano while maintaining control of his ever tumbling sheet music—marked the high point of Keaton's comeback. (Agee had also assisted Chaplin in editing the *Footlight* novel into a manageable screenplay.)

The tragic comedy *Limelight* story allows the once famous, but now almost forgotten, Calvero a second chance before dying in the wings as his protégé dancer Terry is on stage in a tour de force ballet performance—as movingly sentimental as "The show must go on," or as touchingly appropriate as two saved souls helping each other achieve their dreams. Plus, given that Chaplin had always wanted to play Jesus on screen, his choice of the name Calvero, so close to the place where Jesus was crucified (Calvary), suggests, given the neglected Calvero's miracle-like role in the rebirth of Terry, that Chaplin had finally created a scenario in which he could flirt with playing Jesus Christ.

Granted, it is an egotistical act for an artist's work to portray his death; yet other than Bob Fosse staging his own demise in *All That Jazz* (1979), Calvero/Chaplin's passing is a unique movie moment which goes beyond ego. For instance, one can play with the concept of dark comedy, in a personality comedy film which does *not* readily bring that genre to mind. Calvary is the Latin word for "skull." No one knows for sure why the place where Jesus was crucified was known as "the skull," beyond the knee-jerk explanation that it was an execution site, since "the skull" is a widely recognized symbol for death. Fittingly, *Limelight*'s end presents the increasingly dark comic dilemma feel that the world should end, à la W.H. Auden's poem "Funeral Blues" (also known as "Stop the Clocks," 1938), life goes on. Calvero has also shown Terry that life and death should be natural and not wasted in suicide.

As a writer/professor postscript to *Limelight*, there is always a challenge to make older films relevant to college students. Knowing that my favorite "golden age" comedian is Chaplin,

4. Charlie Chaplin

Silent comedy greats Charlie Chaplin (right) and Buster Keaton briefly team in *Limelight*.

while Steve Martin holds that distinction for modern-day funnymen, one of my students asked what was each artists' most underrated movie, and could I make any connection between the two, beyond the comic link. I pinpointed *Limelight* and Martin's *Shopgirl* (2005).[34] Hopefully this brief addendum, which is fleshed out shortly, will provide additional insight into the ongoing legacy of Chaplin's film.

As previously noted, Chaplin's movie came out when he was being hounded by America's reactionary right. His saving grace during the McCarthy witch hunting was his successful marriage to Oona O'Neil, 35 years his junior. In *Limelight* Chaplin's leading lady, Clair Bloom, is close to Oona in both age and appearance. Yet art does not completely imitate life here because, while Bloom and Chaplin's characters do fall in love, he focuses on nursing her back to health and orchestrates a romance with someone closer to her age (Sydney Chaplin).

Chaplin's fatherly Calvero is the most nurturing of figures, consistent with such early watershed Tramp pictures as *The Vagabond* (1916), in which his character cares for another artistically talented young girl (Edna Purviance). But whereas this picture had the Tramp suffer through the fate of unreturned love, Calvero sacrifices romance. Both protagonists rescued lives and played muses to fellow artists. Though saddened that there were limitations to their fate, they were pleased for having done the right thing.

Martin was 60 years old when he adapted his *Shopgirl* novella to the screen, versus Chaplin's 63 at the time his novella became *Limelight*. Both Martin's leading lady and title character for *Shopgirl*, Claire Danes, and Bloom were 20-something actresses. Martin's scenario was a resumé of sorts, too. Danes' character, Mirabelle, is not suicidal but she is a photography artist "dying" in an exclusive Beverly Hills "shopgirl" position. Unlike *Limelight*, however, Martin's sophisticated older businessman Ray only has romance in mind. Still, Ray and Calvero are similar in that their feelings border more on compassion than passion, and each is parental in his attention to the respective young woman.

Though not an artist, Martin's figure has an artistic temperament, which is underlined by his appreciation of her photography and his character's elegantly minimalist residence. The dwelling is reminiscent of the comedian's own starkly modern home, which uses its minimalism to better showcase Martin's collection of 20th century art. In fact, *Shopgirl* often has the freeze frame under glass look of a painting by an artist, Edward Hopper, Martin greatly admires, and whose signature cinema-like 1942 work, *Nighthawks*, is a study of late night loners in New York. *Shopgirl* also showcases a tastefully done nude shot of Danes that comes across as erotic and abstractly artistic—a modern "canvas" that would not be out of place among the sometimes sexy surrealism of Georgia O'Keefe's desert paintings.

As with Bloom, Danes' Mirabelle ends up with a younger lover (Jason Schwartzman). Yet, while the *Limelight* arrangement seems appropriate, the *Shopgirl* viewer genuinely is disappointed that Martin's sophisticated Ray does not commit to the relationship, especially with the lovely Danes being so in love. Granted, Ray professes from the beginning he does not want a permanent coupling but the much-needed attention he showers on Mirabelle, and his delight in giving her gifts seems to have the promise of another May-December romance, à la Billy Wilder's lovely titled 1957 picture, *Love in the Afternoon*, starring Gary Cooper and Audrey Hepburn. And with this in mind, even wistful wishes about Calvero and Terry slip in.

Ultimately, Ray's rejection is more a reflection of the complexity inherent in any modern relationship. However, one wishes his generosity had focused less on the financial and more on the emotional, although even Martin's melancholy close would have been more palatable had there been something like the undisclosed closing whisper between Bill Murray and Scarlett Johansson in *Lost in Translation* (2003). That is, a disconnect that was ambiguous enough to allow the romantic viewer the hope for some future get-together.

Regardless, the greatness of *Limelight* and *Shopgirl* is that two mature artists continue to do what they have done—celebrate the human comedy by way of that most ephemeral phenomenon called love. But these two classics by mature artists also had another, less favorable, link between them. While both were critically acclaimed, each disappeared from theatres fairly quickly. Martin's work was celebrated on the art house circuit, but mainstream America largely lost out. In contrast, because Chaplin was a political hot potato whose re-entry situation resulted in a 20-year, self-imposed exile from the United States, *Limelight* was only briefly in circulation and did not even qualify for Oscar consideration for two decades, when Chaplin, Raymond Rasch, and Larry Russell won a statuette for the movie's haunting score. That same year the formerly blacklisted great actor Edward G. Robinson was awarded a lifetime achievement Oscar, whose citation included, in part, the most hypocritical of Hollywood statements, "a dedicated citizen."[35]

Of course, the logjam of Hollywood's HUAC shame had largely been washed away the previous year when Chaplin was awarded his own lifetime achievement Oscar, which simply said: "[To] Charles Chaplin for the incalculable effect he has had in making motion pictures the art form of the century."[36] The 12-minute standing ovation he received is still the longest on record. And it would have gone on longer but officials stopped it for fear that it could have been detrimental to the health of the emotional octogenarian.

It is difficult to close a chapter on the decade's most provocative comedy by cinema's greatest clown. Innumerable entertainers have said the best way to exit is "leave them laughing." But quoting some of *Limelights'* best lines serves two purposes: the picture is peppered with them, and it more than decimates the random complaint that Calvero's pep talks to Terry might occasionally run long—and keep in mind this is a *suicide minded* girl! *Variety*'s original review best defended the pictures verbal comedy:

> Some of the dialogue is brilliant, almost [more] like fine prose writing than celluloid wordage. For example, "We're all amateurs: none of us lives long enough to be anything else." And "I hate the sight of blood, but it's in my veins."[37]

Other examples would include Calvero's aforementioned crack about not being a sexual threat to Terry as he nurses her back to health: "When you reach my age a platonic friendship can be maintained on the highest platonic level." Also, when Chaplin and Keaton are putting on makeup for their sketch, the latter observes, "If anyone says, 'It's like old times again,' I'm going to jump out the window." And bingo, the line is repeated several more times. (And it works on two levels, within the context of the story and the fact that *the* two silent comedy greats are working again.) When Terry is concerned she will inconvenience Calvero, pretending to be his wife for propriety's sake as he cares for her, he replies, "Not at all. I've had five wives already. One more or less makes no difference to me." When Terry tells Neville (Sydney Chaplin) it is awful he has been drafted for World War I, he answers, "I agree. It's carrying the war too far." Late in the film when Terry is the one attempting to keep up Calvero's spirits, he observes:

> This devotion of yours—it's like a nun—shutting everything else out of your life. Hmm.... We're a strange combination, a nun and a clown.

Again, late in *Limelight*, when he is just getting by he puns his former iconic image, "There's something about working the streets [as a musician] I like. It's the Tramp in me, I suppose."

There are also extended conversations which often end with a comic twist. For example, at one point Terry and Calvero are at the boardinghouse. She is reading the newspaper and he asks:

CALVERO: What's new?
TERRY: War and politics—Europe [is] in [a] race for armaments.
CALVERO: Anything interesting?
TERRY: There's a great deal about Mr. and Mrs. Zancig [mindreaders]. They say they're quite remarkable.
CALVERO: I knew them then. I played with them years ago. It's the old code trick.
TERRY: It isn't genuine?
CALVERO: Of course not.
TERRY: It says here that their minds are so attuned they can transfer their thoughts to each other.
CALVERO: Nonsense!
TERRY: Then how's it done?

> CALVERO: I don't know. But it's not through transference, because I was with him once when he sent a telegram to his wife.

Even at the film's close, as Calvero is close to death in the theatre wings, Chaplin cannot resist some dark humor: "I believe I'm dying. But then—I don't know.... I've died so many times [à la bad reviews]." There are other examples, but one gets the point—he can write comic dialogue. What is even more impressive is that Chaplin has left some "A" material in *Footlights*. For instance:

> TERRY: And how was the play [you attended]?
> CALVERO: Excellent—until the curtain went up.
> TERRY: And *Hamlet*?
> CALVERO: As usual, a most complex performance, so complex nobody knew what ailed him. If Hamlet could only be played without an actor. This one was a temporizing [compromising] lily. He couldn't make up his mind. And neither could the audience....[38]

America's 1952 pushing away of Chaplin makes one think that someone needs to rearrange Geoffrey Cotterell's inspired observation about writers (artists) with Australia's position trading places with America's. Here is how the revised comic tale might read:

> In Australia only the successful writer [artist] is important, in France all writers [artists] are important, in England no writer [artist] is important, in America you have to explain what a writer [artist] is.[39]

How could such a thing happen to Chaplin and *Limelight*? Well, as Scout observes in a novel published eight years later, 1960's *To Kill a Mockingbird*, "I might as well have wanted to see the other side of the moon."[40]

As an addendum to *Limelight*, America's loss of Chaplin to McCarthyism is a tragedy in another way, too. The comedian's bitterness, just as he was peaking as an artist possibly cost the world one more Tramp Film. The artist's following to *Limelight* was the fascinating but flawed payback satire *A King in New York*. Yet, mellowing towards the filmmaker at the time of *Limelight*'s initial New York release, it is quite possible he might have gifted us with one more "little fellow" film. Chaplin later felt he had been wrong to retire Charlie. Indeed, prior to James Agee's premature 1955 death, he had been working on a Tramp script. Chaplin admirer Vittorio De Sica's unforgettable neo-realism film *Umberto D* (1952) gives viewers a suggestion of what might have been. De Sica's picture hauntingly depicts the plight of an elderly pensioner and his dog forced into the streets by poverty. It can be "read" as a long delayed homage to Charlie and his pooch in 1918's *A Dog's Life*.

5

Red Skelton
The Clown (January 29, 1953)

> Oscar Levant's signature line is equally applicable to Red Skelton, "There's a thin line between genius and insanity... and I have erased that line."[1]

Though there is no topping Charlie Chaplin's roller coaster 1952 (see previous chapter), in a multitude of ways, it was the most helter skelter of years for Skelton, too. Before addressing the younger comedian's comedy-tragedy, *The Clown*, with its several parallels to Chapin's *Limelight* (1952), one needs to best set up the calendar year in which it was made. Unlike the HUAC (House of Un-American Activities Committee) problems of Judy Holliday and Chaplin, Skelton's issues were of a more self-inflicted nature. Plus, there were the pressures of trying to sustain a movie career and a hit television series at a time when a season was composed of 39 episodes each year (versus fewer than half that number today).

Ironically, when most of Hollywood was at war with television over viewers (with studios attempting to limit the appearances of their stars on the small screen, despite Martin & Lewis frequently guest hosting the *Colgate Comedy Hour* and Bob Hope's periodic appearances), Skelton had fully embraced the other side. He was arguably the first major movie star to have his own weekly show. The early medium's first star, Milton "Mr. Television" Berle, of whom it was said, "sold more TV sets than any advertising campaign," had previously never been a particular hit in either radio or movies.[2]

So why did Skelton want to so completely join the *enemy*?[3] First, MGM was not a good studio for personality comedians. As *the* dream factory, with the proverbial "more stars than there are in heaven," it exercised tighter control over its performers than any other Hollywood studio, *never* a good situation for improvisational-oriented film clowns. From being the central reason among many for Keaton's crash, to homogenizing the Marx Brothers, MGM was bad news for funnymen. Skelton had little to no control there, even on films in which the comedian was the nominal star. A prime example is 1944's *Mr. Co-Ed*, with Skelton as a songwriter trying to salvage his marriage by following his bride back to school. But sometime during post-production, MGM decided his beautiful swimming sensation starlet screen wife, Esther Williams, could herald a new subgenre. It might be called an aqua-musical category, in which grandiose water ballet numbers, in brightest Technicolor, reminded viewers of Busby Berkeley choreography, gone under the sea. Overnight Skelton's *Mr. Co-Ed* became William's *Bathing Beauty* (1944), and suddenly, second banana Skelton, who had just entered the army, was in a state of shock. Even the comedian's greatest commercial hit as a headliner, the Frank Tashlin influenced *Fuller Brush Man* (1948), was made as a loan out to Columbia Studio. So pencil in *control* as the number one reason for fully embracing TV.

Second, Skelton recognized the phenomenal possibilities for television, likening the new small screen medium to the pioneering days of film. In addition, he was drawn to the informal familiarity of "vaudeville in a box." (As noted in Chapter 2, many critics feel the closest thing to the real Martin & Lewis act was preserved on their *Colgate Comedy Hour* spots.) Regardless, Skelton felt

> I consider the medium so intimate that I'm going to devote my first [1951 television] show to introducing myself and family. I'll be knocking at the doors of strangers' homes and asking, "May I come in?" This is the kind of fellow I am. If you like me, I hope you'll ask me back to your home next week.[4]

Fittingly, as corny as this might now sound, Skelton's genuinely heartfelt comment was consistent with a performer who spent an earlier summer touring the United States conducting his own personal radio survey. (Radio stars would often maintain their programs even after moving to TV.) The brainstorm of his like-minded populist manager and former first wife, Edna Stillwell, the trip allowed the comedian to meet and poll his fans on what they wanted from Skelton's highly rated program. Traveling in a station wagon equipped for sleeping, he found this to be groundbreaking radio "research," especially given that the star was doubling as the chief fact finder. Consequently, it was perfectly logical for Skelton to metaphorically ask his potential television audience, "May I come in?"

A third very practical reason for Skelton's radio and television preference simply came down to money. While largely forgotten today, the commercial airways offered Skelton money that dwarfed even a movie star's pay. (One is reminded of Jorge Pasquel's post–World War II attempt to strengthen the Mexican baseball league by luring talented Major Leaguers south with lavish contracts.) Regardless, while Skelton's weekly film salary in the post-war 1940s was approximately $3,000, Skelton made $7,500 a week on radio.[5] (Hedging their bets, and adding to their bank accounts, many programs were on *both* radio and television in the early 1950s.) Granted, Skelton received a modest raise from MGM in 1948 after the success of the Columbia-produced *Fuller Brush Man* had the latter studio bidding for his services. Yet, that same year, Skelton signed a new six-year radio contract worth $3 million. At $500,000 a year, this figured out to nearly $10,000 a week. Moreover, Skelton's eventual 1951 jump to television produced a $10 million, seven-year contract and banner headlines around the country.[6]

The film and television industries, however, were in the midst of a major entertainment war, and like a famous athlete being paid a king's ransom to join a new and/or different league, à la Pasquel's aforementioned Mexican big money attempt to acquire name American players, the signing of a star like Skelton gave a fledgling medium such as television greater legitimacy. Skelton's motivation towards working in radio and television was driven by artistic control (such as owning his small screen program). But these astronomical salary numbers were a factor for a figure born into wretched poverty.

Finally, Skelton believed that television gave him the chance to be a small-screen Chaplin. The creator of cinema's immortal Tramp figure was a huge influence on the mime-orientated

Skelton, from his own Freddie to Freeloader character (created in 1952, no less), to Skelton's later purchase and transformation of Chaplin's old studio into a television production house (after Chaplin's self-imposed exile; see previous chapter). Paradoxically, yet fittingly, the politically conservative Skelton spoke reverently of Chaplin throughout 1951 (when the younger comedian entered television, and his hero was often viscerally attacked for leftist views). One *Kansas City Star* article also provided an especially rich perspective in the multiplicity of ways in which Chaplin citations occur.[7] For example, after reporting, "Red says he hopes to do for TV what Chaplin did for silent movies," the piece added that prominent entertainment biographer Gene Fowler believed "Red is probably the greatest 'sight' comic since Chaplin."[8] Furthermore, the article noted that Skelton even had copies of all Chaplin's films. As if documenting his knowledge of the Tramp filmography, another article from this seminal year for Skelton and Chaplin quoted the former as saying:

> Kids can smell out a comedian who puts himself *above* his audience. That was the great thing about Charlie Chaplin, who is the master of all. There is hunger, pathos, and humbleness in Chaplin.[9]

Within the entertainment industry, Skelton eventually proved a catalyst for more Chaplin positives when much of the general public was being fed McCarthy-fueled condemnation. For instance, when Skelton's television show proved to be an instant hit (during 1951–1952), critics such as the *Chicago Tribune*'s Larry Wolters often compared Skelton to the silent star. His partisans insist he's the funniest fellow since Chaplin. *New York World Telegram* critic Harriet Van Horne was especially moved by an early Chaplin-like small screen Skelton sketch in which he portrayed several types of people who frequent a cocktail lounge (part of the ongoing comedy legacy of Stillwell, who, starting with the donut dunking routine, wrote the comedian so many bits anchored to observing everyday people).[10] Van Horne felt "the best of these characterizations was one that very few other comedians could do: the lonely woman who drinks," which inspired her review title, "Skelton Has Chaplin Tragic-Comic Touch."[11]

A most memorable opportunity occurred during this time when Skelton and second wife Georgia Davis were occasionally able to dine with Chaplin and his wife, Oona O'Neill, at regularly scheduled dinner parties at the home of *Los Angeles Examiner* critic Cobina Wright. Skelton's joy over these meetings was compounded by being able to successfully entertain this comedy master. Davis later confessed, "When he made Chaplin laugh at Cobina's he was so proud."[12] Host and critic Wright was more expansive on Skelton's skills concerning Chaplin: "I have seen that now legendary comic, Charlie Chaplin, hold his sides, doubled over with laughter at Red's antics."[13]

As noted in the previous chapter, here was more proof of a slow thaw setting in for Chaplin in 1952. Moreover, the positives for both comedians would continue for a time that year, before joint catastrophe occurred. Skelton would win two Emmy Awards for the 1951–1952 season, *Best Comedian* and *Best Comedy Program* (which he received as the show's producer). And the early *Limelight* reviews were magnificent, before the government's indefensible action regarding Chaplin's re-entry visa. (As James Hill once wrote, "I am caught between the duty to remember and the desire to erase."[14]) However, the text has addressed this and Skelton's problems were more immediate. Here is Skelton's frank realization following his first small screen season: "After 39 weeks before the camera I can honestly say that for the first time in my life, I've found out how utterly exhausted a human being can be."[15] Plus, as producer Skelton was also involved in nearly every behind-the-scenes facet of the program. On top of that, he was still doing his radio program that necessitated its own original material each week. Thus, it was obvious he could no longer sustain a real film career, and *The Clown* was the last quality picture he would make. Indeed, he would star in only four additional features for the rest of his career, plus the occasional cameo. Hence, one has yet another Chaplin link, since *Limelight* is the legend's last exceptional film, too.

Nonetheless, what is *The Clown*'s scenario, and how does it often bring to mind Chaplin's *Limelight*? Skelton's picture was a remake of King Vidor's *The Champ* (1931), a boxing picture for which title character Wallace Beery won a Best Actor Academy Award (sharing the statuette with Frederic March for *Dr. Jekyll and Mr. Hyde*, 1931). The movie was also nominated for Best Picture, and Frances Marion won the Academy Award for Best Story. Beery is a former heavyweight champion who has fallen on hard times from drinking and gambling addictions. Worse yet, he is continually breaking promises to his forever loyal eight-year-old son Dink (a winning Jackie Cooper), who acts more like the parent than the child. Eventually, shame drives Champ to give custody of the child to his mother and her wealthy husband. However, Dink runs away to be with his father, shortly after Beery's character has signed to fight Mexico's heavy weight champion. Inspired by his child's loyalty, Champ trains hard and manages to win a brutal bout for his son. After a poignant death scene conclusion with his father, Dink finally accepts a life with his sympathetic mother (Irene Rich), whom he always previously had rejected.

The Robert Z. Leonard-directed remake follows the basic parameter of the original, only the Champ is now Dodo the Clown (Red Skelton), and his devoted son Dink is played by another gifted child actor, Tim Considine (now most associated with a period series of Walt Disney TV serials, and the early years of the long-running *My Three Sons* television series, 1960–1972). Dodo is a once famous clown from the *Ziegfeld Follies*' golden years. However, his loving caretaker of a son is also constantly let down in *The Clown* by Dad's drinking and gambling. As in the original story, Dink's mother (Jane Greer) comes back into the story at this time, and Dodo movingly forces his son to be reared by the more responsible parent. Dramatically, only after a heart-wrenching mild striking of the child by Dodo, in the best acting of Skelton's career, he forces Dink to leave. But the steadfast child again runs away to be with Dodo.

In the interim Skelton's character has been given a last chance with an offer of a television program. In that era's movies-versus-TV war, one wonders if this represents a dig at the small screen as the lowest entertainment rung from which to come back, or if at least some Hollywood types were more reticent to acknowledge television as a viable medium. Plus, *The Clown* would be cashing in on the mega-success of Skelton's first TV season. Regardless, as with the original script, Dodo cleans up his lifestyle and manages to be a smashing success, guaranteeing him a long small screen run. However, peppered throughout the picture it has been suggested Skelton's character has a bad heart. (Thus, as with Beery winning, only to die cradled by Cooper, after Dodo's extraordinary program he too passes in Considine's arms, with another mother in the wings.) At this point, it would have been easy for the film to have slipped into six hanky melodrama-land. Yet, as the opening of the *Hollywood Reporter* review states:

> A good combination of mirth and pathos, "The Clown" is a heart-warming, somewhat tragic picture that avoids a soap opera flavor by virtue of two wonderful performances—one by Red Skelton in what

Dodo (Red Skelton) with screen son Tom Considine and character actor Don Beddoe in *The Clown*.

stands out as his most brilliant acting stint to date, the other by young Tim Considine, as fine a child actor as the screen has presented.[16]

Variety said, "Both [actors] turn in heartwarming performances that do much to carry the story."[17] The *New York Times* critic A.W. Weiler added:

> Red Skelton illustrates quite competently that he can read a straight line as well as fall on his face. However, the pratfalls are not missing entirely as he is permitted to run through a couple of his familiar routines.[18]

The two routines Weiler references are an intriguing duo for a period when film and television were on the verge of attempting to play nice. The first comes in the form of a flashback representing Dodo's glory days in the *Follies*. Running several minutes in length, MGM has actually spliced in Skelton's signature sequence from the aforementioned *Bathing Beauty*. Ironically, despite Skelton's sudden second-class status on that film, the movie includes one of his pivotal comic tour de force sequences. Student Skelton is forced to join a ballet class in an attempt to make up with the screen wife, Esther Williams, who teaches at a girls' college.

The ballet sketch was created by Skelton's frequent screen mentor Buster Keaton, who had been reduced to being a gag consultant at MGM. The routine's pièce de resistance was a bit Keaton had borrowed from his father, vaudevillian Joe Keaton. Tutu-attired Skelton finds himself in a girls ballet class, with one leg horizontal to the bar. The drill sergeant-like instructor, Mme. Zarka (Ann Codee, who superbly teams with Skelton), commands the comedian to seemingly defy gravity by lifting his other leg to a parallel position with said bar. Amazingly, Skelton briefly seems to defy the laws of science (with both legs horizontal to the bar) before taking one of his amazing patented pratfalls. Just as Joe Keaton's use of the snippet was a hit on stage, Skelton's rendition is a tour de silly, too. The sketch is so memorable I often use it in my college genre course as a classic recycled embellishment example of a slapstick routine through the ages.

The painful lesson of the ballet bar is followed by a practice in which the large Skelton manages to be most comically nimble on his feet, despite a sticky candy wrapper forever attaching itself to his foot or hand. The comedian always passes it onto another dancer but like a bad penny it keeps being reattached to him. Again, there is also slapstick history. This gummy routine, though used by many comics, is most associated with W.C. Fields, another Skelton comedy hero. Fields had introduced a variation of it in the 1918 *Follies*, with him later periodically using it on the 1920s stage, and then preserving it on film with *The Golf Specialist* (1930). Besides its first-rate comedy, it augments the storyline, since Dodo, like Fields, was supposed to have been a *Follies* star, too.

In any case, when *Bathing Beauty* appeared, many critics had taken MGM to task for its modus operandi of reducing comedy star(s) to supporting players, despite keeping a magnificent Skelton sketch. For instance, the *Hollywood Citizen News*' Nowel E. Redeling said, "It is his [Skelton's] antics—in cold retrospect—which are the entertainment gems ... [and the ballet routine] caused a young lady behind me to become hysterical with laughter."[19] Things have not changed in the passing years; the recycled Skelton sketch remains the comedy highlight of *The Clown*.

However, it is when the second referenced comic segment occurs that a clever phenomenon happens. This *Clown* comedy routine noted by the *Times*' Weiler is actually a reworking of Skelton's most inventive sketch from his *first season on television*. Granted, much early TV was truly "vaudeville in a box," right down to program star(s) opening and closing before a theatre curtain and a live audience, as was the case with Skelton's show. But a notable Skelton exception, more befitting the medium's first real innovator, Ernie Kovacs (1919–1962), was about to appear. At a time when alcoholic comedy bits were still politically correct, most comedians had a hammered anti-hero in their repertoire of comedy characters. Indeed, Skelton's most celebrated comedy sketch was "Guzzler's Gin," in which an on-screen commercial sponsor proceeds to get more drunk each time he demonstrates the product. The bit cemented Skelton's position in 1940s vaudeville, radio, and the movies, especially as demonstrated in his rendition for the *Ziegfeld Follies* (1946).

Ironically, Lucille Ball's more famous 1951 *I Love Lucy* episode, "Vitameatavegamin," is a direct rip-off of Skelton's routine. Regardless, it stands to reason that the comedian would use other variations on being sloshed for humor. In one of Skelton's early small screen sketches, his TV wife is so tired of him coming home plastered that she has their living room furniture bolted to a wall, with all its accompanying surreal configurations, from the apparent new locations of everything from pictures to light fixtures. (It is almost reminiscent of the bizarre home Chaplin's drunken Charlie returns to in *One A.M.*, 1916). Nonetheless, the pickled persona of Skelton's TV character attempting to sit in a chair fastened to the wall is a comic revelation. Suddenly, his character seemed incapable of a basic

Red Skelton recycles a TV sketch for *The Clown*.

tenet of Dean Martin's tipsy alter ego, "You're not drunk if you can lie on the floor without holding on."

These two *Clown* bookend routines, with one spliced from a 1940s film and the second taken from a pioneering 1950s TV show, in which a real-life movie comedian plays a budding TV star, constitutes the perfect delineation of show business' then helter skelter world. And there is also the strange coincidence of *The Clown* and Chaplin's *Limelight* both opening in the latter half of 1952, given their many parallels. Both are comedy-tragedy projects, with each comedian dying at the close, just off stage. The two pictures also hearken back to earlier entertainment periods, in which the filmmakers provide a brief window into the past greatness of these now nearly unremembered clowns, via dreams and reminiscences. Each wants one more opportunity, however brief, to showcase his exceptional past, for two reasons. One, to just be appreciated a final time for his gifts. And second, to reveal this virtuosity to a beloved youngster who has never seen just how awe-inspiringly loved he once was. Each clown's downfall was the result of a vague lost and/or squandered love which had led to self-destructive behavior. Yet, there is hope for the cherished children left behind. *Limelight*'s Terry (Claire Bloom) will go on to be a great ballerina, and Considine's Dink has the security of a loving mother as *The Clown* closes.

Using Dodo as Skelton's name in *The Clown* seems to have had appropriateness both in and beyond the picture. The term dodo probably comes from the Portuguese word "doudo," meaning fool. The dodo bird is also one of nature's most famous extinct creatures, and in popular culture has often become a symbol for extinction, foolishness, and obsolescence—the latter term meaning something that is disused, or antiquated, because a replacement has become available. Skelton's *clown* character plays the fool, lives a life of self-destructiveness, and dies after a substitute has become available—Dink's loving and now wealthy mother.

Nevertheless, how does the luckless Dodo become a symbol for a 1952 Skelton which rivals Chaplin's disconsolate close to the year, including *Limelight* and *The Clown* eventually seen as each artist's last significant film? After all, Skelton will take home two Emmy Awards that year, and garner more kudos for modesty. In beating out favorite Lucille Ball, he said, "I don't like this. I think it [the award for *Best Comedian*] should go to Lucy." Several critics, such as the *Los Angeles Herald Express*' Owen Collins, were impressed: "This is where Skelton endeared himself in our hearts forever."[20]

Plus, *The Clown* was critically acclaimed, and the comedian was finally given substantial praise for his acting capabilities, too. The movie also held a special place in Skelton's pantheon of pictures. This is brought out in his daughter Valentina Maria Skelton Alonso's Foreword to my second biography of her father.[21] But the exposition demands a brief setup for the telling. In early 1957 nine-year-old Valentina's younger brother Richard (then eight) was diagnosed with leukemia. Later that year, while the disease was in remission, the family did a great deal of traveling—an attempt to jam a lifetime of experiences into a few months. But Red, well aware of all the attention Richard was getting, wisely sensed that Valentina was feeling neglected. Thus, what follows is a special memory of a father-daughter date and the film to which he chose to introduce her to his film alter ego:

> My first real experience of realizing how talented dad was happened when on a summer vacation in Honolulu, Hawaii, in 1957. He said, "There is a movie playing called *The Clown* [still showing five years after its 1952 release], I'd like to take you to see it." So, Dad and I went to the movie. We sat down with popcorn and soda. The show began. It was black and white and I realized that it was Dad up on the screen. He was *The Clown* ... [despite the humor I] was so sad it made me cry. I felt the pain of that clown and his sadness. At the end of the movie I turned to Dad and said, "That was you on the screen." I gave him a hug and held his hand as we walked out of the theatre. I realized my dad's talents then as a hero; I was taken by him. [And] I commend ... Wes ... for helping me to understand more about my father.[22]

So again, how could Skelton's 1952 rival Chaplin parallel to this period for negativity? Ironically, TV could be detrimental for movie people in two ways. While one normally hears about movie careers being hurt by television, a negative TV factor is not always addressed. Skelton was *the* major movie star to make headlines by executing a total leap to the "boob tube." But early in the 1952–1953 season his formerly high profile positive press promptly turned sour—Skelton's ratings were abysmal. (It would take years for his program to recover.) This was *the* illustration of the aforementioned "glass furnace" phenomenon. The comedian had plowed through years of sketches, which could have lasted a vaudevillian a lifetime, since these performers played a single city date only once or twice a year, if that. Routines were honed and repeated forever to a non-mass market.

However, once a classic sketch was done on early TV's 39-episode season, with viewers glued to a limited program selection (CBS, NBC, ABC, and, for a short time, DuMont), millions of viewers simultaneously saw the routine. Thus, TV audiences expected comparable classic material 38 more times each season. As Skelton later confessed, "In my first year on TV I used up a hundred and sixty-five routines. Some of it was stuff I'd spent years putting together."[23] Plus, he had initially vetoed a live audience his second season, despite enjoying immediate feedback, because the cumbersome size and amount of equipment necessary for pioneering TV made spectators viewing haphazard. Eventually, the second season went to what the industry called a "stop-and-go" method. Individual scenes were live but there were breaks between segments. This allowed Skelton adequate time for various costume changes, as well as morphing into one of his different comedy characters (such as his early pivotal country yokel, Clem Kadiddlehopper). And here was another problem; Skelton attempted to play as many of his various comedy alter egos each episode. This got old, as well as difficult for writers to both integrate all the characters and manage to produce polished material. In later years, the problem would be dissipated, in part, by building a program around just *one* of his characters each episode, such as his greatest and most multifaceted figure, Freddie the Freeloader.

So how did he stay on TV if his ratings plummeted? Well, in the industry's infancy long-term contracts were honored. This was then easier to orchestrate, because programs usually only had one sponsor to placate. Sadly for Skelton, there were also bigger problems with which to deal. For example, 1952 was the year Skelton and Edna Stillwell parted company professionally. Though long divorced, she had guided Skelton's career into the 1950s, watching over every detail, from producing the radio program to standing in the wings with a fresh shirt when he came off wet with sweat. More importantly, she had been a sister-like cheerleader for a comedian from the most dysfunctional childhood.

While all this would be difficult for man/child Skelton, he was practically in meltdown mode after the first season, not unlike the comedian's breakdown near the close (1945) of World War II. Performers need more love than most people, or to paraphrase a line from Francois Truffaut's Oscar-winning *Day for Night* (1973), "That's why we kiss and/or hug so much whenever we meet." With that in mind, the broadside of bad reviews were devastating for him, especially after the amazingly unmitigated success of his first season. Granted, anyone would be upset but for the fragile Skelton, who had had so much of his career orchestrated by a devoted first wife, the criticism was extremely hurtful. Indeed, many industry insiders, such as influential columnist Louella Parsons, blamed Skelton's fall, in part, on Stillwell's recent absence.

History still has yet to reveal the ultimate catalyst for Stillwell's exit but the general consensus is that second wife Davis was responsible. When the Skeltons had the most public of temporary splits in late 1952, Stillwell and the crushing TV ratings were again in the news. Parsons suggested the domestic donnybrook was caused by the couple's disagreement over Skelton's desire to bring Stillwell back to save the sinking series.[24] (Skelton was always sensitive to claims that Davis wore the pants in the family, and he had even written Parsons the previous year, 1951, to explain that Stillwell's initial leave had been health related.[25])

Interestingly, the only solid point of contention to hit the late 1952 newspapers seemed to directly reaffirm Skelton's man/child tendencies, and subtextually hint at the comedian's dangerous drinking problem. For example, Davis told the *New York World*:

> He'd come in at four o'clock in the morning—he often worked very late at night—and want to play with them [the children]. Then they'd have terrible colds [after these abnormal play times]. I finally told him, "Red, I'll have to lock my [bedroom] door [the children's rooms were through her suite]. I can't allow my babies to get up at that hour."[26]

This is reminiscent of an observation made by Steve Allen, the multi-talented performer/writer whose media criticism/history is sadly neglected. In what is still the best book on 1950s TV comedians, *The Funny Men* (1956), he entertainingly observes:

> I have never known a successful comedian who was not somewhat neurotic. The unsuccessful ones must be in even worse condition.... A difficult early life seems to be an essential requirement for admission to the ranks of eminent clowns.[27]

In doing numerous biographies of "funnymen," including Charlie Chaplin, the Marx Brothers, W. C. Fields, Laurel & Hardy, Red Skelton, Joe E. Brown, Robert Benchley, and Will Cuppy, I would have to concur with Allen. But maybe an observation made by Robin Williams speaks most directly to Skelton's second wife's dilemma. Williams compared being married to a comic with owning a cobra:

> Basically, there's a certain amount of novelty, and the novelty is showing the cobra to your friends—but comics can be nasty. Along with our desperate insecurity, sometimes we're equipped to be vicious.[28]

Nonetheless, this now brings one full circle back to *The Clown*. While several previous parallels had been noted between that picture and Chaplin's *Limelight*, there was a key difference. While Chaplin's autobiographical work was years in the making, Skelton's personal history ties to *The Clown* seem more unexpected—both in their immediacy and/or foreshadowing. After all, following all the earlier Skelton hurrahs, the public had now suddenly rejected him. And even before the ratings fiasco, he struggled with aping the creative workaholism of his hero (Chaplin). Plus, the pressure of a newly formatted forthcoming TV season, and a tendency to self-medicate (via alcohol), had him near a breakdown.

Nonetheless, his personal and *Clown* similarities are uncanny, beyond the depth of their entertainment falls. Both Skelton and Dodo exacerbated bad situations by unrestrained drinking. At times in *The Clown* Skelton's title character is so self-destructive he seems bent on suicide (another *Limelight* parallel, à la Terry). Regardless, in 1952 and early 1953 Skelton *was* suicidal. The Doppler effect of reality and fiction was made more complex by the fierce but flawed fatherly love of both Dodo and Skelton himself. Moreover, while Skelton lives and Dodo dies, the children involved in these two stories are best served by their mothers—the estranged wife of each clown.

Indeed, the Skelton autobiographical ties to *The Clown* do not stop there. While his fictional character was the dumb Dodo, Skelton's career-building comedy character, in a menagerie of roles, was the aforementioned Clem Kadiddlehopper, a first cousin to his *Clown* character. Indeed, Skelton's cast of comedy figures, often even predating his popular 1940s radio program, were often Dodo-like dolts, such as the comedian's punch-drunk fighter, Cauliflower McPugg. Besides, as has been already established, just as the childish Dodo needed constant parenting, *even* if it was by his own screen child, the real Skelton was of a similar ilk, with his nickname for first wife Stillwell being "Mommie."

Plus, as previously alluded to, during the early 1950s (part of *Limelight*'s long gestation period), Skelton was building a friendship with his film idol. (Skelton would later even visit Chaplin when the legendary figure established his Swiss residency.) Also, though they embraced opposite ends of the political spectrum, this text has barely touched on all the Skelton role model/TV blueprint plugs he showered on the beleaguered Chaplin often in the early 1950s. Thus, is it not possible that a link connects the lengthy creation of *Limelight* with *The Clown*? Do not these factors (especially the building friendship with Chaplin) and the many other direct and indirect tangential ties between each man and his "fictional" figure in these two pictures suggest that *The Clown* was more than a mere remake of a boxing picture?

Nevertheless, while all the comedians and their focus films discussed so far in this text have been impacted by television and/or McCarthyism, Skelton's movie/TV situation is the most unusual. First, by embracing the new medium so fully, it essentially ended his film career; there was not enough time. Second, as hypothetically suggested in Allen's hitherto noted *The Funny Men*, despite Skelton initial TV kudos, maybe his second season nosedive also involved a concluding component. That is, perhaps viewers had also held him to a higher standard, "we had, oversold ourselves" on what a *big film star* could do on the *small screen*.[29] Third, whether or not one accepts Allen's idea, the premise is indirectly reinforced by the fact that it took years before a TV star (of any genre) managed to become a legitimate movie star.

As a footnote to TV giving Dodo a brief second chance before his death, the medium still was shrinking movie audiences throughout the 1950s. With that development, a collective actors' shudder over losing work continued across the decade. For example, the *New York Herald Tribune*'s review of *The Clown* appeared on the same page as a critique of Betty Davis' down and out performer in *The Star* (1953). Though a straight melodrama, the critique opening, if "Ziegfeld Follies" is substituted for "Hollywood," would not have been out of place in the *Clown* critique, "As a has-been Hollywood star trying to stop the clock, Davis suffers a lot of tension and egoistic anguishes."[30] There is no mention of TV, yet the subtextual message is clear. And as with *The Clown* and *Limelight*, there is a certain autobiographical touch to *The Star*, given that the maverick two-time Oscar-winning Davis' career was in one of her many declines, and she was playing a headstrong former Academy Award winner. Thus, while the *Herald Tribune* credited *The Clown* as having a "measure of distinction," the two critiques might have appeared as one.[31] Nevertheless, while all decades are periods of transition, the 1950s occupy a unique hold on that phenomenon.

Be that as it may, with back-to-back chapters anchored in comedy-tragedy, perhaps it is time to stop swooshing around the dark basement and embrace an intermission from angst-ridden laughter. The following chapter returns one to broad clown comedy, smothered with parody, and film's most successful *sometime* comedy team.

6

Hope & Crosby
The Road to Bali (January 30, 1953)

> As Bing Crosby is about to do a *Road to Bali* number, Bob Hope breaks film's fourth wall by turning directly to the audience (camera) and helpfully suggesting, "He's gonna sing, folks. Now's the time to go out and get popcorn."

There's nothing inherently new about comic direct address, even involving a musical put-down. For example, when Chico Marx goes into one of his patented piano solos in *Horse Feathers* (1932), Groucho warns viewers, "I've got to stay here but there's no reason why you folks shouldn't go into the lobby until this thing blows over." But direct address does announce that the focus film has entered *parody* land, as was the case with Bob Hope's *Son of Paleface* (1952, see Chapter 3).[1] And as was formerly noted, *personality comedies* are often tied to parody, since the cornerstone clown is invariably fish-out-of-water funny as a manly leading figure in the genre being spoofed. Indeed, this is a basic component of parody.[2] However, direct address embraces the most fundamental element of a spoof—calling attention to being a movie. That is, looking at the audience is something film characters are not supposed to do. It destroys the genre of reality—which is precisely what a parody picture is all about.

Bali was Hope & Crosby's sixth "Road" film, and as with the others (as well as the concluding *Road to Hong Kong*, 1962), all are loose parodies of action adventure films. One might exemplify this statement and everything else addressed thus far by noting a particular *Bali* sequence. The scene in question involves Hope & Crosby wandering through an island jungle when they see Humphrey Bogart dragging his tiny tramp steamer through an infested marsh (a film clip from 1951's *The African Queen*, for which Bogart won an Oscar). The comic surprise inclusion again breaks any perception of *Bali* reality, as well as making Hope & Crosby all the funnier by comparing them to a *real* action film figure.

Not surprisingly, Hope milks the moment with more direct address and another parody ingredient. First, Hope & Crosby run toward Bogart's Oscar. Hope instantaneously grabs the statuette with jealous fervor: "Give me that. You've got one." The comedian then goes into a droll acceptance speech, which leads to him speaking to the audience. Second, the parody scene is funny without one either having seen *The African Queen*, known about

Bogart's Academy Award, or been aware that Crosby had also won an Oscar for *Going My Way* (1944). Parody, like any form of laughter, should be amusing without viewer expertise on the subject being kidded. It should be obvious, however, that the genre is progressively more entertaining the greater one's familiarity with the topic being spoofed.

Regardless, as with previous "Road" pictures, the plot seems optional. Indeed, as with most personality comedies lathered with parody, these films are character-driven. But to put *Bali* in period perspective, *New York Journal American* critic Jim O'Connor's very enthusiastic review had some fun with the "story":

> Crosby and Hope don't seem to bother about a plot. So why should you or I? While rolling in the aisle [with laughter] at the Astor [theatre], I did seem to gather that the script had something to do with Australia and a voyage to Bali and cannibals and sunken treasure and deep sea diving and a sea monster called Boga Tan [a giant squid] and a volcano and a native prince doing his dirtiest to louse up the love life of Dottie ["Road" picture regular Dorothy Lamour] and Bing and Bob.[3]

With very little tweaking, this could serve as the generic formula for any "Road" picture, fitting, as the *Brooklyn Eagle* review noted, "the pattern established by all the others."[4] This reinforces, as one sees *Bali* as personality comedy, two main characteristics of that comedy genre. First, the sometime team of Hope & Crosby is maintaining a consistent comedy shtick. This involves a constant witty repartee centered around women, Crosby taking advantage of Hope, and references to the movies. Musical interludes were also a norm, usually showcasing Crosby, when the genre still had a variety show tendency.

Second, O'Connor's casually eclectic *Bali* overview underscores that Hope & Crosby, like most film clown outsiders, are frequently nomadic, with direct literary ties to such picaresque heroes as Don Quixote and Huck Finn. Appropriately, cinema's greatest clown, Chaplin's Charlie, is a wandering Tramp, who often closed pictures by literally shuffling down life's highways. Closer to home, Hope & Crosby teamings are *Road* pictures. In fact, some installments, such as *Bali*, devote time to charting their helter-skelter movements on a map.

Not coincidentally, the "Road" pictures began at a time (1940) when America was on the verge of entering a world war and the country was much more cognizant of the world around her, though Hope & Cosby kept the destinations exotically escapist. Regardless, the nomadic norm complements clown comedy in several ways. First, it gives them an endless supply of new settings for humor, from the *Bali* duo being song-and-dance men in a Melbourne, Australia, theatre to a layover at a princess' palace (Lamour) on an unidentified island. And sometimes the mode of transportation can even become a comic end in itself. For example, they escape shotgun marriages in Melbourne (a typical opening to a "Road" picture) by catching a train out of town. However, Crosby travels first class and anti-hero Hope journeys *no class* under the train, with his partner periodically lowering him bundled scraps out the window. When they both have to ditch the train, after one of their almost fathers-in-law appears, Hope and Crosby manage to ship out with a load of sheep for such a protracted time their long beards help mask their cover.

A second comic reason for travel is that placing a clown in some unlikely setting can be an ongoing joke itself, and is often a parody starting point, too. For example, *Bali* Bob in a diving bell suit, both above and below water, is a wonderful sight gag misnomer in and of itself. Though not in a comic league with Buster Keaton's still yet to be matched diving suit sequence from *The Navigator* (1924), Hope effectively exploits the sequence for laughs.

Bob Hope (center) is tricked again by Bing Crosby as Dorothy Lamour looks on in the *Road to Bali*.

Examples range from Lamour fogging over his diving bell window with a passionate kiss, to Hope finding both the treasure *and* the giant squid Bogo Tan (also used in Cecil B. DeMille's 1942 *Reap the Wild Wind*, which won an Oscar for special effects).

A third movie motivation for clown travel is the opportunity to introduce a broad cross-section of supporting comedy characters, from the Outback's almost fathers-in-law, to the less than comely native girl Crosby mistakenly conjures out of a nontraditional snake charmer's basket. (Hope had unexpectedly used the same illusionist flute technique to bring forth the most lovely of ladies.) *Bali* also features an evil prince and his henchman who could also double as upscale treasure-seeking pirates. However, because there are an unprecedented number of *Bali* cameos (to be addressed shortly), this "Road" picture has less room for the series' normal army of kooky characters.

Of course, before proceeding further, one should make note of Hope & Crosby's take on the series. Hope's favorite description of his "Road" character came from a *Saturday Evening Post* article the same year (1953) as *Bali*'s release: "Fate is determined to make [him] a jerk. He brags and blusters but there isn't a child over five who can't outwit him, disarm him or steal his pants."[5] But as Hope observed of these pictures, "We put more emphasis on the 'boob' aspect of his 'Road' character."[6] That is, Hope's alter ego in a solo outing like *Son of Paleface*, anti-hero or not, would not be quite so gullible to all the risks "Road" shenanigans through which Crosby put him.

Crosby's perspective on the series that same year, from his 1953 *Call Me Lucky* memoir, considered

> the basic ingredient of any "Road" picture is a Rover Boys-type plot [juvenile fiction figures of Crosby's youth obsessed with pranks and flirtatious behavior], plus music. The plot takes two fellows, throws them into as many jams as possible, then lets them clown their way out.[7]

Crosby, however, has left a key element out of his "Road" series definition. He does not consider the difference between these "two fellows." Though they are both women-chasing boy/men con artists, Crosby is invariably in charge of their misadventures—misadventures which usually put Hope at risk. For example, in need of money (another "Road" norm), Crosby manages to have his partner go down in a diving bell, despite knowing the danger involved. Thus, with a dark comedy tone, an *Esquire* reviewer of a comparable situation in the *Road to Utopia* (1946), reported, "Theatre ushers report that spectators all laugh at Hope and identify themselves with Crosby."[8]

Yet, through the decades since then, the self confused Bob Hope clone Woody Allen has so peppered his films with Ski Nose–like direct address—which makes the viewer chiefly identify with the character most aware it is a movie—today's audiences (especially my college students) gravitate to a more humorous fourth wall-breaking Hope. For instance, a *Bali* direct address tally favors him 9–1 over Crosby, with one shared example. Beyond the chapter opener, Hope is chummy with the audience in a myriad of ways. Early in the picture a topless native boy from a neighboring island walks by and Hope asks Crosby, "Do you suppose … [that is true of the women, too]?" When Crosby pooh-poohs the idea, Hope turns to the camera and observes, "Stick around folks, he could be wrong, you know."

Upon the first appearances of Lamour, she finds the duo bickering.

> LAMOUR: Do you always fight over girls?
> HOPE: What else could we fight over? We have no money. [He then turns to the camera and with tax awareness states] That's for Washington.

Indeed, Hope addresses the *Bali* camera so much, to review the ones not already noted might necessitate packing some food and getting into comfortable clothing. However, the tour de force example—actually one could count it as compounded direct address of Frank Tashlin cartoon-like brilliance—occurs at a *series* of *Bali* endings.

The catalyst for these multiple conclusions is that Lamour chooses Crosby over Hope (the "Road" standard), and Ski Nose goes back to his previously used flute and snake charmer's basket. Once again, he produces a "wingding" of a woman—Jane Russell in her *Son of Paleface* saloon garb. Since he won her heart in that picture, Hope is more than satisfied. Despite that, Russell also decides to go off with Crosby. Hence, Hope hastily turns to the audience and says, "Stay right where you're at, folks, this picture isn't over yet!" As Crosby and company head off toward ménage à trois land, Hope keeps turning back toward the audience and repeating, "Stay right there," to no avail. Only now, "The End" sign starts to rise from the bottom of the film screen and Hope does his best to push it down. Yet, as the conclusion emblem begins to pull the comedian up, he shouts to everyone in and out of the movie, "Get the writer, get the producer, get my agent, get my girl." Once poor Bob has been removed like a venetian blind going up, the phrase, "Positively the end" appears.

And what of Crosby's one foray into direct address territory, with the help of Hope? It occurs after Bing asks Bob how he managed to survive both getting out of his diving suit and wrestling with the giant octopus—something to which the screen viewer has also not been privy. Hope starts to explain but stops to look at the audience, as if to underline its impossibility (again, the self-consciousness of parody). Bob's silent direct address is briefly copied by Bing, before they both walk away from the camera and Ski-Nose pantomimes his miracle. The sequence concludes with Bing returning to the foreground of the screen and giving a physical shrug of the shoulders to the viewer—he still cannot make sense of film's use/need for the periodic "suspension of disbelief." Consequently, Hope still essentially remains the audience's inside man to this movie parody.

In point of fact, most comedy teams have one designated direct address individual. It both minimizes overuse of the comic surprise of breaking the fourth wall, and allows audience members to be more engaged with the picture by having their own single funny fifth columnist. For example, while Hope was the designated one in his occasional teamings with Crosby, Groucho was that person among his "men from Marx," and Oliver played that part with Stanley in the Laurel & Hardy films.

As noted earlier, all this is not to say that both Hope and Crosby often consciously quip about Hollywood in their nonstop "Road" show bantering. Yet, as with *Bali*'s comically crazed multiple endings, Hope seems to be the one most plugged into the parody process. For instance, when the duo first gets to Lamour's gorgeous palace, which is densely populated with willing and equally gorgeous women, there is an off-screen moan. Crosby asks his partner, with what seems genuine surprise, "What was that noise?" Without missing the proverbially beat, Hope replies, "It's [the swashbuckling womanizer] Errol Flynn. He can't stand it." And there is little visual response that Crosby comprehends Hope's tongue-in-cheek explanation.

As a postscript to Hope's more direct link to the audience than the comedian's norm, he also used his occasional partner as an in-joke "Road" gag in his solo films. For instance, at the close of arguably the best Hope picture, *My Favorite Brunette* (1947), when the comedian is saved from death row, the extremely disappointed executioner (Crosby) has a comic conniption.[9] And before *Son of Paleface* (see Chapter 3) even opens, Hope amusingly knocks Crosby as some poor character actor on the studio lot. Indeed, a funny Bing put-down might occur anywhere in a Hope picture. For instance, it happens in the middle of *Off Limits* (1953), when the comedian plays a distraught fight manager stuck in a bar trying to find out how his boxer (Mickey Rooney) is doing during a televised fight. Hope even manages a compound joke here, knocking *early television* and *Crosby*. Thus, as Hope frantically battles poor TV reception as he changes channels in search of the match, Crosby's image comes up. Hope quickly comments, "More static," and keeps searching.

Actually, even though I have referenced the other Hope films as "solo" outings, there is a "team" element to his and most clown's independent outings, too.[10] To illustrate, little Charlie Chaplin invariably cast himself opposite a mammoth villain, and when W. C. Fields was in his henpecked persona, he invariably played against a variety of busybody shrews.[11] Hope embraced this "team" effect in two ways. First, beyond the "Road" pictures themselves, there was a "team" effect to his regular uses of Crosby as a comic punching bag in Hope's individual pictures—a fitting comic revenge, considering how Bing constantly tricked him in the "Road" series. Audiences looked for these Crosby digs as much as they expected to see one of Alfred Hitchcock's signature cameos in his films.

Second, whether directly teamed with Crosby, or on an allegedly individual cinema outing, Hope was a team unto himself.[12] That is, by the late 1930s, on the eve of the "Road" films, Hope had created a comedy character which could fluctuate between the most cowardly and incompetent of comic anti-heroes and the cool, egotistical womanizing wiseguy. This was a breakthrough development in the world of personality comedians, with numerous screen clowns (such as Red Skelton and Danny Kaye) soon emulating him. But Hope was the unquestionable master, whether in his "Road" pictures, or spoofing film noir detectives in the aforementioned classic *My Favorite Brunette*. Plus, it is a clown legacy that is now the standard. Years later, Woody Allen would confess:

> There are certain moments in his older movies [of which *Bali* was a special favorite] when I think he's the best thing I have ever seen. It's everything I can do at times not to imitate ... [that back and forth movement from cocky to coward]. It's hard to tell when I ... [copy him], because I'm so unlike him physically and in tone of voice but once you know I do it, it's absolutely unmistakable.[13]

Mixed in with the duality of Hope's persona, also replicated by Allen, is Ski Nose's sexual ego. Though on display throughout *Bali*, the exemplar crack has him observing, "Some of us have it [an erotic desirability] and some of us don't. I feel like such a cad having so much of it."

As this chapter has demonstrated, therefore, *Bali* very much continues the basic "Road" picture template. Yet, there are some specific differences. For example, this is the only "Road" adventure filmed in color. This enhanced the exotic escapist settings for which the series was known. Also, in the movies' ongoing battle with TV, a major rallying cry was "Give them something not available on the small screen." Well, in 1953 the number of color TVs in America was so negligible one could honestly say film owned the *rainbow* phenomenon. And in the early 1950s, while other less expensive color processes were in existence, nothing could touch the bright hues of this "Road" film's *Technicolor*. Indeed, the color factor was taken so seriously, it even impacted a Hope and Crosby bagpipe routine early in the movie. With the duo wearing authentic Scottish plaid kilts, several types were screen-tested, with MacTavish plaid winning because it tested best in Technicolor.

Another *Bali* difference, as noted by Hope biographer Charles Thompson, was that while the comedy duo had always bantered at each other's expense throughout the series, on this occasion "they turned the film into an even greater vehicle for their personal routines."[14] Although Crosby invariably got the girl (in *Bali*'s case, two girls), the witticism winner was unfailingly Hope, such as calling Crosby merely a "collapsible [Perry] Como." And on another occasion, when the subject of pirates comes up between the naïve South Seas beauty Dorothy Lamour and Crosby, she is surprised that he makes references to pirates in America. (In real life the singer had a part interest in baseball's Pittsburgh Pirates.) At this point Hope appears and the team bicker back and forth about Crosby's Pirates and Hope's hometown Cleveland Indians, for which he also had stocks. Both get in some clever cracks. However, Hope delivers the coup de grâce closing quip: "At least they're [the Cleveland Indians] in the major leagues," implying Bing's Pirates were a minor league farm team. By ratcheting up what Thompson has called the duo's "personal insult routines," *Bali* is merely playing to Hope's comedy philosophy, which fittingly uses baseball as a metaphor:

> You have to get over to the audience that there's a game of wits going on and that if they don't stay awake, they'll miss something, like missing a baseball someone has lobbed to them. What I'm really doing is asking, "Let's see if you can hit this one!" That's my whole comedy technique. I know how to telegraph to the audience the fact that this *is* a joke, and that if they don't laugh right now, they're not playing the game and nobody has any fun.[15]

These observations by Thompson and Hope imply *Bali* had more "Road" series saturation comedy (the quicker the jokes come, the more likely one scores a laugh), while it once again validates a statement made earlier about a basic parody truism. That is, a successful parody needs to be funny in and of itself—yet the more you know the funnier it gets. Thus, Hope's Cleveland Indians joke versus the Pirates being some baseball nonentity is hilarious. The humor quotient immediately goes up when one knows the duo are also part owners of the clubs.

A third *Bali* difference from the "Road" norm is its pioneering use of multiple movie cameos, with even an increased number of film capitol references. Actually, this is implied by the working title of the picture—the *Road to Hollywood*. And in point of fact, while Hope and Crosby get to more than one exotic island in this installment of the series, the duo never does reach Bali.

Furthermore, the cameos are often inspiringly used. Though one is hard-pressed to top Bogart's *African Queen* clip, and the subsequent fight over his Oscar, conceivably a better example materializes in an extended dream sequence. Shortly after a festive evening ceremony involving an East Indian rope trick, a bit of comic stage magic in which a coil of rope stiffens and enables someone to climb out of sight—Hope, Crosby, and Lamour all turn in for the evening. As they sleep on their separate cots (the censorship code still exists), comic book-like speech, or image bubbles, appear over all their heads and reveals their romantic dream subjects. Both Bob and Bing are fantasizing about Dorothy, but she is dreaming of Martin & Lewis, with the accent on a handsome Dean Martin staring directly at the camera/audience. Martin visibly takes precedence, since Jerry Lewis' expression closely resembles Harpo Marx's famous "Gookie" expression, which was inspired by observing the contortions through which a neighborhood cigar roller put his face in the line of duty—popping eyes and a rolled out tongue protruding from puffed out checks.[16] Critic/personality Alexander Woolcott likened the expression to the mask of a "Neanderthal idiot."[17]

Nevertheless, Lamour might have contributed to the dream sequence, given the following story from her memoir, *My Side of the Road* (1974). During one patch of shooting *Bali*, both Hope and Crosby were struggling with their lines:

6. Bob Hope & Bing Crosby 79

A casual moment on the *Bali* set with Bob Hope and Dorothy Lamour.

"Hal [Walker, director]," I called, "better warm up Martin & Lewis. They're not only funnier but younger." Everybody laughed except the boys [Hope & Crosby], "*You'd* better be careful how you talk to us," Bob [affectionately] said, "You can always be replaced by an actress."[18]

Regardless, Lamour's cinema dream life is especially funny because it builds upon *Bali*'s increased Hollywood focus, and suddenly makes her character more interesting. That is, while Hope & Crosby are always fighting over Lamour on their "Road" trips, she is seemingly always loyal to both of them, while "the boys" are frequently distracted sexually by all the beautiful girls that grace these pictures.

The dream sequence also anticipates a comparable scene in Steve Martin's later acclaimed *L. A. Story* (1991). Martin's zany la la land weatherman falls for a visiting London journalist (Victoria Tennant, Martin's real wife, 1986–1994), except he is seeing a sexy, kooky spokesmodel SanDeE (Sarah Jessica Parker). Tennant is taken with Martin, too, but has promised to attempt reconciliation with her ex-husband (Richard E. Grant). However, by a sprinkling of movie serendipity, each couple happens to take an allegedly romantic weekend at the same upscale hotel getaway ... in adjoining suits. Moreover, when each twosome bed down, the cartoon bubbly imagery matches the comic surprise of the *Bali* sequence. While Martin and Tennant fantasize about each other, the alternate pair visualizes a young Mel Gibson!

As an addendum to the apparent *Bali* influence on the Martin-written *L.A. Story*, the comedian might also have been inspired by the *African Queen* sequence of the "Road" picture. In co-writing *Dead Men Don't Wear Plaid* (1982) with director Carl Reiner (an early Martin collaborator) and George Gibe, the three build a whole picture around the concept of the Hope & Crosby sequence with the Bogart clip. *Dead Men* is essentially a collage picture involving clips from 18 film noir classic, combined with new black and white footage of a nourish-attired and acting Martin. As edited by Bud Molin, the film has the comedian interacting with a pantheon of noir performers, including Bogart, Alan Ladd, Burt Lancaster, Barbara Stanwyck, and Veronica Lake. Though essentially a one-joke movie, it still manages to be an engaging postmodern look at film noir. Even if neither *L.A. Story* nor *Dead Men Don't Wear Plaid* had a direct link to *Bali*, the Hope & Crosby picture was a pioneering catalyst for this sort of parody-driven personality comedy. Other examples might include Hope disciple Woody intercutting historical footage, like the World War I Kaiser, into his first film as a director, the 1969 mockumentary *Take the Money and Run*, or his use of subtitles to reveal what both he and Diane Keaton are thinking during their first encounter of *Annie Hall* (1977).

A final *Bali* difference, paradoxically, has its preceding comic "Road" calamities actually turn back onto themselves. Put another way, *Bali* is rather like a *greatest hits* compendium of all Hope & Crosby's previous pictures. Yes, each installment sends its duo off to crash head-on into an action adventure parody. But *Bali*'s difference here is that it strains out the best of the pool. *New York Daily News* critic Kate Cameron literally says this in her positive review:

> Nearly all the good gags used in other "Road" pictures pop up in this one. Many of them are very funny, especially if you haven't seen them before, and are worth a second laugh, if you have.[19]

There is a certainty in bringing back material which has come up missing in other episodes. For example, Hope & Crosby's "patty-cake" routine returns, which is described by Lamour:

> Whenever a bad guy ... threatens the boys, they stop, bend their knees, and start playing patty-cake. The villain is usually so dumb-founded that he stops to watch them, where upon they flatten him and run.[20]

And Hope even comes home to a *Road to Morocco* (1942) variation of a sketch in which the comedian becomes a monkey. In the original *Morocco* installment, Hope briefly has access to a magic ring. Given the desert heat and his doubts about the object's power, he modestly wishes for a cold Scotch and water. Thus, when the frosted drink instantly appears, Hope is so surprised he blurts out, "I'll be a monkey's uncle." And presto, he is presumably some monkey's uncle, which necessitates burning a final wish to return to his anti-hero norm. Flash forward to *Bali* and Dorothy has an inexplicable platonic fondness for Hope. Finally, she remembers. As a child she had a beloved pet monkey that looked just like the comedian. And in a flashback, with 1950s special effects, the viewer sees Hope's face superimposed over that of some now silly looking simian.

Plus, as was documented earlier, the *Bali* Hope wins the humor crown from Crosby, which is the way it was intended to be all the time. To illustrate, Crosby confesses precisely those thoughts on the series' formula, just before its first installment, the *Road to Singapore* (1940):

> I was intrigued with the idea of working with Bob and Dottie [Lamour] because it seemed to me that it would be a winning combination. A foreign land ... the natives ... the music.... Dottie in a sarong [Hollywood's designated sexy icon for her after films like *The Jungle Princess*, 1936], *Bob being the Clown* [my italics], and me singing the ballads—it was one helluva formula for a series.[21]

To paraphrase historian Dominic LaCapra, "Many artists are good for thinking about but only a few, after their own time has passed, continue to be good enough with which to continue a dialogue."[22] The multi-faceted Hope merits such inclusion. After all, the comedian's definitive biographer, Richard Zoglin, makes such a case in his book, *Hope: Entertainer of the Century* (2014).[23] Woody Allen said of the study, "For me it's a feast."[24] And it is a thesis I have long embraced for an artist whose career, like his life (1903–2003), covered most of the 20th century.

Though there would be one final series exercise, *The Road to Hong Kong* (1962), it really deserves a qualifying asterisk. "The boys" were now too old for their "Road" "Rover Boys" personae, a common problem with the alter egos of most comedians as they age. For example, Jerry Lewis' dysfunctional juvenile antics as a surrogate wannabe younger brother to the cool Dean Martin worked effectively when they were a team. But as a solo his age soon made such actions almost creepy, as if we were to laugh at a special needs adult. The Jerry Lewis–like Jim Carrey has now run into the same problem. Of course, exceptions do exist. Groucho's persona was always that of the witty dirty old man, and age only enhanced that character. Regardless, *Hong Kong*, simply lacked the energy level of previous "Roads," with cameos now grown into parts taking time away from Hope & Crosby, aging or not. And Lamour is all but dropped. The actress, who was even billed above Hope in the first "Road" outing, was now merely reduced to a cameo in the finale.

Bali, with its *greatest hits* status, as well as being a critical and commercial success barely behind Martin & Lewis' *Scared Stiff* (1953) at the box office, would have been a perfect close to the "Road" series.[25] (Indeed, *Stiff* was even a remake of Hope's 1939 *Ghost Breakers*, with Hope & Crosby also having a cameo in the Martin & Lewis picture.) And speaking of the younger duo, many of *Bali*'s reviews had that same almost hysterically positive nature found in the Martin & Lewis critiques. For example, the *New York Journal American*'s *Bali* notice opened:

> SINGARAJA [The old capital of Bali]! That's all you need to know about the new picture which opened yesterday at the Astor Theatre, if you are a Crosby-Hope fan as I am in any picture with Crosby and Hope in it is a funny picture because Bing and Bob always are funny.[26]

Bob Hope breaks up Bing Crosby on the set of *Bali*.

The *New York Herald Tribune* said, "Theirs [Hope & Crosby] is a soothing kind of entertainment, with an occasional roar [of laughter] in the midst of many chuckles, and it is all too rare in modern screen comedy."[27] And the *Brooklyn Eagle*'s review had *Journal American* verve:

> Regardless of where a "Road" picture goes, it leads to fun and romance…. The most enjoyable part of "Road to Bali" is the spirit in which Bob, Bing and Dottie draw the customers right along with them

on their nonsensical excursion. There's something about their evident enjoyment of their own antics [spiked with scripted "ad-libs"], and the easy, relaxed atmosphere that pervades the whole production that makes the audience feel as if they're not merely watching but sharing the same adventures.[28]

Variety added, "the framework is there on which to hang a succession of amusing quips and physical comedy dealing with romantic rivalry and chuckle competition between the two male stars."[29] And even the *Hollywood Reporter*, which had some questionable quibbles, such as too thin a plot—in a *Road* picture?—ultimately confesses:

> Bing Crosby and Bob Hope hit the road again with some amiable tomfoolery, with Dorothy Lamour once more decorating the zany expedition ... [they] romp through the nonsense with all their customary good-natured and amusing nonchalance ... and clowning with happy results.[30]

The best line ever written by Hope's comedy contemporary friend and co-star of the *Road to Utopia* (1946), Robert Benchley, was, "Insanitary runs in my family. In fact, it practically gallops."[31] Arguably, a similar signature citation for Hope emerges from *Paleface* (1948, see Chapter 3) when he happily confesses, "Brave men run in my family." The ease with which he first begins to settle into this comic cowardice persona parallels the beginning of both World War II and the "Road" pictures. And what person in any conflict has not known fear? Hope's screen alter ego, especially in the "Road" movies, was especially happy to embrace and comically verbalize the apprehension of soldier and civilian alike. He also underlined it while entertaining World War II troops:

> I'll admit that I was a little scared when we started ... [this 1943 USO] trip. To tell the truth, I held up the first takeoff half a day before I even got into the plane. Every time they started the motors, my hands pulled my rip cord.[32]

While *Bali* was made well after World War II (1939–1945), the United States was then mired in another conflict, the Korean War (1950–1953). And the "Road" series has always had an odd subtexual connection with war—escapist fare to exotically named places just when Americans were regularly consulting maps for a world conflict, comically confessing it was okay to be fearful, and providing pretty girls and places often unavailable for servicemen.

Bali remains an extremely entertaining work today. But this picture, as well as the preceding five films in this series, received an added boost by the volatile historical backdrop of the period in which they were made, 1940–1953.

7

Tom Ewell/Marilyn Monroe
The Seven Year Itch (June 4, 1955)

> When it gets hot like this, you know what I do? I keep my undies in the ice box!—The Girl (Marilyn Monroe), from *The Seven Year Itch*

The Seven Year Itch is Bill Wilder's adaptation of George Axelrod's long-running (1952–1954) Broadway hit of the same name. Tom Ewell plays a middle-aged Manhattan publishing executive named Richard Sherman, though a better moniker would be the title character of James Thurber's *Walter Mitty*. The setting is a hot New York summer, and Ewell's wife Helen (Evelyn Keyes) and son Ricky (Butch Bernard) begin the story by boarding a train for the summer coolness of Maine. Indeed, it seems as if all the stay-at-home Manhattan moms and their children are heading out of the city for more refreshing places. Suddenly the island is awash with summer bachelors, a tradition a comic opening prologue suggests dates back to Manhattan's original Native Americans.

As with Mitty's motherly wife, Ewell has been given his assignments, which focus on neither smoking nor drinking. Naturally, the subject of other women is not on the list. And being a Mitty-type, he will attempt to follow *orders*. In fact, before he returns to their apartment, Ewell even eats at a health food restaurant. Also, like Thurbers's Mitty, the audience/reader is privy to the nonstop interior monologues of Ewell, including some publishing homework—*coincidentally* reading a manuscript entitled the *Repressed Urges of the Middle-Aged Man*.

As he relaxes at home and hopes the tome will not put him to sleep, a phantom image of his wife appears and affectionately suggests he has no sensuality. Well, this is a catalyst for a defensive Ewell's imagination to promptly go into sexual fantasy overdrive. First, the viewer sees him resisting the advances of his suddenly nymphomaniac secretary. Next, the wannabe lover is a nurse caring for a hospitalized Ewell. This daydream tops the first by giving the nurse appropriately comic dialogue: "Let's steal an ambulance and make a run for the border." But the piece de resistance is the final trance, in which his wife's best friend is on top of him, spoofing the then already iconic beach tryst in *From Here to Eternity* (1953). Fittingly, this follows comedy's rule of threes, in which each example becomes more preposterously funny.

Though Ewell's musings are exceptionally inventive, they are not out of touch with his publishing position—turning out paperback pulp "tough guy" nourish fiction, with luridly provocative covers, even if the subject is a more academically orientated book, like Dr. Brubaker's (Oscar Homolka) aforementioned *Repressed Urges*. Regardless, just after Ewell's sweet but nerdy character briefly gets up from his patio chair reading position, a large potted tomato plant comes crashing down from the balcony above. Initially upset over almost becoming a substance resembling guacamole, his anger turns to anti-heroic lust when the "bomber" from overhead turns out to be more of a bombshell—Monroe's "The Girl."

Subletting the apartment above him for the summer, Monroe is a former model in town to make a TV toothpaste commercial. Between her concern that Ewell thinks she is into splatter forensics, and he being instantly smitten by her beauty, the summer bachelor immediately invites Monroe down for those drinks his wife had made verboten. Again, like Mitty (though the initial ongoing daydreams of Thurber's character had nothing to do with sexuality), even his anti-heroic worm turns, too. Moreover, Mitty's monologue sounds like the cheap noir stories Ewell's company publishes:

> Mitty raised his hand briefly and the bickering attorneys were stilled. "With any known make of gun," he said evenly, "I could have killed … [him] at three hundred feet *with my left hand*." Pandemonium broke loose in the courtroom. A woman's scream above the bedlam and suddenly a lovely, dark-haired girl was in Walter Mitty's arms.[1]

Plus, given that Ewell's character is constantly in and out of fantasyland, the Thurber story from which this quote comes would have made a splendid backup title for Wilder's film, "The Secret Life of Walter Mitty [or Ewell's Richard Sherman]." Regardless, once Monroe arrives, Ewell's every daydream is related to "The Girl." And while he is nearly twice her age and as far from handsome as Elmer Fudd, Monroe does lust after his air conditioning.

With this typically thin personality comedian tale, which invariably bows to character first, chapter analysis can begin. However, a brief addendum is in order, since the focal point is on *two*, rather than one, comedians. Though Monroe and Ewell are not an official team, this dual focus technique was taken for three reasons. First, despite Monroe's iconic sex symbol status, her talents as a comedian are frequently neglected and/or misconstrued. And *The Seven Year Itch*'s huge critical and commercial success is where these misinterpretations began. Second, Ewell is now an even greater neglected comedian, as little known as Monroe is a cultural phenomenon. Again, *The Seven Year Itch* is their common ground, because if students of movies know Ewell at all, it is because of this picture.

Invariably superb in a limited filmography, see especially *Adam's Rib* (1948) and *The Girl Can't Help It* (1956), Ewell's first love was the stage. This came despite ecstatic reviews for *The Seven Year Itch*. For example, the *Hollywood Reporter*'s Jack Moffitt said in his review, "[The picture] may establish Tom Ewell as one of the top comedians of talkie history."[2] And the title for Wanda Hale's *New York Daily News* critique of the picture acclaimed, "Tom Ewell Is Great In 'Seven Year Itch.'"[3] Of course, Ewell first honed his talents in the theatre, including the actor's lengthy run in the original Broadway production of *The Seven Year Itch*, for which he won a Best Actor Tony. Indeed, he was even more acclaimed on stage for the role, with the *Hollywood Reporter*'s Lee Rogow describing the Broadway opening in *Ewellian* terms:

> Both the play and the performance by Tom Ewell are striking examples of what can be sustained by virtuously…. [This] virtuoso job of sustaining is Ewell's, who is off the stage for not one single second during the evening. He is as relaxed as wool socks, but his comedy technique is scalpel sharp.[4]

Besides favoring the stage, there are a litany of other reasons on why Ewell might have neglected movies, ranging from the changes made by movie adaptations, to sometimes being difficult with which to work—though hardly in a league with the often unstable Monroe, which is addressed later in the text (largely in Chapter 12).[5]

The third reason for scrutinizing the duo of Monroe and Ewell in *The Seven Year Itch*, besides it being on extraordinary film (ranking 51st on the American Film Institute's list of America's top 100 movies[6]), is how much Ewell's fantasyland daydreaming persona anticipates Woody Allen's screen alter ego. Though parallels can be drawn between *The Seven Year Itch* and any number of the younger comedian's pictures, it seems most apparent in *Play It Again, Sam* (1973, based on his 1969 play). This crucial link with America's greatest total auteur (Allen), *after* Charlie Chaplin, is examined later in the chapter.

With this foundation in place, it is time to more deeply probe Monroe's persona. Since her partner in hijinks (Ewell) has so fallen through the cracks of time, it was immediately necessary to establish his comedy credentials. In contrast, with Monroe being a quintessential star, it is equally hard to reconfigure her sex symbol image to that of gifted comedian. Indeed, as with Judy Holliday (see Chapter 1), the 1950s unfortunately referred to both as "dumb blondes." And just as with Holliday, there is nothing dumb about either actress' persona. Yet, as was begun in the Holliday chapter, there were distinctive differences between the two. The previous comparison ended with addressing Monroe as a child in a voluptuous woman's body. Wilder's film makes her childlike nature abundantly clear. Even the movie's signature scene, and one of cinema's most iconic images—Monroe standing over a subway grating as the wind from a passing train blows her dress up, exposing her legs—is the action of a child. She and Ewell have just exited a movie screening at Manhattan's Trans-Lux Theatre. As they hear a subway train approaching, she excitedly steps on the grating uttering, "Ooo, do you feel the breeze from the subway?" Monroe so enjoys the totally unselfconscious act, that she does the dress billowing experience again. Moreover, it is childhood squared, because the breeze would not be cooling, since subway vents let out *hot air*, despite a legion of books through the years talking about a cool breeze. Mark it down to an audience's "suspension of disbelief" at the movies. New York in the winter is more evidence of the subway gratings releasing hot updrafts—frequently homeless people camp over them for warmth.

Regardless, Monroe's dress spiraling scene is the act of a youngster, with no thought of any sexually suggestive ramifications. But naturally this is precisely how the image was used, including a 25-foot Times Square billboard over Loews State Theatre, the site of the film's later premiere. Wilder shot on location late at night allegedly to avoid large crowds, despite the press being informed for PR purposes. For added irony, there was little serious thought that any usable footage would find its way to the finished film. Still, Wilder got what he wanted; thousands turned out, and besides the publicity bonanza, there was the then period plus of saying it was partially shot on location. MGM's 1949 production of *On the Town* had scored just such added kudos for shooting background footage in New York—at the insistence of its co-director and star, Gene Kelly. Be that as it may, to no one in Hollywood's surprise, the final subway sequence was filmed back on the Twentieth Century–Fox lot. This ultimate scene would be both more modest than what occurred in New York, and devoid of the controversy that will be addressed later in the text.

Still, Monroe's giggling joy at her swirling skirt is that of an innocent, impulsive child. Of course, every time I think I am getting too cynical about this ongoing misleading depiction of the actress as merely a sex symbol, I see that I am not even keeping pace. The often visceral, yet invariably entertaining, critic David Thomson described the conundrum best when he described Monroe as "half child but not the half that shows … she barely comprehends the world about her."[7] Truman Capote put this little girl in perspective another way when he described his disappointment with Paramount's 1961 casting of Audrey Hepburn as the lead in the studio's adaptation of his novella *Breakfast at Tiffany's*: "Marilyn Monroe was my first choice to play her. I thought she would be perfect for the part. [The character] Holly [Golightly] had to have something touching about her—unfinished. Marilyn had that."[8] Capote was right. The actress still had that little girl component to her persona, but in the post–*Some Like It Hot* period (1959), Marilyn now had a quality which has often been applied to Wilder characters—"a hard-boiled innocence."

Monroe as a child is constantly peppered throughout *The Seven Year Itch* in both image and action. Indeed, her character does not even have a name. She is simply referenced as "The Girl." And when Ewell invites her downstairs for a drink that first night, with much more than just a drink in mind, her response is on the order of a trusting kid being enticed by a stranger bearing candy, even though Ewell's figure is pure milquetoast. The only thing

The Walter Mitty in Tom Ewell suddenly has him thinking he is a great lover, with Marilyn Monroe in *The Seven Year Itch*.

that would remotely qualify as lust for Monroe is that Ewell has air conditioning and she does not. And as a child of the '50s, the rarity of air conditioning could be a major factor in making new summer friends.

If one is still struggling with Monroe as a child when the wannabe Cary Grant Ewell offers to make her a martini, she immediately asks if she can put sugar in it, like so much Kool-Aid. And she soon quietly confesses that she always adds sugar to strong drinks. Plus, later in the movie when they drink champagne, Monroe promptly tells him it is great for dipping potato chips in, too. Ewell eventually attempts to entertain her by playing the piano but the best he can do is "Chopsticks"—just how one might entertain a youngster. What is more, it works. Monroe's character knows the simple number and joins him on the piano bench, getting progressively more involved in the tune. She happily bangs the keys harder, having the most progressfully joyous of times—like a two-year-old who is repeatedly amused by the most repetitive of actions. I am reminded of my daughters as children tirelessly laughing when my cranking of a jack-in-the-box forever produced the same clown as if it were new and different each time.

At this point the Mitty-like Ewell attempts the most awkward of passes at Monroe and both of them take a tumble from the piano bench. He is very embarrassed and profusely apologizes, convincingly confessing that nothing like this has ever happened to him before. In contrast, Monroe is completely nonplussed, telling Ewell it happens to her all the time, like it was just another pile-up at the bottom of the playground slide. Along those same lines, in Norman Mailer's non-fiction/fiction book *Marilyn*, he links her forgetfully forgiving nature to a sympathetic tendency to anyone or anything that needs help and/or love—something especially true in children:

> When she will fall off the piano bench ... and as quickly says to Tom Ewell that he must not feel bad because men always make passes at her ... and [she is] altogether nurturing to the thin quivering banjo-string repressions of thin [anti-heroic] Tom Ewell, she is all that.[9]

To expand further on Mailer's perspective, one only has to examine the discussion Monroe and Ewell were having just before the movie's signature subway breeze sequence. The couple had just seen *The Creature from the Black Lagoon* (1954), a popular 3-D horror film during the production of *The Seven Year Itch*. (It was essentially a well-made B picture with the special effects gimmick of 3-D.) Regardless, the story involves a potential missing link man-like aquatic figure, "Gill-Man," capable of walking upright on land. A small company of scientists had set out on an expedition to the Amazon after a previous search had discovered a fossilized hand-like claw which was presumed to be an unknown creature from the distant past. But when it is discovered that this amphibious humanoid is far from extinct and it has killed the members of the original base camp who had stayed behind, it becomes more of a hunting party. Of course, more people are killed in the attempt. Yet, the only female member of the party (Julie Adams) has captured the attention/adoration of Gill-Man, resulting in a conclusion not unlike *King Kong* (1933), in which it was really "beauty that killed the beast." What follows is the Ewell/Monroe post-movie discussion:

> MONROE: Didn't you just love the picture? I did. I just felt so sorry for the creature at the end [when he was killed].
> EWELL: Sorry for the creature? What did you want him [to] do, marry the girl?
> MONROE: He was sort of scary looking. But he wasn't really all bad. I just think he craved affection. You know, a sense of being loved, and needed.
> EWELL: That's a very interesting point of view.

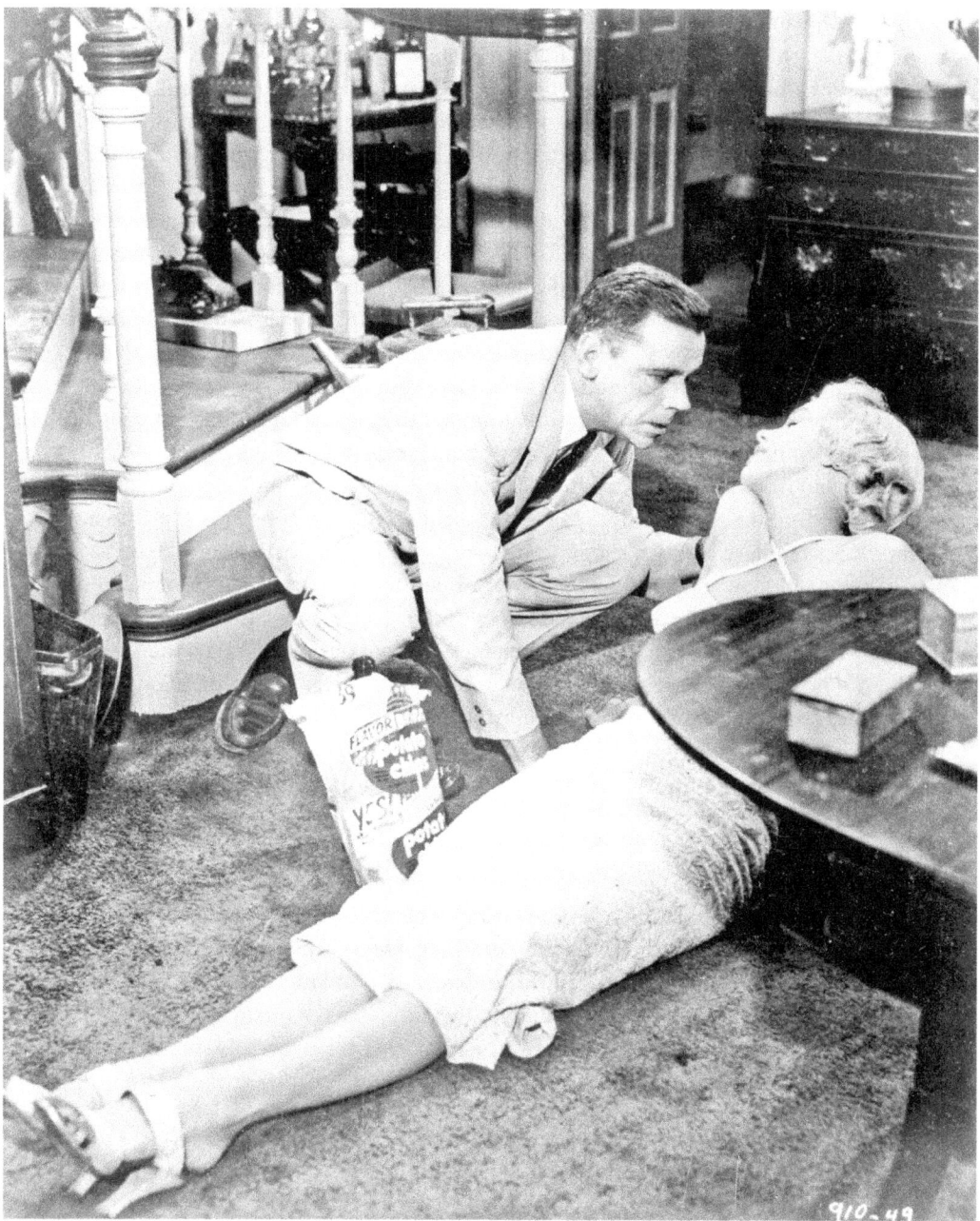

A child-like Marilyn Monroe thinks no more of Tom Ewell's "pass" than that of a male game in *The Seven Year Itch*.

With regard to Monroe, one cannot also help thinking about Mary Shelley's *Frankenstein* (1818), that rare literary classic which is also a staple of popular culture, and James Whale's still definitive 1931 film adaptation of the novel. For example, when the creature's unnerving appearance has scared away all adults it comes across the little girl playing beside a lake. Despite his disturbing countenance and the ability to make only guttural sounds (unlike the novel's articulate figure), the child is unflappable in her joy to have a new playmate. Frankenstein is equally happy to be accepted as normal when the child invites him to play. Her game involves throwing flower petals into the lake and watching them drift away. Sadly, when the blooms are no more, neither is the girl. His full-grown innocence has made him think the next logical step in the amusement is to throw her into the water, where she drowns.

As already suggested, this is the movie persona of Monroe in a nutshell. She still has the innocence of a child, with none of society's learned ills. All she knows is trust and the minute-to-minute bliss of existence. Of course, this has the potential danger of vulnerability. But for now she is neither concerned with judging or being judged. This is reminiscent of a story I heard years ago by some stand-up comedian, with an entertainingly angry Lewis Black perspective, made incredulous by a road trip comment from his young daughter. For several minutes he notes the child has maintained the biggest smile while staring out the window. When he asks what she is thinking about, she simply replies, "Candy." That is the essence of Monroe's "The Girl" character playing "Chopsticks" on the piano, or enjoying champagne-dipping potato chips. Maybe Monroe's little girl topper is that she actually believes the commercial jingle she practices, sans any Tashlin satire. And the fact Monroe almost seems to glow is a product of that unimpeachable youth. Indeed, one could liken it to the little blonde girl in Tom Ford's *A Single Man* (2009, from Christopher Isherwood's novel). While Colin Firth's suicidal title character navigates his last day, the screen is all but black and white, except when he encounters someone special. For example, a short grey sequence in the film suddenly has a brief splash of blue and blonde emanating from the face and dress of a neighbor's child stopping to talk. Then that portion of the screen rewards both Firth and the viewer with all the joyful pulsating color of a partially hand-tinted film frame by pioneering George Méliés, back when nickelodeons were young and innocent, too.

This sense of Monroe's persona constitutes three pivotal developments in the picture. The first is merely establishing her little girl alter ego. The second is her aforementioned childhood insight that the title character in *The Creature from the Black Lagoon* merely "craved affection ... a sense of being loved, and needed." And most importantly, she applies that same kindergarten "play nice" wisdom to Ewell's character and gives him his male dignity back. That is, he has confessed to Monroe that his wife essentially mocks him for her having *no* reason to be jealous that another woman would ever be attracted to him:

EWELL: Let's face it. No pretty girl in her right mind wants me. She wants Gregory Peck.
MONROE: Is that so?
EWELL: Well, isn't it?
MONROE: How do you know what a pretty girl wants?
EWELL: Well, I don't really know. But I imagine—
MONROE: You and your imagination. You think a girl goes to a party with some guy, a great big lug with a fancy striped vest strutting around like a tiger giving you that "I'm so handsome you can't resist me" look. And from this she's supposed to fall flat on her head. Well, she doesn't fall flat on her face. But there's another guy in the room—way over in the corner. Maybe he's kind of nervous and shy, perspiring a little. First you look past him. But then you sort of sense he's gentle and kind and worried and you know he'll be tender with you and sweet. That's what's really exciting. If I were your wife I'd be very very jealous. [She kisses him.] I think you're just elegant.
EWELL: Thank you [the door bell rings].

MONROE: Aren't you going to answer it?
EWELL: [Still stunned by Monroe's kind words and the kiss he can only manage.] The what?
MONROE: The doorbell. Go ahead. I'll put the cinnamon on the toast.

The man at the door is the handsome (6'4") blonde, blue-eyed family friend and romance novelist Tom MacKenzie (Sonny Tufts), who Ewell had fantasized had seduced his wife at the Maine summer camp where the writer was also staying. However, Tufts has merely stopped by to get the kayak paddle Ewell's son failed to take to the resort. Now a tough, reborn Ewell, thanks to Monroe's pep talk, is no longer passive. Indeed, he even recycles parts of Monroe's discourse, such as calling Tufts a "big lug" in a "striped vest" (which the novelist is actually wearing), as he dresses down the man. Moreover, he then decks Tufts and heads off to Maine *with* the paddle himself. Ewell, in Monroe's eyes, had been a variation on the title character from *The Creature from the Black Lagoon*, someone who simply "craved affection ... [and] a sense of being loved, and needed." Ewell's diploma from anti-hero land had actually come moments before, when Monroe told him:

> I have a message for your wife (and then kisses him). Don't wipe it off [the lipstick]. If she thinks it's cranberry juice [once before when Ewell had lipstick on his collar, his wife told him he had so little sex appeal it must be cranberry juice], tell her she's got cherry pits in her head.

Thus, one now even has a biblical validation on Monroe as being childlike, Jesus said, "Out of the mouth of babes [a nice unintended pun] and sucklings you have ordained praise."[10]

Of course, the "God" of any film is the director. And even *Seven Year Itch*'s Billy Wilder seems to have seen Monroe in this picture as childlike, at least as described by Tom Wood's biography of the director. Plus, it is a little girl image on and off the screen. After establishing early that Wilder, like many good directors, attempted to play upon actual characteristics of the actors, Wood chronicles the sequence in which Monroe has managed to open the boarded up stairway and slip into Ewell's apartment:

> "Did I do all right?" she asked [Wilder] in the manner of a child who wants to be told that she had pleased. "You were wonderful," Billy replied [like an affectionate parent], "I never saw anyone sneak downstairs so prettily...." [Later he told the biographer,] "She was scared and unsure of herself [during the shoot, especially because of her abusively disintegrating marriage], so much so I found myself wishing that I were a psychoanalyst and she was my patient."[11]

Though a strained Wilder perspective is more front and center on Monroe and *Some Like It Hot* (1959, see the final chapter), the actress was happy with Wilder for proving she could act. When a 1955 columnist praised her along those lines, she observed complete with a youngster's joke:

> It's due to Billy Wilder. He's a wonderful director. I want him to direct me again. But he's doing the Lindbergh story next. [What eventually became 1957's *The Spirit of St. Louis*, with Jimmy Stewart.] And he won't let me play Lindbergh.[12]

As a postscript to Wilder's more sensitive treatment of Monroe's recognized emergence as an actress, maybe there was a particle of guilt involved. She gave an exceptional performance *despite* an ugly Joe DiMaggio domestic situation to which Wilder had contributed— à la the New York subway grating shoot. Even if it had not been done for PR purposes, Wilder let it get out of hand, with an assist from the controversial newspaper and radio news/gossip columnist Walter Winchell (1897–1972). A Joe DiMaggio biographer describes how the underground wind machine, doubling as passing subway trains sent:

> Marilyn's skirt [up] around her ears. Each time it blew, the crowd [behind police barricades and estimated to be 2,000–3,000 in number] would yell, "Higher!" "More!" Her legs were bare from her high heels to her thick white panties. Photographers were stretched out on the pavement, with their lenses pointed up at his wife's crotch, the glare of their flash-bulbs clearly outlining the shadow of her pubic hair.... The director, Billy Wilder, would recall "the look of death" on [her husband Joe] DiMaggio's face [as the Yankee legend looked on].[13]

Monroe biographer J. Randy Taraborrelli described the shoot as even more provocative:

> Even though Marilyn wore *two* pairs of panties ... under the [extra bright]klieg lights there was still more visible than what Joe would have been comfortable with. [Monroe friend and later biographer] James Haspiel was present for the filming, and he later recalled, "I must confess I had no trouble seeing through Marilyn's sheer panties. I could fully appreciate Joe's anger.... [Yet] In defense of Monroe [as child-like], I am reasonably convinced that in her dressing room she did not see what the powerful klieg lights [put on display]."[14]

Donald Spoto's Monroe biography quotes the man responsible for the subway grating scene idea, Sam Shaw, who was at the New York shoot:

> The location work on Lexington Avenue was of course for the sake of publicity. Everyone knew it would have to be photographed again back in the studio. Wilder ... confirmed this plan in advance, aware that the close-ups would have to be reworked later simply because there was too much ambient noise to record dialogue.[15]

What no one knew going in, however, was the many takes Wilder would shoot, the klieg light factor, and that Winchell was behind a reluctant DiMaggio attending the shoot to get a provocative story. Both the PR happy Wilder won, as did the gossip newsman Winchell, since following the shoot an abusive fight later broke out between Monroe and DiMaggio at their hotel. It was the catalyst for the end of a marriage of less than one year, though oddly enough, they would remain friends until Monroe's 1962 death, as well as him even accompanying the actress to the premiere of *The Seven Year Itch*.

The third reason for closely dissecting the picture is to reveal how closely this movie, à la Ewell's constant strolling back and forth through reality and fantasy represents a template for the basic métier of Woody Allen's later career—film's greatest total comedy auteur for the last half of the twentieth century and counting. Surprisingly, other than a brief aside in Maurice Yacowar's pioneering study of Allen, little has been done to flesh out this significant influence.[16]

The Seven Year Itch and Ewell's playing of its central born-again anti-heroic mold for later Allen alter egos is most enlighteningly showcased, as noted earlier, when compared to *Play It Again, Sam*. First, going well beyond Thurber's short story, and Mitty's always successful cerebral adventures, only intermittently interrupted by a henpecking wife; neither Ewell nor Allen are capable of so basic an escapist joy. Like Chaplin's *Idle Class* (1921) Tramp, who suffers under the same condition, *who* cannot control the content of one's *own* fantasies but the ultimate anti-hero. For example, as Allen's title suggests, his alter ego is hung up on *Casablanca* (1942) as he contemplates a failed marriage. And presto, Allen soon has Bogart (Jerry Lacy) as a sort of fairy godfather of romance. Just when this advice is starting to pay off, Allen's ex-wife (Susan Anspach) enters his imagination and guns down Bogie. Along similar lines, when Ewell finds himself in an innocent but promising dalliance with Monroe, his wife enters his imagination and guns him down. The latter example is especially amusing, since it reminds one of a comic in-the-flesh Judy Holliday shooting haphazardly at Ewell's hilariously disloyal husband in *Adam's Rib* (1950, see Chapter 1).

Second, both Allen and Ewell's characters in these two films are New Yorkers whose jobs are involved with entertainment diversions keying upon film noir and/or tough guy fiction. Allen writes for a movie magazine, and his apartment is basically a shrine to Bogart—the poster figure for film noir, and the movie figure most synonymous with noir writers like Dashiel Hammett and Raymond Chandler. Is it any wonder he becomes Allen's ephemeral mentor? In Ewell's case, he is the premier editor for a publisher which specializes in this sort of literature, even to the extent of disguising material not of the genre with provocatively sexy covers to mask the content.

Third, writing-related lives lead to sedimentary existences which cause relationships problems. Allen's *Sam* partner divorces him "because you're one of life's great watchers. I'm a doer. I want to participate." Ewell's wife is still with him but berates his lack of sex appeal. Moreover, the situation is heightened by two other factors. One, neither of these clowns is very attractive. Secondly, both work in an area of the entertainment industry ripe with tough guy models which might just as well be Marvel Comic superheroes in their distance from anything approaching macho reality.

Fourth, given this background, neither man knows how to successfully interact with women, especially since their careers are so tied up with a film genre base in which relationship skills for males do not even seem necessary. For instance, sexy women just seem to fall all over these private eye types. When Bogart plays Philip Marlowe in *The Big Sleep* (1946), everyone seems out to bed him, including the casino cigarette girl (Shelby Payne), the hat check girl (Lorraine Miller), later Oscar-winning Dorothy Malone's bookstore clerk, Joy Barlowe's cabbie, the casino waitresses (Tanis Chandler and Deannie Best), and the subject of his investigation, Lauren Bacall, as well as her nymphomaniac sister, Martha Vickers. What is a poor anti-hero like Ewell or Allen to do?

Fifth, in *The Seven Year Itch* and *Sam*, both Ewell and Allen are nice guys who suddenly find themselves in similar single situations. Ewell's wife has made him a summer bachelor, while Allen's spouse has left him permanently. Moreover, sexual temptation has, so to speak, literally been dropped into their laps. For Ewell, Monroe has rented the apartment upstairs, and she is always about, egged on by that air conditioning. With Allen, his best friends are the married couple Dick (Tony Roberts) and Linda (Diane Keaton). Except, Roberts is constantly away on business, and lonely Allen and equally lonely Keaton begin hanging out together. Keaton, like Monroe, is a beautiful girl/woman who is both vulnerable and in need of attention.

Sixth, naturally this leads to temptations, especially with Ewell, because as the title implies, happiness in a marriage is said to decline after seven years. However, in both films the men feel initial guilt about this impulse. For Ewell, it is all about loyalty to his wife, while Allen does not want to cheat on his best friend. (In *Sam* a one-night stand does occur, while the 1955 censorship code kept this from happening in *The Seven Year Itch*, though there is a tryst in the play). However, both films end with each highlighted marriage more secure than before. As a paramount postscript to the guilt factor in each man, even Allen's dialogue is often very close to that of Ewell's. For instance, the first time Ewell invites Monroe down for drinks, he immediately regrets it and impatiently says to himself, "It's late. This is ridiculous. She could have been down here already and had her lousy drink." In a comparable situation for Allen, he observes, "Where the hell is she anyhow? By now she could have had her steak and been out of here."

Seventh, each movie spotlights a film which is of pivotal importance to the picture. With Allen's title, *Play It Again, Sam*, the answer is obvious—*Casablanca*. And *Sam* actually uses real footage from the original, as well as recycling camera set-ups and dialogue. *The Creature from the Black Lagoon* is of equal but less obvious importance to *The Seven Year Itch*. While Allen is made more confident by his immersion in Bogie-land, "the creature" works on multiple levels in the other film. First, it poignantly best defines Monroe's little girl persona by having her both fathom and relate to the misunderstood creature—the precise feeling all children go through at some point. Moreover, as *Hollywood in the Fifties* historian Gordon Gow suggests, between her bubbly humor and an implied connection between Ewell and the creature, she manages to create "a certain pathos as the girl who stimulates [makes more confident] a grass widower [someone whose spouse is gone for a prolonged time] suffering from *The Seven Year Itch*."[17]

There are countless other parallels between Ewell's and Allen's alter egos (both in *Sam* and the rest of the younger comedian's oeuvre), from the ongoing fine lines between reality and reverie (increasingly tied to sex and guilt), to periodic health worries and *insecurity* in general. This Ewell/*The Several Year Itch* obvious building block to Allen's later monumental success *cannot* be overstated enough. And what makes it even more interesting is that while Allen took his persona to even more darkly comic existential levels, so did Ewell.[18] For example, in the *New York Times*' 1971 revival review of Samuel Beckett's groundbreaking absurdist play *Waiting for Godot* (1953), about two vaudevillian-like figures (Vladimir and Estragon) ostensibly waiting for a God that never comes, critic Mel Gussow says:

> Ewell's Vladimir is unquestionably the greatest performance of his career.... He has grown from a Broadway comedy star into a classic clown tramp ... who is aware of the tragic dimensions of his character ... but he makes him funnier than he has ever seemed.[19]

Five years before Allen's *Godot* like *Love and Death* (1975), Ewell told *New York Daily News* critic Robert Wahls:

> Maybe I'm also waiting for "Godot." What "Godot" means to me ... [is] how we fill the hours of life while we wait. Some of us wait for fame, some for death, some for God. And we wait to try to occupy ourselves ..."Waiting for Godot" is my "Hamlet." Hamlet "has his [suicidal] soliloquy and as Vladimir I have mine."[20]

Again, one is reminded of Woody Allen, particularly his 2009 film *Whatever Works*, which to paraphrase the comedian, "We're just killing time here, so focus on whatever pleases you, as long as it doesn't hurt other people, do whatever works."

Ironically, despite all its acclaim, *The Seven Year Itch* is an underappreciated movie. Plus, the chapter has demonstrated this "beauty and the beast" movie is multi-faceted. Though it finally showed that Monroe could act, her beauty, as is often the case, continued to distract from her talent for many period critics. And in Ewell's face, like Joe E. Brown's goofy looking puss, the younger comic knew its bonus laughter factor.[21] Of course, though he later admitted to the inherent wisdom in Katharine Hepburn considering his appearance being a plus in serious roles, too, the comedian had to still grimace by her observation after hearing he was being considered for the part of novelist Sinclair Lewis! "Oh, I knew Lewis. Without a doubt, he was the ugliest man I've ever seen. You'd be perfect for the part."[22] Though more often referred to as the comedian with the "homely face and cracked voice," one can safely say Monroe never used either description.[23] This is based on an interview in which Ewell confessed to eating lunch with Monroe every day on *The Seven Year*

Itch. Sometimes she wanted to talk and other times not, but "I found her delightful."[24] (Sadly, given the after effects of the subway grating scene, her lunches were often taken up with studying an Italian American cookbook for DiMaggio.)

So how did period critiques treat *The Seven Year Itch*? The chapter opening sample rave reviews proved to be the norm. *Variety* critic McCarthy Lands said:

> It is a funny picture and a money picture: The title and property are pre-sold values [an assist against TV]: the exploitation possibilities are above average and word-of-mouth comment is bound to be strong; the situation fits Marilyn Monroe tighter than her skirt and the picture undoubtedly restores Tom Ewell to the screen on a bigger and better basis.[25]

Dick William's *Los Angeles Mirror-News* review boldly predicted, "SUMMER'S FIRST BIG MOVIE COMEDY SMASH will be 'The Seven Year Itch.' Marilyn Monroe and Tom Ewell tickle the funny bone in an unrestrained romp."[26] The *Hollywood Reporter* called it "maybe one of the great movie comedies of all time" and stated Ewell is the "first native movie actor who has come within hailing distance of being an American Jacques Tati [then contemporary legendary French comedian/filmmaker]."[27] Another *Hollywood Reporter* piece placed the reader in the theatre:

> A tremendous reception was accorded the picture by the capacity crowd. Previewers broke out with applause several times during the showing, with an ovation at the conclusion. [The] audience rocked with laughter at [the] dialogue, [the] brilliant comic wizardry of Tom Ewell and [the] shining performance of Monroe.[28]

Because of changes to the play by Hollywood censors, despite the distraction of the lovely Monroe, the *New York Herald Tribune* reviewer credited that "only a superb performance by Ewell draws the moviegoer ... back to the true value of the film."[29] The title of the *New York Journal-American* misses Monroe's acting arrival but demonstrates its love for the picture: "Monroe Is Glamorous and Ewell Amusing."[30] In marked contrast, the *New York Telegram and Sun* fully appreciated Monroe's contributions, but again it also notes:

> The real master of mirth is Tom Ewell who brings all the comic wiles that he sharpened night after night in the play. His gift of laughter is sly, every expression and gesture giving a new subtlety to the comic lines and shenanigans of the scenarists.[31]

In fact, this publication goes so far as to credit Wilder's film (a position also shared by the *New York Daily News*) as having a "scenario that expands and improves the original material. They have aroused some of the loudest and most continuous laughter of the year."[32] With all the film's critical praise, this was a position in which few other reviews wavered—high praise, indeed. One's only wish would have been, as scrutinized earlier, the critical kudos would have better interlocked with what Monroe biographer Carl Rollyson also recently "seconded": "She seems infinitely innocent [childlike] and willing to follow every turn of Sherman's [Ewell's] erratic stop-and-go romancing."[33]

With this being said, the following chapter centers on a comedian who will both take home an Oscar for his performance, and later (see Chapter 12) team up with Monroe and a major personality comedian of the Great Depression.

8

Jack Lemmon
Mister Roberts (July 15, 1955)

> Captain [James Cagney], it is I, Ensign Pulver [Jack Lemmon],
> and I just threw your stinkin' palm tree overboard! Now what's all
> this crud about no movie tonight?—*Mister Roberts*' last line

Jack Lemmon's act of defiance against the martinet captain (James Cagney) of a United States Navy cargo ship stationed somewhere in the "backwater" of the World War II Pacific demonstrates that the Ensign has finally followed through with a moxie inspired by his hero—title character Henry Fonda. With fitting anti-heroic humor, the ship is named the U.S.S. *Reluctant*. Though a comedy, Cagney's character is of the same ilk as *Mutiny on the Bounty*'s Captain Bligh. A comic truce between commander and crew is only maintained by Mr. Roberts, who acts as the beloved executive officer/cargo chief of the *Reluctant*. Yet, unlike the name of this "bucket," he is anxious to get transferred to a front line battleship by writing a legion of letters. Yet, he is constantly stymied by a controlling captain who benefits from Roberts' efficiency, the reason for which the original palm tree had been bestowed. Fonda's character only gets his wish for fighting duty when the crew risks court martial by submitting forged paperwork. They also gift him with a gaudy General George Patton-sized "Palm Tree Medal," with the salutation, "[The] Oder of the Palm ... to Roberts for action against the enemy [their captain]." He then leaves by telling Lemmon's character, now the new cargo chief, "I'm counting on you [to not only do your job but be an advocate for the crew against Cagney's captain]." Yet, to put this in perspective, one needs to go back to a conversation at the film's beginning:

> LEMMON: What do you really think of me [after his roommates, William Powell's Doc and Fonda go out of their way to comically create some homemade Scotch for one of the Ensign's romantic misadventures]?
>
> FONDA: Frank [Lemmon], I like you. There is no getting around the fact you're a real likeable guy but—
>
> LEMMON: But what?
>
> FONDA: I also think you're the most hopeless, lazy, disorganized, and in general the most lecherous person I've ever known in my life.
>
> LEMMON: I am not—
>
> FONDA: You are not what?

LEMMON: [Comically, he can only defend himself on the most innocuous of the charges] I'm not disorganized.

FONDA: Have you ever in your life finished one thing you've started out to do? You sleep 16 hours a day [and specialize in avoiding the captain—who later will fail to even recognize the Ensign as one of his sailors].

Now flash forward to the film's near conclusion. It has been over a month since Fonda has been transferred to a battleship in the fierce fighting around Japan's control of Okinawa Island. One senses Lemmon's character is popular and holding his own as the cargo chief. But since even the captain has taken a shine to him, it hardly suggests he is fully looking out for the sailor's rights and/or acting as a buffer between the cantankerous captain and crew, à la Mr. Roberts. Then one day at mail call the thrusts of both Lemmon's character and the film itself make a seismic change from the close of Tom Heggen's original 1946 best-selling novel and his 1948 Tony award–winning play, adapted with producer/director Josh Logan. (The popular Broadway production, 1948–1951, would also star Fonda in the Tony-winning title role.)

Lemmon receives four letters, three of which amusingly reinforce what viewers have grown to relish about his character. The first is from his mother, and, as is his nature, he makes an affectionate joke about it, "All she ever says is stay away from [enemy] Japan."

The gift of creating homemade scotch, with (from left) William Powell, Henry Fonda, and Jack Lemmon in *Mr. Roberts*.

The second has the most sweet-smelling aroma. Thus, the Ensign uses it to embellish his questionable Casanova claims by stating he will read it later, as if it contains some sort of Lady Chatterley naughtiness best savored alone in his bunk. The third letter, which has taken a long time to find him, is from Mr. Roberts. It initially documents with humor that Lemmon's character has always been the same, based upon Fonda meeting one of the Ensign's college friends:

> "[He] 'says that you and he used to load up your car with liquor in Omaha [where Fonda first started acting] and then sell it at an indecent profit to the frat[ernity] boys in Iowa City.'" [At this point Lemmon interjects,] "And we did, too." Then, on a more serious note, he, [Roberts, adds an aside for Doc] I've caught up with that task force that passed me by [one late night on the *Reluctant* he was mesmerized by a rushing armada close by] and I'm glad to be here [on one of its battleships.] I had to be here, I guess. But I'm thinking now of you, Doc, and you, Frank, [Lemmon] and everyone else on that bucket [the cargo ship] and all the other guys that sailed from tedium to apathy and back again, with an occasional side trip to monotony … but I've discovered, Doc, that the unseen enemy of this war is the boredom that eventually becomes a sort of faith and therefore a sort of suicide. And I know now that the ones that refuse to surrender to it are the strongest of all. Right now I'm looking at something [his palm tree medal]. I'd rather have it then the Congressional Medal of Honor. It tells me what I'll always be proudest of, that at a time in the world when courage counted most. I lived among 62 brave [shipmate] men. So, Doc, and especially you, Frank, don't let those guys down.

His final letter comes from the Ensign's old college buddy that Mr. Roberts had referenced in his letter—the partner in those profitable booze trips to Iowa City. As Lemmon reads it his face suddenly and masterfully goes through an understated workshop in anguish, from shock and denial, to pain and anger—all as real as a cloud abruptly passing a shadow over the sun; Mr. Roberts was dead. And ironically, his death had not even occurred at a battle station. A kamikaze plane had hit his ship and the resulting destruction killed him innocuously below deck while he drank coffee in the mess hall. (Historically, the peek in kamikaze attacks occurred at the Battle of Okinawa, in which, as noted earlier, Mr. Rogers' ship was headed.)

Yet, Mr. Rogers' paradoxical death, after he had tried so hard to see military action, plays out much differently in several ways from the darker novel to the film. First, while the quoted passage from Mr. Roberts' letter does not appear in the book—only some general small talk about said letter—the following conversation between his closest friends from the *Reluctant* spell it out more disturbingly:

> Pulver [Lemmon's character] spoke with sudden anguish: "Isn't that rough, Doc? You know how he [Mr. Roberts] batted his head to get off of here [the *Reluctant*]? You know how he wanted to get in the war? And then, as soon as he gets out there, he gets killed." His voice was almost pleading. The Doc nodded and chewed his lip. "That's funny," he said thoughtfully. "Funny?" The Doc looked up. "I don't mean funny, Frank," he said softly. He paused for a moment. "I mean that I think that's what he wanted."[1]

Consequently, this ever so mournful theatre of the absurd moment in the novel is considerably softened in the film. Yes, the movie chronicles yet another preposterous existential joke on us. But the screen Mr. Roberts believes he and the sailors on the "bucket" did accomplish something—they were an integral part in the conflict, and Fonda's character cherishes his goofy palm tree medal. In contrast, the novel's spin on what occurs has more of a *Macbeth* ring to it, life's player "struts and frets his hour upon the stage … it is a tale … full of sound and fury, signifying nothing."[2] Of course, this perspective is further enhanced by the fact that Heggen's novel is both *very* autobiographical, and that he himself committed suicide in 1949, a mere three years after its publication.

A second novel to film difference keys upon how the story's proverbial money scene is taken from the older, more worldly wise, and darkly insightful Doc and given completely to Lemmon's character. Of courage, Mr. Roberts now lives on in the Ensign's act of rebellion, and Cagney's increasingly engaging curmudgeon of a captain (as the number of his meltdowns continue), now has a new but ever so familiar foe. But where is the numb shattering waste of Mr. Roberts' life? As the *Hollywood Reporter*'s critic casually confesses, "[In this] film fare some of the [original] poignancy is underplayed."[3]

Third, changing the tone of the conclusion is made possible by the speed with which Lemmon is allowed to morph into his comic act of insurrection. Unlike the novel, which lingers on the art house-like senselessness of Robert's death—often a painful challenge for mainstream audiences to ponder, the film moves quickly to the slapstick splashdown of yet another symbolic potted palm tree. Needless to say, however, this change in tone to further accent the humor is what makes it a personality comedy, and a breakout movie for Lemmon, who won a Best Supporting Actor Oscar for a character which the *New York Times* described as having "the explosive ebullience of a kid with a live frog in his britches."[4]

Fourth, Lemmon's lively Ensign was not just used to buoy up the ending. When Warners assembled a rough cut, the studio felt the picture played more slowly and seriously, à la the novel and play, then the comic spirit also inherent in the material. Since Lemmon's

The prized palm tree of James Cagney's sour captain in *Mr. Roberts*.

character was essentially behind propelling the majority proportion of both the picture's comedy and story velocity, the actor was summoned to the studio to assist in operation fix it. And Warners had an added challenge here. Both the picture's original director (John Ford), and his replacement (Mervyn LeRoy, a situation to be addressed shortly), tended to "shoot in the camera." That is, the fewer takes of any one sequence they shot made it next to impossible for a studio to drastically re-edit a picture, since there was little coverage footage from which to draw. (When a director did not have the luxury of controlling his own "final cut," minimal extra film stock was the next best defense.) Well, "necessity is the mother of invention" did not become a cliché by accident. Lemmon biographer Will Holtzman noted Warners' idea was to post-synchronize:

> Some harmless, a cappella tune over the long and medium [Ensign] Pulver shots. Jack [Lemmon, also a gifted musician] selected a thirties ditty, "If I Could Be with You," and muttered, hummed, and warbled a handful of renditions which were then superimposed on the sound track. As it worked out, the melody not only picked up the pace by several beats but helped peg Lemmon as the film's [comic] surprise favorite.[5]

Given that it was Warner Bros., one cannot help thinking their gifted animation department had a hand in the idea, since the Ensign's theme song of sorts (he is even singing it when first introduced) is reminiscent of an ever present cocky, casual Bugs Bunny. This is especially true of the sequences in which Lemmon's various renditions of "If I Could Be with You" is heard before viewers even see him, not to mention when one just hears the rendering without a visual. At those times it is like the cartoonish Ensign is everywhere. Plus, Lemmon could not have picked a more appropriate tune, since as *New York Herald Tribune* critic William K. Zinsser described the sailor, "[he's] like the young boy who stirs from his bunk only if he thinks he can lure a girl into it."[6] Ensign and his little ditty really steal the show, with Zinsser's critique title even highlighting the song "A Happy Surprise in Mr. Roberts."

If one still cannot grasp the comic power of Lemmon's ongoing sexual chirping, keep in mind that some critics affectionately referenced him as a "lecherous" joy. Then think of cinema's favorite letch, Groucho Marx, forever getting a laugh as a young *Animal Crackers* (1930) comic every time he warbled what became his theme song, "Hooray for Captain Spaulding." Moreover, further underline the repetitious humor of "If I Could Be with You" for two additional reasons. First, the tune tops a number of other Lemmon gems. For example, his character explaining his alleged radar for immediately knowing some nurses had recently arrived on a nearby island:

> [It] just came to me all of a sudden. I was lying in my bunk [essentially his office] this morning thinking [another laugh line] and there wasn't a breath of air and all of a sudden a funny thing happened. A little breeze came up and I took a deep breath and I said, "[Ensign] Pulver, my boy, there's women on that island."

Other comic treasures include *first* meeting the Captain after having served on the *Reluctant* for *14 months*—talk about reluctant. There was also the Ensign's much praised sudden attempt at being a fifth columnist, when his attempts to make a test run prank of fashioning "a fire cracker for the Captain's bunker [succeeded] only in blowing the [ship's] laundry [area] into a niagara of soapsuds [with Lemmon riding this wave of bubbles some distance]."[7] This also reminds one of a Warner's cartoon.

The second reason that Lemmon's ditty marks the importance of this role is the stunning

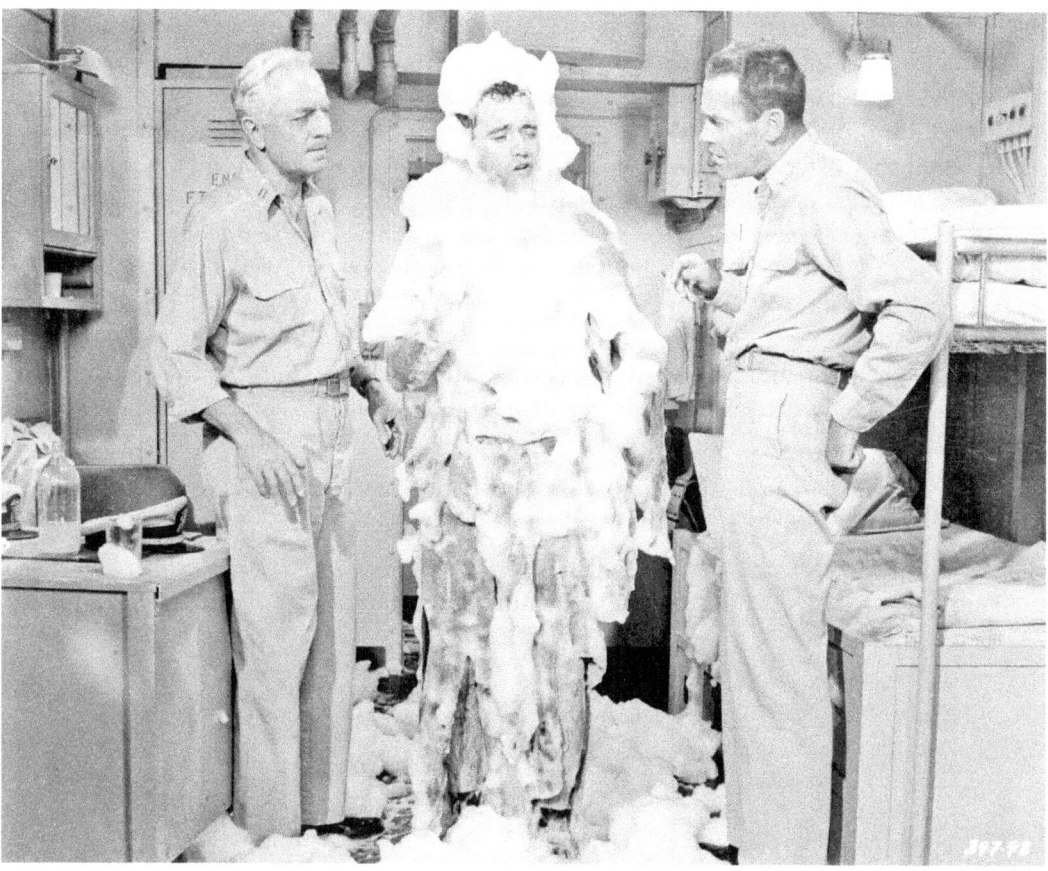

Jack Lemmon's attempt at soapy defiance fails, flanked by William Powell (left) and Henry Fonda in *Mr. Roberts*.

admiration he received both then and in later years. For instance, the *Hollywood Reporter*'s review said:

> Truly brilliant, from the comic side, is Jack Lemmon as Ensign Pulver. Lemmon lives up to all the promise of his performance in "It Should Happen to You" and "Phfft!" [both 1954] showing that without a doubt he is one of our light comedians.[8]

And from the opposite coast, the *Daily News*' Kate Cameron almost exactly replicates the *Hollywood Reporter*'s period praise:

> Jack Lemmon, a fine young comedian ... who made a hit in two Columbia comedies playing opposite Judy Holliday [see Chapter 1] in "It Should Happen to You" and "Phfft!" comes into his own as one of the funniest comedians of the screen in the role of Ensign Pulver. It won't be long now before Lemmon is a star.[9]

Now flash forward a quarter century and film historian Robert Mitchell observes:

> Jack Lemmon's Ensign Pulver is the most engaging character in the film; brash and vulnerable Lemmon, the Academy Award ... made him a major star, and launched his long successful career.[10]

Of course, one really knows a film has made *the* difference in an actor's vocation when a personal family touch is revealed. In Chris Lemmon's warmhearted biography of his father, he shares that the family dog was named "Ensign Pulver."[11] Also, the past was an early validation, maybe even the catalyst for a ritual Jack Lemmon always "would say under his breath" to begin each film take: "It's magic time."[12]

Given this typical personality comedy's thinnest of storylines, in fact, the original novel originally started out as a collection of short stories, the background to the movie is an encyclopedia of melodrama, with an element of humor fittingly involving Lemmon. Prior to *Mister Roberts*, the actor had auditioned for John Ford's sentimental West Point saga *The Long Gray Line* (1955, about the beloved lengthy career of an athletic trainer). In a part which eventually went to Tyrone Power, Lemmon's test had him playing the character at 80. He did not get it. However, the actor had a friend on Ford's staff named Maurice Max. He knew that the director was soon to be casting for *Mister Roberts*. Thus, Max "accidently" later spliced Lemmon's *Long Gray Line* audition at the end of that picture's dailies. Ford said:

> Who the hell was that? [After Max apologized, the director continued,] That's all right. I want to tell you about that kid [Lemmon]. He's a lousy old man but I think he'd make a hell of a Pulver.[13]

Shortly thereafter, Lemmon found himself on *The Long Gray Line* set, neither knowing Ford, nor what his friend had done. When the director and actor eventually met, this is their conversation:

> FORD: You should play Ensign Pulver.
> LEMMON: Well, I wish you'd spread the word, because there's no part in the world that I want more.
> FORD: Spit in your hand.
> LEMMON: Are you out of your mind?
> FORD: It's an old Irish custom. Just spit in your hand [And then he spit in *his* hand. Thus, Lemmon went along and did the same. Ford then took Lemmon's hand.] I'm Ford, you're Pulver.[14]

Now, as Johnny Carson occasionally said, "I told you that story in order to tell you this one." As endearingly charming as the preceding anecdote, it was no secret that John Ford, one of America's greatest directors, had a filmmaking style which could be pigeon-holed as that of a bully—the means justified the end. Indeed, one of William Powell's lines as Doc in *Mister Roberts* fit Ford perfectly, "The Captain of a Navy ship is the most absolute monarch left in this world." And fittingly, in point of fact, Ford actually was an old Navy man.

Naturally, Ford hardly had the corner on the director as tyrant position phenomenon. Arguably the champion of this approach was Stanley Kubrick, probably best documented by Frederic Raphael in his book *Eyes Wide Open: A Memoir of Stanley Kubrick*—the title being a word play upon the name of the film which he co-scripted with the director, *Eyes Wide Shut*, both 1999.[15] There is no doubting the award-winning success Ford and Kubrick achieved, both personally, and often for the performers they put through the ringer. In the case of Ford, maybe the most honest observation comes from a largely affectionate biography of the director by his grandson, Dan Ford:

> [My grandfather] pulled the performance of a lifetime out of Victor McLaglen [in 1935's *The Informer*, for which the actor won the Best Actor Oscar and Ford the Best Director statuette], but he [Ford] also reduced the actor to a trembling wreck. He shook, lost weight, and couldn't sleep at night. At least a dozen times during the making of the picture, McLaglen swore that he was going to quit acting—just after he killed John Ford.... My grandfather's handling of McLaglen raises the question of whether he did it for the picture or for his own pleasure. Wingate Smith [a longtime Ford film associate], who was

there, isn't sure. "You had to wonder where the line was in Jack [Ford]'s mind. Sure he was getting great stuff from Vic, but I also think he enjoyed seeing him suffer. He was like a mean little kid playing with a bug."[16]

Well, a complex *Mister Roberts* encounter between Ford and Fonda ultimately resulted in the director being replaced by Mervyn LeRoy. But somehow LeRoy was able to come in either mid or late in the production, depending upon one's source, and make the movie appear seamless. Though Lemmon was not directly involved in what occurred, it is pertinent to address this donnybrook for two reasons which undoubtedly impacted the young actor. However, first it is necessary to chronicle this behind the scenes melodrama whose clash of personalities was not unlike the actual movie being made. Regardless, when the decision to adapt *Mister Roberts* to the screen was made, Fonda's stage work had kept him off the screen for eight years. Thus, the studio wanted to play it safe with a current popular film star, like William Holden or Marlon Brando. Plus, Fonda was nearly 50, an unlikely age for the character. However, Ford was adamant that Fonda, who had so excelled in several earlier pictures by the director, like *Young Mr. Lincoln* (1939) and *The Grapes of Wrath* (1940), receive the part:

After the studio acquiesced and production had begun, Fonda took early issue with the "edit in the camera," often "one-take" Ford just plowing through a script with so many nuances. Fonda describes the situation as such in his memoir:

> We plodded on. It couldn't have been worse ... [Finally, in one particular sequence] I'd played [on stage] ... for three or four years, I knew how the timing should be ... I don't want to dramatize it but this scene just wasn't flowing. Everyone around us knew it [including producer Leland Hayward]. Everyone, that is except Ford. That was the way he directed. And nobody dared to say a goddam word or he'd be all over you in a second. He was the genius, he was the creator. [Fonda did not call Ford on this but was clearly unhappy.] And at the end of the day's shooting he was told to report to an equally unhappy Ford.] "Pappy [Ford], you know I love you. We've worked on I don't know how many pictures but you must understand that Leland [who also produced the play on Broadway] and me, who have been so close to this property for so many years ... it has a purity that we don't like to see lost."[17]

Ford's arguably definitive biographer, Tag Gallagher, condescendingly described the situation as "an actor who thought he knew more than the director was scarcely a novelty."[18] Yet, given Fonda's long Tony-winning experience with *Mister Roberts*, and an even longer affectionate background with this acclaimed director, certainly some sort of private dialogue was merited between Fonda and Ford. Yet, when it seemed about to happen, with the director summoning Fonda, Ford immediately hit and/or struck him with some object (stories vary). Like Fonda's coolheaded, unruffable Mr. Roberts, the non-violent actor was not about to fight the older, much smaller, sickly one-eyed director. And to Gallagher's credit, he has Ford apologizing to Fonda within the hour. Yet it soon seemed to be a faithless act, a Janus-faced gesture, given the resumption of the shoot:

> From then on, during all the [on-location] filming on Midway [Island], Ford turned to Fonda after each shot. It was embarrassing to the actor because the director had never before done that. It was a glance, a suggestion of approval, a hint of "There. Does that satisfy you?"[19]

Moreover, what is not as widely known, is that there was potential trouble, of Ford's making with James Cagney, the *Reluctant*'s captain. Now, despite the actor's tough guy screen persona from such gangster classics as *Public Enemy* (1931) and *White Heat* (1949), he was really an *everyman* sort of professional, not far removed from his Oscar-winning Best Actor *Yankee Noodle Dandy* (1942) performance as George M. Cohan. Regardless, when Ford and Cagney accidently met at the airport just prior to the shoot, Ford essentially told the actor they would tangle on this production. Sure enough, he soon provoked Cagney on the set, and when the actor would not tolerate Ford's bullying behavior, the director backed down.

No doubt the Fonda and Cagney incidents were catalysts for the alcoholic Ford to start drinking openly while they were shooting. This was something he had never done before. Ford, whose four Best Director Oscars remain a record, was what is clinically known as a "functioning alcoholic," someone who only gets blotto when he is *not* working. Thus, when Ford was too inebriated to direct *Mister Roberts*, actor Ward Bond (a longtime member of Ford's acting troupe and general entourage) and Fonda would consult and keep the Midway production rolling. Ford remained involved in the shooting, to a degree, at the other Pacific locations. But once back in the States the director was hospitalized and soon had surgery for a kidney condition. How serious the situation was has been under debate ever since. But it provided the studio with a non-controversial exit strategy to remove Ford. As noted earlier, director LeRoy was brought in and did such a masterful mop up duty that the film managed to even receive an Academy Award nomination as Best Picture of the year—losing to the modest sleeper hit *Marty* (1955, about a lonely Bronx butcher).

So how does this behind-the-scenes mess pertain to Lemmon? First, this young actor was somehow expected to carry the brunt of the picture's comedy load under the most unfavorable conditions imaginable. Conceivably, the production stress ironically might have assisted the troubled demeanor of Fonda's title character. But to borrow a song title from the then recent *Singin' in the Rain* (1952), Lemmon was expected to "Make 'Em Laugh" in this environment. And what is more, he managed to do it with Oscar-winning finesse. Moreover, who knows? There are so many intangibles involved in winning one of those golden statuettes, maybe Lemmon's remarkable comic performance received additional points based upon the abysmal conditions in which he had to perform.

Second, and more importantly, after reading a great deal about Lemmon, he seems to have always been a fun and agreeable person with whom to work. But one could certainly make a case for that philosophy having been reinforced squared by the often difficult working conditions on *Mister Roberts*. Like that old joke about pain, no matter how stoical the person, ongoing pain is certain to get an individual's attention. One *cannot* help, therefore, but think of this when reading Kevin Spacey's moving "Foreword" to Chris Lemmon's previously noted biography of his father. A 13-year-old Spacey first met Lemmon at a junior high school acting workshop and was later lucky enough to have him as both a friend and mentor as they worked together on several productions. Compare Lemmon's *Mister Roberts* experience to what Spacey later said about his acting guru:

> If you ask me what I learned in his presence, the answers come tumbling out. Most important, I learned about behavior, for he exemplified the way you should treat people around you—always making sure your co-workers feel important and confident, and are having an enjoyable experience. I realized that being an actor—in Mr. Lemmon's case, not just an actor but also a major film star—elevates your responsibility because everyone around you looks to you as a leader. Playing a major character in a film or stage production puts an actor at the center of the experience, and the likeability and relatability of the actor can have an enormous effect in creating a pleasurable atmosphere for everyone involved.[20]

Going hand-in-hand with the amicable working philosophy was Lemmon's ill-used (by Ford) co-star Cagney, whose authoritative biographer, Patrick McGilligan, found the older actor describing the director with one word—"Malice."[21] Not surprisingly, Lemmon and Cagney would become close friends. And an added bonus for Lemmon was that Cagney also did some mentoring that is evident in the younger performer's acting in *Mister Roberts*, and especially the later *Some Like It Hot* (1959, see Chapter 12). For Cagney,

> all movement is or should be an extension of rhythm. "All actors should dance," he told Jack Lemmon during the filming of *Mister Roberts*. And, known as a fanatic who skipped lunch regularly to practice his dance steps, Cagney's passion for dance, and his assertion that all actors should be versed in footwork, give further documentation to Cagney's devotion to rhythm.[22]

The rhythm recommendation especially hit home with Lemmon because of his passion for music, especially with his gift as a pianist. And given that timing is crucial for both music and comedy, Cagney was merely reinforcing what Lemmon was quickly learning. Moreover, through the years an appreciable number of extraordinary comedians have periodically displayed their musical skills, be it Chico and Harpo Marx, or John Belushi and Steve Martin.

Years later (1993) Lemmon would do a voiceover commentary for a *Mister Roberts* video, further fleshing out the shoot, particularly with regard to Ford, Fonda, and Cagney. Indeed, it was Cagney who forewarned Lemmon about Ford's control factor, à la *The Informer* tale noted earlier. Now keep in mind, Lemmon was the most diplomatic of people when discussing something or someone who had been difficult with which to work. So what follows represents strong language for Lemmon:

> [Ford] would pull tricks on actors; he was famous for it, to get a certain performance, or a certain reaction from them that he wanted on film. I personally, as an actor, I kind of resent that because what it's basically saying is, "I don't think you're good enough as an actor [to get what I want]. I'm going to trick you into doing it." That's why I've always resented it. But he's [Ford] famous for it.[23]

Being the respectful, deferential Jack Lemmon, he does not note either Ford's physical attack on Fonda or the director's confrontation with Cagney. Of course, while Lemmon mentions the lifelong friendships he developed with Cagney and Powell, for the director he could only muster, "Pappy Ford was pretty tough."

Moreover, reading between the lines, Lemmon cannot help but establish the growing powder keg developing between Ford and Fonda. For example:

> Hank [Fonda] was not happy with the film because Ford was adding an awful lot of stuff that was not in the script ... putting touches in that were his. And most of them were things he had me doing that never did end up on the screen, thank God. They were funny, but they shouldn't have been there. They were almost like a burlesque sketch at times. He had [Ensign] Pulver doing crazy things, like leaning on guns that had just been shot in practice and they were hot and I'd jump a mile because I burned myself and kinds of different things.... He spent damn near a whole day just shooting me and making things up.

Fonda was becoming visibly upset. Between a camera set-up the two actors talked:

> LEMMON: You're not very happy about this, are you? [And Lemmon's perspective on Fonda mirrored how Spacey felt about Lemmon.]
> FONDA: Hell no; it has nothing to do with *Mister Roberts*....
> Lemmon: I agree with you.
> FONDA: There's nothing much you can do about it because he's the director. But if you can, screw it up. [Lemmon laughs.]

However, as noted earlier, Ford, like Lemmon, was aware of Fonda's growing exasperations, which resulted in the childishly feeble punch. Lemmon provides even less background on

Ford's confrontation with Cagney, beyond disclosing that the director attempted to pull one of his Victor McLaglen–like tricks on the two actors. Yet, Cagney and Lemmon were able to anticipate it. However, it is hardly difficult to imagine another attempted Ford trick ticking off Cagney.

Lemmon's voiceover also reveals there was actually an uncredited third *Mister Roberts* director, Josh Logan, after the picture had seemingly wrapped. Once again, Ford comes across as petty and egotistical. That is, the most pivotal sequence reshot was the poignant letter revealing *Mister Roberts'* death. Lemmon had never been happy with how he played it. But Ford's quick and dirty shooting approach to this signature scene upset more than the soon-to-be Oscar-winning Lemmon. When producer Logan reviewed the rough cut, he also found the scene lacking. So it was redone and Lemmon was more than pleased with the results. Nonetheless, when the actor later made a courtesy visit to the recuperating Ford, the old curmudgeon had gotten wind of Logan's do-over and grilled Lemmon about the actor really thinking the original *Ford* version was more appropriate. Lemmon, the consummate gentleman, politely agreed and left. That was filmmaking with Ford.

So how did *Mister Roberts*, with its old cluttered cargo ship, a regular landfill on water whose captain and the original director had Jackson Pollocked souls, fare with the public and critics? Commercially, it outgrossed all other 1955 films except the gimmicky *Cinerama Holiday*.[24] And as already suggested earlier in the chapter, the critics lined up to lionize *Mister Roberts* and Jack Lemmon, with *Cue* magazine being the most colorful in its kudos, calling it

> a wonderful, whamdinging salty saga of the salty heroes in denim: a classic, serio-comic howler about the unhappy lads who never peered through a gunsight in anger ... [and] Jack Lemmon as the wobble-brained young Ensign Pulver is hilarious.[25]

Variety added:

> From bestseller to hit play to click [hit] pic [picture] is the box-office parlay for Mister Roberts ... with the kind of entertainment that means handsome grosses in the keys [large cities] and elsewhere ... [with] Jack Lemmon a big hit as Ensign Pulver.[26]

Further kudos came from the *New York Herald Tribune*:

> The movie has just as many laughs, but it's more than a comedy ... Pulver is one of the rare birds of modern fiction and he gives the movie most of its humorous moments. Jack Lemmon plays the role with relish. It is fun to watch the calculated ... [character].[27]

The *Hollywood Reporter* credited it with being a "throwback to the good old days when solid laughter was still regarded as audience bait," while the *New York World-Telegram and Sun* said it all in its review title, "'Mister Roberts' Hilarious."[28] One's perfect close, however, to this wave of critical admiration would have to be the *New York Times'* last line of its review, "To 'Mr. Roberts' and all hands involved in one of the season's greatest pleasures: 'Well done.'"[29]

Not bad for a picture bathed in behind the scenes melodrama.

9

Martin & Lewis
Artists and Models
(December 22, 1955)

> Maybe next time Hal Wallis, the the film's producer, will let [co-star Shirley] MacLaine and Jerry [Lewis] go it together, without Dean [Martin] or anyone to get in the way.[1]—*New York Times* critic Bosley Crowther

This statement helps explain why Martin & Lewis were treated as a team in *Sailor Beware* (1952, see Chapter 2), whereas their 1955 *Artists & Models*, despite still carrying the Martin & Lewis moniker, is best designated as Lewis' premier solo outing. Much had changed in the intervening years. Martin's team participation in the duo had been so minimalized by Lewis that the two were on the verge of a non-speaking status which would herald their 1956 split. Lewis, like a cat with a ball of string, had become obsessed with every facet of filmmaking. Obviously, there is nothing wrong with such dedication. Indeed, he might have strengthened the duo, as an equally consumed Stan Laurel did with his Oliver Hardy partnership. However, as Martin noted in Chapter 2, when Lewis' ego saw himself as the second coming of Chaplin, which was fortified by his unfairly getting the lion's share of the team's early critical attention, he could not help to notice that Chaplin never had a partner. Martin was eventually diminished in every facet of the team, from photo shoots to script discussion. One is reminded of the expression in blues folklore of "being at the crossroads"—meaning selling one's soul to the dark side.

Though there would technically be two other Martin & Lewis films, the ironically titled *Partners* and *Hollywood or Bust* (both 1956, and both done with Martin & Lewis communicating only through mediators), *Artist and Models* was an indirect coup d'état by way of the behind the screen addition of Frank Tashlin. This was the first time Tashlin would co-write and direct a Martin & Lewis film. (He also carried the same credits on the even more stressful *Hollywood or Bust*.) Any possible unintended Tashlin contributions to the team split would have been a result of his background in writing comic strips and animation. That is, his creative mindset was naturally geared to the live-action cartoon character named Jerry Lewis. And no one by Lewis' own admission would have a greater impact on the comedian's career, including co-writing and/or directing six of Lewis' early solo films. Indeed, when historian/director Peter Bogdanovich asked the comedian that very mentoring question, Lewis replied in capital letters, "Mr. Tashlin, spelled T-A-S-H-L-I-N. He's my teacher."[2]

Thus, with no hidden agenda to hide, like simply preferring Lewis over Martin, feasibly the talents Tashlin brought to *Artists and Models* further hastened the Martin & Lewis break-up, since the director and the comedian were more simpatico. One might liken it to when writer/director Leo McCarey megaphoned the Marx Brothers' greatest picture, *Duck Soup* (1933).[3] Though he obviously did not break up the team, McCarey's pioneering work in silent comedy immediately had him naturally gravitate towards the speechless Harpo. The result was the most creatively expansive cinematic role Harpo ever had. Indeed, this even included using Groucho, film's most verbally saturation comedy-oriented comedian short of Robin Williams, to be part of a silent pantheon scene in world cinema—*Duck Soup's* comic mirror sequence. Groucho will comically attempt to fool what purports to be an extension of himself (Harpo as his reflection).

Moreover, Tashlin's involvement in *Artists and Models* plausibly further sealed the inevitable Martin & Lewis split because the story, like most personality comedies, was little more than a pastiche of pieces and fragments which was Tashlin's métier. That is, the movie was about a comic strip addict (Lewis) and a painter-turned-cartoonist (Martin) who mined his friend's comic strip-driven nightmares for material. Moreover, one could argue that this premise breaks the basis Martin-Lewis formula, in which the cool surrogate older brother (Martin) is always looking out for Lewis' anti-hero. In contrast, in *Artists and Models*, Martin's character is facilitating Lewis' nightmares in order to obtain story material. Regardless, Tashlin was afforded the most fittingly favorable subject of his life. Is it any wonder that film critic Robert Mundy wrote *Artists and Models* is "arguably Tashlin's masterpiece?"[4]

As so happens with any comedian, especially a superior one like Lewis—he is often pushed to a higher level by an extraordinary director. Thus, make no mistake about it, *Artists and Models* is Lewis at his best. As Bogdanovich observed:

> *Artists and Models* is a spectacularly destructive view of comic-book mentality [starting with Lewis as Exhibit A]. Being an extremely able craftsman [Tashlin] is probably the most inventive visual-gag constructionist of the talkies; Tashlin took the outrageous, impossible humor of cartoons and connected it humanly to live action.[5]

Along the same lines, French critic Roger Tailleur added:

> *Artists and Models* ... is obviously the most Tashlinian of Tashlin's films, the sum total of his past life and career. It is a defense and illustration of the illustrated magazine, an explosion of [positive] fireworks for the comic book, [satirically] distributed to newborn infants and placed into the shackled hands of the world. [The previous year the United States Senate Subcommittee on Juvenile Delinquency focused on the "crime and horror" comic books of the day. Because of the negative press, comic book companies created a self-regulatory ratings system known as the *Comics Code Authority*.][6]

Consequently, moving through the film, what are some of the cartoon-like scenes which favor Lewis? First, early in the picture roommates Martin and Lewis are fighting, after Jerry's schlemiel of a character has lost them yet another job. Trying to lighten the mood, Lewis suggests when you pretend, your dreams comes true. Consequently, he goes to a piece of plywood in the apartment (related to the supplies of wannabe painter Martin) and plunks his finger down as if it were a piano. And sure enough, his imaginary keyboard magically produces music. Naturally, incredulous Martin cannot believe what he is seeing and hearing and gives it a try, but nothing happens. Jerry explains one has to concentrate and again creates his sorcerous sounds. Eventually this segues into the musical number, "When You Pretend," with the assistance of that "piano" accompaniment.

Second, Jerry later discovers that an illustrator has moved into their apartment building. Thinking she (Dorothy Malone) might be able to help Dean's aspirations to be a painter, he knocks on her door. But Malone's flatmate model (Shirley MacLaine) answers dressed as Bat Lady, which so startles Jerry he leaves vapor trails getting away. Paradoxically, however, comic book-crazed Jerry soon realizes he is infatuated by the character. Indeed, he is so attracted to this figure that MacLaine, who has an implausible interest in him, cannot even get Jerry to recognize she is the same person.

Flash forward to the next day. Martin has grilled Lewis enough to realize that with an illustrator/cartoonist in the apartment complex, he just might find a similar job with her publisher. When Dean and Jerry arrive at Malone's studio, Tashlin manages to take Lewis to cartoonland in three different water cooler-related ways. An extended filming of his face through the glass looks like viewing a blowfish at an aquarium. There is also the obligatory kiss causing the water to boil. The catalyst for the final cartoon embellishment of the water cooler comes from child star George "Foghorn" Winslow, whose deep voice and deadpan delivery make it seem like he could be an animation refugee, too. ("Foghorn" also had brief but memorable turns in such other classic pictures as *Monkey Business*, 1952, and *Gentlemen Prefer Blondes*, 1953.) Regardless, here he plays a passing brat trying to tip over the office cooler, only to have Jerry catch it spigot down, with the water emptying inside the front of his pants. As a fitting cartoon-like narrative finale voice to the scene, "Foghorn" observes, "Looks like Niagara Falls." (The scene's sexual innuendo will be addressed later in the chapter as one of Tashlin's auteur components.)

Third, though the term *incongruity* would seem to describe any sentence which includes the names of sophisticated comedy director Ernst *Lubitsch* and the Lubitsch-admiring, cartoonish Frank *Tashlin, Artists and Models* finds a modest way. Lubitsch's pioneering early sound films often had sequences in which the story was, for a time, moved along by a song passing from one character to another in another location. While it works along the lines of a smooth comic operetta transition for Lubitsch, Tashlin's *Artist and Models* juxtapositions it for surprise comic effect. For instance, Malone and MacLaine are sunbathing on their apartment's roof. Unknown to Malone, her almost boyfriend, Martin, secretly comes up, and with MacLaine as an ally, the radio is turned on and he sings a beautiful rendition of a song she loves, "Innamorata" (sweetheart).

When the ruse is up and Martin and Malone kiss, MacLaine slips away and begins to also sing a lovely rendition of "Innamorata" on the steps leading to the roof. She is thinking of her wannabe boyfriend, Lewis. Suddenly she hears him coming up the stairs to also sunbathe. He is weighed down with every possible item for a day at this urban "beach," including a folding deck chair, various sunscreen lotions, a pillow, sun reflectors, a naval officer's hat, and so on. MacLaine has quietly wrapped herself around the 45-degree banister accompanying the stairs to the roof, as an unassuming Lewis reaches the landing just below her. Suddenly she bursts into a comic, overly raucous rendition of "Innamorata," which so surprises Jerry he goes straight up, with his sunning accouterments flying sixty-eleven directions. As her decimal level singing levels off, Shirley flirts with him as she does quasi-ballet movements with the banister. Lewis ignores her and methodically picks up all his supplies. Once this is accomplished and he is at the base of the final set of stairs, Shirley again momentarily ups the volume of "Innamorata," like a quarterback briefly cranking up his cadence to draw the opposition offside, and once more Jerry is startled and everything goes airborne. But Jerry is a regular Sisyphus and repeats the drill. However, this time before he can patiently gather things again, she affectionately attacks him and they both go into a joint impromptu ballet-like number on the landing's parallel banister-turned-dance bar.

However, Jerry soon jumps down and MacLaine performs a more polished ballet routine on the bannister/dance bar as she stops singing. Lewis indirectly acknowledges he is flattered by her attention by a brief comic rendition of a ballerina. Shirley remains so involved in her dance that she seems oblivious to Jerry the schlimazel as he now artfully and ever so quietly (since MacLaine has stopped singing) again retrieves his beach items and even manages to get to the door at the top of the stairs when MacLaine belts out "Innamorata" yet again. And for this big cartoon-like finish, not only are his things broadcast every which way, he ends up sliding back down the stairs on the folding deck chair turned sled. Lying on the floor exhausted, after this simple attempt to rest in the sun, the still energized Shirley lies down beside him—hyper Jerry has met his match in manic behavior.

Of course, all these pratfalls by Jerry are the perfect lead into the picture's piece de resistance cartoonish scene. That is, Jerry's in need of a chiropractor. When the specialist gets him on the table, he uses Lewis like a mattress that needs breaking in—climbing all over him. Then Jerry's legs are bent to comic grimacing proportions, as if he were made of rubber instead of bone and sinew. But the cartoon proportions are just beginning. Next, the chiropractor bends Lewis' legs like so many pretzels. With that, the specialist comes full circle in what might be called "wrestling therapy" by physically joining Jerry the pretzel. Three additional people will soon also be directed to join something moving from medicine to modern art. However, at some point in this live-action cartoon Lewis shoe horns himself from the pretzel, and starts directing this exercise in visual contrariness himself, before leaving them to fend for their twisted selves.

Such live action borrowing from animation was not new to American sound era comedy. For example, Laurel & Hardy's *Way Out West* (1937) gives Stan the ability to use his thumb like a cigarette lighter, and late in the film Ollie's head is stretched a good ten feet straight up, as well as executing a 360-degree rotation. Yet, such actions were not the norm for Laurel & Hardy.[7] Indeed, despite the team's comedy pantheon status, these late career animation antics come off as cheap jokes, because they are inconsistent with their long one-foot-in-reality comedy base. No matter how funny the bit, it is verboten to use material outside one's persona ... or soon one does not have a persona. What was unique about Tashlin, and eventually Lewis, was this cartoonish movie mindset dominated their careers. Yes, Lewis had been successful prior to Tashlin with more traditional comedy fare. But the comedian was only 30 when he began collaborating with Tashlin, and the director's influence soon dominated Jerry's solo work. Moreover, Lewis' earlier manic comedy with Dean sometimes bordered on the edge of cartoonland, too.

Given *Artists and Models* is being treated as Jerry's best solo work from the 1950s, what were other Tashlin auteur components which further accented Lewis' comedy in this film? First, Tashlin was never afraid to milk a given comic situation to near perpetuity. In fact, one such example has already been demonstrated by Lewis' "Innamorata" sequence with MacLaine. And as critic Noel Simsolo has observed, these "episodic gags" often meant

As funny as a "seemingly" solo Jerry Lewis could be, he still worked best with a partner, as showcased by this Shirley MacLaine sequence in *Artists and Models*.

"regulating Dean Martin to the back seat behind Jerry Lewis, a man whose body generates an uncontrollable, destructive energy."[8] Regardless, *the* example, which is all Lewis, is best called the "messenger sequence." That is, the team's old walk-up apartment only has one first floor public phone for the tenants.

Unfortunately, Martin & Lewis live several flights up, and when the landlady screams that Martin's character is wanted on the phone, he is in the bathtub. Naturally, he sends Lewis down to check out who wants him. Sadly, boy/man Jerry is incapable of multi-tasking information. Accordingly, Lewis quickly dashes down and back to tell Dean a publisher has called. Martin asks what the publisher wants. So a tired Jerry again does the up/down loop in order to inform his partner the man wants to meet Martin. Frustrated but still lounging in the tub, Dean once more directs Jerry to go back and determine where the publisher wants to meet. But this final round trip has Lewis so winded he cannot speak. Hence it allows Tashlin to then utilize Jerry's mime skills to inform his buddy the location of the power lunch. The setting is the legendary New York Stork Club in half an hour. (Tashlin's restaurant is well-chosen, since the term "stork" gives Lewis a rich subject with which to pantomime, as well as reflecting the director's preference for animals over people.)

Consistent with the previous statement, a second Tashlin auteur component helping

Lewis' comedy is that the director's humans often exhibited animal characteristics. Nothing better describes the simian appearance and actions of Lewis—an analogy the comedian himself started by comparing his teaming with Martin as that of the singing organ grinder and his monkey. Moreover, Tashlin's children's fables, like *The Bear That Wasn't* (1946), had animals being taken advantage of by humans attempting to make them conform to arbitrary standards—something the director abhorred.[9] And Tashlin constantly has Lewis being threatened with dreaded conformity, such as when *The Better American Forum* TV program attempts to use the comedian as an anti-comic book pawn.

Plus, as the phone scene demonstrates, Jerry comes off as more of a loyal puppy than a person. And even though it is the dashing back and forth which has made his character too winded to talk, this inability to speak plays to Lewis inherently animal-like state. Of course, the film's most wildlife figure is the aforementioned "Foghorn" Winslow, who simply bites people. Yet, Tashlin comically peppers Lewis with animal-related humor. For example, while his nightmares are full of scary figures, the superhero of these colorful snoozes is Vincent the Vulture. In fact, at one point in Lewis' sleep he comically describes Vincent as "the defender of truth and liberty and a member of the Audubon Society." As a child of the '50s, to this writer that sounds very much like the mantra of my hero, Superman, who stood for "Truth, Justice, and the American Way."

Third, Tashlin further arms Lewis with added laughs by making the comic's goal to be a children's author whose central character is a mouse. But before expanding upon this twist, keep in mind that as late as 1962 Tashlin "was awed [to have worked] ... at Disney' [studio]" in 1939 and 1940 as story director for the Mickey Mouse series.[10] Tashlin's primary uncredited work at the time was an aborted project called *Mickey and the Beanstock*. At that time Mickey would have been best described as an overly friendly naïve character who believed in magic beans and was full of plans, which seldom came to fruition. Maybe a one-word capsulization of Mickey's world might best be found in the name of his close friend, "Goofy."

This sounds a lot like Lewis at the start of *Artists and Models* singing that "When You Pretend" everything works out, even if there is a "wolf at the door"—which naturally again reminds one of Disney, as in *The Three Little Pigs* (1933, that year's Academy Award–winning Best Animated Short Subject). Naturally, the Big Bad Wolf comes to all three of their houses. But thanks to the work of Practical Pig, who has built his home of bricks, while his lazy brothers had constructed flimsy dwellings and taunted Practical Pig by singing the song which became an immense hit during the 1930s, "Who's Afraid of the Big Bad Wolf," they are saved. Coming full circle back to Lewis' plywood piano, a final link to this Disney cartoon is an ending in which Practical Pig scares his siblings by plunking on his piano, as if the Wolf has returned.

Tashlin's linking Jerry to a mouse has several other almost subliminal insightful meanings, such as the vulnerability of its use in John Steinbeck's 1937 novella, *Of Mice and Men*, in which the creature represents a false metaphorical sense of safety for Lenny. And while no one is suggesting an *Artists and Models* demise for Lewis, he definitely, as usual, needs looking after. Moreover, one just naturally thinks of mice as pests, who are fearfully meek and with no sense of animal kingdom assertiveness. Obviously, all these descriptions are quintessential illustrations of Lewis' persona. Plus, one can come full circle back to other period cartoon mice which might bring Lewis to mind, from MGM's "Tom (cat) and Jerry (mouse)" cartoon series, to Warner Bros.' "Looney Tunes" animated figure, Speedy Gonzales, who had just become very popular shortly before *Artists and Models*. Plus, given Tashlin's love of comic speed and/or the chase—defining characteristics of Gonzales—is it any wonder that Jerry is frequently going at warp speed? This is especially true of the sequence in which he is so startled by MacLaine's Bat Lady that he runs into the wrong apartment. And instead of the security associated with Dean's presence, his meteoric mouse of a man finds himself in a fat lady's bedroom. Now he really accelerates into Gonzales speed and manages to find the protection of Dean and their apartment. Yet, rest assured, before the movie's close, Jerry will be padded out in an elaborate mouse costume.

Fourth, Tashlin, and no doubt the legacy of Chaplin, manage to provide Jerry with a funny but more modest variation of the Tramp dining upon a cooked boot in *The Gold Rush* (1925). Yet, think minimal here. Instead of Charlie and his companion Mark Swain "feasting" upon the visual puns of spaghetti-like boot laces, wishbone like nails, and turkey à la leather, Jerry is reduced to making a banquet out of a single bean. He extends the bit by delicately cutting this micro-meal into parts, and noisily savoring each bite. But after adding a touch of salt and pepper, he loses the last morsel of a meal by accidently burying it under a bungled attempt to add some ketchup.

Naturally both men would prefer a steak but that seems more than unlikely, so Dean goes to bed early. However, Jerry remains up, and in a generally pre-air conditioned period, an open window allows him to overhear a heated argument between two neighbors several stories up. Though the couple is never seen, the voices perfectly mimic the loud squabbles between Ralph Kramden (Jackie Gleason, including one of his signature lines, "Hardee Har Har") and his TV wife Alice (Audrey Meadows) on the celebrated series with the ironic name, *The Honeymooners*. And the spoof is especially timely, because *The Honeymooners* was always a sketch on Gleason's various variety shows in the 1950s and '60s, *except* for 1955, when it appeared one season as a regular 39-episode series. (*Artists and Models* opened in 1955.)

Not surprisingly, the volatile "Ralph" ends up tossing the steak out the window and Jerry's character manages to catch it. Lewis offers to share it with Dean, but his disbelieving pal stays in bed. Also, coming shortly after the musical number "When You Pretend," it provides unlikely credibility to that philosophy. But a better, more fitting, ideology for Jerry would be the hoary axiom often mistakenly attributed to the Bible, "God protects children and fools."

Interestingly, as the focus films of this study work their way through the decade, while TV will continue to periodically be satirized, there is also a growing tendency to just affectionately spoof the medium, à la the *Honeymooners* reference. This is a change from the early 1950s, as in Bob Hope's cracks about TV censorship issues in *Son of Paleface* (1952, see Chapter 3). The reason behind this softening attitude had three-parts—the small screen was not going away, the movie industry was finding a new source of revenue by producing TV shows, and affectionate parody in-jokes could be funny. While such spoofing was unique neither to Tashlin nor the movie industry in general, such barbs were another basic component of Tashlin the auteur. And as such, the phenomenon provided both more comedy for Lewis here, as well as becoming a key later element of the solo Lewis as auteur, such as the creative closing twist to self-consciously demonstrate his *The Patsy* (1964) is only a movie.

Regardless, Tashlin takes it to TV in various ways, usually by way of Lewis. For example, the comedian's steak courtesy of *The Honeymooners*, or his observation after being kidnapped in a mouse costume, "If I want mystery I'll watch [Jack Webb's pioneering TV police drama] *Dragnet*." On the flip side, Tashlin's Lewis is the focal point of the aforementioned witch-hunting TV show *The Better Forum*. Moreover, the film's comic book editor (Eddie Mayehoff) had earlier drolly defended violence in his medium by noting of TV, "[The] Night before [last] I counted thirteen murders, four stabbings, nine suffocations, four poisonings on two channels in one hour." (Mayehoff is a familiar face in Martin & Lewis films, having also appeared in the duo's *That's My Boy*, 1951, and *The Stooge*, 1952.)

Tashlin does not limit his parody and/or satirical use of Lewis to just TV. After a few of Jerry's nightmare monologues start to inexplicably include a partial numerical rocket formula, suddenly the FBI is involved. (Do not attempt to make any sense of this unfathomable incorporation of the Cold War—Paramount did not.) Nevertheless, it then becomes legitimate to include spying surveillance into the movie. And bingo, there is an agent whose face is obscured by a pair of binoculars in a window overlooking Mayehoff's office. When another spy asks what he can see, one hears a faultless impersonation of Jimmy Stewart saying, "Well, it looks like Todd [Martin] told Murdock [Mayehoff something] and he's leaving. Of course, I can't see so well from this *rear window* [italics mine]."

To Tashlin's credit, not every spoof is set up by Lewis' character. Such is the case in an aforementioned sequence in which the two women are sunning on the roof, and Malone asks MacLaine who is singing "Innamorata" on what she assumes is the radio. Not knowing it is really Martin, who has quietly joined them on the roof, MacLaine answers, "He's the one that had that big hit 'That's Amore [Love].'" (Martin's 1953 recording was so popular it had become his signature song until his 1964 mega-hit "Everybody Loves Somebody Sometime," which even knocked the Beatles' "A Hard Day's Night" from Billboard's number one slot.)

As a postscript to this Tashlin auteur component, and consequently that of his disciple Lewis, too—drawing attention to the fact one is watching a movie—is an unusual but related Tashlin factor. The director was a major fan of Jack Benny, seemingly a far cry from the manic cartoonish Lewis. Yet, the Tashlin-Benny connection is multi-faceted, from the director's attack on America's obsession with success and money (Benny's persona is almost romantic about money in his miserliness), to Tashlin's kidding the very commercialism upon which it is built, such as references to *The Honeymooners*, *Rear Window* and "That's Amore." However, of equal importance in this Tashlin-Benny link is how the comedian unintentionally inspired the disjointed narratives of which the previous sudden intrusion of the Cold War into *Artists and Models* represents a prime example. Of Tashlin's animation days at Warner Bros. he later confessed:

> A lot of our humor came from Benny... [He] was on Sunday nights, when Jack was very, very big. We'd come in Monday morning, all of us were talking about Jack.... [He] had running jokes ... there'd be a knock on the door, Mr. Kitzel [Arthur Artie Auerbach, Benny cast member] would stick his head in the door and say one line. The rabbit [Bugs Bunny] started doing that—"What's up, doc?" Bing, door closes, out. We'd get all of this from Jack Benny. We really stole from all over.[11]

And obviously Tashlin has brought this fragmentation to his live action work, especially in *Artists and Models*, which is so definitive of his oeuvre.

What makes this Tashlin/Benny bond all the more intriguing is that the comedian starred in a 1937 version of *Art and Models*. Granted the two films are so different that many filmographies do not note the Benny film, as was often the case when such drastic changes were made.¹² However, while Benny's picture is a much less biting indictment of cultural conformity and consumer society, it does embrace the garbled storyline of a Tashlin picture. Plus, the older comedians' film is also self-conscious about being a movie. For example, Benny and *one* of the comedian's film fiancées, Gail Patrick (which the picture revels in ending *without* revealing whether Patrick or second fiancée Ida Lupino becomes the bride), enter a room in which the comedian's very popular period radio program is playing. This is the catalyst for the following dialogue:

> BENNY: Very clever fellow. I've always liked him.
> PATRICK: Oh really? I've never cared for him.
> BENNY: Oh well; everyone to their own taste.

The fact that Benny takes the slam so diplomatically anticipates another parallel with Tashlin. Though the director is constantly satirizing America's rampant commercialism as it races towards mass conformity, Tashlin acknowledges that he successfully operates in that same gaudy world, too, even though his message is often missed (satire's sad fate) by most of his viewers. As Benny saw the arbitrary absurdity and/or randomness of it all, so did Tashlin. As critic Ian Cameron has noted of the filmmaker:

> [It is] A synthetic world, a world whose artificiality Tashlin does not like. But when Tashlin doesn't like things, instead of attacking them with open hate, he simply finds them funny. There is in his films a dual approach to his subjects. An obvious affection for movies, stars, rock 'n' roll, horror comics, is coupled with a desire to use laughter to prick the bubble of illusion around them. His films are celebrations as much as satires.¹³

Whether one calls it satire, theatre of the absurd, or black comedy, there is usually an initial sadness/resignation before the laughter. One might liken it to John Huston's human comedy, *The Treasure of the Sierra Madre* (1948), in which Walter Huston encourages his fellow miner Tim Holt to join him in laughter after they realize their fortune in gold dust has blown away—laugh or go crazy.

Before continuing with Lewis' heavily influenced Tashlin persona, one must note that the director did not totally neglect the solo gifts of Dean Martin in *Artists and Models*. As critic David Ehrenstein observed, "Tashlin was a comedy director capable of working with almost *anyone*, tailoring his talents to suit the star at hand."¹⁴ Martin's "Lucky Song" routine of strolling and dancing along the avenue after acquiring some cartoon cash is every bit as charming as Bob Hope's "Silver Bells" street song sequence in *The Lemon Drop Kid* (1951, which an unbilled Tashlin co-directed with Sidney Lanfield). Martin, with his patented happy-go-lucky ultra-cool charisma, begins by passing a comic book stand. He then buys a carnation and begins his promenade by singing his up tempo *bullyboo bullyboy* "Lucky Song." Soon Dean becomes a singing pied piper as his parade collects a biracial cast of children and a small black jazz combo—trumpet, trombone, clarinet, and a hand drum. (Martin had always been a big fan of the Mills Brothers.) Dean's procession briefly thins to a delightful strolling duet with the unbilled little Nancy Abbate in a pink polka-dotted jumper. Eventually the scene comes full circle back to the stand and all the children get loads of comics. With the cavalcade coming to a stop, the viewer is next treated to Dean doing a casually slick tap dance number, which the petite Nancy perfectly duplicates. This back and forth continues before they blend into a briefly dancing team for the most pleasant *almost* finale (Dean needs to finish both the song and return to his moving children's menagerie). They march up/down with one foot on the curb and the other on the street. This finishes as he and his undersized followers begin to bend and hop over each other, as if to anticipate what is known in New York as "Johnny on the Pony." But in this case there is no piling on each other's backs. Nonetheless, it is an enchanting bit, a fugitive from back in the days when Martin & Lewis were actually a team. Now *Artists and Model*'s arguably two best routines, Jerry's misadventures with MacLaine trying to get to the sunbathing roof, and "The Lucky Song" do *not* even feature Martin & Lewis together. However, interestingly enough, each sequence succeeds by way of another, unofficial teaming.

Despite this delightful number *Artists and Models* is essentially Lewis' movie. But as is often asked, "Where does Frank Tashlin END and Jerry Lewis begin?"[15] Given what has already been written in this text (see also 1952's *Sailor Beware*, Chapter 2), it is a valid question. Lewis does, however, adhere to the *most basic* parameters of the personality comedians, both pre– and post–Tashlin. That is, Lewis has an easily definable shtick, he puts a high premium on physical/visual humor, is very much the underdog outsider, and often works best in some sort of team, whether it is an official duo (à la Martin), or the arbitrary coupling, such as the winning *Artists and Models* pairings with MacLaine.[16] That being said, like some of the best rhythm and blues riffing, or the music of your choice, this is the result of starting with a solid framework from which to creatively improvise. When Tashlin started working with Lewis, the writer/director essentially took the comedian in directions he was seemingly predisposed to go.

That being said, Lewis' persona is unusual. Win, lose, or draw, Chaplin's Tramp tended to soldier through whatever the obstacle, even after his nervous breakdown in *Modern Times* (1936).[17] And when society eventually turned on him, he transitioned to the darker world of *Monsieur Verdoux* (1947).[18] For Lewis, Chaplin was the template for everything, from the delicate balancing act of creating a persona capable of moving from comedy to pathos and back again, to the behind-the-screen filmmaker having total control. While Lewis managed the latter for a short time (but never on the creative level of Chaplin), he could not take his screen alter ego from comedy to pathos without slipping into bathos/sentimentality. One wonders if part of this failure could simply start with the monikers he attached to his comedy character. For Chaplin the Tramp was the "Little Fellow," while Lewis referenced his screen clown as "The Idiot." If the latter is his mindset going in, one is much more likely to have any comedy transitions slide into pity and the overly sentimental world which is bathos. This is best demonstrated by a Bogdanovich interview with Tashlin, concerning one of the director's later Lewis collaborations. When asked whether writer/director Tashlin was content with how *CinderFella* (1960) was edited, he responded:

> No, [producer/star] Jerry was so fond of the drama in *CinderFella* that, despite my strong objections, he cut most of the gags and left only the basically serious [sentimental] storyline. I felt the film was ruined by that.[19]

Lewis' aforementioned organ grinder monkey alter ego position slips into this same analogy. Even the comedian's first viewpoint of Martin & Lewis, as "Sex [Martin] and Slapstick [Lewis]," is a less than promising perspective on getting to like Jerry's screen character.[20] It also reinforces the position that from the beginning he felt he was the funny one. As noted in Chapter 2, that just was not the scenario. For example, the team's early press agent Jack Keller noted:

An *Artist and Models* sequence in which Dean Martin and Shirley MacLaine seem to be anticipating the happier Rat Pack days ahead.

> In every team, straight man and comedian, the comedian gets all the attention. Well, Dean *wasn't* a straight man. In his own way he was just as funny as Jerry. But people didn't bother to evaluate.[21]

Regardless, as also suggested in Chapter 2, the forerunners to Lewis' persona have much more in common with an Eddie Bracken, or a Danny Kaye (with whom Tashlin would later work), characters who are essentially physically and/or mentally handicapped. For instance, in yet another early Lewis description of his "Idiot" screen character, "I was walking around counting my nostrils ... [and whining], 'If I go out with girls, I get pimples.'"[22] (This could have been Bracken dialogue straight out of 1944's *Miracle of Morgan's Creek*.) Lewis' screen character was essentially surrealistically demented—a live action cartoon/comic book character, closer to The Three Stooges than Chaplin. (Indeed, during the 1950s and 1960s, there even was a Lewis comic book series.[23]) It is difficult to segue from that to pathos.

In contrast, Harry Langdon's screen character was a baby, oblivious to the world around him, not unlike Peter Sellers' Inspector Clouseau, and to paraphrase Frank Capra, "Safe only by the grace of God." Buster Keaton, "The Great Stone Face," was Langdon's opposite; his character was straight out of 1953's *Waiting for Godot*, decades before Samuel Beckett even penned his absurdist *killing time* play about a nonexistent God. But in some sort of cling to the wreckage philosophy, Keaton went about his stoic deadpan ways. He knew even in a nihilistic world, things could get worse; thus, reveal as little as possible for safety's sake and maintain that poker face. And Laurel & Hardy were "two minds without a single thought," as Kurt Vonnegut wrote of them in *Slapstick* (1976, to whom the novel is dedicated):

> The fundamental joke with Laurel and Hardy, it seems to me, was that they did their best with every test. They never failed to bargain in good faith with their destinies, and were screamingly adorable and funny on that account.[24]

The duo was like a spoof of Greek mythology's Sisyphus, who was punished for his self-serving craftiness by being forced to roll a large boulder up a hill, only to have it roll back down, with Sisyphus then fated to repeat his action for eternity. In fact, Laurel & Hardy's *The Music Box* (1932, the first Academy Award winner for Best Live Action Comedy Short Subject), is essentially a variation on that story. Except in this case, the duo is hired to deliver a large crated piano to a home up an extremely long stairway. However, this giant box seems to have anthropomorphic characteristics, and manages to roll back down every time the team almost accomplishes its goal, necessitating that the two repeat the process. The team was *not* being punished for any craftiness, a trait foreign to their beings but are simply doggedly persistent in attempting a task some unknown entity has assigned them, à la the clownish team of Vladimir and Estragon inexplicably *Waiting for [the existentialistic] Godot*. This is the inherent dignity Vonnegut attaches to Laurel & Hardy, adrift in this absurd world. Thus, with all these comedians—Chaplin, Langdon, Sellers' signature figure of Clouseau, Keaton, Laurel & Hardy and so many more—the "clowning" glory of adding pathos came easily. Yet, with Lewis, one is more inclined to embrace the 1969 view of celebrated comedy historian Raymond Durgnat:

> If Lewis enjoys universal approval the reason is simple: he is the incarnation of all average man's repressions (eroticisms, sadism, masochism, hysteria ... destructive violence.... Lewis is the symbol of bad taste considered as one of the fine arts.... This monster named Jerry fascinates us by the double game of attraction-repulsion.[25]

Much of this legacy lives on in the more recent work of Jim Carrey, Adam Sandler, and Will Ferrell (except when he shifts to his innocent persona, as in 2003's *Elf*). All this does not say there cannot be great humor linked to such comedians but sans the pathos—which Lewis said was his goal. Thus, Durgnat can still write:

> Any idiot can play the fool but only Jerry Lewis can play so many idiots simultaneously. He is imbecility sunk to the height of genius. He appears to have the mentality of a child of six but a six-year-old primed to explode into every emotion which he has been suppressing since he was one. He doesn't so much emote, as disintegrate into an emotional gamut ranging through Donald Duck, the Frankenstein monster, Pluto, Cheeta [the first woman to become the comic book, *Cheetah*, in 1943], [*Mad Magazine*'s] Alfred E. Neumann.[26]

Most of these Durgnat characters with whom Lewis seems densely populated are from the cartoon world, and short of feeling some compassion for poor Wile E. Coyote never capturing the irritating Road Runner, it is hard to work up much pathos for most cartoon characteristics.

Jerry's "Idiot" worked as long as he maintained his adolescent appearance, which helped make *Artists and Models*' basic premise of a kid obsessed by comics work so effectively. Yet, his movie character had an unusually short shelf life. While age invariably hurts the alter ego of most comedians, such as Harpo Marx's wrinkles eventually being detrimental to his pixie persona, Lewis' comedy window was extremely small. Goofy Jerry was that demented six-year-old needing massive quantities of Ritalin. As such, he was hysterical, as long as he was *not* your kid—or as W. C. Fields once said when asked if he liked children, "I do if they're properly cooked." Nonetheless, once Lewis got past his puberty/simian-like period, and looked his age, Lewis' comedy antics threatened to suggest he was mocking the mentally handicapped. One could draw a parallel of sorts with The Three Stooges. Their days of comic violence lasted longer. But once the team's short subjects from the 1930s and 1940s gave the Stooges' career a second act, via 1950s TV kiddie shows, their new movies showcased old men whose hitting and eye poking made one grimace over possible injury, rather than elicit laughs.

If pathos is anathema to cartoons/comic strips, cruelty and pain are not. Just think of Wile falling off yet another cliff, or being flattened by the ever present anvil. It is minimalized in *Artists and Models,* yet the aforementioned chiropractic pretzel scene first showcases Jerry suffering leg twisting cartoon pain. However, once he breaks free from this unnatural human mangled amalgamation, he directs the equally painful placement to other people's limbs. But his tendencies in this direction escalated as a solo non-adolescent-looking Lewis tweaked his style. Ironically, the cruelty factor is most substantial on Lewis' solo masterpiece, *The Nutty Professor* (1963), which placed 99th in the American Film Institute's "Top 100 Comedies."[27] The overriding ruthlessness comes by his savaging of a Dean Martin–like figure (Buddy Love), with Lewis playing both Love and the title character. Paradoxically, even as a solo he needs a variation of his former partner, callous or not.

This later increasingly hard-edged egotistical Lewis was also true of his stand-up comedy act in the 1970s and 1980s. One of his favorite routines was to request a handkerchief or tie from the audience, with the logical expectation the comedian was going to perform some sort of zany magic trick. Instead, the end result was Lewis cutting up the object and gifting the audience member with one of *his* own.[28] The result was usually more along the lines of spectator shock and/or nervous laughter—helped along by the implication his handkerchief or tie was a blessing which overruled any special value a patron might have attached to his own.

While the early Lewis screen persona was a frantic figure miles apart from the almost slow motion figure that was Langdon, they seem to have had two fatal characteristics in common. Neither one would fully respect and follow their mentors (for Langdon it was Frank Capra[29]), nor could either manage to sustain his own do-it-all "Chaplin Disease." It seems a fair assessment, given the earlier question asking, "Where does Frank Tashlin END and Jerry Lewis begin?" And the legendary critic Raymond Durgnat went a step further: "It's impossible to separate the work of Tashlin from that of Jerry Lewis."[30]

Yet, during the making of *Artists and Models*, a film which was such a valentine to Lewis that this book is defining it as his best *solo* picture of the 1950s, the comedian was still questioning Tashlin's every decision. Thus, at one point the director kicked an incredulous Lewis off the set! "I mean it, Jerry. Off! You're a discourteous, obnoxious prick, an embarrassment to me and a disgrace to the profession."[31] And it was not limited to victimizing Tashlin, or Lewis minimizing Martin:

> Jerry and [producer Hal] Wallis were fighting openly on the set. It was hardly their first set-to but Jerry was feeling increasingly powerful as a filmmaker in his own right.[32]

No less a critic/film historian than David Thomson has called Wallis, who first put Martin & Lewis in film, one of the great executives in movie history (and this from a Bette Davis biography addressing the scope of the producer's career).[33] And when the London-born Thomson focuses his insightfully fiendish wit on Lewis, he best capsulizes the comedian's current standing in the United States:

> To live in America is to experience the native incredulity at Lewis being taken seriously. Few things are held against the whole of France more fiercely than French love of Lewis.[34]

To Lewis' credit, the aforementioned Tashlin quote comes from a text the comedian co-authored, but sadly it is the same book with the throat-choking hypocritical titled *Dean & Me: A Love Story*.[35] Moreover, Lewis' honesty here is not unlike when his screen character laughs at Hedda Hopper's hat during *The Patsy*. Both diverse actions are well taken. But in each case he then ruins the action by immediately drawing attention to it, as if to pat himself on the back about being so heartfelt and/or decent. Regardless, as noted in the text's examination of Martin & Lewis' *Sailor Beware* (1952, see Chapter 2), the comedian is still incapable of either giving Martin credit beyond being a great straight man, or toning down his own ego. One wonders how different things might have been for Lewis if he had ever really owned up to reality, as Langdon eventually had. For example, after Chaplin, Langdon had been one of Bob Hope's early comedy favorites. As a young comedian Hope was later able to meet Langdon on the vaudeville circuit. But for Hope,

> it was a sad encounter with a boyhood idol.... Langdon had lost his movie career ... [and as] I learned later, he had done himself in by masterminding his own pictures. He had forgotten that a clever little guy named Frank Capra had directed the best Langdon features. One day between shows, Landon told me, "Young man, if you ever go out to Hollywood and become a star—and I think you could—don't make my mistake. Don't try to convince yourself that you're a genius."[36]

While Lewis had more post–Tashlin success than Langdon sans Capra, the result was eventually the same, a shortened or intermittent film career. Next came a public's loss of interest in Langdon, and a lack of creditability for Lewis, unless one was under ten, or French. And this comes from a Martin & Lewis fan. (Their pictures were often re-issued during my teen years in the 1960s and early 1970s). But by the time of Lewis' solo *The Family Jewels* (1965, in which he plays seven parts), I knew that the creative cheese was off the cracker. My generation was experiencing an early form of "binge watching," and for us, the solo Lewis just stopped being funny. For someone who prided himself on knowing everything about film, Lewis seems to have missed the classic dark comedy lite picture, *Kind Hearts and Coronets* (1949, in which Alec Guinness did a tutorial on playing multiple parts, ultimately "essaying" eight roles).

In fairness to Lewis, one could argue that 1960s *reality* had set in, and demented comedy hardly seemed relevant. Except those balanced Martin & Lewis films still seemed funny. And the carryover casual coolness of Martin's "what the..." persona made him an even bigger star in the 1960s. So what about the French? They continued to embrace Lewis for two quite different reasons. At ground level, his screen character seemed, in their minds, to represent a satire of what was once called "the ugly American"—loud, obnoxious, self-absorbed and, all in caps, I-D-I-O-T-S. (This was a perspective painfully reinforced by my spending the summer of 1970 abroad.) In contrast, on a French intellectual level, the birth of Lewis the filmmaker also paralleled the early 1950s explosion of interest in what the French defined as the *auteur [author] theory*, in which one individual could put his or her signature on the most collaborative of art forms. And for a time both Lewis and Tashlin were able to accomplish this task. Of course, French and American comradery seems to have diverged sometime early after Lafayette. To paraphrase Mark Twain, when angered he was fond of saying, "That's Un-American; that's Un-British; that's French."

Regardless, how did *Artists and Models* do upon its initial release? It was critical and commercial success but not on a caliber with their early years. For example, when 1952's *Sailor Beware* appeared, the duo was number one at the box office, while in 1955 they had slipped to number seven.[37] While still significant, a more telling math lesson comes form the following equation: in 1952 two of their pictures were among the annual top ten moneymakers. *Sailor Beware* was fifth followed by their *Jumping Jacks* at number six.[38] Conversely, in the team's final two years, 1955 and 1956, none of their pictures made the top 20 box office charts.

There were still raves, such as the *New York Herald Tribune* calling it "one of the funnier Martin & Lewis pictures."[39] But for once you were just as likely to have a critic, such as the *New York Daily News'* Wanda Hale, opine, "There they are [Martin & Lewis], bigger than they have ever been but twice as tiresome."[40] *Variety*'s critic, William Brogdon, was tepid, observing, "It is the kind of nonsense ... that fans of the team like and usually buy ... [but making it clear that any positives noted came] with the critic's reservations already stressed."[41] However, as a foreshadowing of the future, he did seem genuinely refreshed by the Martin routines using "Innamorata" and "The Lucky Song."

The ho-hum response pattern is captured perfectively in the *New York World-Telegram and Sun* review title, "'Artists Models' Just More Martin and Lewis."[42] But like the *Time* critique, neither assessment does much more than recite the convoluted plot.[43] The chapter has already opened with the *New York Times'* crack about the neglect of Martin, and essentially also takes a ho-hum attitude, though critic Bosley Crowther does confess that Tashlin's cartoonish "scene in which he [Jerry] and several masseuses get into a snarl of arms and legs ... is convulsively funny."[44]

Only the *Hollywood Reporter* appears to give the picture a rave from start to finish, beginning with this opening:

> A lavish, colorful laughfest, "Artists and Models" is a hilarious piece of dementia spiced with gorgeous femmes, lively tunes and tastefully rich backgrounds that gain in splendor from exquisite Technicolor. The laughs keep coming in this merry romp that leaves one resolved that if Dean Martin and Jerry Lewis ever again speak of splitting up they should be sentenced to star in a remake of "Aaron Slick of Punkin Crick" [a 1955 hillbilly movie].[45]

Plus, the title for this piece has an interesting foreshadowing with regard to a team about to fold its tents, notwithstanding the hillbilly film threat—"Martin and Lewis, MacLaine Sparkle." That is, the title says one thing, and the critique says two other subtextual things. First, it correctly says MacLaine stole the picture:

> Shirley MacLaine ... is merely terrific. This delightful pixie is definitely headed for stardom. She has a magnetic personality, dances with genuine grace even when clowning, has a good voice when she sings straight and has a rare sense of comedy. She fits perfectly into the Martin & Lewis style of rowdy humor.[46]

And Dean, despite minimal time with Jerry, finally receives equal ink time with his "partner": "Martin was never better ... [and 'Innamorata' is] bound to be another solid hit for Martin, who sings it in wonderful voice."[47]

Despite this being arguably Lewis' best picture, from his MacLaine stairwell number, to the pretzel masseuse routine, this should also be seen as a launching pad of sorts for both Martin and MacLaine, whose solo careers would soon eclipse Lewis.' Moreover, Martin and MacLaine would become something of an unofficial team themselves, starring in seven more pictures together, while she also became an informal member (with Dean of yet another larger troupe—Frank Sinatra's "Rat Pack").

While Tashlin's later writing and directing influence on Tony Randall is further examined in 1957's *Will Success Spoil Rock Hunter* (see Chapter 11), what of Lewis' legacy, especially as filtered through *Artists and Models*? First, this is a major transition picture for him, if his two most praised sequences are examined. The first was the extended routine with MacLaine, which was built upon his difficulties in getting his folding beach chair to the roof. It was more of a *traditional* comedy sketch, despite its surrealistic overtones. Most major comedians who preceded him, at some time, explored the comic mysteries of a collapsible deck chair. For example, Lewis worshipped Chaplin, claiming to have seen all his films, and read everything he could about his idol. Thus, Jerry would have been well aware of the funniest bit in Chaplin's *A Day's Pleasure* (1919), in which the Tramp has a wrestling match with said chair.

Other such examples are too numerous to count. Yet, two would seem most memorable to note. From the golden age of American film comedy, one of the best bits in W. C. Fields' greatest picture, *It's a Gift* (1934), has him becoming so discombobulated by his folding deck chair that he uses it for kindling. In contrast, by the mid–1950s Lewis was well aware of France's auteur fascination with his work. Yet, even if he was not, anyone seriously interested in 1950s comedy would have seen France's legendary Jacques Tati's international hit film *Mr. Hutlot's Holiday* (1953), which involves an inspired routine in which Tati's bumbling title character mightily struggles with one of these chairs. And as an important rider, as it relates to Lewis and Tashlin, is the focus of this Oscar-nominated Best Original Screenplay. The inept Mr. Hulot is so shish-kebabbed by modern society's obsession with the latest material goods, which subtextually satires both American-style consumerism, and the increasingly fast forward world—are the same targets as Tashlin's Lewis.

The second pivotal *Artists and Models* Lewis sequence is the pretzel routine—a cartoonish component which will come to represent taking personality comedy in an entirely new direction. It is not that such scenes were unheard of. In Chaplin's *Easy Street* (1917), the Tramp's Mutual film nemesis Eric Campbell is the neighborhood bully whose fighting prowess was occasionally heightened by having a dummy thrown into the mix. What was different about Tashlin's Lewis was both the added frequency of cartoonland occurring, and the transparency with which it materialized. Plus, Lewis was Tashlin's ideal comedian to send "down the rabbit's hole," since the demented comedian was already predisposed to be an animated figure, an obvious precursor to the rubber-faced caricature Jim Carrey in *The Mask* (1994). Even without Tashlin's added push, Lewis had already found a historic niche to survive, after a fashion, for America's perennial anti-hero—be, or appear to be, mad as a hatter. Nevertheless, depending on one's tastes, do you really want to be down a rabbit hole?

10

Danny Kaye
The Court Jester (February 2, 1956)

> I wasn't born a fool. It took work to get this way.
> —a frequently uttered Danny Kay comment

The only improvement in having Danny Kaye and Jerry Lewis in back-to-back chapters would have been to reverse the order, since the latter comedian, consciously or not, built upon the nearly demented Kaye persona. That is, both comedians were in America's anti-heroic little man mold of being caught in the uncaring snare of the modern world. Yet, as previously discussed in this text, while other comedians found various ways to survive, Kaye and his contemporary 1940s funnyman, Eddie Bracken, spontaneously fell into the oblivious safety of becoming unbalanced. Possibly, Mack Sennett notwithstanding, little in comic American film falls prior to B.C. (Before Chaplin), this march towards jumping the rails in the increasingly stressful contemporary world might be traced to Charlie's assembly line breakdown in *Modern Times* (1936). Yet, while he recovered, the Bracken-Kaye-Lewis movement towards the early Jim Carrey has been to simply become unhinged in this seemingly equally unhinged world. One could argue, as Alan Dale does in *Comedy Is a Man in Trouble* (2000), that Lewis is "simply underdeveloped," yet it still does not address the fact that once he outgrew his juvenile persona, his career tanked.[1]

Moreover, this direct Kaye-Lewis link is reinforced by Kurt Singer's pioneering English biography of the former comedian, *The Danny Kaye Saga* (1957), which notes "The British press [has] called this young man 'the only satisfying idiot in show business in thirty years.'"[2] Plus, as the previous chapter recorded, Lewis' own name for his screen character was the "Idiot." But the ultimate statement for Kaye's alter ego having a frequently demented disposition comes from the comedian's definitive biography, Martin Cottfpried's *Nobody's Fool: The Lives of Danny Kaye* (1994): "[From 1945 on] Kaye's by-now-settled screen persona ... [was] schizophrenic."[3] The secret of that schizophrenic alter ego is marvelously captured in Cottfpried's subtitle, "The Lives of Danny Kaye," which also bleeds into his personal life, which will be addressed shortly.

As a related aside, just as Lewis's greatest popularity since the mid–1950s has been in France, during this same time period Kaye's most significant popularity has been in Great

Danny Kaye more than fits his title in *The Court Jester*.

Britain, which has fueled the comedian into being the most appreciable of Anglophiles. In fact, with an ego to match Lewis,' when Bob Hope played the Palladium, he had some fun at Kaye's "hat size" expense:

> I wanna tell you it's great to be in London. Danny Kaye nearly refused me a re-entry permit—but I made it.... He loves it here in London, you know. He always gets the best of everything—he even has mono-grammed fog.... He visits me when he comes to America. You should see his dressing room here—two mirrors and a throne.[4]

10. Danny Kaye 125

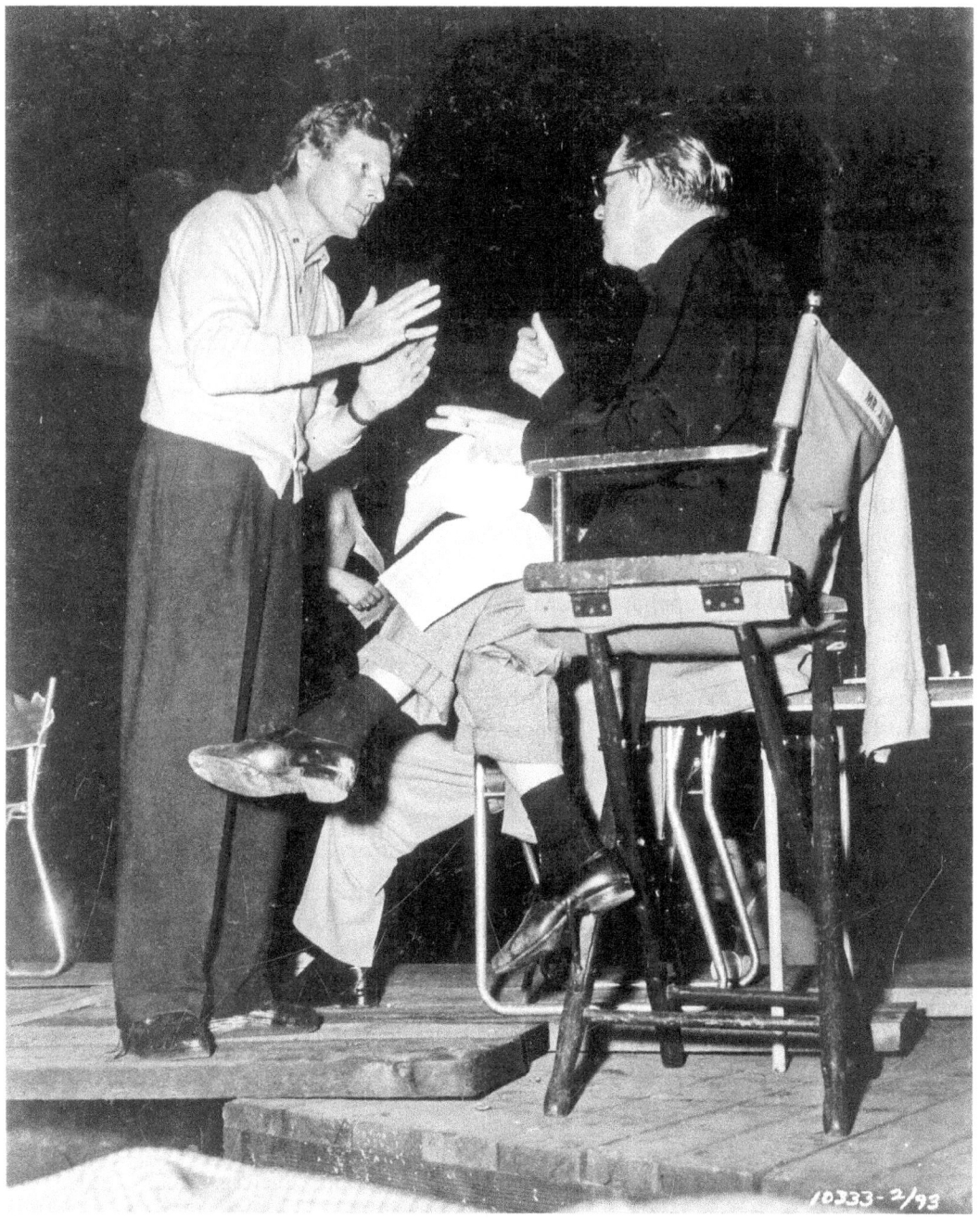

Danny Kaye and co-director/co-writer Melvin Frank on the set of *The Court Jester*.

Egos aside, when one reviews some of Kaye's best film work prior to *Jester*, the loopy parallels anticipating Lewis are all the more apparent. For example, in *Wonder Man* (1945), Kaye plays "two super-identical twins." Estranged for years, one has become the entertainer Buzzy Bellow, whose description bears a striking resemblance to a Lewis persona yet to be formed—a loud, zany nightclub performer. Unfortunately for Buzzy, he witnesses a murder and soon joins the victim on the other side. But death merely represents an inconvenience in search of justice, as Buzzy's spirit enlists the services of his brother to double for him. However, this sibling switch has several problems, beyond the comic shock of a ghostly reconciliation. The other twin, one Edwin Dingle, is a quiet professorial type writing a history book. And before retribution can be accomplished, Dingle the duplicate must not only be a dead ringer (a literal fate if Buzzy's killers have their way); he must become a funny facsimile of his show business brother, or this exact exercise in Doppelgänger righteousness cannot happen. Thus, Dingle must periodically be possessed by Buzzy. The results are what one would anticipate of Lewis, or later see a variation of in Steve Martin's *All of Me* (1984, in which the spirit of Lily Tomlin takes over half of his body—from the novel *Me Two*).

Another Kaye vehicle which obviously lends itself to the bizarre cartoonish world of the future Lewis is the 1947 adaptation of James Thurber's short story, "The Secret Life of Walter Mitty." Kaye's henpecked title character pinballs from one great adventure to another—in his day dreams—as all about him he is harassed by everyone from a domineering mother to a dimwitted fiancée. There are other comparable Kaye-Lewis examples, but the most intriguing one is by the same duo that wrote, directed, and produced *Jester*— Melvin Frank and Norman Panama's *Knock on Wood* (1954).

Yes, Martin & Lewis were a hit team by then. Yet the timing and subject matter of Kaye in the Frank-Panama picture is most fascinating because it opened the year *before* the Lewis-dominated, comic book-oriented *Artists and Models* (1955, see previous chapter). Kaye plays a ventriloquist whose love life is a forever stalled by his jealous dummy—Danny is as demented as Lewis' comic book-driven man/child. Plus, the title tune of *Knock on Wood* is often confused with the seemingly appropriate song "Everyone Thinks I'm Crazy," fittingly from the 1941 animated film *Woody Woodpecker*. And to add to the cartoon confusion, Kaye later sings "The Woody Woodpecker" song in *Knock on Wood*. One cannot help but think that the "batty" baton has been passed from one comedian to another.

Moreover, another parallel between Kaye and Lewis occurs behind the screen, too. They did their best work when teamed with a specific writer/director auteur. For Kaye it was clearly the Frank-Panama duo, while Frank Tashlin served that purpose for the solo Lewis. At first glance, with Frank-Panama starting out as late 1930s radio writers for Bob Hope, one might be quick to posit them as old school versus the cartoonish Tashlin bursting onto the 1950s cinematic scene. Yet, the parallels continue, with regard to their uses of Kaye and Lewis, though the latter's yelling and whining were more like cartoon sound effects, unedited anarchy. In contrast, Kaye's verbal sendups were polished tongue-twisting lyrics and dialogue, like a cartoon on the edge of human perception. And much of it was written by his real life wife, Sylvia Fine. Yet, Frank-Panama hardly needed any assistance along those lines. Parody and witty patter were at the heart of their material. The writing duo were also masters of verbal slapstick. This includes the tricky axiom the team had the title character spy Red Skelton remember in *The Southern Yankee* (1948), "The paper's in the pocket of the boot with the buckle, [and] the map is in the packet in the pocket of the jacket." They even top this with Kaye's *Jester*, which will be addressed shortly.

Frank-Panama do not, however, spoof the 1950s to the darker satirically biting degree of Tashlin. Yet, *Jester* is a near flawless parody of all those elephant-sized epics of old which often bogged down this movie decade. Yet, once again, it was Hollywood bumping shoulders with rival '50s television. Again, in order to pry TV viewers away from their small and invariably black and white screens (complete with rabbit ear antennas, to hopefully defuse an assorted array of bad reception), movies gave viewers big stories on huge Cinemascope screens, in some variety of vivid color (from Vista Vision to Technicolor), and stereoscopic sound. Indeed, 1930s glamour boy Robert Taylor gave his career a second act by starring in such '50s blockbusters as MGM's unofficial swashbuckling trilogy *Ivanhoe* (1952), *Knights of the Round Table* (1953), and *The Adventures of Quentin Durward* (1955, which moved the medieval action from England to France).

Consequently, the time was perfect for *Jester*'s musical comedy spoof of these Knighthood sagas, with a Robin Hood–type character named the Black Fox (Edward Ashley). His mission is to have the true English infant-king recognized, after a usurping villain (Cecil Parker) has seized power as King Roderick I. The parody is enriched by having the king's closet ally, Sir Ravenhurst, be played by Basil Rathbone—who portrayed an extraordinary dueling villain against Errol Flynn's title character in arguably the most significant swashbuckling picture in Hollywood's golden age—*The Adventures of Robin Hood* (1938).

So where does Kaye's Hubert Hawkins fit into what is becoming a most twisted tale? Well, the Black Fox, who Kaye's jester cartoonishly enjoys imitating, with the help of his little carnival friends (the "Hermione Midgets"), feels Hawkins is a mere minstrel. Thus, he is denied being a fighting part of the rebels. But the Fox entrusts him with getting the infant-king to some safe haven, accompanied by Glynis Johns' Maid Jean. On the journey a romance develops between the two. However, their mission takes a new turn when Kaye's character gets the opportunity to enter King Roderick's castle as the monarch's new jester. The Fox has been anxious to obtain a key from the sovereign's private quarters which would open a secret passage to the fortress. Such an entrance would more easily enable the rebels to overthrow the false king.

Rathbone's character has orchestrated obtaining this popular jester from the Italian court, though given the time period, he is known only by reputation. Thus, when Maid Jean and Hawkins' chance to share their lodging one night with the real celebrated entertainer on his way to Roderick's castle, the jester is conked on the head cartoon style and Kaye's Hawkins takes his place. While he briefly struggles to fit in, the king inexplicitly likes him, unlike Woody Allen's medieval court jester episode in *Everything You Always Wanted to Know About Sex* (but were afraid to ask)* (1972), which ultimately results in the loss of his head.

Yet death soon enters the *Jester* world, too. Unknown to the false King Roderick, Rathbone fears he is losing his favored court position. Thus, instead of simply attempting to curry royal favor, he has hired a jester who also doubles as a hit man. So why does Rathbone not figure out quickly that his allegedly Italian jester is not "Guido the ice man," too? Well, the answer lies with the king's daughter, Princess Gwendolyn (Angela Lansbury), who is anxious to find the love of her life, while her father wants to use her as a marrying pawn in an alliance with the powerful warlord Sir Griswold (Robert Middleton). The princess tells her witchy maid-in-waiting Griselda (Mildred Natwick) that if the maid does not produce a real lover, she will meet the fate of Allen's jester.

This is the catalyst for Kaye's standard demented split personality persona to surface, because Griselda puts a spell on the jester and transforms him into a brave, swashbuckling lover who immediately wins the princess' heart. The only catch is that this hypnotic spell comes and goes whenever someone snaps their fingers. Consequently, Kaye is constantly ricocheting between the Jerry Lewis–like prototype he helped create, and a dashing devil-may-care Errol Flynn. And to paraphrase his aforementioned biographer, Martin Cottfpried, Kaye has now "settled into his schizophrenic alter ego." Moreover, since Basil Rathbone's potential court rivals all favor the Princess's marriage to Sir Griswold, Griselda casually poisons them off to protect herself. Not surprisingly, Rathbone is more than happy with his seemingly killer clown. They even develop a chummy, often repeated, swiftly spoken bit of comic dialogue that represents comic gibberish, since it does not mean the same thing to either of them:

> KAYE: Get it.
> RATHBONE: Got it.
> KAYE: Good.

Soon, however, while Rathbone is yet to figure out this jester is not whom he hired, Lansbury's princess is making her love for Kaye's character clear to her father the king. Naturally, he cares nothing for her feelings, since it would negate his plans for an alliance with Sir Griswold. Thus, the vexed king decrees poor Kaye to be executed. Yet, Rathbone's character proves an unlikely liberator to the jester. Thinking that only the Black Fox could have accomplished all that Kaye seems to have done, from killing Rathbone's potential rivals, to winning the princess' hand, he proposes that the jester should be made an official knight. Once that is accomplished, since a mere clown cannot engage in jousting, Kaye's character can legally take on Sir Griswold in mortal combat for the princess.

Rathbones' ever conniving Ravenhurst has done this to eliminate yet another potential rival (Sir Griswold) for influence over the king—assuming that if Kaye is really the Fox, he will make short work of this knight. At this point, *The Court Jester* moves from being a good movie to a truly inspired one. First, Kaye's Hawkins is comically rushed through all the lengthy tests which are normally required to become a knight—including his unwanted assistance in getting over a wall in full body armor. One is reminded of all the fun that Mark Twain had putting his knights through the ringer in the novelist's underrated *A Connecticut Yankee in King Arthur's Court* (1889), such as having a mosquito get inside one suit of armor.

Once the crash course is completed, it is time for Kaye's jester-turned-knight to be challenged to joust Sir Griswold. Glynis John's character, who was caught and brought to the castle shortly after she parted from Kaye (though the baby-king is still safe), encourages her love to accept the fight. She has found the key to the secret passage and promises that the real Black Fox will soon come to his aid. But the tunnel collapses and there is only space enough for Kaye's little people to later help eliminate the king. Yet, they cannot arrive in time to stop the fight.

Next, the princess' witchy maid, Natwick's Griselda, attempts to help Kaye, since her life is on the line, too. Griselda's plan is to poison Sir Griswold's vessel (cup) in the pre-jousting toast between the two combatants. Yet, Kaye's reluctant knight must be warned about which cup to take. What follows is a tongue-twisting exchange which, as one Kaye biographer rightfully suggests, ranks among the best comic dialogues ever written for a screen clown:[5]

> NATWICK: Griswold dies as he drinks the toast.
> KAYE: What?

NATWICK: Listen—I put a pellet of poison in one of the vessels.
KAYE: Which one?
NATWICK: The one with the figure of a pestle [a grinding tool].
KAYE: The vessel with the pestle.
NATWICK: Yes, but you don't want the vessel with the pestle. You want the chalice [often a communion cup] from the palace.
KAYE: I don't want the vessel with the pestle. I want the chalice from the—the what?
GLYNIS JOHN interrupts: The chalice from the palace.
KAYE: Hmmm…
NATWICK: It's a little crystal chalice with a figure of a palace.
KAYE: Does the chalice from the palace have the pellet with the poison?
NATWICK: No. The pellet with the poison's in the vessel with the pestle.
KAYE: The pestle with the vessel.
JOHNS: The vessel with the pestle.
KAYE: What about the palace from the chalice?
NATWICK: Not the palace from the chalice. The chalice from the palace.
KAYE: Where's the pellet with the poison?
NATWICK: In the vessel with the pestle.
JOHNS: Don't you see? The pellet with the poison's in the vessel with the pestle.
NATWICK: The chalice with the palace has the brew that is true.
JOHNS: It's easy. I can say it.
KAYE: Well, then, you fight him.

Kaye, in his bumbling anti-heroic mode, continues to struggle with these directions, making mistake after mistake with this comic life or death axiom. Finally, he repeats it correctly (or is that just the law of averages?). Nonetheless, he proudly repeats it to John's witchy maid. However, soon there is a problem:

NATWICK: There's been a change. They broke the chalice from the palace.
KAYE: [He replies in shock] They broke the chalice from the palace?
NATWICK: And replaced it with a flagon [a drinking container with a lid].
KAYE: A flagon?
NATWICK: With a figure of a dragon.
KAYE: [Distraught] A flagon with a dragon.
NATWICK: Right.
KAYE: And they put the pellet with the poison in the vessel with the pestle?
NATWICK: No, no. The pellet with the poison's in the flagon with the dragon. The vessel with the pestle has the brew that is true.
KAYE: The pellet with the poison's in the flagon with the dragon. The vessel with the pestle has the brew that is true.
NATWICK: Remember that.
KAYE: [Unconvincingly] Yes, thank you very much. [One can almost feel the flop sweat. After all, his demented side has no sense of an epiphany. Mundane reality for a witch seems like deathly gibberish to him.]

While Kaye later had an aversion to discussing a movie career that did not have enough *Court Jesters* in it, even he was no doubt thinking of routines like "the vessel with the pestle" when he observed in 1970 (a year after his last movie): "In a few of those pictures—I hate to use the word but those were classic routines."[6] And one is hardly limited to biographers, or the comedian himself, for highlighting the sketch. Nearly 30 years later, film comedy historian Kathryn Bernheimer included *The Court Jester* in her book, *The 50 Funniest Movies of all Time* (1999), in part, because

> among the all-time great comedy routines, Danny Kaye's dazzling rendition of the ... "chalice from the palace" ranks alongside Abbott & Costello's "Who's on first?" as the funniest ever recorded on film.[7]

And if the picture did not have brilliant bits of wordsmithing like this, there were Syliva Fine's wordplaying songs, such as "The Maladjusted Jester," and ambitious puns like "an unemployed jester is nobody's fool," from her soliloquy, "The Jester's Lament."

Plus, Kaye did not just protect the baby-king, whose royal I.D. was a "Purple Pimpernel—[a primrose flower]" birthmark on his hienie, sometimes the comedian seemed to be reverting to a tyke-like condition himself. For example, Kaye would do anything to convince the false king and his court that he was the well-traveled jester they expected, such as to blurt out randomly in a kiddie voice, "I found a bow and arrow and I learned to shoot. I found a little horn to toot. Now I can shoot and toot; ain't I cute." Sometimes he literally did seem to resort to baby gibberish, such as when Kaye's blather bluffed having been in several European courts with a burst of assorted language sounding gobbledy gook.

This was entirely different from the brilliant mumbo jumbo of German which Chaplin did in his satirical speech as Hynkel/Hitler in *The Great Dictator* (1940). Because part of Chaplin's comedy was to throw in the occasional funny-sounding German word of reference, such "sauerkraut" or "The Katzenjammer" (a reference to a popular American comic strip entitled "The Katzenjammer Kids," which often focused on two bratty German boys that usually resulted in spankings. "Katzenjammer" roughly translates as "wailing cat"). In contrast, Kaye's riffing of the Romance languages was pure comic claptrap.

Thus far, this Kaye overview of *The Court Jester* has concentrated on all its wonderful verbal slapstick. Yet, this brilliant latter half of the picture also showcases a comic array of physical slapstick and simple visual humor. A brilliant example occurs when lightening strikes and magnetizes his suit of armor. Once Kaye is dressed, assorted metal objects of his and Sir Griswold come through mid-air and stick on the comedian, as if some of Natwick's alleged magical gifts have rubbed off on him. This is then eclipsed by the two combatants, Kaye and Robert Middleton's wonderful straight man Sir Griswold, attempt to clankingly walk towards the king prior to the bout. Griswold's knight is a large and imposing figure encased in an equally substantial suit of armor. Not surprisingly, the smaller magnetized metal-attired Kaye is drawn to Griswold's armor. Consequently, they suddenly walk as one, forming a triangle of sorts. That is, Kaye's shoulder armor has him leaning into Griswold, while the comedian's feet keep him semi-anchored.

One is reminded of Chaplin's pre-boxing sequence in *City Lights* (1931), when the comedian's Tramp faces annihilation from Hank Mann's prizefighter. Chaplin's little fellow actually flirts with Mann's Boxer in the locker room, as if to say go lightly on me in the ring. Well, Kaye does not do anything so overt. Yet, as he and Griswold attempt to walk, the comedian is all over him, producing a most odd expression on the normally deadpan Griswold.

There is much more knights-of-old parody in this prolonged sequence, such as the fact-based elaborate lifting system involved in getting heavy warriors on their poor horses. Yet literally the *topper* to the jousting sequence is when Kaye's helmeted head seems to be sliced off by Griswold's weapon. Then slowly the comedian's noodle comes out, like Bert the defense Turtle's head in those 1950s government *Duck and Cover* civil defense films that suggested death from a nuclear apocalypse could be averted by following that axiom. While even as a kid I had serious doubts about this safety tip, it turns out to be pretty effective if one finds themselves jousting and there is a wayward sword coming at you.

However, what makes this a real moon-shot movie is yet to come. Just when the viewer thinks every knighthood stereotype has been parodied, Kaye has a sword fight with one of Hollywood's great fencers, the previously mentioned Basil Rathbone. Their dual works on several levels, beyond actually using a figure associated with straight swashbuckling pictures. First, because of the accomplished fencing abilities Rathbone brought to the part, and Kaye working so hard to approach his foe's skills, the spoofing is pushed to a higher level—"parody of reaffirmation."[8] This approach avoids broad burlesque and, at times, seems to emulate the genre being spoofed. This provides an added comic tension—a sense of thrill comedy—not to be found in transparent parody.

Second, periodically Natwick's Griselda works her magic during the duel, making Kaye fluctuate between anti-hero and a dashing double for the figure he so admires, the Black Fox. This also reinforces Kaye's schizophrenic screen persona. Third, at times, while Kaye is so ensconced in his dazzling devil-may-care Douglas Fairbanks, Sr./Errol Flynn mode, he brings the burlesque full circle back to a comically casual status of undisguised parody, such as almost apathetically fencing while seated. Indeed, I am convinced that Kevin Kline's comic dueling sequences in his underrated portrayal of the senior Fairbanks in *Chaplin* (1992) were inspired by Kaye's bout with Rathbone. Interestingly, however, when the spell is not working for Kaye during his combat, his fearful howling sounds just like that of his demented semi-protégé Jerry Lewis.

Regardless, this being a personality comedy, all ends happily, with Kaye getting the false king deposed, in part, with the help of all those little people managing to squeeze through the partially blocked secret passageway. And even Sir Griswold and his army become allies when he realizes the true heir to the throne is the baby-king. Ironically, however, for Kaye, one of his final duties was a repetition of an early obligation for which he was also answerable; Kaye was responsible for constantly pulling down and pulling up the little coverlet of the underage king in order to prove to all doubters that the youngster had the royal birthmark of the "Purple Pimpernel"—evidently a sovereign tush cannot be exposed for any length of time.

Ironically, as cartoonish as the "Purple Pimpernel" conclusion, or simply its parody in general, the film reminds me of a provocative painting by Kaye contemporary Marsden Hartley, an American Modernist of the 1930s Regionalist School of Art. Fellow Regionalists, like Grant Wood and Thomas Hart Benton, often brought a caricature touch to their work. That is the ambivalence in Hartley's startling painting *Three Friends* (1941). The work is of a standing recrucified Christ supported on either side by a jester and a boxer—marginalized modernized figures in a world yet again gone amiss. *The Court Jester* was an impressive knightly parody of the Middle Ages (best known for its misguided Crusades), made during the fears of the Cold War. The *Jester*'s message, beyond the laughter of clown comedy and parody, was to help viewers forget, at least briefly, the threat of a modern Black Plague, a nuclear apocalypse. Plus keep in mind, the following year Ingmar Bergman took another jester and knight fable, the darkly comic *Seventh Seal* (1957), and showed how human foolishness of that period had more than a little in common with modern man's predisposition

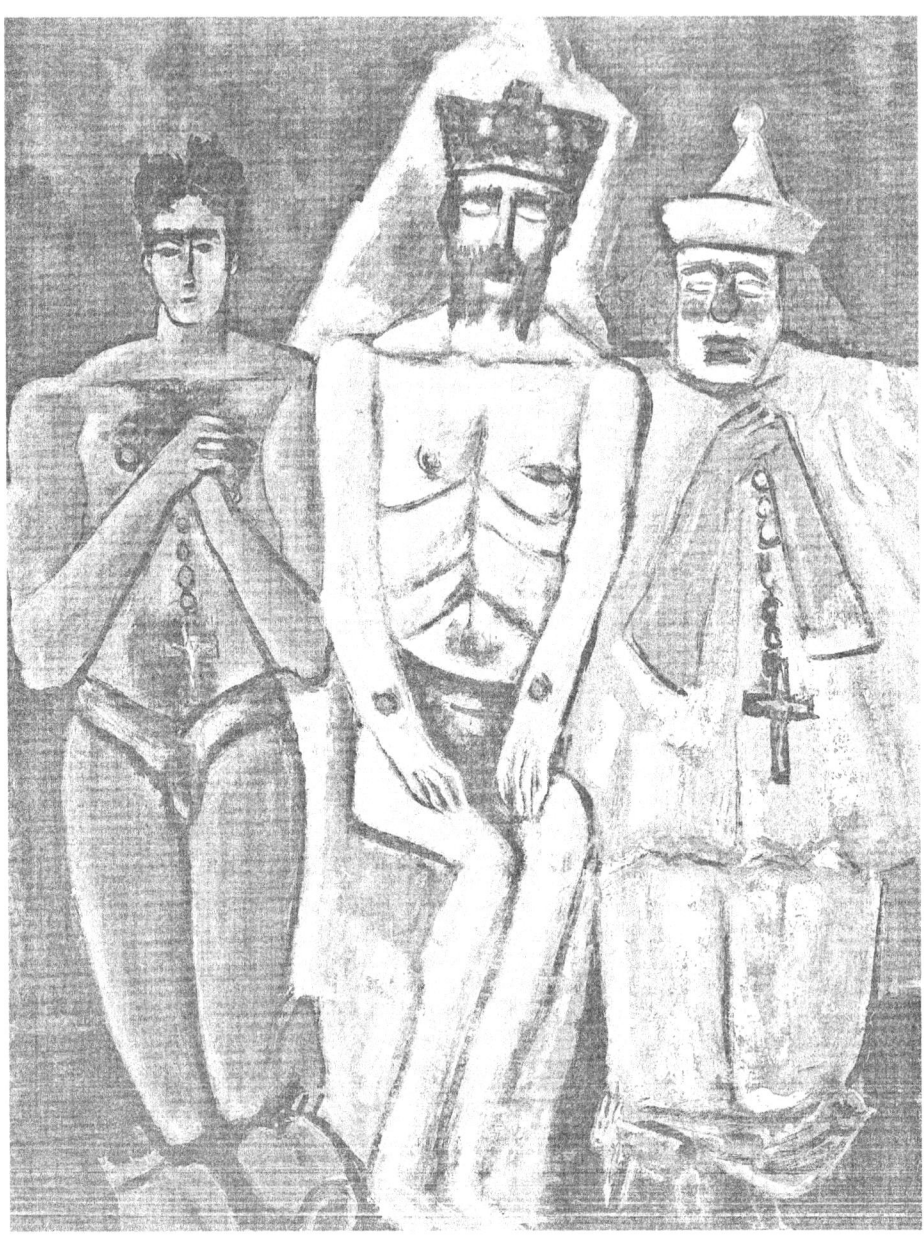

Marden Hartley's darkly comic pertinent painting *Three Friends* (1944). Photograph by Kevin Montague. Gift of Sarahanne Adams Hope in memory of Henry R. Hope, Indiana University Art Museum, 91.28.

for self-destruction, too. Was it any wonder that this time around Hartley's shell-shocked Christ now wanted a jester and a bodyguard? Indeed, Twain's 19th century dark comedy *A Connecticut Yankee in King Arthur's Court* actually combined the silly world of Kaye's jester and Bergman's tale of approaching death with a closing bloodbath. It would seem that mankind needs as many jesters as possible, both for distraction today and for tomorrow's approaching abyss.

Regardless, what was the critical response to the *Jester*, a film the American Film Institute later (2000) listed as one of the top 100 comedies ever made?[9] The movie's period reviews are nearly the best of any of the focus films in this text. For example, under the *New York Journal America*'s critique title, "Danny Kaye in Slick Hatchet Job," reviewer Rose Pelswick wrote:

> Danny Kaye's new comedy is a delightful spoof ... [of] the age-of-chivalry type movie spectacle.... The title role is a natural for the versatile Kaye who sings, dances and clowns superbly, and the supporting players do a grand job of playing their absurdities straight.[10]

The *New York Herald Tribune* added:

> No matter what people say, the age of chivalry is dead. Danny Kaye kills it in his new movie.... Who can ever again watch the likes of Robert Taylor tilting [jousting] at his foes without thinking of Sir Danny. He is funny, of course, in everything he does, and "The Court Jester" gives him a chance to do everything.[11]

The *New York Daily News* stated, under the title "Danny Kaye Rings Bell in Paramount 'Jester'":

> The film is an elaborate production in which Danny is funny, pathetic, courageous, frightened and enduring by turns. He gives a good show, no matter what he is doing, as Danny's sense of comedy is sure and his timing perfect. He is the one great clown the screen can boast of today ... we need a jester like thee.[12]

The entertainment industry's publication, *Variety*, stated, "Costumed swashbucklers undergo a happy spoofing in 'The Court Jester' with Danny Kaye heading the fun-poking and making it click."[13] Even the hard-to-please *New York Times* confessed:

> It stood to reason that somebody would eventually cut loose and do a slam-bang burlesque on recent movies about knighthood and derring-do.... And we are happy to report that it's been leaped at by no less a clown than Danny Kaye, who lands with both feet in "The Court Jester." It's good fun.[14]

Indeed, the same *New York Times* critic, Bosley Crowther, was inspired to write an even more positive, yet personalized, piece on *Jester* just three days after his review. In "Little Things: Being an Appreciation of Small Favors in Films," he adds:

> There's a bit in "The Court Jester" ... that sticks in the mind of this reviewer as the funniest single thing in the film. It is a line tossed off by Cecil Parker, who plays a usurping king in this burlesque [kingdom] ... Mr. Kaye in his heavy suit of armor has been hoisted by a derrick onto his nag ... someone does not remember to unhitch the rope by which he has been raised, so when the horse is whacked and leaps forward, Mr. Kaye is left dangling in mid-air, his armor clanking like a cracked bell. It is a funny scene. However, the thing that got us was Mr. Parker's line.... "Take that horse," he bellows, "and put it back under that man!" Maybe it doesn't sound too funny, written out that way ... but even now, when we recall it and savor the juiciness of that line—the pungency and pithiness of it in sensing the culture of the screen, where the horse is co-equal with the human [see Trigger references in Chapter 3]—it seems the wittiest thing in the film. It clearly states the essential in those tin-suited horse operas.[15]

Yet, here is the rub. *Jester* received all those superlatives. And even the normally money-savvy *Variety* predicted:

> The b.o. [box office] cash jingle should match the audience laugh reaction, meaning the Dena production which Paramount is releasing has bright prospects at the wickets [turnstiles].[16]

However, the picture lost money! Part of the reason was its excessive costs; at $4 million, it was routinely called the most expensive comedy ever made. Still, many movies, such as

The Wizard of Oz (1939), were hits, yet initially lost money because of huge production costs. But *Jester* allegedly only grossed slightly more than an anemic $2 million. Perhaps an answer, or part of an answer, lies in yet another rave review. Under the banner "'Court Jester' Filled with Action Sparkling Humor," *Hollywood Reporter* critic Jack Meffitt opened his critique thus:

> In spite of the fact that the public has been surfeited with bad medieval pictures, this merry iron pants comedy has a good chance of doing well at the boxoffice [sic]. It is loaded with belly laughs and entertainment, due largely to Danny Kaye's ability to keep its humor sparkling and modern in spirit.[17]

Maybe this parody was not timely enough, and the public had just had enough of castles, knights, and blockbusters in general, even if the *Jester* mocked this scenario. And this theory has a more recent precedent. Mel Brooks' *Space Balls* (1987) appeared a full four years after the third installment of the initial *Star Wars* trilogy it was spoofing had been released. And *Space Balls'* mixed critical and commercial response was largely blamed on this time lag. Yet, now the spoof has become a cult classic, and one of Brooks' most popular pictures.

An amusing bit of circumstantial evidence for the conjecture that *Jester*'s disappointing box office returns were the result of a public tired of epic overkill comes from a most unlikely person and setting. The Academy Award ceremony for 1956, the year *Jester* was released, had Jerry Lewis (see chapters 2 and 9) as its Hollywood host, with former Oscar winner Celeste Holm co-hosting from New York. While the 1950s obsession with overblown sagas had been kidded for some time now, possibly the comic coup de grace came from an improbable for Lewis monologue, more befitting a traditional stand-up comic, at an event created to celebrate movies. Lewis, who normally carried his demented alter ego into public settings now sounded more like an "I've gotta tell you" Bob Hope:

> I didn't see all of [the flawed, three-hour-plus-long] *War and Peace* because the kid in front of me grew up. *War and Peace* cost nine million dollars—that's more than the real war cost. [And the equally overlong, overblown] *Giant* cost me three hundred dollars. Three dollars to get in and $297 to pay the babysitter.[18]

Consequently, I would embrace the law of parsimony (also known as Occam's Razor). That is, with all things being equal, usually the simplest explanation is the correct one—people were just tired of these films, even in parody form.

Of course, other masterly movies have not been fully appreciated upon their fledgling appearances, such as Buster Keaton's *The General* (1927), or the Marx Brother's *Duck Soup* (1933). Yet, in most such cases, *both* the public and the majority of the critics missed the boat. Whereas, with the *Jester*, Kaye's mother could have been writing all the reviews.

However, if the law of parsimony does not work for readers, one could argue, I suppose, that Kaye was not the film star he had been in the 1940s. Moreover, because the multi-talented comedian much preferred the stage, his screen appearances had always been intermittent, even during the height of his earlier cinema success. Thus, he had not established the loyal fan film base of other stars. Finally, I have never been fully convinced that the *Jester* received full credit for its overseas market, particularly in Great Britain. For instance, the *Hollywood Reporter* disclosed, under the title "'Jester' Hot in London":

> Following a record-breaking first week at the Plaza Theatre here, Paramount's Danny Kaye grossed [over] $15,000 in the second week. This is the best second week the theatre has had on any picture since 1947, and is only 10 percent below the gross of the initial week.[19]

Still, the simplest answer works best for me.

Regardless, *Jester* is a great picture which has been fully acknowledged along those lines for some time now. Moreover, it also provides a fitting lead-in to Frank Tashlin's use of Tony Randall in the following chapter's focus on *Will Success Spoil Rock Hunter* (1957). In fact, as previously noted, *Jester* auteurs Melvin Franklin and Norman Panama were modest precursors, of sorts, to the cartoonish Tashlin, whether it was *Jester* spoofing 1950s action spectacles, to scripting talking animals in the duo's lengthy treatment of Hope & Crosby's *Road to Utopia* (1946). Indeed, the latter picture's babbling bear would not be out of place in Tashlin's print fables. (See chapters 4 and 9.)

Ironically, along these parallel auteur lines, an excellent chapter transition to what follows would be to close with the *Jester*'s opening credits. In his title costume, Kaye is an entertaining distraction as he dances and sings his way through "Life Could Not Better Be." The topper is Kaye having a pushing match with the credits. Little to no references of this were made in *Jester* reviews. Yet, when Tashlin uses Tony Randal in a more divertingly elaborate satirical opening to *Rock Hunter*'s opening credits, it is a prime source of discussion (see following chapter). Besides yet another example of period neglect for *Jester*, one wonders if Frank-Panama felt like Tashlin on the subject: "I hate credits. Who wants to sit there and read all those names.... I usually have things to distract you during the credits."[20] Nonetheless, on to Tashlin and Randall.

11

Tony Randall
Will Success Spoil Rock Hunter? (September 12, 1957)

> After using Tony Randall as a distracting presence in the credits, the actor later stops the film and observes, "Ladies and gentleman, this break in our motion picture is made out of respect for the TV fans in our audience, who are accustomed to constant interruptions in their programs for messages from sponsors. We want all you TV fans to feel at home, and not forget the thrill you get, watching on your big, 21-inch screens."—from *Will Success Spoil Rock Hunter?*

If Danny Kaye's antics during the opening credits of *The Court Jester* (1956) were distracting, writer/director Frank Tashlin's use of Tony Randall to open *Rock Hunter* is a total blitzkrieg (lightening war), or is that pox, on movie beginnings and television commercials in general. The above quote is later used, however, to fully underline this blistering satire of movie beginnings. That is, humanity in general is a collection of easily manipulated boobs. Moreover, people are such suckers that after Randall delivers his crack about making people "feel at home" with their "21-inch [TV] screens," the giant movie screen is scaled down to seemingly postage stamp-size and all the visual *joys* of early TV reception are reproduced—snowy pictures, rolling images odd distortions and so on. Thus, viewers are not only effortlessly influenced, it is done with this primitive device already nicknamed an "idiot box." Can there be any doubt of the inherent truth in the pioneering theatre of the absurd satirist Georges Feydeau's (1862–1921) frequent observation that comedy artists "think sad first"? However, before Randall's chapter opening quote lowers the boom two-thirds of the way through *Rock Hunter*, what commercial products are skewered during the picture's opening credits? They include one-foot-in-reality exaggerated pitches for everything from beer and hair conditioners, to breakfast cereal and peanut butter. But the most spot-on comic commercial is a laundry advertisement whose housewife complains, "If you're like me, with six dirty children and a big filthy husband."

It is as if Tashlin's Randall has taken one back to the early 1950s and movies' serious battle with the small screen. Ironically, the film is supposed to be an adaptation of George Axelrod's hit Broadway play (1955–1956) of the same name, but Tashlin has made everything go topsy-turvy—redirecting a satire of Hollywood at Madison Avenue hype via television ads, pop culture in general, and a smattering of Hollywood caricature, too, especially with movie opening titles and co-star Jayne Mansfield (who recreates her Broadway spoof of Marilyn Monroe). And not above being a playful hypocrite himself, Tashlin periodically plugs products from his home studio (Twentieth Century–Fox), even his own pictures. For example, the previous year's *The Girl Can't Help It* (1956, also with Mansfield) is mentioned several times—most winningly in *Rock Hunter*' opening orchestrated titles chaos. Randall is stating who is in the film but then cannot remember the name of the picture. Yet, one title he briefly mentions is *The Girl Can't Help It*, only to say, "No, we already did that one." (As a brief addendum, an intriguing double-bill would be *Rock Hunter*'s and Charlie Chaplin's *A King in New York*—both covering the same material the some year, though the master comedian adds political shots at McCarthyism.)

Regardless, after Tashlin's zany version of anti-credits, so adroitly handled by Randall, the actor in voiceover provides a bird's eye view of Manhattan as the picture takes the audience to his title character's advertising agency. We soon meet Rock's immediate supervisor Rufus (Henry Jones), who is in such a state of agitation he is busy self-medicating with liquid fun, because the firm is in immediate danger of losing its king client. The pitchmen cannot come up with an inspired new ad campaign for "Stay-Put Lipstick," and both their jobs are beyond being in jeopardy. This is where Tashlin continues to choreograph a nuanced performance from Randall. *Variety* said:

> "Rock Hunter" should establish him [Randall] as a promising screen comedy talent. He's a fellow who knows timing, and his clowning has a slightly sophisticated touch that hits [the] bull's eye. The picture rests largely on him, and he carries it through with nary a slip. Thanks to some fine shading, he manages to make the transition from hilarity to serious moments [such as the titles sequence to the "Stay-Put-Lipstick" dilemma] without losing the sense of credibility.[1]

Indeed, *Cue* magazine even upped the Randall ante:

> Suffice ... [to say] that Tony Randall, who plays the key role [in *Rock Hunter*] is, as of now, the screen's foremost contender for the title of our No. 1 movie comedian.[2]

Not surprisingly, the journal rather liked the film, too, entitling its review, "The Funniest of 1957: 'Will Success Spoil Rock Hunter?'"[3]

Regardless, to return to a narrative which turned the tables on Broadway's broadside of Hollywood, Randall had come to work that morning with a "Stay-Put-Lipstick" campaign which sounds ever so much like the real Tashlin. The writer/director was a former animator and sometimes writer of animal fables (see chapters 3 and 9). Thus, Randall's idea for the account was a song being sung in a cartoon by three chickens. This was not going to work, and the cocky MC from the titles quickly segues into an anti-heroic Charlie Brown type, sort of a variation of Jack Lemmon.

Rock drags himself back to his office where his secretary/girlfriend Jenny (Betsy Drake) attempts to cheer up her less-than-sexy fiancé. However, naming the slight Tony Randall *Rock* "Hunter" is a joke onto itself, especially when that year's (1957) number one box office star was the strapping *Rock* "Hudson."[4] But this satire will soon only be compounded when the film's Hollywood bombshell Rita Marlowe (Mansfield) later designates him her "Lover Doll" and the star's public buys it, going after him like any product Madison Avenue promotes.

Once Drake's confidence boosting mission fails, Randall's frustrated figure goes home to the apartment he shares with his niece April (Lili Gentile). Unknown to her uncle, she is the leader of a local fan club for the statuesque blonde with the Marilyn Monroe sounding name of Marlowe. Since Mansfield's character is coming to New York early the following morning, Lili has slipped out that night to be at the airport among hundreds of other admirers when Rita lands (think future Beatle-mania). Randall only finds this out by seeing his niece meet Mansfield on the villain of this piece—the TV. He is initially angry with Lili for sneaking out and ditching school, which is comically caught in a brief exchange:

> LILI: How did I look [on TV]?
> ROCK: Like six months of no allowance.

However, Randall soon realizes his niece might have saved his career when a TV announcer refers to Mansfield's "Oh so kissable lips!," à la his "Stay-Put-Lipstick" account. However, prior to Rita's New York landing and Randall's epiphany, viewers meet the actress inflight with her companion/assistant Violet (Joan Blondell). While the veteran actress is now in the "best friend" supporting role portion of her career, in the 1930s she was a staple in many Warner Brother pictures as the sexy wisecracking blonde. It is good casting for several reasons, beyond the fact that Blondell was invariably a plus to any picture in her long Hollywood career. First, she is a time capsule of what Mansfield could have been in 25 years (on screen and off). That is, in Hollywood's pre-code period she had the leeway to be every bit as provocative as a Mansfield in the uptight 1950s. Moreover, for the knowing viewer, she represented an interesting variation on the beddable blonde from another era.

Secondly, while no one then could know the short sad future facing Mansfield in her real/reel life (increasingly poor pictures and a 1967 automobile death), one cannot help thinking some period viewers were considering if she would be able to transition her cartoonish sex appeal into the extended nuanced career of the now character actress Blondell. Third, in the unfortunate 1950 parlance of the "dumb blonde," the younger Blondell offered a distinct variation from Mansfield. Blondell was of the Judy Holliday variety (see Chapter 1). Though she did not have any letters behind her name, she was invariably street smart and made the most of it. In contrast, and again with the wretched chauvinistic 1950s jargon, the screen Mansfield was *the* decade's definitive dumb blonde. Worse yet, Tashlin had written her as a comically cruel spoof of Marilyn Monroe's child/woman blonde. New York critic Bosley Crowther's rare pan of *Rock Hunter* was largely a humor-deprived take on a funny picture—but he did correctly call Mansfield's performance a "leadpipe travesty of Marilyn Monroe."[5]

In Andrew Sarris' watershed auteur study, *The American Cinema: Directors and Directions, 1929–1968*, the critic went after Tashlin's *Rock Hunter* dark comedy cruel streak from another perspective:

> To ridicule Jayne Mansfield's enormous bust in *Rock Hunter* may by constructed as satire, indulgent or otherwise but to ridicule Betsy Drake's small bust in the same film [she is constantly doing breast-enhancing exercises] is simply unabashed vulgarity.[6]

Critic Joe Dante defends the Tashlin perspective on the bigger is better world of the outrageous,

> presenting a cruel and vulgar world in a way that makes it a little bigger than life, so that you can laugh at it ... [removes] that personal insult quality. Whereas today ... [there are] cruel kinds of humor that

are cruelty without humor. They're just cruel, and that's the joke. [The message of black humor is no message.]⁷

In contrast, critic/actor/filmmaker Peter Bogdanovich brought an even broader explanation to his friend's work. Calling it "purposeful ugliness," he shared:

[Tashlin was] among the saddest of men; he seemed personally injured by the ugliness in the world, perpetually disappointed and dismayed by life in civilized modern society. When I asked him what his pictures basically were about, he answered, "I guess it's the nonsense of what we *call* civilization."⁸

When Bogdanovich mentioned to Tashlin that many of his movies had bosomy women, and were full of gags about oversized breasts, one further understands that, unlike the three-dimensional Holliday and Monroe, Mansfield was simply a blonde cardboard target for the director's frustration about both his era and gender. Tashlin stated:

Yeah, well, that's part of the thing. The immaturity of the American male—this breast fetish. You can't sell tires without breasts. Imagine a statue with breasts like [Jayne] Mansfield's—imagine *that* in marble. We don't like big feet or big ears but we make an idol of women because she has outsized breasts.⁹

To reinforce Tashlin's use of Mansfield as merely a big-breasted prop, contrast it with Billy Wilder's comments on directing Monroe in *The Seven Year Itch* (1955, see Chapter 7), and *Some Like It Hot* (1959, see Chapter 12). Though she had been difficult with whom to work, the legendary director later described Monroe as having an authentic identity, rather than a sexual appeal:

When you got her to the studio on a good day she was remarkable. She had a quality that no one else ever had on the screen, except Garbo. No one [with whom Wilder had worked]. She [Monroe] was a kind of real image, beyond mere photography. She looked on the screen as if you could reach out and touch her.¹⁰

Of course, misogyny is often at the heart of W. C. Fields, or Laurel & Hardy's fry pan-toting spouses, to the Marx Brothers' eternal mocking of Margaret Dumont and otherwise pursuing anything in a skirt. Indeed, Chico's nickname is drawn from chasing "chicks" (women). What makes Tashlin's misuse of Mansfield mean but merry is its dumb blonde cardboard contrast (prop) versus the witty but less than manly Randall. This is underlined by her equally dumb former boyfriend—Tarzan wannabe actor Bobo (Mickey Hargitay), the macho "B" actor one punch away from being ugly. (In real life this former "Mr. Universe" would also become Mansfield's next husband.)

It is a foregone conclusion that once Randall bargains with his Mansfield crazy niece for the blonde's New York address, her less than sexy uncle will be the unlikely "Lover Doll" used to make Bobo jealous. Plus, if Randall plays along as the unlikely boyfriend, Mansfield will endorse "Stay-Put Lipstick." The reason this works can be demonstrated by why the Tashlin co-scripted *Love Happy* (1949), the Harpo Marx picture with a tag-along Chico, *did not*.

Harpo was the silent brother, though his assorted sound effects might make that claim hard to substantiate in court. Regardless, his non-verbal persona (often with Chico as translator), was more effective when he clashed with and bested Groucho, the best verbal saturation comedy bully in film. Yet, Groucho was forever a Harpo prop. Their surreal playing field clashes drove the team. Of course there were additional explanations why *Love Happy* was an interesting failure, including the significant fact that the beloved pixie (Harpo) was now in his 60s. Yet, the pivotal reason, despite a curtsey cameo or two by Groucho, was that Harpo did not have his contrasting prop character with whom to do comic battle. A similar team within a team analogy for the Marxes would be those films in which Groucho did not have his favorite contrasting dumb prop to best—"fifth Marx Brother" Margaret Dumont, who so contributes to their best work, such as *Duck Soup* (1933).

The *Love Happy/Rock Hunter* connection is also strengthened by their similar conclusions. In the former film, movie newcomer Monroe is made to be the most basic of comic sexual props because she is ever so briefly used as eye candy for a comically leering Groucho. But before a flash forward to the *Rock Hunter* ending, one needs to set up the situation. That is, in the latter picture, Mansfield and Blondell have had a heart-to-heart talk about the boy/man they each let get away years before. However, in a surprise *Rock Hunter* finish, an unbilled Groucho appears yet again; he is Mansfield's long lost love! And while the viewer has already seen reels of Mansfield as a Tashlin prop dumb blonde, this conclusion is the topper.

After she expresses stupefaction at both his sudden appearance and the fact that even in their past Groucho had never even tried to kiss her, the mustached one, with those sexually driven elevator eyebrows and his honed comic lecher voice replies, "I could never get that close." This has to be Tashlin's quintessential dumb blonde coup de grace—verbally equating Mansfield to the size of her breasts, which were further enhanced by 1950s Hollywood seemingly giving all pretty women added breast inches with cone-shaped pointed brassieres.

Will Success Spoil Rock Hunter?'s most unlikely of couples, Tony Randall and Jayne Mansfield.

Not surprisingly, many of the film's earlier comic lines, after the satirical montage opening attacking commercials, have to do with sex. For example, when Mansfield's character makes it clear to the world that her new lover is Tony Randall, the actual period print gossip columnist Earl Williams is said to be interested in Mansfield's measurements. But since it is really a hoax, Williams is stonewalled yet given an even more provocative reply, "He [Randall] doesn't know, it was dark." Tashlin also has satirical fun with the alleged power of Randall's kiss. Thus, as if

Tony Randall has a rare spontaneous moment in *Will Success Spoil Rock Hunter?*

back in 1930s filmland, there is a montage of newspaper headlines, including "Lover Doll's Kiss Causes Rita to Faint!," "Lover Doll's Potent Kiss Delays Wedding," and as a backhanded slap at the McCarthy witch-hunting 1950s, "Congress to Investigate Subversive Kiss."

Ironically, despite the phony romance there is something unusually powerful in Randall's first kiss of Mansfield. It comes out of nowhere, as if *The Court Jester*'s (1956, see preceding chapter) witchy lady-in-waiting Griselda (Mildred Natwick) is lurking about in *Rock Hunter*. And this is consistent with studying Tashlin as an auteur, because he is attracted to comic duality in his comedians, from the team of Martin & Lewis, to the predisposition of Bob Hope to fluctuate between a coward and a witty smart aleck.

However, the catalyst for Randall's screen changes is driven by his conflict/confusion between success and talent. He forever thought success was the goal of life and when Mansfield's Rita was suddenly the means to that end he just as suddenly grabbed this Hollywood blonde and gave her the cinema's classic bend over kiss. Their mutual arrangement was still a planned campaign, but that first kiss abruptly made it a doable proposition for Mansfield. And Tashlin has fun satirizing the emptiness of Randall's ultimate success, getting teary over receiving a personal key to the executive washroom, followed by his shock in becoming head of the company. (With regard to washroom wonder in the world of corporate America, one is reminded of Jack Lemmon's early attempts to reach this bathroom key Valhalla in the opening reel of Billy Wilder's later film, *The Apartment*, 1960).

Nevertheless, after Randall's initial glazed-over happiness, he finds achieving success has ultimately left him empty. Luckily for Randall, however, his success has opened the eyes of the company's former top man, La Salle, Jr. (John Williams). As his name might suggest in New York's lofty financial world, he has inherited his position ... and has never been happy, *even* with his own personal bathroom, a notch above Valhalla! William's character has always wanted to be a horticulturist and cross pollinate a new variety of roses—which Tashlin makes happen by the end. But it is an exciting LaSalle, Jr., awakened to a new life, who explains to Randall why he has been so confused that his seeming talent (making commercials) has essentially given him a split personality, with neither half having any fun. The following comments are LaSalle, Jr.'s, but I would argue they represent the most heartfelt dialogue Tashlin had ever written, from the film he always labeled his favorite:

> If talent had anything to do with success, Brooks Brothers would go out of business, television studios would be turned into supermarkets, we're [merely] talking about success ... [not the same animal at all].

The previous thought is summed up with an animal reference because, as suggested in earlier chapters, Tashlin's fables much prefer them to human beings, as would seem to be the case with the writer/director. Randall is like Tashlin's bear in the former cartoonist's fable *The Bear That Wasn't*.[11] That is, a bear wakes up from his winter hibernation and finds his habitat has been gobbled up by a factory. The animal is then convinced by the workers that he is, indeed, a plant employee, and thus the title, *The Bear That Wasn't*. Thankfully, both the creature in Tashlin's fable and Randall realize that neither of them is part of the forever misguided human tendency to both get things wrong, and brainwash creatures into an unfulfilling existence.

Consequently, Randall gives up his *success* as an advertiser and uses his *talent* to find happiness as a chicken farmer. Ironically, as previously noted, Randall's initial pitch for the "Stay-Put Lipstick" campaign was to have been a cartoon sung by three chickens. Regardless, coupled with Tashlin's preference for animals and the country, is to indirectly celebrate where the ever erroring human beings are not. Thus, Randall eventually lives on a farm, his boss becomes a gardener, and the bear gets back to the forest. Paradoxically, even when man does not take over nature, à la the world of Tashlin's bear, human countryside trespassers inevitably get things wrong about animals. For instance, in the Tashlin fable *The Possum That Didn't* (1946), hikers see a smiling possum hanging upside down from a tree, and mistake it for a frown.[12] Naturally, like Mark Twain's negative take on missionaries, they attempt to change a perfectly natural situation because these small-brained humans cannot imagine any way but their way.

Yet, this is ever so innocent compared to Tashlin's last fable, 1951's *The World That Isn't*.[13] In this, his final parable, he depicts a planet so fool heartedly stupid that after much thought some inhabits destroy the (so called) modern world with an atomic bomb. And it produces a giant hole into which mankind threw everything it did not need. It represents nihilism versus hope, because the survivors attempt to build a better world. Indeed, Tashlin's book is reminiscent of James Thurber's 1939 parable *The Last Flower*, in which philistines squared destroy civilization countless times through war, only to rebuild it again and again.[14] However, as the title suggests, it ends with the beginning of yet another do-over. *Maybe* this could constitute hope, yet Tashlin's atomic fable appeared the same year as Robert Wise's original *The Day the Earth Stood Still*, in which the most dignified of aliens (Michael

A Frank Tashlin drawing from his 1950 children's parable, *The Possum That Didn't*. Like Madison Avenue, people mistake his upside down smile for unhappiness and attempt to force things on the possum he neither needs nor wants. Used with permission of Dover Publications, Inc.

Rennie) visits Earth with the warning that if the planet continues to flirt with an atomic war, a superior world will simply destroy the planet for galaxy safety. One more than assumes that earth will *not* be up to the task. In fact, as Stanley Kubrick suggests in his later *Dr. Strangelove or: How I Learned to Stop Worrying and Love the Bomb* (1964), humans will only too soon do the trick themselves. And keep in mind, Thurber's text appeared as World War

II was just beginning in Europe ... seemingly yet another conflict to survive and from which to start again. *But* in 1945 Hiroshima and Nagasaki demonstrated that there were soon to be no do-over worlds. In fact, Tashlin's title suggest just that—*The World That Isn't*.

Yet, Tashlin's title can also suggest hope, because mankind creates a museum containing examples of its ugly past—*The World That Isn't*. Maybe things turn out okay. A promising sign is that if one looks *very* carefully, Tashlin's fable bear and possum make cameo appearances. Maybe this split decision "reading" can be compared to Will Cuppy's *How To Become Extinct* (see Chapter 3).[15] Cuppy, too, used animals to suggest the end of life as we know it. Though the drawings that accompany Cuppy's *Extinct* collection of short essays are by William Steig, each is a perfect extension of Cuppy's perspective. However, Cuppy's comic warnings here and in other texts, use anthropomorphism to make animals an extension of man's foolishness; Tashlin's parables have poor creatures as pure victims of man, until *The World That Isn't*.... It bares noting, moreover, that the year *Extinct* came out paralleled the entry of American into what was now another world war. Plus, Cuppy would commit suicide a few years after the conflict. Though one cannot make a direct link between the war and his suicide à la author Virginia Woolf (1882–1941), the war was a major contributing factor.

Indeed, given Tashlin's *Waiting for Godot* philosophy, it is remarkable he could hold this mindset and make such mainstream movies as *Rock Hunter*, or the previously critiqued *Son of Paleface* (1952, see Chapter 2) and *Artists and Models* (1955, see Chapter 9). Maybe he had something in common with, of all people, 1970s Secretary of State Henry Kissinger, who was once described as "an existentialist who believed in a world without objective truth or inescapable historical patterns ... [in which] positive action [is] rooted in intuition rather than rational thinking."[16] If one thinks Tashlin and Kissinger are an odd coupling, the statesman's comments on the battle of the sexes, whether one is a misogynist or not, certainly applied to all satirists of Thurber or Tashlin's ilk, "Nobody will ever win the battle of the sexes. There's just too much fraternizing with the enemy."[17]

Regardless, in many ways *Rock Hunter* was the satirical retaliation film Chaplin should have made with *A King in New York*, after his 1952 American re-entry visa was denied (the comedian had always retained his British citizenship). Though undoubtedly he could have had the ruling reversed, by this time he had had enough of the McCarthy era and gone into voluntary exile in Switzerland. Much of Chaplin's film satirized more universal topics than Tashlin's, such as the comedian's brilliant takeoff on plastic surgery. But his soapbox political agenda in the latter half of the picture, while completely understandable, derails much of the proceeding fun. One should add that while both *Rock Hunter* and *A King* opened in 1957, Chaplin's ongoing bitterness kept him from releasing his film in America until the early 1970s. This followed the country essentially apologizing for the 1952 debacle by giving him his second honorary Oscar (April 10, 1972) "for the incalculable effect he has had in making motion pictures the art form of this century."[18] (At 1928's first Academy Award ceremony Chaplin had been given a statuette "for versatility and genius in writing, acting, directing and producing *The Circus*."[19]) However, this helter-skelter real treatment of Chaplin is perfectly in keeping with the fun but puzzling perplexity of *Rock Hunter*.

Nevertheless, even after Randall's boss, La Salle, Jr., has gifted him with the all-important axiom that talent beats success for happiness, our title character is inundated with a juggernaut of 1950s temptations. They range from Edward R. Murrow wanting him to appear on CBS' immensely popular TV program *Person to Person* (hosted by a reluctant hard news Murrow, almost a caricature himself, hidden behind his haze of cigarette smoke), to famed publisher Bennett Cerf, one of the founders of the publishing firm Random House (as well as a period pop culture personality), coveting any sexy morsels Randall might bring to a book tentatively called, *Always Leave Them Loving*. The name is a comic play upon a hoary but pertinent title to a film like this—*Always Leave Them Laughing*. And it goes without saying that wherever Randall appears, his clothing continues to be ripped off by media-programmed teens. One should add, moreover, that *Rock Hunter* opened the year after the sexually provocative Elvis Presley actually began suffering through these souvenir attacks.

To his credit, by this time a frustrated and disillusion Randall is ever more questioning this kind of manufactured hype, comically demonstrated by his answer to a drink request! "Something simple, a bottle and a straw." But one might also say he is becoming an intellectual teetotaler, à la an observation by a once broadly syndicated newspaper cartoonist whom Tashlin would no doubt have enjoyed Kin Hubbard (1868–1930). Hubbards' print figure alter ego, Abe Martin, once observed, "Flattery won't hurt you if you don't swallow it."[20]

Near the movie's conclusion, however, it almost seems like Randall will still "swallow" the idea of success when La Salle, Jr., lobs in his final potential game changer for Randall, who by now has even received Hollywood's ultimate stab at immortality—his foot and handprints in cement at Grauman's Chinese Theatre. Except fittingly for the increasingly tired and tattered Randall, his arm goes into the gooey wet cement past his elbow. So what is the second succinct sarcastic warning from La Salle, Jr.? "Success will fit you like a shroud." Thus, even with Tashlin cherry-picking the era's signature success distracting" "honors," Randall walks away.

Choosing his chicken farm dream and finally returning to his patient fiancé, Betsy Drake's Jenny, Randall falls in line with the basic Tashlin hero/anti-hero. Even coupled with his other male leads showcased in this text, Bob Hope in *Son of Paleface* (1952, see Chapter 3) and Jerry Lewis in *Artists and Models* (1955, see Chapter 9), each character ends up in a more subdued natural/normal setting, just like Tashlin's *Bear That Wasn't* finally realizes what and who he is as he returns to nature. And my favorite *Rock Hunter* scene still remains that shadowy extreme long shot of Randall in Bobo's (which even sounds like bear) oversized muscle man clothing. With all the stuffing and padded shoulders necessary to make Randall able to wear the garb, his cartoon appearance is not unlike Tashlin's teddy. Moreover, at this earlier point in the picture, like the writer/director's parable bear, both figures have been brainwashed into thinking they are something they are not.

While all films double as a documentary of sorts for the period in which they were made, an additional part of the fun in screening *Rock Hunter* is that the picture is a veritable time capsule of the late 1950s. Tashlin seems to have squeezed in every trend and tendency with which corporate America was bombarding the public. He was sort of a one-man PG precursor to *National Lampoon*. The vivid period detail he brought to his satire, and especially the manner in which he shish-kebabbed television as the pivotal delivery system, is a regular time machine back to the decade. In fact, the specifics Tashlin brings to his late 1950s satire reminds me of the precise attention Stephen King successfully shepherds to the same period in his 2011 time-tripping mystery thriller *11/22/63*, a novel which also pinballs back to the late 1950s. Ironically, the novel *also* suggests that despite the modest hopes of the Thurber and Tashlin fables, even mercy mission time travel cannot save the world.

Yet again, what prompted the association was King's scrutiny of language and jokes during the *Rock Hunter* period. Granted, the works belong to different genres, and this might elicit a loopy first response to their linkage. Still, King's novel includes a 1950s joke pertinent to the Randall internal battle between success and applying one's talent to happiness. However, in the final incarnation of Randall's rural Rock Hunter, he has already demonstrated he would not have emulated the joke's punch line, though it fits the apocalyptic nature of Tashlin's Thurber-like fable, *The World That Isn't*:

> QUESTION: Do you know the problem with German bologna?
> ANSWER: An hour after you eat some, you're hungry for power.[21]

"Hungry for power" seemed to be like the norm of this 1950s world, yet ultimately it is the last thing Randall's movie-ending country character would want. Indeed, even earlier, when power was the movie's catalyst, his title character needed to work himself into a frenzy to play the corporate competitor. He did not even partake of the perks which were essentially being temptingly thrown his way—such as girls, girls girls—which would have been arguably understandable enticements (though merely physical in nature), as he sought an answer to true happiness.

Fittingly, good things also came to other *Rock Hunter* characters, from La Salle, Jr., creating a new rose named after himself, to Joan Blondell's character finding happiness with Randall's loyal but constantly stressed friend Rufus. Consequently, Randall ends the picture with an observation which Tashlin still manages to satirically tweak by closing it with a kidding of trendy 1950 jargon: "We've learned that success is just the art of being happy… [through applying one's talents to what brings us real emotional joy] and being happy *is just the very living end* [italics mine]." And with that, Tashlin satirically recycles a then up-to-the minute observation with which to close the movie, "And that is the very living end," sans a traditional "The End." As a footnote to Randall's summing up, before Tashlin's '50s hip addition, is yet another pleasing connection to the writer/director's parables. Though written subliminally with adults/parents in mind, these are obstinately children's books. And Randall's "We've learned…" close has the ring of how one underlines the moral of the story to a child.

So how was Tashlin's satirical use of Randall and Mansfield received in *Rock Hunter*? The picture was a critical and commercial success of nearly the elephantine blows the writer/director took to the 1950s. *Cue*'s review headline called the film "The Funniest of 1957":

> [On Broadway the play attacked Hollywood]—here Hollywood has turned the joke on its arch enemy, Television: on the rat race in the industry, and on the most irritating characteristics of TV commercials. The resulting destruction is complete—the comedy is hilarious, the entertainment is magnificent, and the comic performances by the whole cast are out of the world.[22]

The *Christian Science Monitor* congratulated Tony Randall as

> a kind of Alec Guinness in a gray flannel suit [see Guinness' 1951 *The Man in the White Suit*, who] purses his lips, bulges his eyes, and generally expresses well-justified concern…. [The film] makes its points well: that the wide screen can project an exuberance which on the home screen not even Rita's [Jayne Mansfield] boyfriend, the vine-swinging hero of TV's first "adult" monkey series can make.[23]

Variety said:

> This is the kind of snappy, cracking farce that Hollywood hasn't had too much of in recent years…. Tashlin has turned out a vastly amusing comedy that has all the earmarks of a bang up success … [The film] is helped by sock [o] performances, notably by Jayne Mansfield and Tony Randall.[24]

New York Daily News critic Kate Cameron applauded "the fun they [Randall and Mansfield] make of their [satirical] rivals ... [in this] often screamingly funny [film]."[25] The *New York World-Telegram and Sun* went so far as to say:

> The movie is a vastly improved version of the play that zoomed Miss Mansfield to such sudden stardom on Broadway a couple of seasons ago.... But the big man of the achievement certainly must be Frank Tashlin, who re-wrote George Alelrod's play and then produced and directed the rollicking screen version. He will roll up a lot of happiness on the credit side of the ledger.[26]

While the *Newark Evening News* had more lionizing for Tashlin, Randall ultimately received the greatest kudos:

> Frank Tashlin ... [has made] this magnificently funny picture ... and his range is something superb.... The picture, however, may best be remembered as the introduction [actually his second screen appearance] of that fine stage actor, Tony Randall, to the movies. He is the best thing that has happened to Hollywood since Cinemascope. He has a voice with many graduations of expression, he has a lively, alert face that mirrors each thought as it flits across his mind, and he doesn't mind taking a beating in the cause of fun.... Randall can be both slapstick and touching at the same time, and that's real talent.[27]

There are many more critiques along these lines, sometimes even capsulized in the review titles, like the *New York American*'s headline, "Sizzling Jayne Zips Through Zany Film."[28] And unlike last chapter's *Court Jester*, which was much applauded but lost money, *Rock Hunter* was a hit at the box office, too. Randall was our master of ceremonies to what Peter Bogdanovich later paradoxically described as "not a pretty age, and so, unfortunately, too many critics did not see the often bitter and devastating satire behind the laud and façade."[29]

Ironically, as so often happens in American satire, critics praised *Rock Hunter*'s surface for substance instead of its dark hollow underbelly. It was the nadir of Andy Warhol soup cans. As *Village Voice* critic J. Hoberman later wrote of Tashlin's work, and by extension, the closest he ever came to his screen alter ego's (Randall) confusion:

> One aspect of modernism is its almost painful self-consciousness. The art object is not "aware" that it's an artiface but mindful of its place in the history of artiface as well.[30]

Again, as suggested by both Bogdanovich and the title of Hoberman's essay, Tashlin was "Cartooned In." Sadly, the satirist's attempt to make people aware that the real world does not exist when juxtaposed with all the media with which the public is bombarded often goes unrecognized. Bob Fosse said it in so many ways by way of a song—"'Just Give Them the Old "Razzle Dazzle."'" Critic Dave Kehr later summarized:

> More than most of his contemporaries, Tashlin was attuned to the ways in which our own desires betray us and how easily it can be manipulated to sell things.... The most absurd figure in Tashlin's films is not a heavy-bosomed blonde but the pathetic male in a pure, helpless state of arousal, continually provoked by the eroticized environment that surrounds him.[31]

The title of the *New York Times* essay from which the Kehr quotes come also helps define Randall's comedy persona: "When Unmanly Men Met Womenly Women." That is, Randall's character does not succumb to a media-manufactured Mansfield but ultimately embraces human emotion. The urban corporate world usually makes him seem less than manly; no air seems to vibrate when he is around, except for the occasional prick to some commercial product, like the aforementioned opening film titles. Tashlin is creating a sensitive real person versus Mansfield's prop dumb blonde.

Ironically, while Randall's greatest future success will come in the world *Rock Hunter* satirizes (TV), in both this film and his small screen work he is invariably sensitive and fair to a fault. When he does act more assertive, those scenes when the movie's image is reduced to the stamp-like size of TV screen—he is still being real. Tashlin's molding of Randall's movie alter ego effortlessly slips into the anti-heroic little man of American 20th century humor. But by the time of Randall's signature pop culture legacy, as Felix Unger in the television adaptation of Neil Simon's play *The Odd Couple* (1970–1975), his sensitivity had evolved into a rather womanly prim, fastidious figure.

Nevertheless, like 1940s comedy star Eddie Bracken, whose career is irrevocably tied to director Preston Sturges, Randall's film persona will be forever linked to Tashlin.[32] Though Randall only did one picture with Tashlin, it both jump-started his career and established his frustrated anti-heroic alter ego, whatever the screen size. In contrast, when Tashlin worked with Mansfield on both *The Girl Can't Help It* (1956) and *Rock Hunter*, Mansfield and Randall might have become a completely different hit "odd couple."[33]

Tashlin's time at the top, like that of Sturges, would be relatively short. And his oeuvre is now too often neglected and misunderstood. Part of the problem might be likened to a recent film title, *Very Semi-Serious* (2015). Period audiences and critics tended to enjoy but stopped at his brash, seemingly surface satire, and failed to dig deeper. Unfortunately, at the time, he simply seemed to produce products that were to be enjoyed or endured, and sometimes audiences could not tell the differences. Regrettably, no one up to now has deciphered Tashlin's films and characters by way of his fables, especially *The World That Isn't*. In that text's aforementioned museum of the ugly past, or man as the "Nomadic Savage," one of the exhibits is called "Primitive Worship."[34] It depicts a male bowing down to a big-breasted woman, with a movie camera and a film light in the background. As suggested before, satire comes out of sadness.

12

Lemon & Curtis/ Monroe/Joe E. Brown

Some Like It Hot (March 30, 1959)

> "Nobody's perfect."—Joe E. Brown's (Osgood Fielding III)
> classic closing line to fiancée Lemmon (Jerry/Daphne)
> in *Some Like It Hot* (1959), after discovering she is a he

The American Film Institute (AFI) ranks the above quote as one of the 100 greatest lines ever uttered in a United States film, logging in it at number 48.[1] However, what really makes Billy Wilder's (see Chapter 7) *Some Like It Hot* such a fitting conclusion to this study of 1950s personality comedians is that AFI has ranked the picture the foremost American film comedy in history.[2] Moreover, it also boasts the best and most varied clown cast of the decade, including the inspired reemergence of Joe E. Brown, a personality comedian frequently ranked among the annual top 10 box office stars of the 1930s.[3] Such casting further embellishes a picture that begins in 1929, a game plan which will be expanded upon later in the chapter.

Once again, as in most plot-driven personality comedies, the story line is minimal. One might simply sum up *Hot*'s scenario as hinging upon two musicians (Tony Curtis and Jack Lemmon) witnessing a Chicago gangland garage murder obviously inspired by tabloid history's most well known mob mass execution, the "Saint Valentine's Day Massacre." (Orchestrated by Al Capone, it also took place in 1929 Chicago.) The musicians go "underground" for protection by disguising themselves as women and joining an all-girl band, Sweet Sue's (Joan Shawlee) Society Syncopators, which is leaving for a Miami booking. Thus, Lemmon's base fiddle-playing Jerry becomes Daphne, and Curtis' saxophonist virtuoso morphs from Joe to Josephine. The band includes the hard-drinking singer Sugar (Marilyn Monroe), determined both to never fall for another two-faced saxophone player, and to marry a millionaire.

Ironically, the only millionaire romance either "girl" has involves Lemmon's Daphne and Brown's Osgood, who if a question of gender is not enough, is over half again "her" age. And naturally, while both musicians are smitten by Monroe, she will naturally end up with saxophonist Curtis. But at first Monroe thinks she is snaring a millionaire, since the

The "girl" band, with Tony Curtis (far left), Jack Lemmon, and Marilyn Monroe in *Some Like It Hot*.

actor manages to not only play Joe and Josephine, he also wins her romantically as "Shell Oil, Junior." What is more, Curtis does the part with an exaggerated Cary Grant accent. (The actor so admired Grant that during World War II he had enlisted in the submarine corps after seeing the performer in the "Silent Service" film *Destination Tokyo*, 1943.)

Yet before examining the fascinating multi-faceted variations of personality comedy on display in *Hot*, one must note the many types of comedy genres at work, all of which enhance the clown perspective. First, *Hot* is a dark comedy inspired by a famous multiple murder mob hit, which also includes booze packed in a coffin and delivered by a hearse, and a speakeasy in a mortuary. This might seem tame today, but that was not the case in the late 1950s.[4] Curtis recalled Bill Wilder telling him:

> Before it was made, *Hot* was considered too controversial to be a comedy. It had ... all those murders. I remember talking to David [*Gone with the Wind*] Selznick. He was a very smart man and a marvelous producer. I told him a little about *Hot*. He said, "The Valentine's Day Murder? You're crazy. You mean real machine guns, and blood, in a comedy? It'll be a total failure." I said, "Well, I think I'll try it anyway."[5]

Second, *Hot* is a parody of gangster films. The movie does not qualify as a spoof of the reaffirmation variety, in which the action is so close to the genre being lampooned (à la the original *Scream* trilogy, 1996, 1997, 2000) that a viewer could assume, for this particular example, s/he was watching a trio of horror films.[6] However, a few *Hot* scenes, such as the catalyst garage mass execution sequence, are played realistically enough to flirt with the reaffirmation phenomenon. Such circumstances, especially for a 1959 audience, simply enhance the dark comedy—broad comedy abruptly cutting to visceral violence—and back again.

Moreover, parody films frequently intensify their power to burlesque a genre by casting actors associated with their category. For instance, when Bob Hope's *My Favorite Brunette* (1947) spoofed film noir, one of the best scenes included a cameo by noir regular Alan Ladd, with the comedian even enriching the laughs by working the actor's name into the dialogue. Consequently, Wilder's *Hot* has done the same thing by casting George Raft and Pat O'Brien in the picture. With Raft as head mobster Spats Columbo, and O'Brien as Detective Mulligan, Wilder has especially elevated the humor.

Raft was one of the definitive movie gangsters of the 1930s. Indeed, he became a star opposite Paul Muni in *Scarface* (1932), part of *the* definitive gangster trilogy which put the genre on the map early in the decade. (The other two were 1930's *Little Caesar* and 1931's *Public Enemy*.) Plus, by using Raft, Wilder could further heighten the parody humor level for gangster aficionados. For example, in one *Hot* sequence a low level mobster, Johnny Paradise (Edward G. Robinson, Jr., son of the 1930s gangster-stereotyped actor who played the title character of *Little Caesar*) is casually flipping a coin and Raft sarcastically cracks, "Where did you pick up that cheap trick?" Truth be told, Raft had introduced this now *signature* gangster gesture in *Scarface*. (The motion is even used in the mobster portion of a fantasy sequence in Gene Kelly and Stanley Donen's 1952 *Singin' in the Rain*.) *Scarface* director Howard Hawks had felt that relative Hollywood newcomer Raft was nervous in his role and suggested flipping the coin as something to do with his hands, and it soon became a prominent symbol of the genre.

O'Brien had also played in numerous 1930s gangster films, too. But as with his *Hot* good guy detective role, the actor invariably played the counterweight positive figure to the mobster in these pictures. This is best exemplified by *Angels with Dirty Faces*, Warner Bros.' top grossing film of 1938. Iconic screen tough guy James Cagney plays the boyhood chum of O'Brien, who has grown up to be a priest. It was a popular gangster plot dichotomy of the time. That is, though Cagney's charismatic killer elicits sympathy by having had a tough childhood, his chum O'Brien had the same background, too. Consequently, there was no cutting Cagney any slack.

Hot's 1930s gangster reunion was also bolstered by casting George E. Stone in a cameo as Toothpick Charlie, one of the hoods killed in the garage. Stone was a character actor most recognized for playing Runyonesque gangsters. Ironically, with regard to *Hot*, he was probably best known as Rico's (Edward Robinson, Sr.) sidekick in *Little Caesar*. The paradox was that the elder Robinson was supposed to play Spat's (Raft) rival mobster kingpin Little [author's italics] Bonaparte. However, Robinson and Raft had gotten into a well-publicized fistfight on the set of the movie *Manpower* (1941), and Robinson backed out of the *Hot* part when Raft was cast. One wonders if Wilder suggested to the still angry Robinson that the part might have been cathartic, since Little Bonaparte has Spats and his entourage crew killed at the end of *Hot*.

Besides Wilder casting actors synonymous with the genre to bolster *Hot*'s parody component, the director had an added motive in using these veteran actors. He wanted to strengthen *Hot*'s period ambience, which was another plus in using personality comedy star Joe E. Brown, though the clown was not on Wilder's initial radar. Interestingly, there ended up being several intriguing backstories to Brown's selection. First, ironically, while today's viewer finds his millionaire, Osgood Fielding III, a delightfully harmless dirty old man, Wilder had some concerns that late 1950s audiences would find this character something of an off-putting letch. Thus, Wilder wanted to make an inherently provocative part palatable. He needed to select the most age-appropriate, wholesome actor possible for the role. And there were few major 1930s screen clowns with a more squeaky-clean persona than Brown. Moreover, Brown's performance both defuses any sense of controversy *and* somehow graces this old womanizer with a sense of poignancy. Still, *Hot* was a pioneering example of the American film industry system experimenting with a rating system, by being given an "M" classification—"For Mature Audiences." The once very powerful Catholic Legion of Decency went even further, labeling it "B" for being "morally objectionable in part to all"—one notch below their "C" (condemned category).

A young Joe E. Brown in the baseball uniform of his Warner Bros. Studio team (circa 1935).

There was an additional bonus in casting Brown of which Wilder was not cognizant. *Hot* taps into this then controversial plot point with direct links to the comedian's early career. Just as his Osgood character falls for a man in drag (Lemmon), Brown's title character in his picture *The Circus Clown* (1934) does the same thing—he is smitten by a female-impersonating bareback rider. Paradoxically, this gender mistaken identity turn was perceived as more provocative in the 1950s than the 1930s. For example, *Variety*'s strictly hohum take on this earlier plot twist was "Old gag of the country lout falling for a female impersonator serves to induct Brown into the circus."[7] Moreover, as with Raft's coin flipping signature characteristics, Wilder will eventually add one of Brown's own equally defining screen persona traits to the *Hot* script—another positive for parody aficionados. Osgood's pet phrase, "Zowie," a term for anything which excited him, had been a regular part of Brown's 1930s screen vocabulary.

As a surprise *Hot* second backstory to Brown's casting, as often happens in movies and life, sometimes the most fortuitous things fall into place by chance. The comedian's movie rebirth happened like that. Both Wilder and Brown were serious baseball fans. In fact, the Austrian-born director was often fond of saying he learned English in America by listening to baseball games on the radio. Yet as monumental as Wilder' love of the game, Brown topped it. He grew up playing the sport, was once under consideration for being signed by the New York Yankees, was a pioneering collector of baseball memorabilia, owned a part interest in a minor league team, captained his own Warner Bros.' team in the 1930s, and among his best films were the baseball trio: *Fireman, Save My Child* (1932), *Elmer the Great* (1933), and *Alibi Ike* (1935). Indeed, author and celebrated sports writer Ring Lardner was behind the original storylines for the latter two pictures. I even felt driven to title my 2006 biography of the comedian: *Joe E. Brown: Film Comedian and Baseball Buffoon*.[8]

Regardless, despite Wilder and Brown being such fans of the game, there were no major league teams west of the Mississippi until 1958, when the Brooklyn Dodgers moved to Los Angeles, and the New York Giants relocated to San Francisco. And Wilder's casting for *Hot* paralleled the opening of the Dodger's second California season. Naturally, such rabid fans as Wilder and Brown were at the Dodgers' opening day game (1959) at the city's old Memorial Coliseum, where the team played their first four years in Los Angeles. Being a baseballer insider, Brown was down on the diamond. Now keep in mind, the director knew just what he wanted in the Osgood character—all the factors just enumerated. But nobody had yet clicked for him until this game. Wilder explains:

> There was a loudspeaker on the field behind home plate, and people talking, and now comes the next speaker and it's Joe E. Brown. And I said, "That's our guy. *That's the guy!*" He did the part ... and was the nicest guy. You have to be alert, you know? You have to sit there, always, and say, "Is that the best I can do?"[9]

So when one quantifies the added bonus Brown features also just noted, as well as the giant mouth for which Brown was known (often nicknamed "the Grand Canyon")—which Wilder loved—this was undoubtedly "the best" the director could have done.

The third comedy genre happily lurking beneath *Hot*'s surface is screwball comedy—American farce. Earlier in the chapter, it was noted that Curtis also played a Cary Grant-sounding millionaire, Shell Oil Junior. Just having Grant in a film does not make it a screwball comedy. But he was the genre's most significant male lead, especially during its 1930s heyday.[10] For example, in the latter half of the decade his classic screwball comedy resume included *The Awful Truth*, *Topper* (both 1937), *Holiday*, *Bringing Up Baby* (both 1938), *My Favorite Wife*, and *His Girl Friday* (both 1940). While Grant could assume varied takes on his screwball comedy persona, his template for *Bringing Up Baby* best serves how Curtis played *Hot*'s Junior. That is, Grant's *Baby* persona was the most passive of absentminded professors and Curtis replicates just that characterization in *Hot*, when he is not doubling as Joe or Josephine.

Hot does not have screwball comedy's frequent triangle configuration of an anti-heroic male and two controlling women, one dominatingly practical and the second a more positive free spirit. Yet, though Curtis' character is actually pulling all the strings, one could metaphorically build a case for the genre's trio arrangement. That is, Jerry and Joe are a couple of sorts, with Lemmon's character often sounding like a motherly nagging wife. And Monroe's Sugar is definitely a free spirit, and while she does not come across as farce's almost stalking lover, à la Katharine Hepburn in *Bringing Up Baby*, she is the one pursuing Junior.

Also keep in mind that *Hot* pretends, via Curtis, to address a key component of screwball comedy: a male somehow tied to a death-like rigidity. For example, *Bringing Up Baby* is again a seminal model. Grant's character is a timid professor whose world revolves around reconstructing a giant *dead* brontosaurus skeleton. Hepburn comes into his life often accompanied by a dangerously sexy, very much *alive* leopard—equally symbolic of Hepburn. Thus, she awakens him from his obsession with a prehistoric past to the present tense ... present and tense, but also alive and in love. In *Hot*, Curtis' Junior also collects dead objects—clam *shells* (representing his Shell Oil wealth)—and pretends to be impotent, sexually dead. Monroe's Sugar also takes it upon herself to bring Curtis romantically back to life by throwing all her physical attributes at, and on, him. With tongue firmly-in-cheek irony, this is one case in which rigidity represents very much coming to life.

As a final addendum to *Hot*'s screwball comedy subtext, keep in mind that while Wilder excelled in a multitude of genres, beyond his special talents for a variety of comedy types, nothing came easier for him than screwball farce. For example, prior to directing, Wilder was a writer with such strong screwball credits as *Bluebeard's Eighth Wife* (1938), *Midnight* (1939), and *Ball of Fire* (1941, all co-scripted with Charles Brackett). But he wanted to be a writer/director. However, at that time a Hollywood caste system of sorts existed, in which talent was generally restricted to their area of expertise.

Along related lines, one writer whose work Wilder greatly admired, Preston Sturges, also helped change the system, at least as it pertained to writers who were wannabe directors. Sturges essentially gave Paramount one of his scripts if he could direct it. The result was *The Great McGuinty* (1940), which won an Oscar for Best Original Screenplay and allowed Sturges to become a writer/director of predominantly screwball comedies. Wilder basically made the same offer to Paramount with his screwball comedy screenplay *The Major and the Minor* (1942, with Brackett co-scripting). Wilder had decided to go with his genre strength as a writer, and the movie's immediate critical and commercial success then allowed him to also wear dual hats. Interestingly, there are also several parallels between Sturges' screwball triumph *The Palm Beach Story* (1942) and *Hot*: including elaborate mistaken identity ploys, real milquetoast millionaire Rudy Vallee being not unlike Curtis' wealthy character, comically using instant examples of wealth (from Wilder's Shell Oil Junior, to

Vallee's character, John D. Hackensaker, being less than a veiled reference to John D. Rockefeller), and physical affluence in both films being tied to yachts.

Of course, the most interesting connection between Wilder's screwball comedy forte past and *Hot* is that *The Major and the Minor* was also tied to a sexually provocative case of mistaken identity played out on a train, too. The "Minor" (Ginger Rogers) is a young Iowa woman who has moved to New York City but finds it wanting. However, in trying to get home she only has money enough for a child's train fare. Thus, she disguises herself as a 12-year-old. While managing to obtain a ticket, suspicious conductors soon are on to her, and Rogers finally finds a sanctuary in the private compartment of Ray Milland's "Major." He never suspects a thing, and with charming innocence Milland allows what appears to be a frightened child, traveling alone, to stay overnight in his compartment. Obviously, nothing happens, yet the sequence has an amusingly erotic ambience to it, which more than anticipates elements of *Hot*. In fact, at one point there is a bad storm in the night, and Milland comes down from his berth to comfort Rogers in hers, assuming "the child is frightened." The sequence is almost a template for a *Hot* signature scene in a train berth soon to be examined, in which one party does not know the true identity of the other.

Regardless, with *Hot*'s backdrop of additional comedy genres surveyed (black humor, parody, and screwball comedy), it is time to focus upon the chapter's principle task of examining a rich assortment of personality comedian configurations. First, the logical starting point is the multifaceted nature of the team which drives the story. *Hot* was loosely inspired by the French film *Fanfares of Love* (1936) and its German remake *Fanfaren das Liebe* (1951), which were about two struggling musicians who would do anything for work, such as dressing up like women to play in an all-girl band. The title is an entertainingly telling pun upon the story, since "fanfare" means a short flourish played upon a brass instrument, and in *Hot*, Monroe and saxophone-playing Curtis have what will undoubtedly be a short romantic flourish. But this clever wordplay is neglected in *Hot* literature.

Be that as it may, the reason Wilder and writing partner "Izzy" I. A. L. Diamond (though born Itek Dominic, he enjoyed claiming his initials stood for Interscholastic Algebra League) found the original story promising but too thin was its lack of a second act. That is, their characters' motive was simply trying to obtain musical work, à la Lemmon and Curtis, before the garage shooting. Thus, the original duo would wear disguises for *any* sort of booking, whether it was blackface to get into a jazz combo, or drag for an all-girl band. It was a funny but limited premise, especially since they could easily return to their real identities if a traditional opportunity presented itself. But Wilder wanted his twosome *perilously stuck* in mascara and women's clothing. Finally, he came up with the perfect dark comedy hook, which Wilder labeled "the hammerlock"—witnessing a gangland massacre and fearing for their lives.[11] As the writer/director's definitive biographer, Ed Sikov, observed:

> Diamond and Wilder understood precisely what it would take to force an American man even to play at being a woman [not just briefly dressing like one] in the [repressive] 1950s—the threat of death.[12]

And Wilder knew repression, from losing family in Hitler's death camps, to seeing McCarthyism hound the one actor with whom "Billy once said he'd work for free if he could get him. That was Charlie Chaplin ... [an artist he considered] an authentic genius."[13]

So who was Wilder's manufactured comedy team going to be for *Hot*? As with most studio pictures of that era, United Artists pitched some safe name stars, like Bob Hope and

Danny Kaye, who while outstanding comedians (see chapters 3, 6, and 10), were, if nothing else, too old for the parts. Moreover, to play in drag realistically, they would have been stretching the feminine believability factor Wilder was after. But with his clout he was not listening. The writer/director wanted Frank Sinatra and Tony Curtis, though soon after approaching Curtis, Wilder told him Sinatra was out. In the actor's second autobiography he has Wilder explaining:

> He'll [Sinatra] have to dress up as a woman every day, and I just can't see Frank doing that. I knew what he meant. Along with Frank's arrogance came oversized insecurities.[14]

There are discrepancies between the two Curtis memoirs, most pointedly about his relationship with Monroe. Regardless, in his first go around Curtis simply said Sinatra had lost interest with the part. But the "arrogance" comment connects with something from Sikov's Wilder biography. The writer/director greatly admired Sinatra's talent, even believing his greatest gift could have been acting, if he had focused on film. Yet, Wilder feared the performer would have been egotistically unreliable: "I'm afraid he would run after the first take—'Bye-bye kid, that's it. I'm going. I've got to see a chick!' That would drive me crazy."[15] Given the major trouble Wilder anticipated he would have with the unstable Monroe (to be addressed shortly), Wilder no doubt made a good choice.

Curtis had always been set to be one of the musicians, given his striking good looks. Wilder wanted someone so attractive that the viewer would accept that Sugar (originally set to be played by Mitzi Gaynor) would be immediately entranced by him. Lemmon was the wild card, someone who had impressed Wilder in *Operation Mad Ball* (1957). They ran into each other at a Hollywood restaurant and the writer/director briefly pitched the cross-dressing part. Wilder's status resulted in an immediate yes from Lemmon, who later confessed:

> If anybody else had said ... [the nature of the role], I would have run like a jackrabbit. Go in *drag*? Since it was Billy Wilder, I said, "Fine, I'll do it if I'm free to do it, and if I'm not I'll get free."[16]

Though Curtis had been on Wilder's short list almost from the start, the actor had not been aware of his status. Also, his response was similar to Lemmon's, and was just as casually offered by Wilder. In yet another book by Curtis (with Mark A. Vieira), he gushed:

> I was a star but not in Billy Wilder's part of the firmament. As far as I was concerned, he was way up there, beyond my reach, making pictures with legends like Tyrone Power and Marlene Dietrich.[17]

However, while both actors rate audacious points for taking these then controversial roles, the added risk Curtis was assuming is best set up by Lemmon's comments in Don Widener's biography of the actor:

> Friends told me I could be ruined because the audience would think I was faggy or had a yen to be a transvestite ... the picture was a minefield for actors. I finally decided the real trap was to never *think* of that trap.... The only way to play it was to let it all hang out and just go [with it], trusting that Wilder would say, "Cut," if it got out of bounds.[18]

Why the extra merits for Curtis? Since the beginning of his film career the actor's androgynous beauty had created ongoing rumors that he was gay and threatened his career. Now he was going to play a part in drag. Moreover, studies of *Hot* never seem to hypothesize that just maybe this was why Curtis initially struggled more than Lemmon at the beginning of their cross-dressing scenes. Moreover, comically but not consciously, it was not until well into the shooting that they realized, to a degree, the duo were channeling their mothers, with Lemmon actually suddenly seeing a resemblance.

The brilliance of their teaming is its multifaceted scale, set within the framework of the aforementioned other comic genres. First, in *Hot*'s hilarious pre-drag sequences, when Lemmon and Curtis play a conventional comedy duo, one is seeing the prototype of the future periodic teaming of Lemmon and Walter Matthau—often with the latter comedian playing the huckster type, while Lemmon is the malleable nebbish. This is best showcased by Wilder's later *The Fortune Cookie* (1966), in which Matthau plays Lemmon's crooked brother-in-law lawyer, William H. "Whiplash Willie" Gingrich. Fittingly, Lemmon's perfectly named anti-hero, Harry Hinkle, is browbeaten to go along with a lucrative false insurance claim. Matthau would win a Best Supporting Oscar for the role, which came as no surprise to Wilder, who had wanted him for the Tom Ewell part in *The Seven Year Itch* (1955, see Chapter 7). But Matthau had then been too little known to play opposite Monroe.

These solo stars, Matthau and Lemmon, would go on to periodically team (see Chapter 6 on Hope & Crosby), with and without Wilder. Examples would range from the director's underrated take on the often refashioned *Front Page* (1974), to Gene Saks' adaption of Neil Simon's *The Odd Couple* (1968, which spawned the classic TV show of the same name, 1970–1975). This small screen version would further add to the resume of Tony Randall (see Chapter 11), who reprised Lemmon's role. Wilder considered *Hot* the best film he made with Lemmon: "After a certain time I guess you are prone to regard your most successful picture as your best."[19]

As the old comic set-up goes, "I told you that story to tell you this one." The reason this is Wilder's best Lemmon film is because he teamed Lemmon *with* Curtis. The prototype duo of Lemmon and Curtis is *better* than Lemmon and Matthau. With Curtis' good looks and smoother Slick Willie ways, he could, to borrow an alleged line from American legend Davy Crockett, who coincidentally was also a 1950s pop culture phenomenon, Curtis "could smile a raccoon out of a tree." For example, early in *Hot* Lemmon and Curtis suddenly need a car to get them from Chicago to a one-night booking at the University of Illinois (Urbana). As the team leaves the talent agency, Lemmon thinks the time constraints are impossible, but Curtis counters, "Don't crowd me." And before they even exit said establishment, his character approaches a secretary named Nellie (Barbara Drew) who is really upset at Curtis' Jerry, who has just stood her up for a date. Yet, when he turns his spell on poor Nellie about borrowing her car, the woman does not have a chance:

CURTIS: What are you doin' tonight?
DREW: Tonight? Why?
CURTIS: Cos I've got some plans.
DREW: I'm not doing anything
CURTIS: Really?
DREW: I just thought I'd go home and have some cold pizza [she had prepared it for their broken date].
CURTIS: Then you won't be needing your car?
DREW: My car? Why, you …. [Curtis turns on the charm]
LEMMON: [Lemmon, in the film's only direct address line to the viewer, states,] Isn't he a bit of terrific?

In no Lemmon and Matthau teaming does one find such a superlative audience-directed kudo for hucksterism. Moreover, there is a good reason. Matthau's amusing con artists invariably resemble used car salesmen played by President Richard "Tricky Dick"

Nixon. In reality, no one would be taken in by Matthau. But in Curtis' handsome heyday, there were no impossibilities. Indeed, this might best be documented by Blake Edward's *The Great Race* (1965), in which Lemmon and Curtis co-star but appear as rivals in a slapstick 1908 car race. With Lemmon cast against type as a villain, Curtis' definingly dressed in white dashing hero has a smile, which, via Frank Tashlin–like special effects, *sparkles* in one sequence (see chapters 3 and 9).

Nonetheless, there are also layers to his Lemmon and Curtis team—"teams" within their teams. For instance, the twosome are a traditional male comic duo along the lines of a Hope & Crosby, stars who occasionally worked together, with each being funny. They are also a drag couple. Third, Curtis was a team onto himself—brilliantly playing three parts: Joe, Josephine, and the Cary Grant–like Junior. Sadly, however, Curtis sometimes felt like just a straight man for Lemmon.[20] This is reminiscent of the continuing neglect for Dean Martin's comic gifts when paired with Jerry Lewis (see chapters 3 and 9). Yes, Curtis fed a number of lines to Lemmon. But Curtis' fluctuating three-for-one "trio" is the film's comic tour de force. While Lemmon's comedy line count is higher, Wilder is amusingly generous with Curtis, too. For example, when Lemmon/Daphne first sees Curtis dressed as Junior, with designs on Monroe's Sugar, it appears that Lemmon might blow his friend's cover, until his inspired Cary Grant offers up the most entertainingly fitting dark comedy threat! "I heard a very sad story about a girl who went to Bryn Mawr. She squealed on her roommate and they found her strangled with her own brassiere." Moreover, after 30-plus years of countless *Hot* screenings for my college classes and friends, another Curtis line which consistently gets the biggest laugh, short of Brown's close (to be addressed later in the chapter), involves Sugar discovering that Junior supposedly played water polo:

MONROE: Isn't water polo terribly dangerous?
CURTIS: I'll say. I had two ponies drowned under me.

Yet, the most fascinatingly funny sequence in which Curtis creates a major laugh sequence occurs both without him saying word one, and while he juggles elements of *all* his *Hot* characters. This occurs just after the aforementioned brassiere strangling threat made by Curtis, while in Junior mode. All three actors are on a Miami Beach, before the band's opening that night. Sugar and Lemmon's Daphne have gone out to get some sun, while Curtis' Josephine claims she just wants to soak in a hotel room tub. Naturally, this is Curtis' cover to dress in a stolen yachting costume and "accidentally" meet Sugar on the beach. After his orchestrated chance meeting, Sugar is anxious to immediately introduce Daphine to this handsome young millionaire. Now a Jerry-Joe game is on. Daphne hurries them back, hoping to catch a roommate still dressed as Junior and/or attempting to morph back into Josephine.

However, surprise of surprises, Josephine is *in* the tub with a bubble bath up to her/his neck. Sugar shares her good news but soon has to leave because her roommate is locked out of their room. Once she leaves, an angry Daphne starts to read Josephine the riot act over his actions, provoking Lemmon's normally anti-heroic Jerry to anger:

What are you tryin' to do to that girl, puttin' on a millionaire act? And that phony accent? Nobody talks like that. [Another large laugh line]. I've seen you pull some low tricks on women. This is without a doubt the trickiest, lowest, meanest... [At this point Curtis starts to emerge from the tub in which the bubble bath has hidden the fact he is still dressed as yachtsman Junior, with only his head made-up as Josephine. Now an equally angry Joe/Curtis kicks in.] I'm [Lemmon] not afraid of you. I'm thin but I'm wiry. You're gonna get hurt. When I'm aroused, I'm a tiger. Joe. Don't look at me like that. It was all a joke. I didn't mean any harm. I'm gonna press the [wet yacht] suit myself. [At this point Lemmon is saved by a ringing phone.]

Possibly the Rosetta Stone behind Wilder's creating Lemmon and Curtis teams within teams, or simply the densely character-packed Curtis, was inspired by the director's admiration for the Marx Brothers. The group's wit was often broken down to comedy between Groucho and Chico; Chico and Harpo; Groucho and Harpo, with Chico translating; Groucho and frequent co-star, Margaret "the fifth Marx Brother" Dumont; and in the Marx's Paramount period, Groucho and Zeppo (with the youngest brother retiring before they moved to MGM, 1935). Moreover, in *Duck Soup*'s (1933) celebrated mirror sequence, and the moments leading up to it, one cannot tell the difference among Groucho, Chico, and Harpo. Indeed, Wilder later confessed to paying tribute to the team in *Hot*:

> The Pullman berth party is my homage to the [Buster Keaton–created] stateroom scene in *Night at the Opera* [1935], though no one could have done it better than the Marx Brothers. When the bullets fall out of the gang's [sic, a gangster's] trousers in *Some Like It Hot*, I am doing another homage to them, to that great scene in *Animal Crackers* [1930] when the silverware falls out of Harpo's sleeves. I wish I could have made a Marx Brothers picture, and I talked about it with them but it's one of those never-was films.[21]

Marilyn Monroe just on the verge of diving into Daphne's (Jack Lemmon) train berth in *Some Like It Hot*.

In fact, arguably Lemmon and Monroe's greatest *Hot* sequence is the Pullman berth party, and its build-up. However, before addressing this sequence, one last thing merits noting about Wilder and teams. He never wrote alone. And his literary "teamings" had one key connection with the Lemmon-Curtis dynamic, and its continuation with Lemmon and Matthau. The comic bullying so often at the heart of these twosomes arguably sprang directly from the writer/director's own creative process. One of the reasons his great scripts flowed from a revolving door of partners was a bit of the bully in Wilder. For example, Ernest Lehman, his co-writer/adapter on *Sabrina* (1954, from the Samuel A. Taylor play), suffered a nervous breakdown for his troubles. Lehman later commented on Wilder's team writing style, even beyond his constant slurs: "Billy has to take over your whole life. You don't just collaborate on a script with him. He has to change what you wear and what you eat."[22] No wonder Wilder had a fondness for the comically controlling Groucho and his men from Marx; Wilder's methods were the embodiment of the mustached one.

Regardless, the Lemmon and Monroe berth party sequence has a memorable lead-in. Like most good writing, the script comically references it with a priceless twist later in the film. That is, the groundwork for the berth party begins with Lemmon/Daphne ogling the scantily clad women band members from the top bunk as they prepare for bed:

> When I was a kid, Joe [talking to Curtis' Josephine], I dreamed I was locked up overnight in a pastry shop. And there were goodies all around. Jelly rolls, mocha éclairs and Boston cream pie and cherry tarts.

Curtis' response, besides amusingly telling him, "We're on a diet," was to give Lemmon an all important mantra to constantly repeat: "I'm a girl. I'm a girl." The later comic reversal of this maximum also suggests Lemmon has taken the phrase to heart. Thus, after a short period in Miami, Curtis has conned Lemmon into a date with Brown, in order to facilitate his own romance with Monroe. However, when Junior/Curtis comes back from a perfect evening with Sugar/Monroe, he finds his roommate in rare form:

> CURTIS: What happened? [The question is directed at a very happy Daphne/Lemmon.]
> LEMMON: I'm engaged.
> CURTIS: Congratulations. Who's the lucky girl?
> LEMMON: I am.
> CURTIS: What?
> LEMMON: Osgood [Joe E. Brown] proposed to me. We're planning a June wedding.
> CURTIS: What are you talking about? You can't marry Osgood.
> LEMMON: Do you think he's too old for me? [The dialogue continues along these lines until a still confused Lemmon describes an annulment/settlement plan.]
> CURTIS: Will you take my advice? Forget about the thing, will you? Just keep telling yourself you're a boy.
> LEMMON: I'm a boy.
> CURTIS: That's the boy.
> CURTIS: I'm a boy, I'm a boy, I'm a ... I wish I were dead. I'm a boy....

(Lemmon would later describe it as probably "the best scene I've ever been in."[23])

Returning from this flash forward, Lemmon as Daphne is tucked in his upper bunk repeating his "I'm a girl" refrain. Unexpectedly, Monroe has climbed up a berth ladder to thank him for saving her job—earlier Lemmon had covered for Monroe when she dropped her flask in front of conductor Sweet Sue, who would have bounced Sugar from the band.

Normally, any scene based upon the Marx stateroom sequence, as is the case with the berth party episode, has its major comic payoff being an army of people spilling out of a tight space head over heels. While *Hot*'s ultimate cascading waterfall of band members is hilarious, one could argue that the witty dialogue throughout the sequence is even more consistently entertaining. For instance, after thanking Lemmon for claiming it was "her" flask, the following exchange occurs:

> MONROE: If there's anything I can do for you....
>
> LEMMON: I can think of a million things. [Suddenly she dives into his berth, with the privacy curtains decidedly closed behind her.] That's one of 'em.
>
> MONROE: It's Sweet Sue. [Their sleepy bandleader has appeared without warning to groggily head for the bathroom.]

Another delectable example occurs just prior to what Lemmon had hoped would be an intimate party with Monroe, before seemingly the whole band crashes their private shindig:

> LEMMON: [He has procured some alcohol and cups.] Oh, I tell you my dear, this is the only way to travel.
>
> MONROE: Put on some lights. I can't see what I'm doing.
>
> LEMMON: No lights. We don't want them [the band] to know.
>
> MONROE: But I might spill some.
>
> LEMMON: So spill it. Spills, thrills, laughs, and games. This may even turn out to be a surprise party.
>
> MONROE: What's the surprise?
>
> LEMMON: Not yet.
>
> MONROE: When?
>
> LEMMON: Better have a drink first.
>
> MONROE: That'll put hair on your chest.
>
> LEMMON: No fair guessing.

Unfortunately for Lemmon, their little "clambake" is overheard and soon becomes the most densely populated of parties. Then, when the girls begin to put ice down Lemmon's back after he develops the hiccups, and his secret threatens to become a mass "unveiling," he pulls the emergency cord. The train immediately begins to stop, and it is an instant Niagara Falls of musicians tumbling out of Lemmon's top berth. Funny stuff, but the proceeding banter is still arguably superior amusement. Moreover, it perfectly fits Lemmon's personality comedian persona. His screen alter ego is the stereotypical anti-hero operating purely upon chance, and doomed to failure.

To better flesh this out, contrast Lemmon's Marx Brothers–inspired sequence with con man Curtis' later love fest with Monroe on Osgood's yacht. Both younger men had had an immediate thing for her. But Lemmon's innocent gregariousness had merely resulted in them becoming "girlfriends." As with Walter Mitty, he could dream of the random almost "surprise party" with Monroe, but it remained a dream. Moreover, like the ideal schlemiel, he allowed Curtis to browbeat him into a "relationship" with Osgood so his "buddy" could use the millionaire's yacht to win Monroe.

In contrast to Lemmon's absence of a plan, Curtis' mind had immediately gone into overdrive. For instance, before the duo had even checked into the Miami hotel as Josephine and Daphne, Curtis had stolen the suitcase of Sweet Sue's stuffy business manager Beinstock (Dave Barry, whose movie name is an ongoing *Hot* joke). The moneyman had egotistically packed what would pass for a wealthy yacht owner's suit, complete with a captain's cap. So what is the theft tie-in? Curtis had discovered on the band's train trip south that Sugar was on the lookout for a millionaire, and since Miami was at that time a magnet for moneyed playboys on the water...

Most importantly, however, Curtis' scheme encompassed what Wilder considered one of the script's most notable ideas: how to put a new spin on the movie's obligatory Monroe sex scene. Since any man would want to make love to her, Wilder turned it around, saying "I made her the *seducer* [in the love scenes with an allegedly impotent Curtis/Shell Oil Junior on Osgood's yacht]."[24] Thus, Wilder's insight further underlined the con man astuteness of Curtis' character. Moreover, it totally meshed with Monroe's persona. She was the same child/woman who attempted to bolster co-star Tom Ewell's anti-hero in *The Seven Year Itch* (1955, see Chapter 7), while even finding a comparable sympathy for the unloved *Creature from the Black Lagoon* (1954).

Of course, while Ewell, like Lemmon, genuinely needed helped, Curtis' huckster had opportunistically worked out a successful plan to make Monroe do all the sexual heavy lifting. The only redeeming quality had Curtis' character falling in love with her. Consequently, true to form, *Hot*'s underdog Lemmon could not make any progress with Monroe, even when she jumped into his upper berth while conniving Curtis had her voluntarily steaming over his glasses with foreplay. It seems that Wilder had made all these sexual Slick Willie components (something for which he himself was once known) come together in "watertight" fashion, to pun the yacht setting. Yet, the script ratchets up things to an even more impermeable state via the manner in which Curtis' confidence man is able to manipulate Monroe.[25] Yes, it is a brilliant stroke to make Junior impotent, thus encouraging Monroe to do some "sexual healing." Moreover, making Junior's impotence the result of a lost love is an excellent variation of the old chestnut of turning pity/sympathy into sex. However, given that *Hot* nicely doubles as a dark comedy, the manner in which Junior's first and only girlfriend has died is Wilder's coup de grâce gift to the audience and con man Curtis:

MONROE: What happened?
CURTIS: I don't want to bore you.
MONROE: You couldn't possibly.
CURTIS: Well.... It was my freshman year at Princeton. There was this girl. Her name was Nellie. Her father was the vice president of Hupmobile [a popular 1920s automobile]. She wore glasses, too. That summer we were at the Grand Canyon. We were on the highest ledge watching the sunset, when suddenly we got the impulse to kiss. I took off my glasses. She took off her glasses. I took a step towards her. She took a step toward me.
MONROE: [Gasps.]
CURTIS: Yes. Eight hours later they brought her up by mule.

Now, while Curtis' artificial ruse is working masterfully upon the yacht, Wilder is regularly using a swish pan to also showcase Brown/Osgood's more traditional courtship of Lemmon on land. Ultimately, the latter couple tango until dawn (bitingly trading a long-stemmed rose in each other's mouths with each turn). And the humor gets an added boost with a blindfolded orchestra backdrop. Both Lemmon and Curtis return to their hotel rooms in love ... which results in Curtis' aforementioned attempt to reprogram the "engaged" Daphne/Lemmon with a new mantra "I'm a boy..." And this represents the logical moment to move forward to both the picture's last personality comedian (Brown), and its much ballyhooed conclusion. As a background set-up, murder witnesses Curtis and Lemmon have been discovered in Miami by the mob, and the movie's two couples (Monroe and Curtis, and Lemmon and Brown) are motor boating to an escape on Osgood's yacht:

> Lemmon: [He is still made-up as Daphne.] Osgood [Brown], I'm gonna level with you. We can't get married at all.
> Brown: Why not?
> Lemmon: Well…. In the first place, I'm not a natural blonde.
> Brown: Doesn't matter.
> Lemmon: I smoke. I smoke all the time. [Osgood's mother, who one never sees, is dead against her son being involved with a smoker.]
> Brown: I don't care.
> Lemmon: I have a terrible past. For three years I've been living with a saxophone player [Curtis].
> Brown: I forgive you.
> Lemmon: I can never have children.
> Brown: We can adopt some.
> Lemmon: You don't understand, Osgood. [Lemmon pulls his wig off.] I'm a man.
> Brown: [In a perfect deadpan] Well, nobody's perfect.

This is one of cinema's quintessential funny sequences. As noted earlier, the American Film Institute included Brown's "Well, nobody's perfect" in its 100 most substantial quotes.[26] Brown's surprise deadpan acceptance, sans neither a double take nor bug-eyed shock, completely sells the scene. And Wilder and Diamond, who had originally only included the line as filler until they thought of something better, accomplish the forever difficulty closing task to a funny film—to comically top all that has come before. Moreover, the line continues to resonate over time. It originally produced laughs via comic surprise, not to be taken literally. Today, the humor remains but one wants to suddenly rethink the whole Brown character. One might liken it to the sequence in *Bringing Up Baby* (1938), when Katharine Hepburn has taken all of Cary Grant's clothing and he is forced to put on a woman's frilly dressing gown. When Hepburn's screen aunt (Mae Robson) asks why he is dressed that way, an exasperated Grant jumps in the air and says, "I just went gay all of a sudden." This funny sequence did not originally obtain its humor upon today's meaning for "gay."

Regardless, though tradition has long decreed that we transcend our comic favorites (indeed the oldest of comedy theories is that of superiority), we still enjoy the odd comment from the fool which might make us reconsider our position on him. For instance, maybe his entertaining idiocy is something of a pose, and we label him a "wise fool," or "crazy like a fox." However, perhaps the surprising observation is not so much insightfully wise but rather revealing an entirely different comedy agenda for our character. Conversely, the fool's startling comment might only be an accidental exercise in comic absurdity. Any of these observations could be applied to Brown's closing line. Whether one interprets this as the height of comic absurdity, some sort of mind game, or the revelation that his character is really a poser who swings both ways, the line is now much more likely to provide a provocative finish to the picture—a close which does not close but rather opens new questions.

During Brown's 1930s heyday, his screen persona was generally an energetic straight arrow whose modest intelligence never hindered occasional bouts of ego. As noted earlier, Wilder had cast him against type to soften and/or avoid criticism from viewers who might have found his dirty old man offensive. Yet that description only describes *Hot*'s initial introduction of Osgood, which culminates in an off camera pass at Lemmon's Daphne. As the movie progresses, Brown's character, both as written and played, seems incapable of suppressing his original screen persona's innate sweetness. For example, when Osgood comes ashore planning to take Daphne back to a yacht on which the crew has been dispatched, and a lovely dinner laid out, "her" refusal (enabling Curtis to implement his plan) barely upsets Brown's figure. He immediately suggests a little "roadhouse" at which they can go dancing. Indeed, he seems especially taken with music, having shared in his original invitation how happy he was to have a "new batch of Rudy Vallee records [a popular period singer and later actor]." Consequently, when Osgood is so unfazed by Daphne being a man, one could also argue that this represents neither comic absurdity, nor the surprising revelation he is not a heterosexual. At an age when companionship often usurps sex, Osgood's inspiringly stunning non-response could also be read as embracing a comically asexual friendship. After all, he has been married over a dozen times (his "ma-ma" was keeping track); why not give mere companionship a try? One is reminded of a comment from singer David Bowie, whose work as a gifted painter only became more broadly appreciated after his 2016 death: "Art should be open enough for me [the viewer] to develop my own dialogue with it."[27] Though similar comments have been expressed before, it seems especially relevant here, given that Bowie's many musical stages invariably involved a blurring of gender lines. Regardless, farce has always been driven by tolerance, and what says that better than "Well, nobody's perfect?"

However one interprets this close, it is most telling that the film ends with Osgood and Daphne instead of Junior and Sugar. It suggests that with all the seeming roadblocks to a relationship between the former "couple," they ironically have a better chance for success than the twosome played by Curtis and Monroe. Indeed, if a viewer watches the film enough, and focuses on Daphne's face at the close, instead of Osgood, one almost feels as if he has worn "her" down to submission. I am reminded of the romantic stalker-like Barbara Streisand line to Ryan O'Neal at the close of *What's Up, Doc?* (1972, a loose remake of *Bringing Up Baby*), "You can't fight a tidal wave." Moreover, even Lemmon's broader playing of Daphne (both physically and verbally), versus Curtis' restrained Josephine, is reminiscent of a younger "crater-mouthed" Brown, especially when he played in drag during the 1930s. In fact, Wilder had hired a famous female impersonator to assist Lemmon and Curtis in their transformations but eventually Lemmon's resistance had driven him off.

Regardless, the greatness of the film and its focus personality comedians demand a lengthy addendum about the trying circumstance under which it was made—an increasingly unstable Monroe. Much later, the always diplomatic Lemmon observed:

> Tony had his hands full with Marilyn [having the most scenes with her]. She was ill at the time but we didn't know that until later. All we knew then was that she was driving everybody nuts. You might do forty takes with Marilyn, or you might do one, and Billy's gonna print the one that's best for her. I figured that out fairly early and made up my mind, if I let this [pressure] get to me, it's gonna hurt my performance.[28]

Even Lemmon, however, could be pushed by Monroe to reveal a harsher but interesting assessment of how the actress worked to find her screen persona:

> Marilyn had a kind of built-in alarm system. It would "go off" in the middle of a scene if ... [it] was not right for her, and she would just stop.... She would stand there with her eyes closed, biting her lip and kind of wringing her hands until she had it worked out ... she didn't mean to be selfish—it was

the only way she could work.... [But] she didn't give a damn about the director, the other actors.... [However] it was fascinating. I don't think Marilyn had a great talent—what she had was an ability to use *completely* the talents she did have.[29]

Still, Lemmon was tactful, and his comments came after Monroe's death. But Wilder and Curtis publicly lowered the boom on the actress immediately after the movie was completed. For instance, Wilder was widely quoted as saying since he was the only director to do two movies with her, the Director's Guild should give him a Purple Heart. And Curtis told anyone who would listen that making love to Monroe was like kissing Hitler, and maybe that was unfair to the dictator, since he had never tried to kiss Hitler. However, with the passage of time, these comments were heavily toned down. In fact, it occurred fairly early, once the movie was a critical and commercial hit.

Of course, for Wilder, he did not just have to deal with the long delays caused by Monroe. There was an added humiliation he had to endure daily on the set. At the end of a shot Monroe would first look to her personal acting coach (Paula Strasberg) as to whether the sequence worked, rather than director Wilder. The sardonic Wilder went into attack mode early, as in asking Strasberg, in so many words, whether the scene worked for her? This somewhat leveled the playing field but Monroe's deferring to Strasberg would continue throughout the shoot. After making *The Seven Year Itch* with Wilder, she had moved back to New York and joined Lee Strasberg's Actors Studio, famous for the Method—literally becoming the screen character. (Paula Strasberg was Lee's wife.) Wilder would later provocatively place part of the blame for the multi-faceted train wreck which was Marilyn on the Strasbergs:

> I'm not convinced she needed training. God gave her everything. Before going to the Actors Studio she was like a tightrope walker who doesn't know there's a pit down there she could fall into. Now she knows about the pit, and ... she's self-conscious.[30]

Still, Lemmon finding her "fascinating," despite the frustration she brought to the set, is best explained by Monroe biographer Carl Rollyson:

> She wanted to know her characters and how her acting had to be all of a piece. It had to come organically out of herself—even the smallest gestures and seemingly innocuous expressions. Sugar Kane could easily have been just a stereotype, a figure in a farce, but in playing her Monroe generated a substantial personality, a wholeness that transcends caricature.[31]

Monroe's little girl persona was still intact from *The Seven Year Itch*. Despite what her physical appearance did to men, "as if fed on sexual candy," she remained the child that needed mothering and love but was usually only fated to be further derailed by sensing this hollowness in others.[32] Still, her characters invariably tried to help, even if this amounted to the "big girl" sexuality she offered Curtis' impotent Junior. Monroe biographer Donald Spoto has credited Wilder with having "noticed [since *The Seven Year Itch*] that Marilyn had matured as an actress ... 'with her own natural instinct for reading a line.'"[33] Otherwise she could not have effectively kept this child persona while recognizing her own weakness in a monologue to Curtis' Josephine:

> You fall for them and you love 'em—you think it's going to be the biggest thing since the Graf Zeppelin [an airship named after flight pioneer Graf (count) Ferdinand Zeppelin]—and the next thing you know they're borrowing money from you and spending it on other dames and betting the horses.... Then one morning you wake up and the saxophone is gone and the guy is gone, and all that's left behind is a pair of old socks and a tube of toothpaste, all squeezed out.... So you pull yourself together and you

go on to the next job, and the next saxophone player, and it's the same thing all over again.... [Yet, she will remain loyal to Curtis' Josephine, even when she discovers he is yet another male saxophone player and not millionaire Junior].

Given that Monroe has become one of Hollywood's most seminal icons, it stands to reason that she is the *Hot* personality comedian who garners the most attention. Moreover, her instability and personal issues have always dominated any examination of the picture. Yet, as this text has demonstrated, Curtis' chronicling of the film, though sometimes entertainingly inconsistent, has generally gone unnoticed, just as his winning portrayal of three characters has been underrated. (Coming full circle, a senior aged Curtis would also even briefly play Brown's Osgood character in a stage production of *Hot*.) And his later success as an abstract painter has a potential tangential comic tie to the picture. Thus, before examining the critical and commercial period reaction to the movie, it seems fitting that one credit the neglected Curtis' litany of reasons on why making *Hot* "drove him slightly mad," and make for an off-beat summation of the movie.[34]

Just off camera there were often buckets of ice water for the male co-stars' feet, given their need to wear and walk in women's shoes, which was made worse by Monroe's *long* delays in getting to the set. When in female mode, Lemmon and Curtis wore an otherworldly garish green makeup which photographed skin tone for this black and white movie (the reason why it was not shot in color—the standard stipulation in Monroe contracts). Before each take, as noted earlier, Lemmon would always get in the mood by saying, "Magic time!" Though a charming tradition, when Monroe would routinely flub her lines dozens of times, one would also hear "Magic Time!" ad nauseam. Plus, given that the gowns the fellows wore made bathroom breaks difficult, long delays were an added challenge, though Curtis eventually designed a special under garment funnel system for secret relief. And finally, he not only had the most scenes with the line-forgetting Monroe (many times her dialogue was posted on off-camera cue-cards), he often found himself in the most unusual scene settings, such as the fully clothed bubble bath sequence, which went on for prune skin–producing hours. Thus, is it any wonder that Curtis' future paintings were often of a surrealistic nature?

Later studies of *Some Like It Hot* would sometimes suggest it opened to mixed reviews, but solid word of mouth quickly turned it into a commercial hit. But any reference to mixed reviews is pure *poppycock*. *Variety*'s early critique, a month *before* its world premiere at Times Square's recently remodeled *Loew's State Theatre* showplace began:

> "Some Like It Hot," directed in masterly style by Billy Wilder, is probably the funniest picture of recent memory. It's a wacky, clever, farcical comedy that starts off like a firecracker and keeps on throwing off lively sparks till the picture ends.[35]

But the *Variety* praise which, without a doubt, would have most pleased Wilder, included the word "Lubitsch"—"the scene on the train, where the 'private' Pullman berth party of Lemmon and Miss Monroe in their nightie is invaded by guzzling dames, represents humor of Lubitsch proportions."[36] Director Ernst Lubitsch (1892–1947) had been Wilder's friend and mentor, with the younger man having co-scripted the master's groundbreaking comedy *Ninotchka* (1939, billed as "Garbo Laughs"). In later years Wilder would even have a sign over his office door asking, "How would Lubitsch do it?"

The *Hollywood Reporter*'s equally early review, under the title, "'Some Like It Hot'

Certain To Be Even Hotter At B. [Box] O. [Office]," had as strong an opening to its critique as *Variety*'s:

> "Some Like It Hot" is another supersonic, breakneck, belly-laugh comedy which should be a blockbusting bonanza ... [and] proof that when the making of pictures is ... handed over to men whose only purpose is to create amusement, they are still the world's best means of entertainment.[37]

The reviews also provided further documentation of Lemmon's Daphne being in the earlier broad Brown tradition the older comedian brought to his drag characters:

> Lemmon's wildly uproarious impersonation of a Mack Sennett–type bathing beauty recalls the lampoons of shrill femininity which brought [Brown contemporary] Bert Savoy [who specialized in cross-dressing comedy] stardom in the Ziegfeld Follies.[38]

Hollywood Reporter critic Jack Moffitt was also a critical clairvoyant in assessing both the film's sweeping appeal *and* the ease with which it put over its dark comedy structure: "[being] masterful ... in making the audience accept killing as a part of comedy.... This should be a winner in any town in any state for the [co-producing] Mirisch organization."[39]

The following month's star-studded Times Square opening garnered comparable praise, best summarized by the caption of Kate Cameron's *New York Daily News* critique: "Gallop, Don't Amble to 'Some Like It Hot.'"[40] Cameron quickly added:

> [This] is the funniest comedy I've seen in years. There aren't many of the hundred and four minutes of running time that doesn't find the audience laughing its head off at the antics of Jack Lemmon, Tony Curtis and Marilyn Monroe.[41]

Cue magazine simply let the event write the review:

> I'm sure this must be a very funny picture, because in the theatre I couldn't hear a tenth of the dialogue for audience laughter, rolling and reverberating through the house in endless waves of ... thunder, yaks, yowls, giggles, guffaws, shrieks, and screams.[42]

Another novel way to praise the picture came from *New York Herald Tribune* critic Paul V. Beckley, who, after giving the film kudos, entered into the fun by adding some comedy of his own. For example, "A good deal of it if not downright bawdy is certainly playing piano on the premises."[43]

Other publications pumped out more traditional praise, such as Rose Pelswick's *New York Journal American* opening with all capital letters, "CALL IT THE MOST HILARIOUS ENTERTAINMENT of this or any year and you come close to describing 'Some Like It Hot.'"[44] Tonier publications, lionized the movie, too. For instance *The New Yorker* called it "a jolly, carefree enterprise in which some of the old phonetic nonsense of Mack Sennett is restored to the screen."[45] The magazine also stated a pattern from the other reviews, given all the assembled personality comedian talent, "none is more effective than Jack Lemmon."[46] Even the always hard to crack *New York Times* ultimately had to admit, in what sounded rather like *The New Yorker*:

> Both [Lemmon and Curtis] take to slapstick, doubletakes and mugging as though they were charter members of the Keystone Kops. They give vigorous, top-flight performances that add greatly to the wacky goings-on.[47]

So much for the later urban legend that the movie opened to "mixed reviews." *Hot* would be the third top grossing film of the year, after *Auntie Mame* and the *Shaggy Dog* (both 1959).[48] Surprisingly, given the great cast performances, Lemmon would be the only actor nominated for an Oscar—though as noted, he received the most attention in the reviews. Lemmon lost the Best Actor Oscar to Charlton Heston in *Ben Hur* (late 1959, which became a box office juggernaut in 1960). (Lemmon and Monroe would, however, win Golden Globes as Best Actor and Best Actress in the Musical/Comedy category.) Wilder was nominated for both Best Director and Best Adapted Screenplay (with I. A. L. Diamond) Oscars, but William Wyler won the former statuette for *Ben Hur*, and the writing award went to Neil Paterson for *Room at the Top* (1959). (The Writers Guild of America did recognize the Wilder and Diamond script as the Best-Written Comedy.)

In terms of *Hot*'s personality comedians, the film would most benefit Lemmon for one key reason; Wilder felt:

> "He has the greatest rapport with an audience of anyone since Chaplin. Just by looking at him people can tell what goes on in his heart." Before teaming up with Lemmon, Wilder's connection to his comedy characters tended to be more detached. Now, with Lemmon, he could reveal (however hesitantly and cruelly) some of his own hidden sweetness and bumbling insecurity.[49]

Writer/director Cameron Crowe would best summarize this scenario in his book *Conversations with Wilder* (1999): "[Jack Lemmon was the only one] who truly brought your words and your style to life."[50] Wilder would do for Lemmon in the following decade, in pictures

One of cinema's most iconic closing lines now adds ambiguity to its meaning—Joe E. Brown (left) tells his fiancé Daphne (Jack Lemmon), "Well, noboby's perfect" after discovering she's a he in *Some Like It Hot*.

like *The Apartment* (1960), *Irma la Douce* (1963), and *The Fortune Cookie* (1966), what Frank Tashlin had done for Bob Hope and Jerry Lewis in the 1950s (see Chapters 3 and 9). And as previously noted, many auteurs have helped mold and/or tweak personality comedians, such as Preston Sturges modifying Eddie Bracken's and Harold Lloyd's screen characters in the 1940s, or Leo McCarey making adjustments to the 1930s Marx Brothers and Eddie Cantor.[51]

Though this book has demonstrated that Tashlin had the most significant writer/director cartoonish impact on the 1950s, one would be remiss in not coming full circle back to Wilder being responsible for Monroe's best and most defining personality comedy performances of the 1950s, both with *Hot* and the earlier *Seven Year Itch*. Though she was so difficult with whom to work, especially in *Hot*, he mustered the patience and the superlative talent to showcase her screen persona's inherent child/woman nature. These were her legacy pictures, though John Huston followed the template in her greatest dramatic role, the vulnerable divorcee to surrogate father figure Clark Gable in the *Misfits* (1962, which was written by her then husband, Arthur Miller). Regardless, unlike the satirical *object* she would have been in Tashlin's hands, Wilder made her comically poignant and three-dimensional.

Before closing the chapter, one must include Wilder's favorite post-shooting *Hot* story. After a number of years, the director revealed on the late night talk show circuit, that one sneak preview audience response card stated, "I laughed so hard I peed in my girlfriend's hand." Maybe Wilder was so good with personality comedians because these later years revealed he was the most amazing of raconteur jesters. Indeed, this sardonic wit, and its connection to *Hot*, lived on after his death. His tombstone reads:

BILLY WILDER
I'M A WRITER
But Then
NOBODY'S PERFECT

Epilogue
The Question of Quality
1950s Film Clowns

> Early in *Some Like It Hot* (1959), when Jack Lemmon and Tony Curtis are still working members of a 1929 *male* band, the former musician expresses doubts about job security. Curtis attempts to calm Lemmon by comparing their position to a series of things which could never happen, "Why paint everything black?... Suppose the stock market crashes. Suppose Mary Pickford divorces Douglas Fairbanks. Suppose the Dodgers leave Brooklyn...."
> His assurances are suddenly cut short by a job-ending police raid.

Naturally, Curtis' litany of comforting guarantees would all eventually crumble, too. His position is often the two-part perspective of many personality comics. First, do not think, or as entertainer/comedy historian Steve Allen wrote during the 1950s, "he *relieves* you of the responsibility [to think]."[1] Indeed, clown comedy is the most mind candy-driven of all the laughter genres. In an earlier decade book on the subject, *Film Clowns of the Depression: Twelve Defining Comic Performances* (2007), I found that Charlie Chaplin was one of the few comedians to focus on the economic crisis, though the Marx Brothers briefly allude to the subject on their way to satirizing government in *Duck Soup* (1933).[2] Second, if a somber subject cannot be dodged, trivialize it, as Curtis attempted to do. That seemed to be the message of a second decade text I did on the subject, *Forties Film Funnymen: The Decade's Great Comedians at Work in the Shadow of War*.[3] Other than Chaplin's title characters in *The Great Dictator* (1940) and *Monsieur Verdoux* (1947), and Ernst Lubitsch's use of Jack Benny in *To Be or Not to Be* (1942), the other pivotal 1940s comedians downplayed the conflict by staying "in the shadow of war."

Now there is nothing wrong with mind candy mirth, or trivializing the traumatic. After all, most viewers embrace the clown as a comforting escape from the real world. Certainly, that is the conclusion Joel McCrea's wannabe serious film director ultimately comes to in Preston Sturges' classic *Sullivan's Travels* (1942). Searching for the harshness of life, McCrea's character gets more than he bargained for when he wrongly ends up on a Southern chain gang. Yet, one night the convicts are given the chance to see a Disney cartoon personality comedian, *Playful Pluto* (1934), and the laughter which ensues provides him with an epiphany maybe best capsulized by film critic/historian David Thomson: "There is something to be said for silly movies that make you laugh."[4]

That particular *Sullivans' Travels* scene and its sensible suggestion is also the catalyst for an equally pertinent memorable line from Steve Martin's movie director in Lawrence Kasdan's *Grand Canyon* (1991). After surviving a robbery/shooting, Martin's escapist filmmaker chides his best friend (Kevin Kline) for not having seen and absorbed *Sullivan's Travels'* point—"That's part of your problem, you haven't seen enough movies. All of life's riddles are answered in the movies."

Whether or not one subscribes to that axiom, personality comedy has been the most pervasive genre throughout the history of essentially escapist mainstream movies. For example, I grew up in the latter half of the Western film heyday. That is, between 1940 and the mid-1960s, roughly one in four American films was a Western, and there were 20-plus horse operas on primetime TV. Yet today, the genre is barely visible. However, throughout that mini-Western renaissance, personality comedies were as strong as ever, just as now the genre happily chugs along during the present obsession with sci-fi/fantasy and horror. Thus, personality comedy through the years has been the genre which most frequently has had to dodge society's more humorless subjects.

Now, as already implied with references to the Depression and World War II, every decade seems to have the proverbial eight-hundred-pound gorilla casting a dark silhouette over the proceedings. For the 1950s subject of this text, the shadow was a two-part variation of the same thing. For most Americans it was the Cold War and the Doomsday Clock—the symbolic tick tock face representing a countdown to a possible global catastrophe. Established in 1947 at the University of Chicago, the closer scientists set the clock to midnight, the closer the world was to global disaster. For most of its history, especially during the ongoing communist paranoia of the 1950s, the Doomsday Clock concerned itself with fear of a nuclear holocaust brought on by a war between the United States and what was then the communist Soviet Union. Indeed, the catalyst for the clock, and its locations, were all tied to these events. That is, an international group of scholars called the "Chicago Atomic Scientists" had been involved in the World War II atomic bomb-producing Manhattan Project.

Consequently, the fear of a mushroom cloud ending to life as we knew it was a 1950s given, especially after the Soviets developed their own bomb in 1949. Yet, it did not impact most people directly beyond, say, a random question like, should my new suburban house have a bomb shelter? (This was a question my parents had to address, with my father declining. His reason actually anticipated a later *Twilight Zone* (1959–1965) episode in which "friends" fought each other over the only shelter in the neighborhood.) Regardless, if one were a Hollywood filmmaker, any hint of even past Soviet sympathies meant Congress' House Un-American Activities Committee (HUAC) would scare the film industry into blacklisting you out of a job. Ironically, this perspective is merely a variation on personality comedian/auteur Mel Brooks' take on the genre: "Tragedy is when I cut my finger. Comedy is when you fall into an open sewer and die."[5]

Nevertheless, the ramifications of McCarthyism made 1950s comedians, and entertainment in general, all the more politically innocuous. In a 1958 *Newsweek* article Groucho Marx observed, "If Will Rogers [1879–1935] were to come back today, he couldn't make a living. They'd throw him in the clink [prison] for being subversive."[6] Paralleling this piece, the man from Marx expanded on comedy's 1950s decline in a *Los Angeles Mirror-News* column entitled, "Groucho Diagnoses Our Ailing Comedy," focusing the blame on the communist witch hunting of Senator Joseph McCarthy (1908–1957):

> Everybody became afraid to say what they were thinking. This affected comedy and comedians. There used to be a lot of comedians telling political jokes. Bob Hope is the only one left.... Many people don't seem to realize that the first thing which disappears when men are turning a country into a totalitarian state is comedy and comics.[7]

In this text, HUAC activity could be so out of touch with reality that the only political picture addressed, and a patriotic one at that—*Born Yesterday* (1950, see Chapter 1)—could have a dishonest businessman be decoded as a communist attack on capitalism? Thankfully, these assaults on the film and its star, Judy Holliday, were seen as pure lunacy by most viewers. Still, it set a chilling tone for the decade to follow. And Holliday was blacklisted for a time, given her earlier leftist views.

Of course, most obviously, though it had nothing to do with Charlie Chaplin's *Limelight* (1952, see Chapter 4), HUAC was a major contributing factor in hounding the comedian out of the country. Here was another early-in-the-decade warning about keeping the laughs innocuous. Moreover, like the townsfolk in the McCarthyism allegory *High Noon* (1952, written by the soon to be blacklisted Carl Foreman), Hollywood had hardly rushed to Chaplin's aid. At best, even a major Chaplin fan—though admittedly a conservative one—the ironically nicknamed "Red" Skelton, would only limit his comments about Chaplin, whose work had so influenced his, to praising the *comedy* gifts of the man who gave cinema its most iconic figure—the Tramp (see Chapter 5). As Groucho added, Bob Hope was the most high profile funnyman to counterattack, which merits recycling Ski Nose's most pointed jab from Chapter 3:

> No wonder there's so much confusion in Washington.... Everybody back there spends all their time under their desks.... If they're not practicing for an H-bomb attack they're hiding from McCarthy.[8]

Hope or not, the added paradox was that 1950s personality comedy, a genre which normally leads the pack in playing it safe, was thus "dumbing it down" even more. However, there were some subtextual attacks on the American establishment. For example, the Frank Tashlin-directed Martin & Lewis of *Artists and Models* (1955, see Chapter 9) has fun with the Congressional hearings and the inherent *dangers* of comic books! And Tashlin's molding of Tony Randall in *Will Success Spoil Rock Hunter?* (1957, see Chapter 11), is an inspired mockery of both capitalism and its lemming consumers. Of course, it is not without its provocative smokescreens—starting with Jayne Mansfield's breasts as a marketing metaphor for a decade of "bigger is always better."

Inexplicably, there is a pertinent recent quote for the subject at hand in Stephen King's time-tripping novel *11/22/63* (2011, about averting John F. Kennedy's assassination), which is largely set in the same year (1958) as the aforementioned Groucho quotes. King observed, "Time is a tree with many branches."[9] That is, if anything remotely positive came from the blacklisting stain on American film, and on our history in general, it possibly assisted in catapulting the emergence of the cartoon-trained Tashlin to being the most influential live-action personality comedian-molding director of the 1950s.

Hypothetically, based upon the previous decade studies of personality comedians, few film clowns would have acted upon the subject anyway. Winston Churchill's 1946 speech warning that "an iron curtain has descended across the continent [of Europe]" would no doubt have convinced all but a few "Chaplins" and "Marx Brothers" to be cautious. Yet, at least the option was still there, bleak as it might be. Of course, it was also a question if those lemming-like audiences Tashlin's comedians shish-kebabbed so well would follow. However, like any entertainment pendulum, personality comedians in particular became so darkly political during the turbulent 1960s and early 1970s, former comic activist Steve Martin completely changed directions with his "wild and crazy guy," seeing the need for a safety valve of silliness. In his memoir, *Born Standing Up* (2007), he observed:

> I cut my hair, shaved my beard, and put on a suit. I stripped the act of all political references, which I felt was an act of defiance [and no doubt healing]. To politics I was saying, "I'll get along without you very well. It's time to be funny [without a message]."[10]

But it was *his* choice. The world of laughter will always have its George Carlins, who feel it is "the duty of the comedian to find where the [status quo] line is drawn and *cross it deliberately*."[11]

Ironically, another threat to the quality and/or diversity of 1950s' cinema personality comedians simply came from the talent-draining medium of TV. As noted throughout the text, the first half of the decade represented a war for audiences between film and TV, though the small screen's *Colgate Comedy Hour* was like a second home to frequent guest hosts Martin & Lewis and Abbott & Costello. However, Red Skelton was the only "A" status film comedian to jump ship and fully embrace what was then the grueling 39-episode seasonal norm of network television. Other major cinema clowns, like Bob Hope, merely dabbled in the medium. Additional early TV personality comedian stars often had one of two previous relationships with the movies.

The first scenario involved comedians who had been in the movies but had never become stars. This is best exemplified by TV's initial superstar Milton Berle (1908–2002). His monumental popularity had him being credited with selling so many TV sets he was affectionately nicknamed "Uncle Miltie" and "Mr. Television." His screen career, though modest, stretched as far back as being a child actor in American cinema's first comedy feature, *Tillie's Pictured Romance* (1914, with Charlie Chaplin). Others in this category would include Jackie Gleason, Phil Silvers and Eve Arden.

The second film comedian to TV star grouping were prominent big screen performers who never quite garnered star status. This group would include Jack Benny, Lucille Ball, Burns & Allen, and Martha Raye. Indeed, for a short time between the late 1930s and mid–1940s, Benny could arguably be called a film star. But his focus was always radio, and after a few film failures, he became his own worst enemy. That is, by forever lampooning his movie career, much of Benny's radio and later TV audiences bought into his self-deprecating filmography.

Regardless, moving on to this study's focus film clowns, there are several parallels to address. First, it is obviously possible to find a way to label every decade one of transition for a multitude of subjects. And thus it is for personality comedians. Yet, I would label the 1950s the twentieth century's *seminal* decade of change for this genre. While all the key figures highlighted herein are still most associated with comedy, for the first time the majority are not strictly pigeonholed as screen clowns. Indeed, for some, even Chaplin's *Limelight* (1952), or Red Skelton's *The Clown* (1953), might place tragedy before their clown components.

This diversity phenomenon is best demonstrated by Jack Lemmon's filmography. While he won an Oscar for *Mr. Roberts* (1955) and would be nominated for another statuette in Billy Wilder's *Some Like It Hot* (1959), four of his six future Academy Award nominations would be for dramas: *The Apartment* (1960, another Wilder comedy), *Days of Wine and Roses* (1962, an alcoholic problem film), *Save The Tiger* (1973; he wins an Oscar for a picture about moral decay in America), *The China Syndrome* (1979, a thriller about a nuclear power plant cover-up), *Missing* (1982, a father searches for his son after a U.S.–backed Chilean coup), and *Tribute* (1980, a quasi-comedy about a flawed dying entertainer making amends).

Moving to Tony Curtis, while arguably his best ever performance was in *Some Like It Hot*, it took that picture to fully showcase/reveal his comic talents. But other than *Operation Petticoat* (1959, with his idol Cary Grant), Curtis' other signature roles, in a career which sadly peaked in the mid–1960s, are anything but comedies. And two of the three predated *Hot*: *Sweet Smell of Success* (1957, in which he is outstanding as a press agent in a nourish drama), *The Defiant One* (1958, Curtis is Oscar-nominated in a problem film as a runaway convict handcuffed to Sidney Portier), and the title character in the murder thriller *The Boston Strangler* (1968). Curtis' inclusion here is based upon his unacknowledged three-character stealing of the American Film Institute's greatest comedy, *Hot*, as well as inadvertently being part of the template for the future best *sometime* comedy team since Hope & Crosby—Lemmon & Walter Matthau.

Judy Holliday, Marilyn Monroe, and Jayne Mansfield all conjure up comedy images, with Holliday even winning an Academy Award for her linchpin play/film *Born Yesterday* (1950, see Chapter 1). Yet more importantly, two of these three represent a distinctly serious difference from what the period flippantly called the "dumb blonde," and indiscriminately lumped together. Holliday's persona was anything but dumb, and it was beginning to morph into a more multi-faceted figure. Monroe was a struggling child/woman stripped of control yet forever bordering on something sober. Only Mansfield was victimized as a mere prop—more cartoon than character. Yet, both Holliday and Monroe had the potential for dramatic breakouts, though their short, troubled lives provided few opportunities. That being said, Monroe showed the most potential, especially with the near career beginning nourish *Niagara* (1953), or *The Misfit*'s troubled divorcée (1961, opposite her childhood idol/father figure Clark Gable). Ironically, with Monroe's 1962 suicide, the two films form perverse bookends to what might have been, since *Misfits* was her last picture.

A final fascinating defense mantra—"more than a 'dumb blonde'"—comes from the Oscar-nominated Cathy Moriarty, who became a star overnight for her performance as the teen bride of prizefighter Jake Le Motta (Robert De Niro) in Martin Scorsese's *Raging Bull* (1980). First seeing Judy Holliday on TV at 14, Moriarty later observed:

> My favorite movie moment was from a movie I saw growing up, *Born Yesterday*, with Judy Holliday.... It became my all-time favorite movie.... The scene that made the greatest impression on me was when Judy Holliday finally gets mad at [bully] Broderick Crawford and talks back to him.... He was shocked when she stood up to him. It seemed to come out of no where but it didn't. She had discovered her own confidence and became more of a whole person.... I loved that.[12]

Moriarty no doubt drew upon that scene when she had to stand up to a much more frightening man in *Raging Bull*, and received an Academy Award nomination.

Jerry Lewis was that rare 1950s clown who remained in the old school personality comedian pigeonhole. However, for much of the decade he was teamed with a funny multi-talented

Dean Martin's (center) persona radiates bemused coolness as he walks the Las Vegas strip (circa 1960) with two fellow Rat Pack members, Frank Sinatra (left) and Peter Lawford.

performer (Dean Martin) who seldom received his comic due until *after* he split with Lewis. Moreover, an added paradox for Martin was that before his gift for laughter was fully validated, there almost seemed to be a need to demonstrate his serious acting chops in such memorable movies as *The Young Lions* (1958, with Marlon Brando), and *Rio Bravo* (1959, with John Wayne). The final Martin paradox was when his 1960s devil-may-care drift fully coalesced, he comically blew by Lewis with a "what the fuck" attitude which anchored "Rat Pack" coolness. And this carried over to his immensely popular television program, *The Dean Martin Show* (1965–1974), and his guilty pleasure Matt Helm spoofs of James Bond.

Even veteran personality comedian superstar Bob Hope would flirt with semi-serious properties in the 1950s, his last decade of consistently strong pictures. Hope would stretch his acting talents with two excellent biography films. The first chronicled the story of how vaudeville headliner Eddie Foy put his children in the act after the death of his wife—*The Seven Little Foys* (1955). The show-stopper scene, moreover, would further demonstrate Hope's versatility as he kept pace with James Cagney as George M. Cohan in a superlative table top dance duet inspired by *Yankee Doodle Dandy* (1942). The second profile picture was a winning minimally comic portrayal of the entertaining ne'er-do-well New York City Mayor Jimmy Walker—*Beau James* (1957).

For Danny Kaye, the 1950s found him increasingly drawn to serious roles ... in real life, devoting an even increasing amount of time to the Untied Nations International Children's Emergency Fund (UNICEF). This included the film *Assignment Children* (1955), in which Kaye traveled the world to showcase the plight of third world youngsters. His close ongoing link to UNICEF would anticipate Jerry Lewis' later long association with the Muscular Dystrophy Association and his annual Labor Day Telethons. These yearly TV fundraisers would, ironically, eventually usurp Lewis' film identity to younger viewers.

Indeed, this dovetails into the second set of parallels with these featured 1950s clowns. It is a fascinating anomaly that so many film comedians who found great success during the decade's war with TV would later and/or simultaneously be featured on the small screen. Besides Martin's aforementioned program, and Martin & Lewis earlier periodically hosting the *Colgate Comedy Hour*, there was: *The Red Skelton Show* (1951–1971); Hope's ever increasing TV specials; *The Tom Ewell Show* (1960–1961), and Ewell's later prominent part on Robert Blake's *Baretta* (1975–1978); *The Danny Kaye Show* (1963–1967); Tony Randall's plethora of programs, with the best being featured on *Mr. Peepers* (1952–1955) and *The Odd Couple* (1970–1976); and Tony Curtis co-starring with Roger Moore in *The Persuaders* (1971–1972), and heading a group of positive con artists in *McCoy* (1975–1976, inspired by the hit film *The Sting*, 1973).

The third similarity to be found among these 1950s personality comedians is that two pivotal directors driving several of their pictures, Frank Tashlin and Billy Wilder, had an ever increasingly misanthropic view of society. (Of course, one might also add Chaplin and his 1957 British-produced *A King in New York*, after HUAC had contributed to his 1952 bouncing from the country. In fact, the film shares many parallels with Tashlin's use of Tony Randall in 1957's *Will Success Spoil Rock Hunter?* Yet, Chaplin's *King* falls outside the "made in America" parameters of this study.)

Obviously, this 1950s pricking of humanity should come as no surprise with the growing existence, though under-appreciated presence, of post–World War II dark comedies from pantheon directors like Chaplin's *Monsieur Verdoux* (1947), Alfred Hitchcock's *Rope* (1948), and Preston Struges' *Unfaithfully Yours* (1948).[13] Granted, Chaplin's personal baggage dragged down the tale of a *widow*-shopping Bluebeard, but the public had no individualized objections with the other two celebrated directors, whose films also failed at the box office. Like it or not, the public had to accept the fact that the world had finally caught up to that old Darwinian pun: "Evolution was more than just monkey business."

This text keyed most on the 1950s as Tashlin's decade to mold and/or distort film clowns, with his children's parables (see chapters 3, 9, and 11) being a decoder ring of understanding—the director often anthropomorphically using animals to create his own special brand of misanthropy. Moreover, whether Tashlin preferred Trigger in *Son of Paleface* (1952) or comically debasing Jayne Mansfield into the decade's only true dumb blonde in *Will Success Spoil Rock Hunter?*, he did it with a cartoonist's relish.

The title of another Tashlin-directed Mansfield picture, *The Girl Can't Help It* (1956), impeccably summarized not only Mansfield's plight but that of what H. L. Mencken called "the booboisie" (bourgeois) in general, as well as now becoming a *boob*oisie pun when Mansfield is involved. (This picture's opening credits also rival the satirical beginning of *Will Success Spoil Rock Hunter?*, with Tom Ewell standing in for Tony Randall.) Is it any wonder that the 1950s personality comedian with whom Tashlin worked best was Jerry Lewis' self-described "Idiot" screen persona? Wilder played a softer but no less condescending puppeteer to his clowns, too. He enjoyed manipulating Monroe in *The Seven Year Itch* (1955), though he did grant her a semblance of that child/woman persona. Plus, as in Tashlin children's animal friendly parables, she is the only one to show compassion for the *Creature From the Black Lagoon* (1954). And while Monroe's character was more of an asexual baby feline than a sex kitten, Wilder emphasized the latter. Of course, he also "painted" Manhattan as intercourse central.

Plus, Joe E. Brown's "nobody's perfect" closer line to *Some Like It Hot* is just a delayed reaction variation to Tashlin's title *The Girl Can't Help It*—humanity's forte is weakness. And the nuances of the *Hot* line, delivered by seemingly the most simplistically defined and least analyzed of the film's characters, Brown's Osgood, suddenly makes him the most diabolically consistent cast member. Moreover, the catalyst for all *Hot*'s genre-driven components is dark comedy—personality comedians witnessing a murder. Appropriately, Wilder was no stranger to black humor, with it being a key component of his noir classics, *Double Indemnity* (1944) and *Sunset Blvd.* (1950), not to mention his overtly dark comedy *Stalog 17* (1953).

However, while Tashlin's career faded quickly after the 1950s, one can trace Wilder's increasingly misanthropic impact on his personality comedians (especially the much favored Jack Lemmon) immediately. For example, in Wilder's 1960s commercial and critical hit *The Apartment*—winning him Oscars for directing, writing (with I. A. L. Diamond), and producing (winning Best Picture)—one can "read" Jack Lemmon's likeable neurotic in two ways. His character, C. K. Baxter, is attempting to get ahead in a gargantuan corporate office, with nonentity imaginary reminiscent of King Vidor's *The Crowd* (1928), by loaning out his apartment key to superiors for sexual liaisons. However, a young woman to whom Baxter is attracted, Shirley MacLaine's elevator girl, naively falls for one of these office Casanovas. And when it does not work out, she attempts suicide in Baxter's apartment. As critic David Thomson has observed:

> How is Baxter going to live with his compromise [for success] after the suicide [attempt] and his need to nurse her back to health in his apartment?... Is Lemmon a heroic actor or a fumbling wretch?[14]

This is a far cry from Chaplin's *Limelight* (1952, see Chapter 4), when his post–Charlie character nurses another naïve and near-suicide child/woman back to health in his apartment for strictly altruistic reasons.

Wilder's penchant for painting future personality comedians in dark hues would not cease, though two film examples will suffice. In *Kiss Me, Stupid* (1964), the writer/director reduces Dean Martin's comic coolness to cruel crassness in a film which failed with both critics and the public, though recent revisionists are attempting to resurrect its status. And while Wilder had a modest hit with *The Fortune Cookie* (1966), his personality comedians continued to grow faulty. Granted, Walter Matthau's shyster lawyer won a Best Supporting Oscar for being such a cartoonishly nefarious character (more shades of Tashlin?). But to not have found him amusing would be like dishing the animated quasi–Soviet spies Boris and Natasha from the then Cold War contemporary *Rocky and Bullwinkle Show* TV show. Indeed, in the United Kingdom, *Cookie* even had a cartoonish title: *Meet Whiplash Willie*.

The more problematic personality comedian element of *Cookie* is Jack Lemmon's character. He is so easily manipulated by both his crooked brother-in-law (Matthau) and a gold digger ex-wife (Judi West) that for most of the film he is willing to go through with a fraudulent physical injury claim, despite the growing guilt of the individual allegedly responsible for the "accident." It is not that Lemmon is devoid of humor in this first teaming with Matthau. But his screen persona has changed dramatically from *Mr. Roberts* (1955, see Chapter 8), in which his Ensign Pulver ultimately becomes the feisty first defense of the crew against James Cagney's comic villain of a captain.

There will always be delightfully distracting mind candy comedians, such as Jim Carrey representing an obvious portal to the past of pioneering neurotics like Danny Kaye and Jerry Lewis. Yet, as previously noted, today one invariably includes many favorite clown whose work is not limited to broad comedy—such as Carrey's finest film being arguably the bittersweet romantic comedy/sci-fi vehicle *Eternal Sunshine of the Spotless Mind* (2004). Of course, what never changes is that frequently the personality comedian's persona will be tweaked by an auteur like a Tashlin or a Wilder. With *Eternal Sunshine*, Carrey stretches his comedy with Charles Kaufman's inspired Oscar-winning screenplay.

All in all, the 1950s closed with film's television war essentially over, though some older stars still minimized time on the small screen to maintain their movie mystique. Sadly, blacklisting was only slowly beginning to crack. The year after *Some Like It Hot* was released the most high profile victim of HUAC, Hollywood Ten writer Dalton Trumbo, would be the first blacklisted writer to receive a screen credit under his own name. But the pictures would be memorable epics—*Spartacus* and *Exodus* (both 1960). Credit for this breakthrough would go to the former film's star and quasi-producer Kirk Douglas, and *Exodus*' producer/director Otto Preminger. Yet McCarthyism had crumbled enough that well before *Hot* was even a Billy Wilder thought, criticism Marilyn Monroe received for defending playwright husband Arthur Miller when he appeared before HUAC quickly dissipated.

Strangely enough, one might even close, with another pertinent, out of left field, sci-fi reference to the President Kennedy's assassination, combined with a bizarre dark comedy twist on *Forrest Gump* (1994). That is, in an episode of the original *X-Files* television series (1993–2002) addressing Kennedy's death, "The Smoking Man" observes, "Life is like a box of chocolates. A cheap, thoughtless, perfunctory gift that nobody ever asks for."[15] Consequently, whenever has society not needed silly clowns to distract us from the world around us? Is that not why a definitive theatre of the absurd production such as Samuel Beckett's *Waiting for Godot* (1953) forever uses loopy characters like Vladimir and Estragon to distract audiences from the fact that neither God nor anything else awaits one after death? Even more fitting, it was written in the disturbingly dumbing down 1950s, with a pioneering production even starring one of this book's featured personality comedians, Tom Ewell (see Chapter 7). Life is all we have, so without our diverting clowns, we must fall back on the death warning of another 1950s artist, poet Dylan Thomas, whose signature work/admonition begins with the opening words of its title, "Do Not Go Gentle…"

Yet, I prefer not to end on such a black note. If I were so inclined, I would at least phrase it along dark *comedy* lines, such as paraphrasing W.B. Yeats, another poet from Thomas' homeland, "Being Irish, one has an inherent sense of tragedy that sustains one through those brief times of joy."

Consequently, coming full circle from the Prologue's goal of self-discovery, this text, in part, has been a personal exercise in time-tripping to my cinema past, and what the French might call a "concours de constances"—a confluence of circumstances. Regardless, I think of writers as locksmiths, using words to double as a key in order to better unlock some mystery. Since part of this mystery is self-directed, I can honestly say much has been clarified for me. Yet, in taking the journey I am now well aware of the old proverb, "The past is unpredictable." And yes, my ancestry is Irish.

Filmography

December 27, 1950—*Born Yesterday* (Columbia Pictures, 103 minutes). Director: George Cukor. Screenplay: Albert Mannheimer, based on Garson Kanin's play. Stars: Judy Holliday (Billie Dawn), Broderick Crawford (Harry Brock), William Holden (Paul Verrall), Howard St. John (Jim Devery), Frank Otto (Eddie), Larry Oliver (Norval Hedges), Barbara Brown (Mrs. Hedges).

February 1, 1952—*Sailor Beware* (Paramount Pictures, 108 minutes). Director: Hal Walker. Screenplay: James Allardice, Martin Rackin; adapted by Elwood Ullman, from a play by Kenyon Nicholson and Charles Robinson. Stars: Dean Martin (Al Crowthers), Jerry Lewis (Melvin Jones), Corinne Calvet (plays herself), Marion Marshall (Hilda), Robert Strauss (Lardoski), Leif Erickson (Commander Lane), Don Wilson (Mr. Chubby), Betty Hutton (unbilled cameo).

October 2, 1952—Son of Paleface (Paramount release of a Robert L. Welch production, 95 minutes). Director: Frank Tashlin. Screenplay: Tashlin, Welch, and Joseph Quillan. Stars: Bob Hope (Junior), Jane Russell (Mike), Roy Rogers (play himself), Bill Williams (Kirk), Lloyd Corrigan (Doc Lovejoy), Paul Burns (Ebeneezer Hawkins), Iron Eyes Cody (Indian Chief), Trigger (Rogers' unbilled horse).

October 24, 1952—*Limelight* (United Artist release of a Charles Chaplin production, 145 minutes). Director/Screenplay: Charles Chaplin. Stars: Chaplin (Calvero), Claire Bloom (Terry), Sydney Chaplin (Neville), Buster Keaton (Partner—memorable short part), Norman Lloyd (Bodalink), Marjorie Bennett (Mrs. Alsop), Wheeler Dryden (Doctor and Clown), Nigel Bruce (Mr. Postant), Snub Pollard (Musician), Charles Chaplin, Jr. (Pantomime Policeman), Geraldine, Michael, and Josephine Chaplin (Very brief unbilled cameos).

January 29, 1953—*The Clown* (MGM release of a William H. Wright production, 91 minutes). Director: Robert Z. Leonard. Screenplay: Martin Rackin; adapted by Leonard Praskins, from a Frances Marion story. Stars: Red Skelton (Dodo Delwyn), Tim Considine (Dink Delwyn), Jane Greer (Paula Henderson), Loring Smith (Goldie), Philip Ober (Ralph Z. Henderson).

January 30, 1953—*Road to Bali* (Paramount release of Harry Tugend production, 90 minutes). Director: Hal Walker. Screenplay Frank Butler, Hal Kanter, William Morrow; from Butler/Tugend story. Stars: Bob Hope (Harold Gridley), Bing Crosby (George Cochran), Dorothy Lamour (Lalah), Jane Russell, Martin & Lewis, and Bob Crosby (brief unbilled cameos).

June 4, 1955—*The Seven Year Itch* (20th Century–Fox release of Charles K. Feldman Group production, 105 minutes). Director: Billy Wilder. Screenplay: Wilder and George Axelrod adapt the latter's play. Stars: Marilyn Monroe (The Girl), Tom Ewell (Richard Sherman), Evelyn Keyes (Helen Sherwood), Robert Strauss (Kruhulik), Sonny Tufts (Tom McKenzie), Oscar Homolka (Dr. Brubaker), Victor Moore (plumber).

July 15, 1955—*Mr. Roberts* (Warner Brothers, 123 minutes). Director: John Ford and Mervyn LeRoy. Screenplay: Frank Nugent and Joshua Logan's adaptation of the Thomas Heggen and Logan play based upon Heggen's novel. Stars: Henry Fonda (Lieutenant Roberts), James Cagney (The Captain),

William Powell (Doc), Jack Lemmon (Ensign Pulver), Betsy Palmer (Lieut. Ann Girard), Ward Bond (C. P. O. Dowdy), Phil Carey (Mannion), Ken Curtis (Dolan), Harry Carey, Jr. (Stefanowski), Nick Adams (Reber).

December 22, 1955—*Artists and Models* (Paramount release of Hall Wallis production, 109 minutes). Director: Frank Tashlin. Screenplay: Tashlin, Hal Kanter and Herbert Baker; adapted by Don McGuire from a play by Michael Davidson and Norman Lessing. Stars: Dean Martin (Rick Todd), Jerry Lewis (Eugene Fullstack), Shirley MacLaine (Bessie Sparrowbush), Dorothy Malone (Abigail Parker), Eddie Mayehoff (Mr. Murdock), Anita Ekberg (Ansta).

February 2, 1956—*Court Jester* (Paramount Pictures, 101 minutes). Director/Screenplay: Norman Panama and Melvin Frank. Stars: Danny Kaye (Hawkins), Glynis Johns (Maid Jean), Basil Rathbone (Sir Ravenhurst), Angela Lansbury (Princess Gwendolyn), Cecil Parker (King Roderick), Mildred Natwick (Griselda), Robert Middleton (Sir Griswold), Edward Ashley (Black Fox), John Carradine (Giacomo).

September 12, 1957—*Will Success Spoil Rock Hunter?* (20th Century–Fox release of Frank Tashlin production, 94 minutes). Director: Tashlin. Screenplay: Tashlin, adaptation of George Axelrod play. Stars: Tony Randall (Rock Hunter), Jayne Mansfield (Rita Marlowe), Betsy Drake (Jenny), Joan Blondell (Violet), John Williams (La Salle, Jr.), Henry Jones (Rufus), Lili Gentle (April Hunter), Mickey Hargitay (Bobo).

March 30, 1959—*Some Like It Hot* (United Artists release of a Billy Wilder production for the Mirisch Company, 119 minutes). Director: Billy Wilder. Screenwriter: Wilder and I. A. L. Diamond; suggested by a R. Thoeren and M. Logan story. Stars: Marilyn Monroe (Sugar), Tony Curtis (Joe/Josephine/Jr.), Jack Lemmon (Jerry/Daphne), Joe E. Brown (Osgood Fielding III), George Raft (Spats Colombo), Mulligan (Pat O'Brien).

Chapter Notes

Preface

1. Ed Sikov, *On Sunset Boulevard: The Life and Times of Billy Wilder* (New York: Hyperion, 1998), 427.
2. Bob Hope (with Linda Hope), *Bob Hope: My Life in Jokes* (New York: Hyperion, 2003), 90.
3. See the author's *Film Clowns of the Depression: Twelve Defining Performances* (Jefferson, NC: McFarland, 2007); and *Forties Film Funnymen: The Decade's Great Comedians at Work in the Shadow of War* (Jefferson, NC: McFarland, 2010).

Prologue

1. Katy Lederer, "Last Gathering," *New York Times*, December 27, 2015, Book Review section: 9.
2. See the author's *Film Clowns of the Depression: Twelve Defining Performances* (Jefferson, NC: McFarland, 2007); and *Forties Film Funnymen: The Decade's Great Comedians at Work in the Shadow of War* (Jefferson, NC: McFarland, 2010).
3. Jim Knipfel, *Quitting the Nairobi Trio* (2000; rpt. New York: Berkley Books, 2001), 1.
4. Andy Borowitz, *The 50 Funniest American Writers: An Anthology of Humor from Mark Twain to the Onion* (New York: Library of American Humor, 2014).
5. Buster Keaton (with Charles Samuels), *My Wonderful World of Slapstick* (Garden City, NY: Doubleday, 1960), 271.
6. Katie Roiphe, "Dying with Nothing to Say," *New York Times*, March 20, 2016, Sunday Review section: 8.
7. Holland Cotter, "Alexander and the Days of Peak Greek," *New York Times*, April 15, 2016, C-19.
8. Margalit Fox, "Geoffrey H. Hartman, Scholar Who Saw Literary Criticism as Art, Dies at 86," *New York Times*, March 21, 2016, B-7.
9. James Charlton, ed., *The Writer's Quotation Book* (1980; rpt. New York: Penguin, 1985), 52.

Chapter 1

1. Maria DiBattista, *Fast-Talking Dames* (New Haven: Yale University Press, 2001).
2. See the author's *Personality Comedians as Genre: Selected Players* (Westport, Connecticut: Greenwood Press, 1997).
3. See the author's *Parody as Film Genre: "Never Give a Saga an Even Break"* (Westport, Connecticut: Greenwood Press, 1999).
4. See the author's *Populism and the Capra Legacy* (Westport, Connecticut: Greenwood Press, 1995).
5. Lewis Nichols, "New Arrival," *New York Times*, February 10, 1946, section 11:1.
6. "Judy Holliday, 42, Is Dead of Cancer," *New York Times* (June 8, 1965), 1.
7. Kenneth Tynan, "The Current Cinema: Summer [and] Judy Holliday," *The New Yorker* (July 25, 1970), 54.
8. Danny Peary, *Close-Ups* (New York: Simon & Schuster, 1978), 44.
9. Ronald L. Smith, *Who's Who in Comedy* (New York: Facts on File, 1992), 218.
10. Will Holtzman, *Judy Holliday: A Biography* (New York: G. P. Putnam's Sons, 1982), 246.
11. Emanuel Levy, *George Cukor, Master of Elegance* (New York: William Morrow, 1994), 73.
12. Karen Judson and Carlene Harrison, *Law and Ethics for Health Professions* (1994; rpt. New York: McGraw-Hill Professions, 2013), 34.
13. Gary Carey, *Judy Holliday: An Intimate Life Story* (London: Robson Books, 1983), 102.
14. Katharine Hepburn, *ME: Stories of My Life* (New York: Alfred A. Knopf, 1991), 246–247.
15. Robert Emmet Long, ed., *George Cukor Interviews* (Jackson: University Press of Mississippi, 2001), 142.
16. James Curtis, *Spencer Tracy: A Biography* (New York: Alfred A. Knopf, 2011), 577.
17. *Ibid.*, 578.
18. Long, ed., *George Cukor Interviews*, 142.
19. Sam Roberts, "Mary Keefe, 92, Model for Rockwell's 'Rosie the Riveter,'" *New York Times*, April 25, 2015, B-14.
20. Molly Haskell, *From Reverence to Rape: The Treatment of Women in the Movies* (New York: Holt, Rinehart and Winston, 1973), 241–242.

21. Marjorie Rosen, *Popcorn Venus: Women, Movies & the American Dream* (New York: Coward, McCann & Geoghegan, 1973), 278.

22. Again, see the author's *Personality Comedians as Genre: Selected Players*.

23. See the author's *Laurel & Hardy: A Bio-Bibliography* (Westport, Connecticut: Greenwood Press, 1990).

24. Richard Zoglin, *HOPE: Entertainer of the Century* (New York: Simon & Schuster, 2014), 68.

25. Martin Amis, "There Is Simply Too Much to Think About," *New York Times*, May 3, 2015, Book Review section: 20.

26. Harold Myers, "'Born Yesterday' [Review]," *Variety*, November 22, 1950.

27. Only attributed to Lincoln two decades after his death, Lincoln quotation texts generally omit it. For example, Louise Bachelder, ed., *Abraham Lincoln: Wit and Wisdom* (Mount Vernon, NY: Peter Pauper Press, 1965).

28. David Thomson, "Frank Capra," in *The New Biographical Dictionary of Film* (New York: Alfred A. Knopf, 2003), 133.

29. Myers, "'Born Yesterday' [Review]."

30. Otis L. Guernsey, Jr., "On the Screen: 'Born Yesterday,'" *New York Herald Tribune*, December 27, 1950, 16.

31. "Holliday Triumphs in Her Own Role," *Hollywood Reporter*, November 17, 1950, 3.

32. Kate Cameron, "Judy Holliday Tops in 'Born Yesterday,'" *New York Daily News*, December 27, 1950, 60.

33. "Judy with a Punch," *Christian Science Monitor*, January 9, 1951.

34. Hollis Alpert, "SRL Goes to the Movies," *Saturday Review*, January 6, 1951.

35. Tynan, "The Current Cinema: Summer Judy Holliday."

36. John Offer, *Jean Arthur: The Actress Nobody Knew*. (New York: Limelight Editions, 1997), 156.

37. "'Born Yesterday' Becomes a Film After Much Travail," *New York Herald Tribune* (December 24, 1950), section: 5:3.

38. Cobbett Steinberg, *Real Facts: The Movie Book of Records* (New York: Vintage, 1978), 345.

39. Thomas F. Brady, "Film of Kanin Play Attacked on Coast," *New York Times*, December 1, 1950, 31.

40. "2 Catholic Vet Groups Picket 'Yesterday' in Rap at Holliday-Kanin," *Variety*, March 28, 1951.

41. Corey, *Judy Holliday: An Intimate Life Story*, 143.

42. *Ibid.*, 146.

43. "MPAA Protests Review on 'Yesterday,'" *Hollywood Reporter*, December 4, 1950, 8.

44. Mark Merbaum, *Born Yesterday*, in *Magill's Survey of Cinema*, Ed. Frank N. Magill (Englewood Cliffs, N.J., 1980), 210.

Chapter 2

1. Shawn Levy, *Rat Pack Confidential* (New York: Doubleday, 1998), 100.

2. Cobbett Steinberg. *Reel Facts: The Movie Book of Records* (New York: Vintage, 1978), 405–406.

3. *Ibid.*, 406.

4. Jerry Lewis and James Kaplin, *Dean & Me (A Love Story)* (New York: Doubleday, 2005), 160.

5. See the author's *Film Clowns of the Depression: Twelve Defining Comic Performances* (Jefferson, NC: McFarland, 2007); and *Forties Film Funnymen: The Decade's Great Comedians at Work in the Shadow of War* (Jefferson, NC: McFarland, 2010).

6. See the author's *Personality Comedians as Genre: Selected Players* (Westport, Connecticut: Greenwood Press, 1997).

7. Jane Corby, "Dean Martin and Jerry Lewis in 'Sailor Beware' at Mayfair," *Brooklyn Eagle*, February 1, 1952, 8.

8. William Brogdon, "'Sailor Beware' [Review]," *Variety*, December 5, 1952.

9. Rose Pelswick, "Martin-Lewis Best Film, a Zany, Hilarious Show," *New York Journal American*, February 1, 1952, 10.

10. Kate Cameron, "Martin and Lewis at Mayfair [Theatre] in Laugh Maker," *New York Daily News*, February 1, 1952, C-14.

11. Bosley Crowther, "'Sailor Beware' [Review]," *New York Times*, February 1, 1952, 17.

12. Jerry Lewis and James Kaplin, *Dean & Me*. There are many such references in this text (see p. 43), as well as other texts.

13. *Ibid.*, 99.

14. Ronald L. Smith, *Who's Who in COMEDY* (New York: Facts On File, 1992), 283.

15. James Ursini, *Preston Sturges: An American Dreamer* (New York: Curtis Books, 1973), 133–134.

16. "Million Dollar Madmen," *Quick*, October 8, 1951. 56.

17. Jerry Lewis (with Herb Gluck), *Jerry Lewis in Person* (New York: Atheneum, 1982), 143.

18. See the author's *Laurel & Hardy: A Bio-Bibliography* (Westport, Connecticut: Greenwood Press, 1990).

19. See the author's *Forties Film Funnymen: The Decade's Great Comedians at Work in the Shadow of War* (Jefferson, NC: McFarland, 2010), 46–58.

20. See the author's *The Marx Brothers: A Bio-Bibliography* (Westport, Connecticut: Greenwood Press, 1990); and *Groucho & W. C. Fields: Huckster Comedians*. (Jackson: University Press of Mississippi, 1994).

21. Jerry Lewis (with Herb Gluck), *Jerry Lewis in Person*, 138.

22. Jerry Lewis and James Kaplan, *Dean & Me*, 20–22.

23. Jerry Lewis, *The Total Film-Maker* (1971; rpt. New York: Warner Paperback Library, 1973).

24. See the author's *Leo McCarey: From Marx to McCarthy* (Lanham, Maryland: Scarecrow Press, 2005).

25. See the author's *Charlie Chaplin: A Bio-Bibliography* (Westport, Connecticut: Greenwood Press, 1983); and *Chaplin's War Trilogy: An Evolving Lens in Three Dark Comedies, 1918–1947* (Jefferson, NC: McFarland, 2014).

26. See the author's *Film Clowns of the Depression:*

Twelve Defining Performances (Jefferson, NC: McFarland, 2007).

27. James Agee, "Comedy's Greatest Era," *Life*, September 3, 1949.

28. See the author's *James Dean: Rebel with a Cause* (Indianapolis: Indiana Historical Society Press, 2005), 119.

29. Corinne Calvet, *Has Corinne Been a Good Girl?* (New York: St. Martin's Press, 1983), 185.

30. *Ibid.*, 191.

31. *Colgate Comedy Hour* (June 5, 1955) CBS. On *The Martin & Lewis Show* DVD. Genius Entertainment, 2003.

32. Dean Martin and Jerry Lewis on *Person to Person* (1954) CBS. YouTube. Uploaded by Soapbxprod, November 11, 2011.

33. Michael Freedland, *DEAN MARTIN: King of the Road* (London: Robson Books, 2004), 67.

34. *Sailor Beware* ad noting, "The Navy Needs Men," *New York Herald Tribune*, January 27, 1952, Section 4:3.

35. "Million Dollar Madmen," 55.

36. *Ibid.*

37. Alton Cook, "Jerry and Dean Unified in Navy This Time," *New York World Telegram and Sun*, February 1, 1952, 16.

38. Otis L. Guernsey, Jr., "On the Screen: 'Sailor Beware,'" *New York Herald Tribune*, February 1, 1952, 13.

39. *Ibid.*

40. Crowther, "'Sailor Beware' [Review]."

41. *Ibid.*

42. "Martin and Lewis Tee Off P.A. Tour," *Hollywood Reporter*, February 12, 1952, 14.

43. Steinberg, *Reel Facts: The Movie Book of Records*, 345.

44. *Ibid.*, 344–347.

Chapter 3

1. Jane Corby, "Bob Hope Aided by Trigger in a Western-Style Comedy," *Brooklyn Eagle*, October 2, 1952, 4.

2. Cobbett Steinberg, *Reel Facts: The Movie Book of Records* (New York: Vintage, 1978), 344–345.

3. Tim Brooks and Earle Marsh, *The Complete Directory to Prime Time Network TV Shows: 1946-Present* (New York: Ballantine Books, 1979), 539.

4. "'Son of Paleface' Hilarious," *Hollywood Reporter*, July 14, 1952, 3.

5. *Son of Paleface* ad (noting Bob Hope's appearance), NY *Times*, October 1, 1952, 39; Roy Rogers Madison Square Garden ad, *New York Daily News*, October 3, 1952, 61.

6. Bosley Crowther, "'Son of Paleface' [Review]," *New York Times*, October 2, 1952, 32.

7. See the author's *Parody as Film Genre: "Never Give a Saga an Even Break"* (Westport, Connecticut: Greenwood Press, 1999.

8. Frank Tashlin, "'Son of Paleface' Went Thataway," *New York Times*, October 5, 1952, Section 2:5.

9. Richard Zoglin, *HOPE: Entertainer of the Century* (New York: Simon & Schuster, 2014), 283.

10. Tashlin, "'Son of Paleface' Went Thataway."

11. For example, see the *Son of Paleface* ad, *New York Times*, October 1, 1952, 39.

12. Kate Cameron, "Bob Hope & Trigger Paramount Co-Stars," *New York Daily News*, October 2, 1952, 65; Corby, "Bob Hope Aided by Trigger in a Western- Style Comedy," 4.

13. Corby, "Bob Hope Aided by Trigger in a Western-Style Comedy," 4.

14. Cameron, "Bob Hope & Trigger Paramount Co-Stars," 65.

15. *Ibid.*

16. Frank Tashlin, *The Bear That Wasn't* (New York: Dover, 1946).

17. Cameron, "Bob Hope & Trigger Paramount Co-Stars," 65.

18. Otis L. Guernsey, Jr., "On the Screen: 'Son of Paleface,'" *New York Herald Tribune*, October 2, 1952, 30.

19. Tashlin, *The Bear That Wasn't*, last line (no page numbers).

20. Will Cuppy, *How to Tell Your Friends from the Apes* (1931; rpt. Boston: Nonpareil, 2005); also see the author's *Will Cuppy: American Satirist* (Jefferson, NC: McFarland, 2013).

21. Rose Pelswick, "Hope and Jane Russell in Fine and Funny Film," *New York Journal American*, October 2, 1952, 22.

22. Stefan Kanfer, *Ball of Fire: The Tumultuous Life and Comic Art of Lucille Ball* (London: Faber and Faber, 2003), 155.

23. Crowther, "'Son of Paleface' [Review]."

24. *Ibid.*

25. Emily Herbert, *Robin Williams: When the Laughter Stops, 1951–2014* (London: John Blake Publishing, 2014).

26. "'Son of Paleface' Hilarious," *Hollywood Reporter*.

27. Guernsey, Jr., "On the Screen: 'Son of Paleface.'"

28. "'Son of Paleface' [Review]," *Variety*, July 16, 1952.

29. Alton Cook, "New 'Paleface' Chip Off Old Block," *New York World-Telegram and Sun*, October 2, 1952, 24.

30. "Bob Hope and *Friends*," *Look* magazine, August 26, 1952.

31. Rose Pelswick, "Hope and Jane Russell in Fine and Funny Film."

32. Cobbett, *Reel Facts: The Movie Book of Records*, 405.

33. *Ibid.*

34. Bob Hope (with Melville Shavelson), *Don't Shoot, It's Only Me* (New York: G.P. Putnam's Sons, 1990), 165.

35. *Ibid.*, 166.

36. Raymond Strait, *Bob Hope: A Tribute* (New York: Pinnacle Books, 2003), 318.

37. Bob Hope (with Linda Hope), *Bob Hope: My Life in Jokes* (New York: Hyperion, 2003), 86.

38. Strait, *Bob Hope: A Tribute*, 299.

39. *Ibid.*, 315.

40. Zoglin, *HOPE: Entertainer of the Century*, 288.

41. *Ibid.*

42. Hope with Linda Hope, *Bob Hope: My Life in Jokes*, 90.

Chapter 4

1. Bosley Crowther, "'Limelight' [Review]," *New York Times* (October 24, 1952), 27.
2. Gene [Gene Moskowitz], "Limelight [Review]," *Variety*, October 8, 1952.
3. Edwin Schallert, "Genius Touches Flit, Flash in 'Dictator,'" *Los Angeles Times*, November 15, 1940, Part 1:18.
4. See the author's *Chaplin's War Trilogy: An Evolving Lens in Three Dark Comedies, 1918–1947* (Jefferson, NC: McFarland, 2014.)
5. Charles Chaplin, *My Autobiography* (1964; rpt. New York: Pocket Books, 1966), 458.
6. John McCabe, *Charlie Chaplin* (Garden City, NY: Doubleday, 1978), 203.
7. Charles Chaplin, Jr. (with N. Rau and M. Rau), *My Father, Charlie Chaplin* (New York: Random House, 1960), 202.
8. John Beaufort, "An Assault from Mr. Chaplin," *Christian Science Monitor*, April 19, 1947, 8.
9. Theodore Huff, *Charlie Chaplin* (1951; rpt. New York: Arno Press and the New York Times, 1972), 308–309.
10. *Ibid.*
11. Eugene Smith, "Chaplin at Work: He Reveals His Movie-Making Secrets," *Life*, March 17, 1952, 117.
12. See the author's aforementioned *Chaplin's War Trilogy: An Evolving Lens in Three Dark Comedies, 1918–1947*.
13. Mason Wiley and Damien Bona, *Inside Oscar* (1986; rpt. New York: Ballantine Books, 1993), 853.
14. See the author's *Charlie Chaplin: A Bio-Bibliography* (Westport, Connecticut: Greenwood Press, 1983); and his *Film Clowns of the Depression: Twelve Defining Comic Performances* (Jefferson, NC: McFarland, 2007.)
15. Alton Cook, "Chaplin's *Limelight* a Film Masterpiece," *New York World Telegram*, October 24, 1952, 20.
16. Archer Winsten, "Chaplin's 'Limelight' Now Showing," *New York Post*, October 24, 1952, 52.
17. Otis L. Guernsey, Jr., "On the Screen: 'Limelight,'" *New York Herald Tribune*, October 24, 1952, 14.
18. Anthony Leviero, "Chaplin Is Facing Barriers to Re-Entry from Abroad," *New York Times*, September 20, 1952, 1.
19. *Ibid.*, 16.
20. Cristina Nehring, "Quite Contrary," *New York Times*, May 10, 2015, Book Review section: 29.
21. Leviero, "Chaplin Is Facing Barriers to Re-Entry from Abroad."
22. "Chaplin to Return Here, He Declares," *New York Times*, September 23, 1952, 9.
23. Elie Wiesel, *Open Heart* (2011; rpt. New York: Alfred A. Knopf, 2012), 20.
24. Claire Bloom, *Limelight and After* (1982; rpt. New York: Penguin, 1983), 91.
25. *Ibid.*, 91–92.
26. David Robinson, *Chaplin: His Life and Art* (New York: McGraw-Hill, 1985), 551.
27. Joe Franklin, *Joe Franklin's Encyclopedia of Comedians* (Secaucus, NJ: Citadel, 1979), 313.
28. Barry Anthony, *Chaplin's Music Hall: The Chaplins and Their Circle in Limelight.* (New York: I. B. Tauris, 2012).
29. David Robinson, "Evolution of a Story," in *Footlights with the World of Limelight*, ed. Robinson (Bologna: Cineteca Bologna, 2014), 13.
30. Charlie Chaplin, *Footlights*, in *Footlights with the World of Laughter*, ed., David Robinson (Bologna: Cineteca Bologna, 2014), 33–34.
31. *Ibid.*, 48.
32. Stephen Weissman, M.D., *Chaplin: A Life* (New York: Arcade Publishing, 2008, with an "Introduction" by Geraldine Chaplin).
33. James Agee, "Comedy's Greatest Era," *Life* magazine, September 3, 1949. See also *Agee on Film, Volume 1* (1958 rpt. New York: Grossett & Dunlap, 1969).
34. See the author's "Stepping Out of Character," *USA Today Magazine*, January 2009.
35. Wiley and Bona, *Inside Oscar*, 969.
36. *Ibid.*, 966
37. Moskowitz, "'Limelight' [Review]."
38. Chaplin, *Footlights*, 59.
39. James Charlton, ed., *The Writer's Quotation Book* (1980; rpt. New York: Penguin, 1986), 39.
40. Harper Lee, *To Kill a Mockingbird* (1960; rpt. New York: Harperperennial, 2006), 256.

Chapter 5

1. For example, the author used it to open his novelized memoir of the comedian, as well as inspire the book's title, *I, Red Skelton Exit Laughing Or, a Man, His Movies and Sometimes His Monkeys* (Albany, GA: BearMan Fiction, 2011).
2. Tim Brooks and Earl Marsh, *The Complete Directory to Prime Time Network TV Shows: 1946–Present* (New York: Ballantine Books, 1979), 403.
3. The author has written extensively on the comedian; especially his award winning *Red Skelton: The Mask Behind the Mask* (Indianapolis: Indiana Historical Society Press, 2008), with a Foreword by the comedian's daughter, Valentina Maria Skelton Alonson.
4. Hedda Hopper, "Helter Skelton!" *Chicago Tribune*, June 17, 1951.
5. Red Skelton photo showcase with text, *Look* magazine, May 14, 1946, 39.
6. See "$10,000,000 TV Pact for Procter and Gamble and Red Skelton," *Long Beach Press Telegram*, May 3, 1951.
7. Jack Quigg, "Fantastic Capers by Red Skelton Are a Prelude to His TV Shows," *Kansas City Star*, May 13, 1951.
8. *Ibid.*
9. Sid Ross, "Red Skelton … His Plane Was in Trouble," *Parade* magazine, September 23, 1951, 9.
10. Harriet Van Horne, "Skelton Has Chaplin Tragic-Comic Touch," *New York World Telegram*, February 18, 1952.

11. Ibid.
12. Georgia Davis Skelton, "Do Comics Make Good Husbands?" *Screenland*, June 1952, 58.
13. Cobina Wright, "Red Skelton Rates as 'Comedian with a Heart,'" *Los Angeles Examiner*, May 13, 1951.
14. "Briefly Noted," *The New Yorker*, July 6 & 13, 2015, 87.
15. Red Skelton (subbing for syndicated columnist Erskine Johnson), "TV Proves Tougher Nut to Crack for Entertainment's Funniest Nut," *Bingham Press*, September 4, 1952.
16. "Skelton Great in Heart-Warming Pic [Ture]," *Hollywood Reporter*, December 23, 1952, 3.
17. William Brogdon, "'The Clown' [Review]," *Variety*, December 24, 1952.
18. A. H. Weiler, "'The Clown' [Review],'" *New York Times*, January 29, 1953, 25.
19. Lowell E. Redelings, "Red Skelton Highlights New Musical," *Hollywood Citizen News*, June 28, 1944.
20. Owen Collins, "Red Skelton Wins 2 'Emmys' at Annual TV Academy Banquet," *Los Angeles Herald Express*, February 19, 1952.
21. Valentina Maria Skelton Alonso, "Foreword," in the author's *Red Skelton: The Mask Behind the Mask* (Indianapolis: Indiana Historical Society Press, 2008), xi.
22. Ibid.
23. Steve Allen, "Red Skelton," in Allen's *The Funny Men* (New York: Simon and Schuster, 1956), 274.
24. Louella Parsons (syndicated), "Red Skelton Moves Out; Ex-Wife Has Role in Row," *Seattle Post*, December 4, 1952.
25. Red Skelton, letter to Hedda Hopper, January 31, 1951, Hedda Hopper Collection, Special Collections, Margaret Herrick Library, Academy of Motion Picture Arts and Sciences, Beverly Hills, California.
26. "Wife Pins Skelton Rift on Dawn Visits to Kids,'" *New York World*, December 4, 1952.
27. Steve Allen, "Jackie Gleason," in Allen's *The Funny Men* (New York: Simon & Schuster, 1956), 145.
28. Emily Herbert, *Robin Williams: When the Laughter Stops* (London: John Blake Publishing, 2014), 205.
29. Allen, "Red Skelton," 265.
30. Otis L. Guernsey, Jr. "On the Screen: 'The Star,'" *New York Herald Tribune*, January 29, 1953, 15.
31. Joe Pihodna, "On the Screen: 'The Clown,'" *New York Herald Tribune*, January 29, 1953, 15.

Chapter 6

1. See the author's *Parody as Film Genre: "Never Give a Saga an Even Break"* (Westport, Connecticut: Greenwood Press, 1999).
2. See the author's *Personality Comedians as Genre: Selected Players* (Westport, Connecticut: Greenwood Press, 1997).
3. Jim O'Connor, "Pretty Girls, Gags, Crosby and Hope," *New York Journal American*, January 30, 1953, 11.
4. Jane Corby, "Bob Hope, Bing Crosby Meet D. Lamour Again in a 'Road,'" *Brooklyn Eagle*, January 30, 1953, 6.
5. Bob Hope (with Melville Shavelson), *Don't Shoot, It's Only Me* (New York: G. P. Putnam's Sons, 1990), 34.
6. Ibid.
7. Bing Crosby (with Pete Martin), *Call Me Lucky* (New York: Simon & Schuster, 1953), 95.
8. Jack Moffitt, "Back to Utopia," *Esquire*, April 1946, 63.
9. See the author's chapter "Bob Hope: *My Favorite Brunette* (1947), in *Forties Film Funnymen: The Decade's Great Comedians at Work in the Shadow of War* (Jefferson, NC: McFarland, 2010), 150–164.
10. Gehring, *Personality Comedians as Genre: Selected Players*.
11. See the author's *W. C. Fields: A Bio-Bibliography* (Westport, Connecticut: Greenwood Press, 1984), and *Groucho & W. C. Fields: Huckster Comedians* (Jackson: University Press of Mississippi, 1994).
12. See the author's "Bob Hope's the *Cat and the Canary* (1939)," in *Film Clowns of the Depression Twelve Defining Comic Performances* (Jefferson, NC: McFarland, 2007).
13. Eric Lax, *Woody Allen: A Biography* (New York: Alfred A. Knopf, 1991), 25.
14. Charles Thompson, *Bob Hope: Portrait of a Superstar* (New York: St. Martin's Press, 1981), 102.
15. Arthur Frank Wertheim, *Radio Comedy* (New York: Oxford University Press, 1979), 102.
16. See the author's *The Marx Brothers: A Bio-Bibliography* (Westport, Connecticut: Greenwood Press, 1987).
17. Alexander Woolcott, "A Strong, Silent Man," *Cosmopolitan*, January 1934, 108.
18. Dorothy Lamour (as told to Dick McInnes), *My Side of the Road* (1974; rpt. London: Robson Books, 1980), 190.
19. Kate Cameron, "Bob and Bing Back on Road, Bound to Bali," *New York Daily News*, January 30, 1953, 44.
20. Lamour, *My Side of the Road*, 89.
21. Ibid., 87.
22. Andrew Delbanco, *Melville: His World and Work* (New York: Random House, 2005). 12.
23. Richard Zoglin, *Hope: Entertainer of the Century*. (New York: Simon & Schuster, 2014).
24. Woody Allen dust jacket blurb for Richard Zoglin's *Hope: Entertainer of the Year* (New York: Simon & Schuster, 2014).
25. Cobbett Steinberg, *Reel Facts: The Movie Book of Records* (New York: Vintage, 1978), 346.
26. O'Connor, "Pretty Girls, Gags, Crosby and Hope," 11.
27. Otis L. Guernsey, Jr., "On the Screen: 'Road to Bali,'" *New York Herald Tribune*, January 30, 1953, 15.
28. Corby, "Bob Hope, Bing Crosby Meet D. Lamour Again in a 'Road,'" 6.
29. William Brogdon, "'Road to Bali' [Review]," *Variety*, November 19, 1952.
30. "Crosby-Hope Farce Pleasant Nonsense," *Hollywood Reporter*, November 18, 1952, 4.
31. See the author's *"Mr. B" Or, Comforting Thoughts*

About the Bison: A Critical Biography of Robert Benchley (Westport, Connecticut: Greenwood Press, 1992).

32. Bob Hope (with Linda Hope), *Bob Hope: My Life in Jokes* (New York: Hyperion, 2003).

Chapter 7

1. James Thurber, "The Secret Life of Walter Mitty," in *My World and Welcome to It* (1942; rpt. New York: Harcourt, Brace and Company, 1944), 77.
2. Jack Moffitt, "'Seven Year Itch' Packed with Laugh Entertainment," *Hollywood Reporter*, June 3, 1955, 3.
3. Wanda Hale, "Tom Ewell Is Great in 'Seven Year Itch,'" *New York Daily News*, June 4, 1955, 18.
4. Lee Rogow, "'The Seven Year Itch': Itchcraft," *Hollywood Reporter*, November 21, 1952, 3.
5. Wes D. Gehring, Phone Interview With Film Historian Conrad Lane, August 17, 2015.
6. *AFI's 100 Years ... 100 Laughs*, CBS TV Special, First aired June 13, 2000.
7. David Thomson, *The New Biographical Dictionary of Film* (New York: Alfred A. Knopf, 2003), 609.
8. Donald Spoto, *Enchantment: The Life of Audrey Hepburn* (New York: Three Rivers Press, 2006), 206–207.
9. Non-fiction/fiction is when a writer has a biographer-like knowledge of a subject but wishes to fill in some blank spots with educated assumptions: Norman Mailer, *Marilyn* (1973; rpt. New York: Random House, 2012), 39. I did a similar thing after writing two Red Skelton biographies, with the result being my *I, Red Skelton: Exit Laughing, or a Man, His Movies and Sometimes His Monkeys: A Novelized Memoir* (Albany, GA.: BearManor Press, 2011).
10. Matthew 21:16.
11. Tom Wood, *The Bright Side of Billy Wilder, Primarily* (Garden City, NY: Doubleday, 1970), 110–111.
12. *Ibid.*, 113.
13. Richard Ben Cramer, *Joe DiMaggio: The Hero's Life* (New York: Simon & Schuster, 2000), 367.
14. J. Randy Tarraborrelli, *The Secret Life of Marilyn Monroe* (New York: Grand Central Publishing, 2009), 243–244.
15. Donald Spoto, *Marilyn Monroe: The Biography* (1993; rpt New York: Cooper Square Press, 2001), 283–284.
16. Maurice Yacowar, *Loser Take All: The Comic Art of Woody Allen* (New York: Frederick Ungar, 1979), 52.
17. Gordon Gow, *Hollywood in the Fifties* (New York: A. S. Barnes, 1971), 146.
18. See the author's *Genre-Busting Dark Comedies of the 1970s: Twelve American Films* (Jefferson, NC: McFarland, 2016).
19. Mel Gussow, "Stage: Ewell in Waiting for Godot," *New York Times*, July 29, 1971, 43.
20. Robert Wahls, *New York Daily News*, "Footlights," August 22, 1971.
21. See the author's *Joe E. Brown: Film Comedian and Baseball Buffoon* (Jefferson, NC: McFarland, 2006).
22. Dwight Chaplin, "After the Gun Fire Stops, Enter Tom Ewell Smiling," *TV Guide*, October 30–November 5, 1976, 13.

23. "Tom Ewell, Actor, Is Dead at 85; Monroe Co-Star in '7 Year Itch,'" *New York Times*, September 13, 1994.
24. Wahls, *New York Daily News*.
25. McCarthy Lands, "'The Seven Year Itch' [Review]," *Variety*, June 8, 1955.
26. Dick Williams, "'The Seven Year Itch' [Review]," *Los Angeles Mirror News*, included in a *Hollywood Reporter* collage of review ads for the picture, June 16, 1955, 6–7.
27. Moffitt.
28. "'Seven Year Itch' New York Sneak Jams Broadway," *Hollywood Reporter*, June 2, 1952.
29. William K. Zinsser, "'The Seven Year Itch' [Review]," *New York Herald Tribune*, June 15, 1955, 4.
30. Rose Pelswick, "Monroe Is Glamorous and Ewell Amusing." *New York Journal-American*, June 4, 1955, 14.
31. Cook, "'Itch' Should Make Scratch," *New York World-Telegram and Sun*, June 4, 1955, 8; *Hollywood Reporter* collage of review ads for *The Seven Year Itch*.
32. Cook, "'Itch' Should Make Scratch."
33. Carl Rollyson, *Marilyn Monroe: A Life of the Actress* (Jackson: University Press of Mississippi, 2014), 94.

Chapter 8

1. Thomas Heggen, *Mister Roberts* (Boston: Houghton Mifflin, 1946), 218.
2. William Shakespeare, *The Tragedy of Macbeth*, Act 5, Scene 5 (1606).
3. Milton Luban, "'Mr. Roberts' Comedy Riot with Huge B.O. Potential," *Hollywood Reporter*, May 24, 1955, 3.
4. A. H. Weiler, "'Mister Roberts' [Review]," *New York Times*, July 15, 1955, 14.
5. Will Holtzman, *Jack Lemmon* (New York: Pyramid Publications, 1977), 47.
6. William K. Zinsser, "A Happy Surprise in 'Mr. Roberts,'" *New York Herald Tribune*, July 24, 1955, [Entertainment section]: 1.
7. *Ibid.*
8. Milten Luban, "'Mr. Roberts' Comedy Riot with Huge B.O. Potential."
9. Kate Cameron, "'Mr. Roberts' at Music Hall a Honey of a Film," *New York Daily News*, July 15, 1955, 52.
10. Robert Mitchell, *Mister Roberts*, in *Magill's Survey of Cinema*, Frank N. Magill, ed. Englewood Cliffs, NJ: Salem Press, 1980), 1124.
11. Chris Lemmon, *A Twist of Lemmon* (Chapel Hill, NC: Algonquin Books, 2006), 109.
12. Kevin Spacey, "Foreword," in Chris Lemmon's *A Twist of Lemmon* (Chapel Hill, NC: Algonquin Books, 2006), x.
13. "[Jack Lemmon Interview]," *American Film*, September 1982, 16.
14. *Ibid.*
15. Frederic Raphael, *Eyes Wide Open: A Memoir of Stanley Kubrick* (New York: Orien Publishing, 1999).

16. Dan Ford, *Pappy: The Life of John Ford* (Englewood Cliffs, N.J.: Prentice-Hall, 1979), 86.
17. Henry Fonda (as told to Howard Teichman), *Fonda: My Life* (New York: New American Library, 1981), 232–233.
18. Tag Gallagher, *John Ford: The Man and His Films* (Los Angeles: University of California, 1986), 346.
19. Henry Fonda (as told to Howard Teichman), *Fonda: My Life*, 234.
20. Kevin Spacey, "Foreword," ix.
21. Patrick McGilligan, *Cagney: The Actor as Auteur* (New York: Da Capo Press, 1975), 209.
22. *Ibid.*, 208–209.
23. Jack Lemmon voice-over bonus material on *Mister Roberts* (1955; Warner Brothers Entertainment, 2005), DVD. (Unless otherwise noted, additional quotes are from this DVD.)
24. Cobbett Steinberg, *Reel Facts: The Movie Book of Records* (New York: Vintage, 1978), 346.
25. Jesse Zunser, "A Sea-Going Classic Immortalized Onscreen," *Cue*, July 16, 1955, 13.
26. William Brogdon, "'Mister Roberts' [Review]," *Variety*, May 25, 1955.
27. William K. Zinsser, "A Happy Surprise in Mister Roberts,'" *New York Herald Tribune*.
28. Milten Luban, "'Mr. Roberts' Comedy Riot with Huge B.O. Potential"; Alton Cook, "'Mister Roberts' Hilarious," *New York World-Telegram and Sun*, July 15, 1955, 10.
29. A. H. Weiler, "'Mister Roberts' [Review]."

Chapter 9

1. Bosley Crowther, "'Artists and Models' [Review]," *New York Times*, December 22, 1956, 20.
2. Peter Bogdanovich, "Frank Tashlin: The Possum's Smile," in Bogdanovich's *Who the Devil Made It: Conversations with Legendary Film Directors* (New York: Ballantine Books, 1997), 769.
3. See the author's *Leo McCarey: From Marx to McCarthy* (Lanham, Maryland: Scarecrow Press, 2005); and *The Marx Brothers: A Bio-Bibliography* (Westport, Connecticut: Greenwood Press, 1987).
4. Robert Mundy, "Frank Tashlin: A Tribute," in *Frank Tashlin*, eds. Claire Johnston and Paul Willenen (London: Vineyard Press, 1973), 9.
5. Peter Bogdanovich, "Frank Tashlin: The Possum's Smile," 771.
6. Roger Tailleur, "Anything Goes," in *Frank Tashlin*, eds. Claire Johnston and Paul Willenen (London: Vineyard Press, 1973), 25.
7. See the author's *Laurel & Hardy: A Bio-Bibliography* (Westport, Connecticut: Greenwood Press, 1990).
8. Noël Simsolo, "The Coordinator of Disorders," in *Frank Tashlin* eds. Roger Garcia and Bernard Eisenschitz (London: British Film Institute, 1994), 54.
9. Frank Tashlin, *The Bear That Wasn't* (1946; rpt. New York: Dover, 1995).
10. Mike Barrier, "Interview," in *Frank Tashlin*, eds. Claire Johnston and Paul Willenen (London: Vineyard Press, 1973), 52, 131.
11. *Ibid.*, 47.
12. For example, see Patti Lewis' *I Laffed Till I Cried: Thirty-Six Years of Marriage to Jerry Lewis* (Waco: WRS Publishing, 1993).
13. Ian Cameron, "Frank Tashlin and the New World," in *Frank Tashlin*, eds. Claire Johnston and Paul Willenen (London: Vineyard Press, 1973), 86.
14. David Ehrenstein, "Frank Tashlin and Jerry Lewis," in *Frank Tashlin*, eds. Roger Garcia and Bernard Eisenschitz (London: British Film Institute, 1994), 44.
15. *Ibid.*, 43.
16. See the author's *Personality Comedians as Genre: Selected Players* (Westport, Connecticut: Greenwood Press, 1997).
17. See author's *Charlie Chaplin: A Bio-Bibliography* (Westport, Connecticut: Greenwood Press, 1983).
18. See the author's *Chaplin's War Trilogy: An Evolving Lens in Three Dark Comedies, 1918–1947* (Jefferson, NC: McFarland, 2014).
19. Peter Bogdanovich, "The Nonsense of Civilization," in Bogdanovich's *Who the Devil Made It: Conversations with Legendary Film Director* (New York: Ballantine Books, 1997), 775.
20. Richard Gehman, *That Kid: The Story of Jerry Lewis* (New York: Avon Books, 1964), 127.
21. *Ibid.*
22. "Million Dollar Madmen," *Quick*, October 8, 1951, 56.
23. For example, see *The Adventure of Jerry Lewis* (New York: National Comics Publications, Nov.-Dec. 1959). Author's collection.
24. Kurt Vonnegut, *Slapstick* (New York: Delacorte Press, 1976), 1.
25. Raymond Durgnat, *The Crazy Mirror: Hollywood Comedy and the American Image* (New York: Horizon Press, 1969), 47.
26. *Ibid.*, 234.
27. *American Film Institute's 100 Years ... 100 Laughs*, CBS television special broadcast, June 13, 2000.
28. The author has seen the comedian several times in concert, including an October 7, 1978, appearance at Ball State University (Muncie, Indiana).
29. See Frank Capra's *Frank Capra: The Name Above the Title* (New York: Macmillan, 1971).
30. Durgnat, 233.
31. Jerry Lewis and James Kaplan, *Dean & Me: A Love Story* (New York: Doubleday, 2005), 274.
32. Shawn Levy, *King of Comedy: The Life and Art of Jerry Lewis* (New York: St. Martin's Griffin, 1997), 192.
33. David Thomson, *Bette Davis* (New York: Faber and Faber, 2009), 34.
34. David Thomson, *The New Biography Dictionary of Film* (New York: Alfred A. Knopf, 2003), 521.
35. Jerry Lewis and James Kaplan.
36. Bob Hope and Bob Thomas, *The Road to Hollywood* (Garden City, NY: Doubleday, 1937), 12.
37. Cobbett Steinberg, *Reel Facts: The Movie Book of Records* (New York: Vintage, 1978), 405–406.
38. *Ibid.*, 345.
39. William K. Zinsser, "'Artists and Models' [Review]," *New York Herald Tribune*, December 22, 1955, 11.

40. Wanda Hale, "The Paramount [Theatre] Shows Martin & Lewis Film," *New York Daily News*, December 22, 1955, 64.
41. William Brogdon, "'Artists and Models' [Review]," *Variety*, November 9, 1955.
42. Alton Cook, "'Artists and Models' Just More Martin and Lewis," *New York World-Telegram and Sun*, December 22, 1955.
43. "Cinema: 'Artists and Models,'" *Time*, January 9, 1956, 86.
44. Bosley Crowther, "'Artists and Models,'" *New York Times*, December 22, 1955, 20.
45. Milten Luban, "Martin and Lewis, Maclaine Sparkle," *Hollywood Reporter*, November 9, 1955, 3.
46. *Ibid.*
47. *Ibid.*

Chapter 10

1. Alan Dale, *Comedy Is a Man in Trouble* (Minneapolis: University of Minnesota Press, 2000), 187.
2. Kurt Singer, *The Danny Kaye Saga* (London: Robert Hale Limited, 1957), 14.
3. Martin Cottfpried, *Nobody's Fool: Danny Kaye: The Lives of Danny Kaye* (New York: Simon & Schuster, 1994), 120.
4. Charles Thompson, *Bob Hope: Portrait of a Superstar* (New York: St. Martin's Press, 1981), 96.
5. Cottfpried, 219.
6. Eric Pace, "Danny Kaye, Limber-Limbed Comedian, Dies," *New York Times*, March 4, 1987, D-23.
7. Kathryn Bernheimer, *The 50 Funniest Movies of All Time* (Secaucus, N.J.: Citadel Press, 1999), 113.
8. See the author's *Parody as Film Genre: "Never Give a Saga an Even Break"* (Westport, Connecticut: Greenwood Press, 1999).
9. *American Film Institute's 100 Years ... 100 Laughs*, CBS television special broadcast, June 13, 2000.
10. Rose Pelswick, "Danny Kaye in Slick Hatchet Job," *New York Journal American*, February 2, 1956, 16.
11. William K. Zinsser, "Screen: "The Court Jester,'" *New York Herald Tribune*, February 2, 1956, 12.
12. Kate Cameron, "Danny Kaye Rings Bell in Paramount 'Jester,'" *New York Daily News*, February 2, 1956, 19.
13. William Brogdon, "'The Court Jester' [Review]," *Variety*, February 1, 1956.
14. Bosley Crowther, "'The Court Jester' [Review]," *New York Times*, February 2, 1956, 19.
15. Bosley Crowther, "Little Things: Being an Appreciation of Small Favors in Films," *New York Times*, February 5, 1956, 111.
16. Brogdon.
17. Jack Meffit, "'Court Jester' Filled with Action, Sparkling Humor," *Hollywood Reporter*, January 27, 1956, 3.
18. Mason Wiley & Damien Bona, *Inside Oscar* (1986; rpt. (New York Ballantine Books, 1993), 276.
19. "'Jester' Hot in London," *Hollywood Reporter*, February 27, 1956, 3.
20. Claire Johnston and Paul Willemen, eds., *Frank Tashlin* (London: Vineyard Press, 1973), 58.

Chapter 11

1. Fred Hift, "'Will Success Spoil Rock Hunter?' [Review]," *Variety*, July 31, 1957.
2. Jessie Zunser, "The Funniest of 1957: 'Will Success Spoil Rock Hunter?," *Cue*, September 14, 1957, 13.
3. *Ibid.*
4. Cobbett Steinberg, *Reel Facts: The Movie Book of Records* (New York: Vintage, 1978), 406.
5. Bosley Crowther, "'Will Success Spoil Rock Hunter?' [Review]," *New York Times*, September 12, 1957, 37.
6. Andrew Sarris, *The American Cinema: Directors and Directions, 1929–1968* (New York: E.P. Dutton, 1968), 141.
7. Bill Krahn, The Outsider: Joe Dante on Tashlin," in *Frank Tashlin*, eds. Roger Garcia and Bernard Eisenschitz (London: British Film Institute, 1994), 136.
8. Peter Bogdanovich, "Frank Tashlin," in *Who the Devil Made It*, ed. Bogdanovich (New York: Ballantine Books, 1997), 772.
9. *Ibid.*, 773–774.
10. Tony Curtis (with Mark A. Vieira), *The Making of Some Like It Hot* (Hoboken, NJ: John Wiley & Sons, 2009), 27–28.
11. Frank Tashlin, *The Bear That Wasn't* (1946; rpt. New York: Dove Publications, Inc.,).
12. Frank Tashlin, *The Possum That Didn't* (New York: Farr, Straus, 1950).
13. Frank Tashlin, *The World That Isn't....* (New York: Simon & Schuster, 1951).
14. James Thurber, *The Last Flower* (1939: rpt. New York: Harper & Row, 1971).
15. Will Cuppy, *How to Become Extinct* (1941; rpt. Garden City, NY: Rinehart, 1951); also see the author's *Will Cuppy: American Satirist* (Jefferson, NC: McFarland, 2013).
16. Mark Atwood Lawrence, "Kissinger the Cynic," *New York Times*, October 4, 2015, Review of Books section: 13.
17. Andrew Roberts, "Kissinger the Idealist," *New York Times*, October 4, 2015, Review of Books section: 13.
18. Mason Wiley and Damien Bona, *Inside Oscar* (1986; New York: Ballantine Books, 1993), 966.
19. *Ibid.* 853.
20. Ray E. Boomhower, "Frank Mckinney 'Kin' Hubbard," in *Indiana's 200, 1816- 2016: The People Who Shaped the Hoosier State*, Linda C. Gugin and James E. St. Clair, eds. (Indianapolis: Indiana Historical Society Press, 2015), 182.
21. Stephen King, *11/22/63* (New York: Scribner, 2011), 152.
22. Zunser.
23. Melvin Maddocks, "Tony Randall Starring in Spoof on TV," *Christian Science Monitor*, September 10, 1957.
24. *Variety*, "'Will Success Spoil Rock Hunter?' [Review]," July 31, 1957.
25. Kate Cameron, "La Mansfield Lights Local RKO Outlets," *New York Daily News*, September 12, 1957.
26. Alton Cook, "'Rock Hunter' Bows at 100 Film

Houses," *New York World-Telegram and Sun*, September 12, 1957, 20.

27. Alan Branigan, "Fast, Funny: That's 'Rock Hunter,' Full of Jibes at TV Husksters," *Newark Evening News*, undated [September 1957], in the *Will Success Spoil Rock Hunter?* file, NY Performing Arts Library, Lincoln Center, NY.

28. Rose Pelswick, "Sizzling Jayne Zips Through Zany Film," *New York Journal American*, September 12, 1957.

29. Peter Bogdanovich, "Frank Tashlin," *New York Times*, May 28, 1972, 7.

30. J. Hoberman, "Cartooned In," *Village Voice*, July 16, 1980, 46.

31. Dave Kehr, "When Unmanly Man Met Womanly Woman," *New York Times*, August 20, 2006.

32. See the author's *Forties Film Funnymen: The Decade's Great Comedians at Work in the Shadow of War* (Jefferson, NC: McFarland, 2010).

33. Bosley Crowther, "'Will Success Spoil Rock Hunter?' [Review]," *New York Times*, September 12, 1957, 37.

34. Tashlin, *The World That Isn't....* Page numbers not noted [84–85].

Chapter 12

1. *AFI's 100 Years ... 100 Movie Quotes*, CBS television special broadcast, June 21, 2005.

2. *American Film Institute's 100 Years ... 1000 Laughs*, CBS television broadcast, June 13, 2000.

3. Cobbett Steinberg, *Real Facts: The Movie Book of Records* (New York: Vintage), 403–404; also see the author's *Joe E. Brown: Film Comedian and Baseball Buffoon* (Jefferson, NC: McFarland, 2006).

4. See the author's *American Dark Comedy: Beyond Satire* (Westport, Connecticut: Greenwood Press, 1996); and *Chaplin's War Trilogy: An Evolving Lens* (Jefferson, NC: McFarland, 2014).

5. Charlotte Chandler, *Nobody's Perfect: Billy Wilder: A Personal Biography* (New York: Simon & Schuster, 2002), 201.

6. See author's *Parody as Film Genre: "Never Give a Saga an Even Break."* (Westport, Connecticut: Greenwood Press, 1999).

7. "'The Circus' [Review]," *Variety*, July 3, 1934.

8. Gehring, *Joe E. Brown: Film Comedian and Baseball Buffoon*.

9. Cameron Crowe, *Conversations with Wilder* (1999; rpt. New York: Alfred A. Knopf, 2001), 42.

10. See the author's *Screwball Comedy: A Genre of Madcap Romance* (Westport, Connecticut: Greenwood Press, 1986); and *Romantic Vs. Screwball Comedy: Charting the Difference* (Lanham, Maryland: Scarecrow Press, 2002).

11. Chandler, *Nobody's Perfect: Billy Wilder: A Personal Biography*, 206.

12. Ed Sikov, *On Sunset Boulevard: The Life and Times of Billy Wilder* (New York: Hyperion, 1998), 409.

13. Tom Wood, *The Bright Side of Billy Wilder, Primarily* (Garden City, New York: Doubleday, 1970), 150.

14. Tony Curtis (with Peter Golenbock), *Tony Curtis: American Prince: A Memoir* (New York: Harmony Books, 2008), 203.

15. Sikov, *On Sunset Boulevard: The Life and Times of Billy Wilder*, 410–411.

16. *Ibid.*, 408.

17. Tony Curtis (with Mark A. Vieirira), *The Making of Some Like It Hot* (Hoboken, NJ: John Wiley & Sons, 2009), 10.

18. Don Widener, *Lemmon: A Biography* (New York: Macmillan, 1975), 166–167.

19. *Ibid.*, 174.

20. Curtis (and Paris), *Tony Curtis: The Autobiography*, 168.

21. Chandler, *Nobody's Perfect: Billy Wilder: The Life and Times of Billy Wilder*, 208.

22. Sikov, *On Sunset Boulevard: The Life and Times of Billy Wilder*, 355.

23. *Ibid.*, 420.

24. Chandler, *Nobody's Perfect: Billy Wilder: The Life and Times of Billy Wilder*, 209.

25. See the author's *Groucho & W. C. Fields: Huckster Comedians* (Jackson: University Press of Mississippi, 1994).

26. *AFI's 100 Years ... 100 Movie Quotes*, CBS Television, first broadcast June 21, 2005.

27. Michael Kimmelman, "Bowie, from State to Easel," *New York Times*, January 15, 2016, C-25 (A reprint of a NYT interview from June 14, 1998).

28. Curtis (and Paris), *Tony Curtis: The Autobiography*, 161.

29. Widener, *Lemmon: A Biography*, 170.

30. Wood, *The Bright Side of Billy Wilder, Primarily*, 153.

31. Carol Rollyson, *Marilyn Monroe: A Life of the Actress* (Jackson: University Press of Mississippi, 2014), 176.

32. Norman Mailer, *Marilyn* (1973: rpt. New York: Random House, 2012), Picture section caption.

33. Donald Spoto, *Marilyn Monroe: The Biography* (1993; rpt. New York: Cooper Square Press, 2001), 399.

34. Sikov, *On Sunset Boulevard: The Life and Times of Billy Wilder*, pp. 422–423.

35. "Some Like It Hot [Review]." *Variety*, February 25, 1959.

36. *Ibid.*

37. Jack Moffitt, "'Some Like It Hot' Certain to Be Even Hotter at B. O.," *Hollywood Reporter*, February 25, 1959.

38. *Ibid.*

39. *Ibid.*, 4.

40. Kate Cameron, "Gallop, Don't Amble to 'Some Like It Hot,'" *New York Daily News*, March 30, 1959, 44.

41. *Ibid.*

42. "'Some Like It Hot' [Review]," *Cue*, undated critique in the *Some Like It Hot* folder in the Performing Arts Library, NY Public Library at Lincoln Center, NY.

43. Paul V. Beckley, "'Some Like It Hot' [Review]," *New York Herald Tribune*, March 30, 1959, 11.

44. Rose Pelswick, "'Some Like It Hot': Oh, Boy, That Marilyn!," *New York Journal American*, March 30, 1959.

45. John McCarten, "The Current Cinema: Sennett, Anyone?," *The New Yorker*, April 4, 1959.

46. *Ibid.*

47. A. H. Weiler, "'Some Like It Hot' [Review]," *New York Times*, March 30, 1959, 23.
48. Cobbett Steinberg, *Reel Facts: The Movie Book of Records* (New York: Vintage Books, 1978), 348.
49. Sikov, *On Sunset Boulevard: The Life and Times of Billy Wilder*, 470.
50. Crowe, *Conversation with Wilder*, 6.
51. See the author's *Film Clowns of the Depression: Twelve Defining Comic Performances* (Jefferson, NC: McFarland, 2007; and *Forties Film Funnymen: The Decade's Great Comedians at Work in the Shadow of War* (Jefferson, NC: McFarland, 2010).

Epilogue

1. Steve Allen, *The Funny Men* (New York: Simon & Schuster, 1956), 197.
2. Wes D. Gehring, *Film Clowns of the Depression: Twelve Defining Comic Performances* (Jefferson, NC: McFarland, 2007).
3. Wes D. Gehring, *Forties Film Funnymen: The Decade's Great Comedians at Work in the Shadow of War* (Jefferson, NC: McFarland, 2010).
4. David Thomson, *Have You Seen...?* (2008; rpt. New York: Alfred A Knopf, 2010), 842.
5. Noah Millman, "The Shortlist," *New York Times*, January 24, 2016, "The Shortlist," Book Review Section: 26.
6. "The Marx Brothers Now," *Newsweek*, March 17, 1958, 104.
7. Hal Humphrey, "Groucho Diagnoses Our Ailing Comedy," *Los Angeles Mirror-News*, March 17, 1958, in the "Marx Brothers Files," Margaret Harrick Library, Academy of Motion Picture Arts and Sciences, Los Angeles; see also the author's *The Marx Brothers: A Bio-Bibliography* (Westport, Connecticut: Greenwood Press, 1987); and *Groucho & W. C. Fields: Huckster Comedians* (Jackson: University Press of Mississippi, 1994).
8. Bob Hope (with Linda Hope). *Bob Hope: My Life in Jokes* (New York: Hyperion, 2003), 90.
9. Stephen King, *11/22/63* (New York: Scribner, 2011), 648.
10. Steve Martin, *Born Standing Up* (New York: Scribner, 2007), 144.
11. George Carlin, *It's Bad for Ya* (USA: MPI Home Video DVD, 2006), 68 minutes.
12. Duane Byrge, ed. *Private Screenings: Insiders Share a Century of Movie Moments* (Atlanta, Georgia: Turner Publishing, 1995), 119.
13. See the author's *American Dark Comedy: Beyond Satire* (Westport, Connecticut: Greenwood Press, 1996).
14. Thomson, *Have You Seen...?*, 43.
15. Jeremy Egner, "A Rabbit Hole of Kennedy Conspiracies." *New York Times*, February 7, 2016, Arts & Leisure Section: 15.

Bibliography

Books

The Adventures of Jerry Lewis. New York: National Comics Publications, Nov.-Dec., 1959.

Anthony, Barry. *Chaplin's Music Hall: The Chaplins and Their Circle in Limelight.* New York: I. B. Tauris, 2012.

Bachelder, Louise, ed. *Abraham Lincoln: Wit and Wisdom.* Mount Vernon, NY: Peter Pauper Press, 1965.

Bernheimer, Kathryn. *The 50 Funniest Movies of All Time.* Secaucus, NJ: Citadel Press, 1999.

Bloom, Claire. *Limelight and After.* 1982; rpt. New York: Penguin, 1983.

Borowitz, Andy. *The 50 Funniest American Writers: An Anthology of Humor from Mark Twain to the Onion.* New York: Library of American Humor, 2014.

Brooks, Tim, and Earle Marsh. *The Complete Directory to Prime Time Network TV Shows: 1946–Present.* New York: Ballantine Books, 1979.

Calvert, Corinne. *Has Corinne Been a Good Girl?* New York: St. Martin's Press, 1983.

Capra, Frank. *Frank Capra: The Name Above the Title.* New York: Macmillan, 1971.

Carey, Gary. *Judy Holliday: An Intimate Life Story.* London: Robson Books, 1983.

Chandler, Charlotte. *Nobody's Perfect: Billy Wilder: A Personal Biography.* New York: Simon & Schuster, 2002.

Chaplin, Charles. *Footlights.* In *Footlights with the World of Limelight,* ed. David Robinson. Bologna: Cineteca Bologna, 2014.

Chaplin, Charles. *My Autobiography* 1964; rpt. New York: Pocket Books, 1966.

Chaplin, Charles, Jr. (with N. Rau and M. Rau). *My Father, Charlie Chaplin.* New York: Random House, 1960.

Charlton, James, ed. *The Writer's Quotation Book.* 1980; rpt. New York: Penguin, 1985.

Cobbett, Steinberg. *Reel Facts: The Movie Book of Records.* New York: Vintage, 1978.

Cottfpried, Martin. *Nobody's Fool: Danny Kaye: The Lives of Danny Kaye.* New York: Simon & Schuster, 1994.

Cramer, Richard Ben. *Joe DiMaggio: The Hero's Life.* New York: Simon & Schuster, 2000.

Crosby, Bing (with Pete Martin). *Call Me Lucky.* New York: Simon & Schuster, 1953.

Crowe, Cameron. *Conversations with Wilder.* 1999; rpt. New York: Alfred A. Knopf, 2001.

Cuppy, Will. *How to Become Extinct.* 1941; rpt. Garden City, NY: Rinehart, 1951.

Cuppy, Will. *How to Tell Your Friends from the Apes.* 1931; rpt. Boston: Nonpareil, 2005.

Curtis, James. *Spencer Tracy: A Biography.* New York: Alfred A. Knopf, 2011.

Curtis, Tony (with Peter Golenbook). *Tony Curtis: American Prince: A Memoir.* New York: Harmony Books, 2008.

Curtis, Tony (and Barry Paris). *Tony Curtis: The Autobiography.* New York: William Morrow, 1993.

Curtis, Tony (with Mark A. Vieira). *The Making of Some Like It Hot.* Hoboken, NJ: John Wiley & Sons, 2009.

Dale, Alan. *Comedy Is A Man in Trouble.* Minneapolis: University of Minnesota Press, 2000.

Delbanco, Andrew. *Melville: His World and Work.* New York: Random House, 2005.

DiBattista, Maria. *Fast-Talking Dames.* New Haven: Yale University Press, 2001.

Durgnat, Raymond. *The Crazy Mirror: Hollywood Comedy and the American Image.* New York: Horizon Press, 1969.

Fonda, Henry (as told to Howard Teichmann). *Fonda: My Life.* New York: New American Library, 1981.

Ford, Dan. *Pappy: The Life of John Ford.* Englewood Cliffs, NJ: Prentice-Hall, 1979.

Franklin, Joe. *Joe Franklin's Encyclopedia of Comedians.* Secaucus, NJ: Citadel, 1979.

Freedland, Michael. *Dean Martin: King of the Road.* London: Robson Books, 2004.

Gallagher, Tag. *John Ford: The Man and His Films.* Los Angeles: University of California, 1986.

Gehman, Richard. *That Kid: The Story of Jerry Lewis.* New York: Avon Books, 1964.

Gehring, Wes D. *American Dark Comedy: Beyond Satire.* Westport, Connecticut: Greenwood Press, 1996.

Gehring, Wes D. *Chaplin's War Trilogy: An Evolving Lens in Three Dark Comedies, 1918–1947*. Jefferson, NC: McFarland, 2014.

Gehring, Wes D. *Charlie Chaplin: A Bio-Bibliography*. Westport, Connecticut: Greenwood Press, 1983.

Gehring, Wes D. *Film Clowns of the Depression: Twelve Defining Performances*. Jefferson, NC: McFarland, 2007.

Gehring, Wes D. *Forties Film Funnymen: The Decade's Great Comedians at Work in the Shadow of War*. Jefferson, NC: McFarland, 2010.

Gehring, Wes D. *Genre-Busting Dark Comedies of the 1970s: Twelve American Films*. Jefferson, NC: McFarland, 2016.

Gehring, Wes D. *Groucho & W. C. Fields: Huckster Comedians*. Jackson: University Press of Mississippi, 1994.

Gehring, Wes D. *I, Red Skelton: Exit Laughing or, A Man, His Movies and Sometimes His Monkeys*. Albany, GA: BearMan Fiction, 2011.

Gehring, Wes D. *James Dean: Rebel with a Cause*. Indianapolis: Indiana Historical Society Press, 2005.

Gehring, Wes D. *Joe E. Brown: Film Comedian and Baseball Buffoon*. Jefferson, NC: McFarland, 2006.

Gehring, Wes D. *Laurel & Hardy: A Bio-Bibliography*. Westport, Connecticut: Greenwood Press, 1990.

Gehring, Wes D. *Leo McCarey: From Marx to McCarthy*. Lanham, Maryland: Scarecrow Press, 2005.

Gehring, Wes D. *The Marx Brothers: A Bio-Bibliography* Westport, Connecticut: Greenwood Press, 1990.

Gehring, Wes D. *"Mr. B" Or, Comforting Thoughts About the Bison: A Critical Biography of Robert Benchley*. Westport, Connecticut: Greenwood Press, 1992.

Gehring, Wes D. *Parody as Film Genre: "Never Give a Saga an Even Break."* Westport, Connecticut: Greenwood Press, 1999.

Gehring, Wes D. *Personality Comedians as Genre: Selected Players*. Westport, Connecticut: Greenwood Press, 1997.

Gehring, Wes D. *Populism and the Capra Legacy*. Westport, Connecticut: Greenwood Press, 1995.

Gehring, Wes D. *Red Skelton: The Mask Behind the Mask*. Indianapolis: Indiana Historical Society Press, 2008. Foreword by the comedian's daughter, Valentina Maria Skelton Alonson.

Gehring, Wes D. *Romantic vs. Screwball Comedy: Charting the Difference*. Lanham, Maryland: Scarecrow Press, 2002.

Gehring, Wes D. *Screwball Comedy: A Genre of Madcap Romance*. Westport, Connecticut: Greenwood Press, 1986.

Gehring, Wes D. *W. C. Fields: A Bio-Bibliography*. Westport, Connecticut: Greenwood Press, 1984.

Gehring, Wes D. *Will Cuppy: American Satirist*. Jefferson, NC: McFarland, 2013.

Gow, Gordon. *Hollywood In the Fifties*. New York: A. S. Barnes, 1971.

Haskell, Molly. *From Reverence to Rape: The Treatment of Women in the Movies*. New York: Holt, Rinehart and Winston, 1973.

Heggen, Thomas. *Mister Roberts*. Boston: Houghton Mifflin, 1946.

Hepburn, Katharine. *Me: Stories of My Life*. New York: Alfred A. Knopf, 1991.

Herbert, Emily. *Robin Williams: When the Laughter Stops, 1951–2014*. London: John Blake Publishing, 2014.

Holtzman, Will. *Jack Lemmon* New York: Pyramid Publications, 1977.

Holtzman, Will. *Judy Holliday: A Biography*. New York: G. P. Putnam's Sons, 1982.

Hope, Bob, and Bob Thomas. *The Road to Hollywood*. Garden City, NY: Doubleday, 1977.

Hope, Bob (with Linda Hope). *Bob Hope: My Life in Jokes*. New York: Hyperion, 2003.

Hope, Bob (with Melville Shavelson). *Don't Shoot. It's Only Me*. New York: G. P. Putnam's Sons, 1990.

Huff, Theodore. *Charlie Chaplin*. 1951; rpt. New York: Arno Press and the New York Times, 1972.

Johnston, Claire, and Paul Willemen, eds. *Frank Tashlin*. London: Vineyard Press, 1973.

Judson, Karen, and Carlene Harrison. *Law and Ethics for Health Professions*. 1994; rpt. New York: McGraw-Hill Professions, 2013.

Kanfer, Stefan. *Ball of Fire: The Tumultuous Life and Comic Art of Lucille Ball*. London: Faber and Faber, 2003.

King, Stephen. *11/22/63*. New York: Scribner, 2011.

Knipfel, Jim. *Quitting the Nairobi Trio*. 2000; rpt. New York: Berkley Books, 2001.

Lamour, Dorothy (as told to Dick McInnes). *My Side of the Road*. 1974; rpt. London: Robson Books, 1980.

Lax, Eric. *Woody Allen: A Biography* New York: Alfred A. Knopf, 1991.

Lee, Harper. *To Kill a Mockingbird*. 1960; rpt. New York: Harper Perennial, 2006.

Levy, Emanuel. *George Cukor, Master of Elegance*. New York: William Morrow, 1994.

Levy, Shawn. *King of Comedy: The Life and Art of Jerry Lewis*. New York: St. Martin's Griffin, 1997.

Levy, Shawn. *Rat Pack Confidential*. New York: Doubleday, 1998.

Lewis, Jerry, and James Kaplin. *Dean & Me: A Love Story*. New York: Doubleday, 2005.

Lewis, Jerry (with Herb Gluck). *Jerry Lewis In Person*. New York: Antheneum, 1982.

Lewis, Jerry. *The Total Film-Maker*. 1971; rpt. New York: Warner Paperback Library, 1973.

Lewis, Patti, *I Laughed Till I Cried: Thirty-Six Years of Marriage to Jerry Lewis*. Waco: WRS Publishing, 1993.

Long, Robert Emmet, ed. *George Cukor Interviews*. Jackson: University Press of Mississippi, 2001.

Mailer, Norman. *Marilyn*. 1973; rpt. New York: Random House, 2012.

McCabe, John. *Charlie Chaplin*. Garden City, NY: Doubleday, 1978.

McGilligan, Patrick. *Cagney: The Actor as Auteur*. New York: Da Capo Press, 1975.

Offer, John. *Jean Arthur: The Actress Nobody Knew*. New York: Limelight Editions, 1997.

Peary, Danny. *Close-ups*. New York: Simon & Schuster, 1978.

Raphael, Frederic. *Eyes Wide Open: A Memoir of Stanley Kubrick*. New York: Orien Publishing, 1999.

Robinson, David. *Chaplin: His Life and Art*. New York: McGraw-Hill, 1985.

Rollyson, Carl. *Marilyn Monroe: A Life of the Actress*. Jackson: University Press of Mississippi, 2004.

Rosen, Marjorie. *Popcorn Venus: Women, Movies & The American Dream*. New York: Coward, McCann & Georghegan, 1973.

Sarris, Andrew. *The American Cinema: Directors and Directions, 1929–1968*. New York: E. P. Dutton, 1968.

Sikov, Ed. *On Sunset Boulevard: The Life and Times of Billy Wilder*. New York: Hyperion, 1998.

Singer, Kurt, *The Danny Kaye Saga*. London: Robert Hale Limited, 1957.

Smith, Ronald L. *Who's Who in Comedy*. New York: Facts on File, 1992.

Spoto, Donald. *Enchantment: The Life of Audrey Hepburn*. New York: Three Rivers Press, 2006.

Spoto, Donald. *Marilyn Monroe: The Biography*. 1993; rpt. New York: Cooper Square Press, 2001.

Strait, Raymond. *Bob Hope: A Tribute*. New York: Pinnacle Books, 2003, 318.

Tarraborelli, J. Randy. *The Secret Life of Marilyn Monroe*. New York: Grand Central Publishing, 2009.

Tashlin, Frank. *The Bear That Wasn't*. New York: Dover, 1946.

Tashlin, Frank. *The Possum That Didn't*. New York: Farr, Straus, 1950.

Tashlin, Frank. *The World That Isn't....* New York: Simon & Schuster, 1951.

Thompson, Charles. *Bob Hope: Portrait of a Superstar*. New York: St. Martin's Press, 1981.

Thomson, David. *Bette Davis*. New York: Faber and Faber, 2009.

Thomson, David. *Have You Seen...?* 2008; rpt. New York: Alfred A. Knopf, 2010.

Thurber, James. *The Last Flower*. 1939; rpt. New York: Harper & Row, 1971.

Thurber, James. "The Secret Life of Walter Mitty." In *My World and Welcome to It*. 1942; rpt. New York: Harcourt, Brace and Company, 1944.

Ursini, James. *Preston Sturges: An American Dreamer*. New York: Curtis Books, 1973.

Vonnegut, Kurt. *Slapstick*. New York: Delacorte Press, 1976.

Weissman, Stephen, M. D. *Chaplin: A Life*. New York: Arcade Publishers, 2008, with an Introduction by Geraldine Chaplin.

Wertheim, Arthur Frank. *Radio Comedy*. New York: Oxford University Press, 1979.

Widener, Don. *Lemmon: A Biography*. New York: Macmillan, 1975.

Wiesel, Elsie. *Open Heart*. 2011; rpt. New York: Alfred A. Knopf, 2012.

Wiley, Mason, and Damien Bona. *Inside Oscar*. 1986; rpt. New York: Ballantine Books, 1993.

Wood, Tom. *The Bright Side of Billy Wilder, Primarily*. Garden City, NY: Doubleday, 1970.

Yacowar, Maurice. *Loser Take All: The Comic Art of Woody Allen*. New York: Frederick Ungar, 1979.

Zolgin, Richard. *HOPE: Entertainer of the Century*. New York: Simon & Schuster, 2014.

Shorter Works

Agee, James. "Comedy's Greatest Era." *Life*, September 3, 1949. See also *Agee on Film, Volume 1*. 1958, rpt. New York: Grossett & Dunlap, 1969.

Allen, Steve. "Jackie Gleason." In Allen's *The Funny Men*. New York: Simon & Schuster, 1956.

Allen, Steve. "Red Skelton." In Allen's *The Funny Men*. New York: Simon & Schuster, 1956.

Alonso, Valentina Maria Skelton. "Foreword." In the author's *Red Skelton: The Mask Behind the Mask*. Indianapolis: Indiana Historical Society Press, 2008, xi.

Alpert, Hullis. "SRL Goes to the Movies." *Saturday Review*, January 6, 1951.

Amis, Martin. "There is Simply Too Much to Think About." *New York Times*, May 3, 2015, Book Review section: 20.

Barrier, Mike. "Interview." In *Frank Tashlin*, eds. Claire Johnston and Paul Willenen (London: Vineyard Press, 1973).

Beaufort, John. "An Assault from Mr. Chaplin." *Christian Science Monitor*, April 19, 1947, 8.

Beckley, Paul V. "'Some Like It Hot' [Review]." *New York Herald Tribune*, March 30, 1959, 11.

"Bob Hope and Friends." *LOOK* magazine, August 26, 1952.

Bogdanovich, Peter. "Frank Tashlin: *The Possum's Smile*." In Bogdanovich's *Who the Devil Made It*. New York: Ballantine Books, 1997.

Bogdanovich, Peter. "The Nonsense of Civilization." In Bogdanovich's *Who the Devil Made It*. New York; Ballantine Books, 1997.

Boomhowser, Ray E. "Frank McKinney 'Kin' Hubbard." In *Indian's 200, 1816–2016: The People Who Shaped the Hoosier State*, Linda C. Gugin and James E. St. Clair, eds. Indianapolis: Indiana Historical Society Press, 2015.

"'Born Yesterday' Becomes A Film After Much Travail." *New York Herald Tribune*, December 24, 1950, section 5:3.

Brady, Thomas F. "Film of Kanin Play Attacked On Coast." *New York Times*, December 1, 1950, 31.

Branigan, Alan. "Fast, Funny: That's 'Rock Hunter,' Full of Jibes at TV Hucksters." *Newark Evening News*, undated [September 1957]. In the *Will Success Spoil Rock Hunter?* file, NY Performing Art Library, Lincoln Center, NY.

"Briefly Noted." *The New Yorker*, July 6 & 13, 2015, 87.

Brogdon, William. "'Artists and Models' [Review]." *Variety*, November 9, 1955.

Brogdon, William. "'The Court Jester' [Review]." *Variety*, February 1, 1956.

Brogon, William. "'Mr. Roberts' [Review]." *Variety*, May 25, 1955.

Bragdon, William. "'The Clown' [Review]." *Variety*, December 24, 1952.

Brogdon, William. "'Road to Bali' [Review]." *Variety*, November 19, 1952.

Brogdon, William. "'Sailor Beware' [Review]." *Variety*, December 5, 1952.

Cameron, Ian. "Frank Tashlin and the New World." In *Frank Tashlin*, eds. Claire Johnston and Paul Willenen. London: Vineyard Press, 1973.

Cameron, Kate. "Bob and Bing Back on Road, Bound to Bali." *New York Daily News*, January 30, 1953, 44.

Cameron, Kate. "Bob Hope & Trigger Paramount Co-Stars." *New York Daily News*, October 2, 1952, 65.

Cameron, Kate. "Danny Kaye Rings Bell In Paramount 'Jester.'" *New York Daily News*, February 2, 1956, 19.

Cameron, Kate. "Gallop, Don't Amble To 'Some Like It Hot.'" *New York Daily News*, March 30, 1959, 44.

Cameron, Kate. "Judy Holliday Tops In 'Born Yesterday.'" *New York Daily News*, December 27, 1959, 60.

Cameron, Kate. "La Mansfield Lights Local RKO Outlets." *New York Daily News*, September 12, 1957.

Cameron, Kate. "Martin and Lewis At Mayfair [Theatre] in Laugh Maker." *New York Daily News*, February 1, 1952, C-14.

Cameron, Kate. "'Mr. Roberts' at Music Hall a Honey of a Film." *New York Daily News*, July 15, 1955, 52.

Chaplin, Dwight. "After the Gun Fire Stops, Enter Tom Ewell Smiling." *TV Guide*, October 30–November 5, 1976, 13.

"Chaplin to Return Here, He Declares." *New York Times*, September 23, 1952, 9.

"Cinema: 'Artists and Models.'" *Time*, January 9, 1956, 86.

"'The Circus' [Review]." *Variety*, July 3, 1954.

Collins, Owen. "Red Skelton Wins 2 Emmys at Annual TV Academy Banquet." *Los Angeles Herald Express*, February 19, 1952.

Cook, Alton. "'Artists and Models' Just More Martin and Lewis." *New York World-Telegram and Sun*, December 22, 1955.

Cook, Alton. "Chaplin's Limelight a Film Masterpiece." *New York World-Telegram and Sun*, October 24, 1952, 20.

Cook, Alton. "'Itch' Should Make Scratch." *New York World-Telegram and Sun*, June 4, 1955, 8.

Cook, Alton. "Jerry and Dean Unified in Navy this Time." *New York World-Telegram and Sun*, February 1, 1952, 16.

Cook, Alton. "New 'Paleface' Chip Off Old Block." *New York World-Telegram and Sun*, October 2, 1952, 24.

Cook, Alton. "'Rock Hunter' Bows At 100 Film Houses." *New York World-Telegram and Sun*, September 12, 1957, 20.

Cook, Alton. "'Mister Roberts' Hilarious." *New York World-Telegram and Sun*, July 15, 1955, 10.

Corby, Jane. "Bob Hope Aided by Trigger In a Western-Style Comedy." *Brooklyn Eagle*, October 2, 1952, 4.

Corby, Jane. "Bob Hope, Bing Crosby Meet D. Lamour Again in a 'Road.'" *Brooklyn Eagle*, January 30, 1953, 6.

Corby, Jane. "Dean Martin and Jerry Lewis. In 'Sailor Beware' at Mayfair." *Brooklyn Eagle*, February 1, 1952, 8.

"Crosby-Hope Farce Pleasant Nonsense." *Hollywood Reporter*, November 18, 1952, 4.

Crowther, Bosley. "Artists and Models.'" *New York Times*, December 22, 1955, 20.

Crowther, Bosley. "'The Court Jester' [Review]." *New York Times*, February 2, 1956, 19.

Crowther, Bosley. "'Limelight' [Review]." *New York Times*, October 24, 1952, 27.

Crowther, Bosley. "Little Things: Being an Appreciation of Small Favors in Film." *New York Times*, February 5, 1956, 111.

Crowther, Bosley. "'Sailor Beware' [Review]." *New York Times*, February 1, 1952, 17.

Crowther, Bosley. "'Son of Paleface' [Review]." *New York Times*, October 2, 1952, 32.

Crowther, Bosley. "'Will Success Spoil Rock Hunter?' [Review]." *New York Times*, September 12, 1957, 37.

Ehrenstein, David. "Frank Tashlin and Jerry Lewis." In *Frank Tashlin*, eds. Roger Garcia and Bernard Eisenstchitz. London: British Film Institute, 1994.

Fox, Margalit. "Geoffrey H. Hartman, Scholar Who Saw Literary Criticism as Art, Dies at 86." *New York Times*, March 21, 2016, B-7.

Gehring, Wes D. "Bob Hope: *My Favorite Brunette*." In *Forties Film Funnymen: The Decade's Great Comedians at Work in the Shadow of War*. Jefferson, NC: McFarland, 2010.

Gehring, Wes D. "Bob Hope's *The Cat and The Canary*." In *Film Clowns of the Depression: Twelve Defining Comic Performances*. Jefferson, NC: McFarland, 2007.

Gehring, Wes D. Phone Interview with Film Historian Conrad Lane. August 17, 2015.

Gehring, Wes D. "Stepping Out of Character." *USA Today Magazine*, January 2009.

Gene [Gene Moskowitz]. "'Limelight' [Review]." *Variety*, October 8, 1952.

Guernsey, Otis L., Jr. "On the Screen: 'Born Yesterday.'" *New York Herald Tribune*, December 27, 1950, 16.

Guernsey, Otis L., Jr. "On the Screen: 'Limelight.'" *New York Herald Tribune*, October 24, 1952, 14.

Guernsey, Otis L., Jr. "On the Screen: 'Road to Bali.'" *New York Herald Tribune*, February 1, 1952, 13.

Guernsey, Otis L., Jr. "On the Screen: 'Sailor Beware.'" *New York Herald Tribune*, February 1, 1952, 13.

Guernsey, Otis L., Jr. "On the Screen: 'Son of Paleface.'" *New York Herald Tribune*, October 2, 1952, 30.

Guernsey, Otis L., Jr. "On the Screen: 'The Star.'" *New York Herald Tribune*, January 29, 1953, 15.

Gussow, Mel. "Stage: Ewell in Waiting for Godot." *New York Times*, July 29, 1971, 43.

Hale, Wanda. "The Paramount [Theatre] Shows Martin & Lewis Film." *New York Daily News*, December 22, 1955.

Hale, Wanda. "Tom Ewell Is Great in 'Seven Year Itch.'" *New York Daily News*, June 4, 1955, 18.

Hift, Fred. "'Will Success Spoil Rock Hunter?' [Review]." *Variety*, July 31, 1957.

Hoberman, J. "Cartooned In." *Village Voice*, July 16, 1980, 40.

"Holliday Triumphs In Her Own Role." *Hollywood Reporter*, November 17, 1950, 3.

Hopper, Hedda. "Helter Skelton!" *Chicago Tribune*, June 17, 1951.

Horne, Harriet Van. "Skelton Has Chaplin Tragic-Comic Touch." *New York World Telegram*, February 18, 1952.

Humphrey, Hal. "Groucho Diagnoses Our Ailing Comedy." *Los Angeles Mirror-News*, March 17, 1958. In the "Marx Brothers Files," Margaret Harrick Library, Academy of Motion Picture Arts and Sciences, Beverly Hills.

"[Jack Lemmon Interview]." *American Film*. September 1982, 16.

"'Jester' Hot in London." *Hollywood Reporter*, February 27, 1956, 3.

"Judy Holliday, 42, Is Dead of Cancer." *New York Times*, June 8, 1965, 1.

"Judy with a Punch." *Christian Science Monitor*, January 9, 1951.

Kehr, Dave. "When Unmanly Man Met Womanly Woman." *New York Times*, August 20, 2006.

Kimmel, Michael. "Bowie, From Stage to Easel." *New York Times*, January 15, 2016, C-25 (A reprint of a *NYT* interview from June 14, 1998).

Krahn, Bill. "The Outsiders: Joe Dante on Tashlin." In *Frank Tashlin*, ed. Roger Garcia and Bernard Eisenschitz. London: British Film Institute, 1994.

Lands, McCarthy. "'The Seven Year Itch' [Review]." *Variety*, June 8, 1955.

Lawrence, Mark Atwood. "Kissenger the Cynic." *New York Times*, November 4, 2015.

Lederer, Katy. "Last Gathering." *New York Times*, December 27, 2015, Book Review section: 9.

Leviero, Anthony. "Chaplin Is Facing Barriers to Reentry from Abroad." *New York Times*, September 20, 1952, 1.

Lubon, Milten. "'Mr. Roberts' Comedy Riot Huge B. O. Potential." *Hollywood Reporter*, May 24, 1955, 3.

Maddocks, Melvin. "Tony Randall Starring In Spoof on TV." *Christian Science Monitor*, September 10, 1957.

"Martin and Lewis Tee Off P. A. Tour." *Hollywood Reporter*, February 12, 1952, 14.

"The Marx Brothers Now." *Newsweek*, March 17, 1958, 104.

McCarten, John. "The Current Cinema: Sennett, Anyone?" *The New Yorker*, April 4, 1959.

Meffitt, Jack. "'Court Jester Filled with Action, Sparkling Humor." *Hollywood Reporter*, January 27, 1956, 3.

Merbaum, Mark. *Born Yesterday*. In *Magill's Survey of Cinema*, ed. Frank N. Magill. Englewood Cliffs, N. J., 1980.

"Million Dollar Madmen." *Quick*, October 8, 1951, 56.

Mitchell, Robert. "Mister Roberts." In *Magill's Survey of Cinema*, ed. Frank N. Magill. Eaglewood Cliffs, NJ: Salem Press, 1980.

Millman, Noah. "The Shortlist." *New York Times*, January 24, 2016, Book Review section: 26.

Moffitt, Jack. "'Seven Year Itch' Packed with Laugh Entertainment." *Hollywood Reporter*, June 3, 1955, 3.

Moffitt, Jack. "Back to Utopia." *Esquire*, April 1946, 63.

Moffitt, Jack. "'Some Like It Hot' Certain To Be Even Hotter At B.O." *Hollywood Reporter*, February 25, 1959.

"MPAA Protests Review On 'Yesterday.'" *Hollywood Reporter*, December 4, 1950, 8.

Mundy, Robert. "Frank Tashlin: A Tribute." In *Frank Tashlin*, eds. Claire Johnston and Paul Willemen. London: Vineyard Press, 1973.

Myers, Harold. "'Born Yesterday' [Review]." *Variety*, November 22, 1950.

Nehring, Cristina. "Quite Contrary." *New York Times*, May 10, 2015, Book Review section: 29.

Nichols, Lewis. "New Arrival." *New York Times*, February 10, 1946, section 11:1.

O'Connor, Jim. "Pretty Girls, Gags, Crosby and Hope." *New York Journal American*, January 30, 1953, 11.

Pace, Eric. "Danny Kaye, Limber-Limbed Comedian Dies." *New York Times*, March 4, 1987, D-23.

Parsons, Louella (syndicated). "Red Skelton Moves Out; Ex-Wife Has Role in Row." *Seattle Post*, December 4, 1952.

Pelswick, Rose. "Danny Kaye in Slick Hatchet Job." *New York Journal American*, February 2, 1956, 16.

Pelswick, Rose. "Hope and Jane Russell In Fine and Funny Film." *New York Journal American*, October 2, 1952, 22.

Pelswick, Rose. "Martin-Lewis' Best Film, A Zany, Hilarious Show." *New York Journal American*, February 1, 1952, 10.

Pelswick, Rose. "Monroe Is Glamorous And Ewell Amusing." *New York Journal American*, June 4, 1955, 14.

Pelswick, Rose. "Sizzling Jayne Zips Through Zany Film." *New York Journal American*, September 12, 1957.

Pelswick, Rose. "'Some Like It Hot: Oh, Boy, that Marilyn!" *New York Journal American*, March 30, 1959.

Pihodna, Joe. "On the Screen: 'The Clown.'" *New York Herald Tribune*, January 29, 1953, 15.

Quizz, Jack. "Fantastic Capers by Red Skelton Are a Prelude to His TV Shows." *Kansas City Star*, May 13, 1951.

Redeling, Lowell E. "Red Skelton Highlights New Musical." *Hollywood Citizen News*, June 28, 1944.

Red Skelton photo showcase with text. *LOOK* magazine, May 14, 1946, 39.

Roberts, Andrew. "Kissinger the Idealist." *New York Times*, October 4, 2005, Review of Books section: 13.

Roberts, Sam. "Mary Keefe, 92, Model for Rockwell's 'Rosie the Riveter.'" *New York Times*. April 25, 2015, B-14.

Robinson, David. "Evolution of a Story." In *Footlights with the World of Limelights*, ed. David Robinson. Bologna: Cineteca Bologna, 2014.

Rogow, Lee. "'The Seven Year Itch': Itchcraft." *Hollywood Reporter*, November 21, 1952, 3.

Roiphe, Katie. "Dying with Nothing to Say." *New York Times*, March 20, 2016, Sunday Review section: 8.

Ross, Sid. "Red Skelton ... His Plane Was in Trouble." *Parade*, September 23, 1951, 9.

Roy Rogers Madison Square Garden ad. *New York Daily News*, October 3, 1952, 61.

Sailor Beware ad noting "The NAVY Needs MEN." *New York Herald Tribune*, January 27, 1952, Section 4:3.

Schallert, Edwin. "Genius Touches Flit, Flash in 'Dictator.'" *Los Angeles Times*, November 15, 1940, Part 1:18.

"'Seven Year Itch' New York Sneak Jams Broadway." *Hollywood Reporter*, June 2, 1952.

Shakespeare. *The Tragedy of Macbeth*. Act 5, Scene 5.

Simsolo, Noël. "The Coordinator of Disorders." In *Frank Tashlin*, eds. Roger Garcia and Bernard Eisenschitz. London: British Film Institute, 1994.

Skelton, Georgia Davis. "Do Comics Make Good Husbands?" *Screenland*, June 1952, 58.

"Skelton Great In Heart-Warming Pic[ture]." *Hollywood Reporter*, December 23, 1952, 3.

Skelton, Red. Letter to Hedda Hopper, January 31, 1951. Hedda Hopper Collection, Special Collections, Margaret Herrick Library, Academy of Motion Picture Arts and Sciences, Beverly Hills.

Skelton, Red (subbing for syndicated columnist Erskine Johnson). "TV Proves Tougher Nut to Crack for Entertainment's Funniest Nut." *Bingham Press*, September 4, 1952.

Smith, Eugene. "Chaplin at Work: He Reveals His Movie Making Secrets." *Life*, March 17, 1952, 117.

"'Some Like It Hot' [Review]." *Cue*, undated. In the *Some Like It Hot* folder in the Performing Arts Library at Lincoln Center, NY.

Son of Paleface ad (noting Bob Hope's appearance). *New York Times*, October 1, 1952, 39.

"'Son of Paleface' Hilarious." *Hollywood Reporter*. July 14, 1952, 3.

"'Son of Paleface' [Review]." *Variety*, July 16, 1952.

Spacey, Kevin. "Foreword." In Chris Lemmon's *A Twist of Lemmon*. Chapel Hill, NC: Algonquin Books, 2006.

Stone, Herb. "'I Married a Witch' [Review]." Rob Wagner's Script, December 1942. In *Selected Film Criticism, 1941–1950*, ed. Anthony Slide. Metuchen, NJ: The Scarecrow Press, 1983.

Tailleur, Roger. "Anything Goes." In *Frank Tashlin*, eds. Claire Johnston and Paul Willenen. London: Vineyard Press, 1973.

Tashlin, Frank. "'Son of Paleface' Went Thataway." *New York Times*, October 5, 1952, section 2:5.

"10,000,000 TV Pact for Proctor and Gamble and Red Skelton." *Long Beach Press Telegram*, May 3, 1951.

Thomson, David. "Frank Capra." In *The New Biographical Dictionary of Film*. New York: Alfred A. Knopf, 2003.

"Tom Ewell, Actor, Is Dead at 84; Monroe Co-Star in '7 Year Itch.'" *New York Times*, September 13, 1994.

"2 Catholic Vet Groups Picket 'Yesterday' In Rap at Holliday-Kanin." *Variety*, March 28, 1951.

Tynan, Kenneth. "The Current Cinema: Summer [and] Judy Holliday." *The New Yorker*, July 25, 1970, 54.

Wahls, Robert. "Footlights." *New York Daily News*. August 22, 1971.

Zinsser, William K. "'Artists and Models' [Review]." *New York Herald Tribune*, December 20, 1955, 11.

Zinsser, William K. "Screen: 'The Court Jester.'" *New York Herald Tribune*, February 2, 1956, 12.

Zinsser, William K. "A Happy Surprise In 'Mr. Roberts.'" *New York Herald Tribune*, July 24, 1955, Entertainment section: 1.

Zinsser, William K. "'The Seven Year Itch [Review]." *New York Herald Tribune*, June 15, 1955, 4.

Zunser, Jessie. "The Funniest of 1957: 'Will Success Spoil Rock Hunter?'" *Cue*, September 14, 1957, 13.

Zunser, Jessie. "A Sea-Going Classic Immortalized On Screen." *Cue*, July 16, 1955, 3.

Weiler, A. H. "'The Clown' [Review]." *New York Times*, January 29, 1953, 25.

Weiler, A. H. "'Mister Roberts' [Review]." *New York Times*, July 15, 1955, 14.

Weiler, A. H. "'Some Like It Hot' [Review]." *New York Times*, March 30, 1959, 23.

"Wife Pins Skelton Riff on Dawn Visits to Kids." *New York World*, December 4, 1952.

Williams, Dick. "'The Seven Year Itch' [Review]." *Los Angeles Mirror News*. Included in a *Hollywood Reporter* collage of review ads for the picture, June 16, 1955, 6–7.

"'Will Success Spoil Rock Hunter?' [Review]." *Variety*, July 31, 1957.

Winsten, Archer. "Chaplin's 'Limelight' Now Showing." *New York Post*, October 24, 1952, 52.

Woody Allen dust jacket blurb for Richard Zaglin's *Hope: Entertainer of the Year*. New York: Simon & Schuster, 2014.

Woolcott, Alexander. "A Strong, Silent Man." *Cosmopolitan*, January, 1934, 108.

Wright, Cobina. "Red Skelton Rates as 'Comedian with a Heart.'" *Los Angeles Examiner*, May 13, 1951.

Documentaries and Concerts: Live and Filmed

AFI's 100 Years ... 100 Laughs. CBS Television Special, first broadcast June 13, 2000.

AFI's 100 Years ... 100 Movie Quotes. CBS Television Special, first broadcast June 21, 2005.

Colgate Comedy Hour. CBS Television, first broadcast June 5, 1955. On the Martin & Lewis Show DVD. Genius Entertainment, 2003.

Jack Lemmon voiceover on *Mister Roberts*. Bonus Feature on 2005 DVD of 1955's *Mister Roberts*, Warner Entertainment.

Person to Person, CBS Television with host Edward R. Murrow interviewing Martin & Lewis, first broadcast in 1954. YouTube. Uploaded by Sopbxprod, November 11, 2011.

Red Skelton in Concert. Ball State University (Muncie, Indiana), October 7, 1978.

Index

Numbers in *bold italics* refer to pages with photographs.

Abbate, Nancy 115–116
Abbott & Costello 4, 13, 21, 27–28, 130, 173
Adam's Rib 10–12, 92
Agee, James 29, 56
All That Jazz 56
All the King's Men 17, 20
Allen, Steve 70, 71, 170
Allen, Woody 29, 75, 77, 80, 81, 86, 92–94, 127
The Apartment 141, 169, 177
Arnaz, Desi 43–44
Arthur, Jean 18
Artists and Models 107–122, *111*, *117*, 144, 145, 172

Ball, Lucille 43–44, 66, 173
"The Banana Man" 3–4
Barry, Joan 49–50, 170
Bathing Beauty 62, 65–66
The Bear That Wasn't 112, 142, 145
Beatles 114, 138
Beckett, Samuel 94, 117, 178
Benny, Jack 114–115, 173
Berle, Milton 46, 61, 173
Blondell, Joan 138–139, 146
Bloom, Claire 52–53, 55–60, 67, 70
Bogart, Humphrey 72
Bogdanovick, Peter 108, 116, 139, 147
Born Yesterday 7–20, *8*, *16*; 172, 174
Borowitz, Andy 4
Bowie, David 164
Bracken, Eddie 26, 117, 123, 148, 169
Bringing Up Baby 154, 163, 164
Brooks, Mel 38, 134, 171
Brown, Joe E. 94, 149, *152*, 153, 160, 162–164, 166, 167, *168*, 177

Bunny, John 27
Burns & Allen 14

Cagney, James 96, 97, *99*, 103–106, 151, 176, 178
Calvert, Corinne 23, 30
Capote, Truman 87
Capra, Frank 7, 15, 16–17, 18–19, 117, 119–120
Carlin, George 173
Carrey, Jim 118, 122–123, 178
Cerf, Bennett 145
The Champ 64
Chaplin, Charlie 5, 19, 24, 29, 31; *Limelight* 48–61, *52*, *54*, *57*, 64, 67–68, 70–71, 172; Red Skelton and 62–63, 66, 67–68, 70–71; 73, 77, 113, 116, 122–123, 130, 137, 144, 155, 168, 170, 172–173, 176–177
Chaplin, Charlie, Jr. 55
Chaplin, Geraldine (daughter) 55–56
Chaplin, Lita Grey (second wife) 55
Chaplin, Oonn O'Neill (fourth wife) 49, 52–53, 55, 57–58, 63
Chaplin, Sydney (brother) 23
Chaplin, Sydney (son) 55, 57, 59
The Circus 50
City Lights 24, 29, 50, 130
The Clown 61–71, *65*, *67*, 173
Cohn, Harry 10–11, 13, 20
Colgate Comedy Hour 4, 30, 61–62, 173
Connecticut Yankee in King Arthur's Court 128, 132
Considine, Tom 64, *65*, 67, 68
Cops 36
The Court Jester 123–135, *124*, *125*, *132*, 136, 141, 147
Crawford, Broderick 7, *8*, 13, 15, 20, 174

The Creature from the Black Lagoon 88, 90–91, 94, 162, 177
Crosby, Bing 72–83, *74*, 135; see also Hope & Crosby
Crowe, Cameron 168
Cukor, George 9–10
Cuppy, Will 43, 144
Curtis, Tony 149–169, *150*, 174, 176

Dale, Alan 123
The Day the Earth Stood Still 142–143
Dean, James 25, 30
DeMille, Cecil B. 38
De Sica, Vittorio 60
DiMaggio, Joe 91, 95
Dinner at Eight 9
Disney, Walt 112, 170
Dr. Strangelove or: How I Learned to Stop Worrying and Love the Bomb 143
A Dog's Life 60
Drake, Betsy 137–138, 145
Duck Soup 41, 108, 134, 140, 159, 170
"Dumb Dora" 14
Durgnat, Raymond 118, 119

11/22/63 145, 172
"Everybody Loves Somebody Sometime" 114
Ewell, Tom 11, 84–95, *87*, *89*, 157, 162, 176–177, 179

Ferrell, Will 118
Feydeau, Georgas 136
Fields, W.C. 66, 77, 119, 122, 139
Finch, Flora 27
Finding Neverland 2
Fine, Sylvia 126, 130
Flynn, Errol 76, 127–128, 131

199

Fonda, Henry 96–99, **97**, **101**, 103–105
Footlights 48, 53, 55–56, 60
Ford, Dan (grandson) 102–104
Ford, John 100, 102–106
Fosse, Bob 56, 147
Frank, Melvin **125**, 126, 135

Gable, Clark 169, 174
The Girl Can't Help It 137, 148, 177
Gleason, Jackie 113, 173
Grant, Cary 150, 153–154, 158, 163, 174
The Great Dictator 48, 50, 55, 130, 170
Guinness, Alec 120, 146

Hargitary, Mickey ("Bobo") 139, 145, 146
Harlow, Jean 9
Hartley, Marsden 1, 131, **132**
Haskell, Molly 12
Hawks, Howard 151
Hawn, Goldie 14
Hellman, Lillian 19
Hepburn, Katharine 10–12, 94, 134, 154, 163
Herman, Pee-Wee 5
Holden, William 7, **8**, 10, 13, 14–15, **16**
Holliday, Judy **8**, **16**, 50, 61, 86, 101, 138, 172, 174; *Born Yesterday* 7–20
The Honeymooners 12, 113–114
Hope, Bob 1, 7; *Road to Bali* **79**, **82**, 115, 120, 124, 126, 141, 145, 151, 156, 169, 172–173, 176; *Son of Paleface* 35–47, **37**, **40**, **45**, 72–83
Hope & Crosby 22, 28, 72–83, 174; *see also* Hope, Bob
Hopper, Edward 58
HUAC 16, 19–20, 32, 49–51, 58–59, 61, 172, 176, 178
Hubbard, Kin 145
Hughes, Howard 36
Huston, John 115, 169
Hutton, Betty 23

"Innamorata" 109–110, 121
Isherwood, Christopher 90
It's a Gift 122
It's a Wonderful Life 17

Johns, Glynis **ii**, 127–129
Jumping Jacks 121

Kanin, Garson 10, 15, 18–19, 50
"The Katzenjammer Kids" 130
Kaye, Danny **ii**, 77, 117, 123–135, **124**, **125**, 156, 176, 178
Keaton, Buster 36, 41, 56, **57**, 59, 61, 65–66, 73, 117–118, 134, 159
Keefe, Mary 12
Kehr, Dave 147

Kelly, Hetty 52–53
The Kid 50
Kind Hearts and Coronets 120
King, Stephen 145, 146, 172
A King in New York 60, 137, 144, 176
Kissinger, Henry 144
Knipfel, Jim 4
Kovacs, Ernie 3, 66
Kubrick, Stanley 102, 143

Lamour, Dorothy 44, 73, **74**, 75, 78–83, **79**, 137
Langdon, Harry 117–120
Lansbury, Angela **ii**, 127–128
The Last Flower 146
Laurel & Hardy 13, 25, 27–28, 50, 76, 110, 118, 139
Lemman, Chris (son) 101–102, 104
The Lemon Drop Kid 115
Lemmon, Jack: *Mr. Roberts* 96–106, **97**, 98, 99, 100, **101**, 141; *Some Like It Hot* 149–169, **150**, **159**, 162, **168**, 170, 174, 177, 178
LeRoy, Mervyn 100, 103–104
Levant, Oscar 61
Lewis, Jerry 5, 13–14; *Artists and Models* 107–122, **111**, 112, 116–117, 123, 128, 131, 134, 145, 169, 174–176, 178; *Sailor Beware* 21–34, **22**, **27**, 27, 28, 30, **33**, 34, 81
Limelight 48–61, **52**, **54**, **57**; 64, 67–68, 70–71, 172
Logan, Josh 97, 106
Lombard, Carole 14
Lost in Translation 58
Love Happy 139–140
Love in the Afternoon 58
Lubitsch, Ernst 109, 166, 170

MacLaine, Shirley 22, 107–110, **111**, 116, **117**, 121–122, 177
The Major and the Minor 153–154
Malone, Dorothy 109
Mansfield, Jane 5, 137–139, **140**, **141**, 146–148, 172, 174, 177
Martin, Dean 21, 24–30, 115–116, **117**, 121, 122, 158, **175**–176, 178
Martin, Steve 57–58, 80, 126, 171, 173
Martin & Lewis 4, 13–14, 28–29, 108, 141; *Artists and Models* 107–122, **111**, **117**, 158, 172–173; *Sailors Beware* 21–34, **22**, **27**, **33**, 35, 45–46, 61–62, 78–79
Marx, Groucho 39, 72, 100, 108–109, 139–140, 159–160, 169
Marx, Harpo 13, 41, 78, 108, 119, 139, 159
Marx Brothers 28, 61, 134, 139, 159, 161, 170, 173
Maslow, Abraham 9–10, 11, 13
Matthau, Walter 157–158, 160, 174, 178

Mayehoff, Eddie 114
McCarey, Leo 108, 169
McCarthyism 1, 5–6, 16, 47–52, 55, 63, 71, 137, 141, 144, 155, 171, 172
Meadows, Audrey 113
Meet John Doe 16–17
Méliés, George 90
MGM 61–62, 66
Miller, Arthur 169, 174
Mills Brothers 115
Misfits 169, 174
Mr. Deeds 15, 17
Mister Roberts 96–106, **97**, **101**, 178
Mr. Smith Goes to Washington 7, 14–15, 17, 19
Monroe, Marilyn 5, 9–10; *The Seven Year Itch* and 84–95, **87**, **89**, 137–140; *Some Like It Hot* 149–169, **150**, **159**, 177–178
Monsieur Verdoux 50, 111, 170, 176
Moriarty, Cathy 174
Murrow, Edward R. 30–31, 144–145

"The Nairobi Trio" 3
National Lampoon 145
Natwick, Mildred 127, 128–131, 141
A Night at the Opera 159
Nurse Betty 12
The Nutty Professor (Jerry Lewis) 14, 26, 119

O'Brien, Pat 151
The Odd Couple (TV) 148
The Outlaw 36

The Paleface 35–36, 44
The Palm Beach Story 154–155
Panama, Norman 126, 135
Paramount 114, 154
Play It Again, Sam 92–94
The Possum That Didn't 142, **143**
Powell, William 96–98, **97**, **101**, 102, 105
Presley, Elvis 145

Raft, George 151–153
Randall, Tony 122, 135–148, **140**, **141**, 157, 172, 176
"The Rat Pack" 21, 25, 122, 176
Rathbone, Basil 127–128, 131
Rear Window 114
Red Channels 19
Rogers, Roy 35–39, **37**, 41–**42**
Rogers, Will 171
Russell, Jane 35–**40**, **37**, **42**, 76

Sailor Beware 21–34, **23**, **27**, **33**, 121
Sandler, Adam 118
Sellers, Peter 117–118
Sennett, Mark 123, 167

The Seven Year Itch 84–95, **87**, **89**, 162, 165, 169
Shopgirl 58
Shoulder Arms 50
Sinatra, Frank 21, 25–26, 122, 156, **175**
A Single Man 90
Skelton, Edna Stillwell (first wife) 62–63, 69–70
Skelton, Georgia Davis (second wife) 63, 69
Skelton, Red 5, 57; *The Clown* 61–71, **65**, **67**, 77, 126, 172–173, 176
Skelton, Valentino Maria (Alonso, daughter) 68
Some Like It Hot 105, 139, 149–169, **150**, **159**, **168**, 170, 174, 177
Son of Paleface 35–47, **37**, **40**, **42**, **45**, 72, 75–76, 113, 144–145, 177
Spacey, Kevin 104–105
State of the Union 17
Steinbeck, John 112
Strasberg, Paula 165

Strauss, Robert 23
Sturges, Preston 26, 148, 154, 169, 170, 176
Sullivan's Travels 170–171

Tashlin, Frank 5, 22, 29, 34; *Artists and Models* 107–122, 126; *Son of Paleface* 35–47; 62, 75, 92, 126, 143; *Will Success Spoil Rock Hunter?* 135–148, **143**, 158, 169, 172
Tati, Jacques 122
"That's Amore" 114
Thomas, Dylan 179
Thomson, David 17, 87, 120, 171, 177
Three Friends 1, 131, **132**
Three Stooges 28, 117, 119
Thurber, James 84–85, 92, 126, 142–146
Tomlin, Lily 126
Tracy, Spencer 10–12, 17
Truffaut, François 69
Trumbo, Dalton 178
Twain, Mark 121, 128, 132, 142

Umberto D 60

Vonnegut, Kurt 118

Waiting for Godot 94, 117–118, 144, 178
Walter Mitty 84–85, 87–88, 92, 126, 161
Warhol, Andy 147
Warner Brothers 100, 113–114, 138, 151–152
West, Mae 18, 45
Wilder, Billy 1, 5, 58; Chaplin idol of 155, 168, 174, 176–178; *The Seven Year Itch* 84–95, 139, 141, *Some Like It Hot* 149–169
Will Success Spoil Rock Hunter? 122, 135, 136–148, **140**, **141**, 144, 172, 176–177
Williams, Robin 44, 70, 108
Winslow, George "Foghorn" 109, 112
The World That Isn't 142, 144, 146, 148

www.ingramcontent.com/pod-product-compliance
Lightning Source LLC
Chambersburg PA
CBHW081557300426
44116CB00015B/2916